THE
Sigmund Freud–Ludwig Binswanger
Correspondence
1908–1938

Edited by Gerhard Fichtner

Translated by Arnold J. Pomerans

Introduction, editorial notes and additional letters
translated by Thomas Roberts

OTHER

Other Press
New York and London

Originally published in German by S. Fischer Verlag GmbH, Frankfurt am Main, 1992

Translation of letters © 2003 by Arnold J Pomerans,
Translation of editorial apparatus, introduction and additional letters
© 2003 by Thomas Roberts

The Sigmund Freud letters
© 1992 by A W Freud et al
by arrangement with Mark Paterson & Sigmund Freud Copyrights

The Anna and Martha Freud letters
© 1992 by the Estate of Anna Freud
by arrangement with Mark Paterson

The Binswanger letters
© 1992 by the Successors to Ludwig Binswanger
by arrangement with Dieter Binswanger, Zurich

The Alphonse Maeder letters
© 1992 by Hannes Maeder, Küsnacht.

The introduction and editorial apparatus
© 1992 and 2003 by Gerhard Fichtner, Tübingen.

Library of Congress Cataloging-in-Publication Data

CIP data for this book is available from the Library of Congress

Contents

Translator's Note to the English-Language Edition

While it is not uncommon for a book to be translated by two or even more translators working together, for two translators to work in isolation on different parts of the same book is very unusual, and the reader deserves an explanation. Prof. Fichtner began editing this correspondence in 1978. Few people are aware of the vast amount of research which goes into an edition of this kind, but to those who are, it will not be surprising that fourteen years passed before the German edition was published. During this period, in the hope of speeding up the publication of an English edition, Arnold Pomerans was commissioned to translate the unedited letters then available, a task he completed in 1987. When the fully annotated German text became available in 1992, no English language publisher could be persuaded to commit themselves to the expense of translating the remaining parts of the book and by the time a publisher was found in 2000, Mr Pomerans was committed to other work and unable even to begin the task for a long time. Thus I, as archivist to Sigmund Freud Copyrights and having a degree of familiarity with the correspondence, was persuaded to step with some trepidation into the footsteps of one of the most renowned translators in this field and translate the editorial apparatus, fourteen additional letters which had turned up in the meantime, including one which came to light only after the publication of the German edition, and parts of a further two letters which had not been available in their entirety to Mr Pomerans. Some of this work has gone well beyond the bounds of straightforward translation, as for example researching the very obscure expression *Mohrenwäsche*, in letter 56F, which called for a much expanded note for the English reader.

This has been a very complex project and, for a variety of reasons, two more years have now passed since the translation was completed, but I, for one, am delighted this important contribution to the history of psychoanalysis is at long last being made available in English.

For those who also have a knowledge of German, and who may read the original alongside this translation (as I hope they will), detailed information about the translation can be found on page 253.

Changes for the English-language edition
Twenty-two footnotes in the German edition are of a linguistic or other nature which renders them superfluous in an English edition. These have been omitted. For this and other reasons, such as the necessary inclusion of an additional explanatory note for the English reader, the numbering of subsequent footnotes has changed.

In accordance with Prof. Fichtner's wishes, patients' names have remained encrypted, even where the identity of the patient, as in at least one instance, has been revealed elsewhere.

American English
British terminology and orthography have been used throughout. The only exception to this is the use of the American word 'intern' to refer to a houseman.

The use of numerals for months, much in evidence in the original, has been avoided, as UK and American conventions differ.

Bibliography
In several instances the publication date given in the German edition of this current work refers to a German translation, where in fact an earlier edition came out in another language. These have been rectified. Relevant works published since 1992 have been added, of which some are of significance in this context, such as the Freud–Ferenczi correspondence and Paul Häberlin's correspondence with Binswanger.

Prof. Fichtner's German edition includes an exhaustive Ludwig Binswanger Bibliography listing all 129 writings known. Very few of Binswanger's works have been translated into English and it was felt that such an all-encompassing bibliography would be of little practical use to the English reader, so the list has been reduced by about 50%. It is assumed that serious scholars with an adequate knowledge of German will refer to the German edition.

Thomas Roberts
Wivenhoe, January 2003

Introduction
Notes on the Transcription
Binswanger's First Visit to Freud

SIGMUND FREUD

Freiberg, Moravia   London
6 May 1856   23 September 1939

LUDWIG BINSWANGER

Kreuzlingen, Switzerland   Kreuzlingen
13 April 1881   5 February 1966

Introduction

'I think you are forcing me too hard into a father pattern which I do not altogether fit into. On the one hand I am the venerable old father deserving of piety and forbearance, sympathy even, because he has such a burden to bear till the end of his days; then I am the sinister despot punishing every free expression with banishment; then I am Cronos who devoured his own children. I heard today that I am one of those people who are sufficient to themselves and therefore cannot accept anything from others. I think all this amounts to illusions in the mirror of transference.'

When Freud wrote these lines at the age of 56 to Johannes Marcinowski[1] in November 1912, the split with Josef Breuer already lay far behind,[2] but the break-up of the friendship with Wilhelm Fliess, to whom Freud had written his last letter in July 1904,[3] was still painful. The defections of Alfred Adler and Wilhelm Stekel were still fresh in the memory[4] and one could already sense the revolt of the 'crown prince' C.G. Jung who, a little later, reproached Freud with 'playing the father'.[5] Enough breaks, then, to make him defend himself from outside voices, perhaps even inside voices, who doubted Freud's ability to conduct friendships with people who developed divergent views and opinions.

Time and again the correspondence between Freud and Binswanger is seen, not least by Binswanger himself, as evidence of a friendship. This friendship lasted a lifetime and grew deeper, despite increasingly divergent opinions about the establishment of psychoanalysis and opportunities to apply it. What was the bond between these two men so different in thinking and temperament? What did Freud expect from the young Binswanger, 25 years his junior, when they first met in 1907? What drew Binswanger to Freud?

Freud himself felt that only after the turn of the century had he come out of that 'splendid isolation' in which he had previously worked and done his research. Indeed, in Vienna from October 1902 on, a circle of like-minded followers in the Wednesday Psychological Society gathered round him for regular discussions in his waiting room.[6] In Zurich, however, psychoanalytic ideas first came to international notice in a university psychiatric clinic: Eugen Bleuler had worked as Director in the Burghölzli Clinic there since 1898. As early as 1893 he had reviewed Freud's translation of Charcot[7] and in 1896 Breuer's and Freud's *Studies on Hysteria*,[8] reviewing both works in a friendly and interested way. In September 1904 the (still largely unpublished) correspondence between Freud and Bleuler[9] began. Freud then heard from Bleuler 'that he and all his staff had been busily occupying themselves for a couple of years with psychoanalysis and finding various applications for it'.[10]

The pleasure and pride Freud must have felt can hardly be overstated, when in the spring of 1906 he could read in the first volume of Jung's *Diagnostischen Assoziationsstudien*,[11] which had just been published, that Jung, Senior Physician at the Burghölzli, had confirmed his discoveries. Thus he achieved threefold recognition: in academic psychiatry, internationally, and from the younger generation. Jung's sending Freud a copy of the *Diagnostischen Assoziationsstudien* sparked off the rapidly intensifying contact between Freud and Jung. In January 1907 Jung made the decision to visit Freud that spring. And it was suggested that Jung should not only be accompanied by his wife on this journey to Vienna in March 1907, but that he should also ask the 26-year-old Binswanger to go with him. This young trainee doctor had been working at the Burghölzli since June 1906 and, as a student of Jung's, carried Jung's word association studies further in his doctoral thesis. He came from a family which ran a renowned private psychiatric clinic and was a nephew of Otto Binswanger, Professor of Psychiatry at the University of Jena. He was thus a model student of Jung's and, because of the word association studies, also a disciple of psychoanalysis.[12]

There is no need to describe the Vienna visit here: Binswanger himself has given us a graphic report of it.[13] But we can guess what hopes Freud wanted to pin on Binswanger because he knew the young man's background. Not only had he met Binswanger's uncle at the conference of the Society of German Natural Scientists and Doctors in Vienna in 1894,[14] he also knew the Binswanger private clinic at Kreuzlingen very well: he had repeatedly referred his own patients there during the 1890s.

This private clinic, the so-called 'Bellevue', had been founded at Kreuzlingen near Constance in 1857 by Binswanger's grandfather Ludwig Binswanger (1820–80) for the treatment of neurological and emotional disorders. He came from a Jewish family in Osterberg, Bavaria. During the 1848 revolution he had been present at an address in front of the Munich town hall entitled 'For the Emancipation of Faith',[15] and had early on aroused the interest of Wilhelm Griesinger[16] and Carl August Reinhold Wunderlich. From 1848 on he had worked as a junior doctor under Wunderlich at Tübingen and had also – no doubt in the hope of an academic career – qualified there as a university lecturer. In 1850, however, he left Germany in order to take up, on Griesinger's recommendation, the directorship of the state lunatic asylum at Müsterlingen, Switzerland. Did he promise himself greater freedom and development opportunities in Switzerland? Perhaps it was no accident that for his 'private lunatic asylum', which he established a few years later, he was able to acquire a plot and a building which during the years 1843 to 1847 had housed the Bellevue émigré printing and publishing house which had published a plethora of revolutionary writings by, among others, Georg Herwegh and Ferdinand Freiligrath.[17]

The concept which Ludwig Binswanger senior wanted to realise with his new establishment was seen as 'revolutionary', if not by himself then certainly by his descendants and in particular his grandson Ludwig.[18] For Ludwig Binswanger senior it went without saying that the instruments of restraint still widely used would not be allowed in his clinic, but the 'novelty that is introduced here is that now the doctor's family is placed at the disposal of the sick, so that we have a combination of (open) clinical handling with family care in the strictest meaning of that word'.[19] Or as the eldest son, Robert Binswanger, wrote of his father: 'His whole life was in the service of his patients

The Bellevue Sanatorium, main building (seen from the park side)

and he devoted himself to them, a sacrifice he made with the greatest willingness, but he demanded the same in full measure as top priority from his family and then from all members of the staff to contribute to the treatment and care of the patients. If any member of staff was obliged to give up his own family life for a time, Father regarded it as his first duty to provide a substitute family as far as he was able, and therefore formed a large family circle out of the whole establishment, over which he presided as the true patriarch.'[20] The business began with 15 patients, most of whom belonged to 'the educated class',[21] and grew over the years to 40 patients.

Robert Binswanger (1850–1910), energetic and impulsive, circumspect and with organisational skills, continually developed his father's concept. The 'intensive care of the patients and the whole family atmosphere of the sanatorium' remained 'essential aspects of the treatment'.[22] But the modern methods of treatment of the time, electrotherapy, hydrotherapy, physiotherapy and medication, indeed occasionally even hypnotic suggestion therapy, were also employed. The aim of the sharpest possible separation between the psychotic and the mentally ill, and as individualised a treatment as possible, led to a large expansion of the establishment. An abundance of buildings

The park of the Bellevue Sanatorium

went up in the parkland; in extreme cases houses for individual patients and their relations were set up. For the 'socially capable' patients, the sanatorium was to offer 'the image of a comfortable Swiss boarding house'.[23] 'But this system demanded as large a number of healthy elements as possible, at the heart of which were pleasure and love and an understanding for our patients, which surrounded them from morning till night. In brief, a larger family circle surrounded the patients.'[24] A particular image of the institution then gradually emerged in public, which Joseph Roth presents, albeit in an ironic way, when he writes in *Radetzky-Marsch* of that 'institution on Lake Constance where pampered lunatics from wealthy homes are gently and expensively treated and the staff are as tender as midwives'.[25]

Soon patients arrived at Kreuzlingen from far and wide. The sanatorium came to the notice of Freud's fatherly friend, Josef Breuer, in 1881 and, in the autumn of that year, he sent Bertha Pappenheim – 'Anna O.', whose agonising symptoms he relieved with his cathartic treatment which became the prototype for psychoanalysis – to Kreuzlingen for a course of treatment for her addiction to morphine.[26] In July 1893 Freud and Breuer sent a joint (female) patient there.[27] And a patient of Freud's from the best circles was treated at the Bellevue

xiii

in the mid-1890s. From his patients' reports, Freud would have been able to form a graphic picture of the sanatorium and its possibilities, that environment, then, which appeared to the young Ludwig Binswanger junior as a world of its own, indeed *the* world.[28]

Ludwig Binswanger (1881–1966) of course grew into this world in which his 'father's' way of life and orders [...] were absolute law'.[29] He had, according to one school report, decided long before his final examinations at grammar school not only to study medicine, but also to become a psychiatrist and his father's successor.[30] While he was a medical student from 1900 to 1906 (in Lausanne, Zurich, Heidelberg and finally back in Zurich), what most impressed him was the personality of Eugen Bleuler, 'for whom we walked through fire and through whom psychiatry became our main subject and our main concern'.[31] Binswanger believed he could prepare for his role in life, psychiatry, nowhere better than in the Burghölzli. From December 1900 C.G. Jung worked there, first as an intern, later as senior physician and outside lecturer (from 1905).[32] After 1906 the medical staff at the Burghölzli included Karl Abraham, Franz Riklin, Max Eitingon and Hermann Nunberg, who to a greater or lesser extent were all to play important roles in the psychoanalytic movement. During the time following his appointment in June 1906, Binswanger appeared to be completely absorbed by his work on his dissertation under the supervision of Jung.[33] He was carried away by that excited atmosphere, as Abraham A. Brill,[34] who at that time was also working at the Burghölzli, later described it: 'Under Jung's leadership, all the junior doctors at the clinic were working on the association experiments; they conducted research daily for hours on end on trial subjects to discover experimentally whether Freud's opinions were right. [...] Freudian principles were not only applied to patients, but everyone at the clinic seemed to be obsessed with psychoanalysis.'[35] Even Binswanger studied Freud's publications intensively at that time.[36]

In the association experiments, each time a word was called out the subject had to say, without reflection, the first word that came into his or her head, whereupon the reaction time (up to the word being spoken) and the change in the electrical resistance of the skin were measured. In the event of conspicuous changes in the values measured indicating 'emotionally charged psychic events' or 'complexes',[37] the subject would be asked for further thoughts and associations. Jung himself used his graduate students as subjects. Two series of experiments – series I and IV – were, as can easily be determined, conducted with Jung[38] and they present a highly informative psychograph of him at this time.[39] What is informative about it for us is not just that Binswanger registered with Jung a distinct 'will to power',[40] but above all that Jung can hardly have expected to travel to Vienna.[41] Binswanger, then, is not only completely bound up in the atmosphere of the Burghölzli, he also knows exactly what his – just six years his senior – supervisor's expectations are, knows that he hopes to be able to solve the puzzle of *dementia praecox* (schizophrenia) by means of psychoanalysis, senses that Jung's impatience to see Freud springs from his 'need [...] for new sensations'[42] – and Binswanger expected to get for himself from the visit a personal introduction through Freud to psychoanalysis.

As the visit progressed it aroused a further expectation in Binswanger. Almost fifty years later he was still singing the praises of 'the easy-going, friendly atmosphere' of the visit and 'Freud's dislike of all formality and ceremony, his personal charm, simplicity, natural openness and kindness'.[43] Did he gain a second father here, and indeed – in contrast to his own – did this one treat him like a partner, not in an authoritarian way?[44]

Thus there arose a concord of expectations on either side, as Freud and Binswanger got to know each other personally: on one side the hope for a breach through the wall[45] between official psychiatry and psychoanalysis, as well as for recognition and the acquisition of one more fellow campaigner abroad; on the other side the hope of being able to assist, under 'fatherly' guidance, in the front line of establishing a new science with a promising future.

After visiting Freud, Binswanger worked with his uncle Otto Binswanger in the Jena University Psychiatric Clinic from April 1907 to June 1908. As early as 29 May his uncle entrusted him with a female patient with severe hysteria ('Irma') who appeared to him to be a suitable case for psychoanalytic treatment. Like many of the early pioneers, Binswanger of course knew psychoanalysis only from the literature and conducted this treatment with great intensity until the end of September 1907. His model was Freud's *Fragment of an Analysis of a Case of Hysteria*,[46] as is shown by the repeated quotations from it and also the form of the titles in Binswanger's publication about this case ('*Versuch einer Hysterieanalyse*').[47] Binswanger seems to have told Jung quite early on how much the daily work with this patient and his involvement with psychoanalysis excited him, for Jung replied to him on 28 June 1907: 'I hope you have success with psychoanalysis, with which you will be able to show people something. You are quite right, Freud's sexual theory is the crown, I too observe that more each day.'[48] In Jena, Binswanger also met the woman who was to become his wife, Hertha Buchenberger, who worked as a nurse in the clinic there.[49]

In July 1908 Binswanger took up a post in his father's establishment and as early as December 1910, when he was not yet thirty, he had to take over direction of the clinic following his father's sudden death. At this time he still believed 'that almost every patient must be analysed',[50] particularly following favourable experiences with one female patient whom he had analysed for six months in 1909 in his father's clinic and whose case ('Gerda') he published as '*Analyse einer hysterischen phobie*'.[51] It took him, Binswanger later wrote, 'ten years of hard work and disappointments' before he realised 'that only a certain number of cases in our institution were suited to analysis'.[52]

This correspondence shows that in the exchange between Freud and Binswanger practical questions about the treatment of patients and about psychoanalysis were foremost, and that Binswanger gratefully adopted Freud's ideas. The critical appraisal of psychoanalysis – which increased as time went by – began when Binswanger was working on the theoretical basics of psychoanalysis. He saw himself, however, all his life as 'on the way' to Freud.[53] What follows is intended to sketch Binswanger's way of thinking – including after Freud's death, – though only so far as it is important to an understanding of the correspondence and to Binswanger's position vis-à-vis Freud.

The first stage of this way was, as we have seen, the debate about psychoanalysis 'in the sense of learning, the learning experience of its teachers through the word and writing of its founder', which began even before Binswanger's first visit to Freud. The second stage was 'putting what had been learned to the test on living people',[54] which began when Binswanger first treated a patient psychoanalytically in Jena. Binswanger rightly pointed out that 'talk of stages along such a way by no means meant that with each new stage the previous ones "disappeared". More often the opposite was the case: if a certain experience appeared on the way, it remained on the way.'[55] Indeed, even those stages in which Binswanger was not expressly in discussion with Freud can be seen as stretches of the way to and with Freud. In the main Binswanger was influenced not only by the literature, but also by his personal intercourse with philosophers and psychologists, poets, painters and musicians, philologists and medics.[56]

Binswanger himself was able to date the beginning of the third stage precisely. In April 1911 he attended a lecture by a disciple of Wernicke, Hugo Liepmann,[57] entitled 'Wernicke's influence on clinical psychiatry',[58] which deeply impressed him. 'On hearing this paper, which was from every point of view exemplary', he decided to place alongside it a counterpart with the title 'Freud's influence on clinical psychiatry'.[59] With this he wanted to replace the instrument of knowledge of psychoanalysis with a *methodological* or *cognitively theoretical* scrutiny, but soon had to recognise that for him 'every prerequisite for a scientific and theoretical presentation and evaluation of psychoanalysis was lacking',[60] although he had intensively pursued his philosophical interests since his schooldays.[61] He saw that he must make a thorough and methodological study of general psychology before he could evaluate psychoanalysis in a cognitively theoretical way. With *Allgemeine Psychologie* [General Psychology] by the neo-Kantian Paul Natorp as a starting point, he began to study Henri Bergson and also Edmund Husserl's[62] phenomenology more and more intensively. Out of the plan for a paper there quickly arose a plan for a book, then finally a two-volume work. The *Einführung in die Probleme der allgemeinen Psychologie*[63] [Introduction to the Problems of General Psychology], published in 1922, was meant as the first volume.[64] Binswanger was disappointed that neither Freud nor Bleuler, to whom he had jointly dedicated the book, could make much of it. With Freud, he should have been prepared for this: he had, after all, noticed on his second visit how 'Freud felt little need of philosophy'.[65] The planned second volume bore the provisional title *Die Psychologie Freuds und der Aufbau der Person.*[66] Its structure was to match exactly that of the *Einführung in die Probleme der allgemeinen Psychologie*: [...] the *definition* of the psychic (its meaningfulness) in the case of Freud was to be the *presentation* of the psychic, 'centring around the theory of psychic conflict and the psychic functions',[67] as well as following Freud's construction and deconstruction of the individual.[68] By August 1917 Binswanger had already shown Freud the first chapter of the 'second part',[69] further chapters were written in 1918,[70] and in 1922, after the publication of the *Einführung in die Probleme der allgemeinen Psychologie*, a large part of the second volume seems to have been completed. Now began a renewed and deeper study of Husserl's phenomenology and Dilthey's and Schleiermacher's hermeneutics, which was certainly strengthened by personal contact with Husserl on the Reichenau on 10 August 1923. A few days later, on

15 August, Husserl visited Binswanger in Kreuzlingen and gave a lecture to a small audience on 'The nature of phenomenology'.[71] Between these two dates, on 12 August, Binswanger wrote the foreword to the second volume, as if he wanted to hold on to what he had achieved and not let himself get too deeply into new discussions.[72] This nevertheless signified the beginning of the complete abandonment of part two. Looking back, Binswanger wrote: 'When I look at the hundreds of pages from that time that I have lying in the drawer of my desk and which will never see the light of day,[73] I do not in any way regret the effort and work I spent on it, because even this stage, in spite of everything, is a *necessary* experience in the whole process of experience which is possible with psychoanalysis.'[74] One remaining fruit of this renewed extension was, however, the short treatise of 1926 on 'Experience, understanding and interpretation in psychoanalysis'[75] in which Binswanger confronts Freud's interpretation experience with the hermeneutic experience in the mental sciences and draws the conclusion that Freud 'had founded the "hermeneutic operation" first and foremost on experience'.[76]

During Binswanger's study of Heidegger's *Sein und Zeit* [Being and Time] after its publication in 1927, his thinking took a 'second change of direction', admittedly not as 'decisive as the one brought about through Husserl himself',[77] but it did begin a new stage. As early as April 1928 Binswanger says in his diary: 'Heidegger begun with him' [Robert, his eldest son, then aged 19].[78] And at the end of January 1929 Binswanger met Heidegger in person after a lecture at the Kant Society in Frankfurt.[79] It is a change of direction from pure phenomenology to a phenomenological ontology and bound up with that a change from a methodological viewpoint to an anthropological one. Out of the attempt to fuse psychoanalytic dream analysis with the consideration of basic patterns of human Being [*Dasein*], and Husserl's phenomenological method with the theory of Being as being-in-the-world, the short paper '*Traum und Existenz*'[80] [Dream and Existence] arose, with the result, characteristic of Binswanger, that expressions like dejection [state of being thrown down, *Niedergeschlagenheit*] and flying high [*Höhenflug*] are not mere metaphors but indicate – inherent in Being – 'a meaning matrix' [*Bedeutungsrichtungen*] of 'rising and falling'[81] and thus their pathological manifestations in melancholy (and mania),[82] the flight of ideas [*Ideenflucht*][83] and delusion [*Verstiegenheit*][84] can also be understood in this way.[85]

That new stage on the way to Freud, which Binswanger himself saw[86] as beginning in the mid-1930s with two invitations to give lectures at the celebration of Freud's eightieth birthday in May 1936, was only the consolidation of the first signs already seen. It was the change from phenomenological ontology to anthropology, or rather, to a research approach with a decidedly anthropological bent.[87]

In the essay on 'Freud and the state of clinical psychiatry'[88] Binswanger asserted that what bound Freud's scientific experience to that of clinical psychiatry was that 'both "reduce" human nature to a scientific scheme or system'.[89] 'The new anthropological avenue of research in psychiatry approaches it not by trapping "man" in biological or natural science categories, nor even mental science ones, but by understanding him ['man'] from his own most particular – indeed human – *being* and trying to describe the original basic *directions* of this being. Thus "mental illness" is taken out of the realm of just a "natural" occurrence, and not seen either as a "mental" matter, but is understood and described from the point of view of the original opportunities of man's being.'[90] And on 7 May 1936 in the commemorative lecture given in Vienna under the title 'Freud's view of man in the light of anthropology'[91] the concept of *homo natura*, the view of man as a pure object of nature, was considered critically and described as 'man's horizon of understanding' of which psychoanalysis and its abstraction form the basis, 'from which horizon of understanding the natural science construction of the psychic apparatus becomes comprehensible in its equally impressive methodological breadth and unity and equally impressive anthropological bias'.[92]

Freud did not live to see the publication in 1942 of the Binswanger work which constituted the concluding high point of this stage, *Grundformen und Erkenntnis menschlichen Daseins*.[93] He could hardly have viewed it as the fulfilment of the promise shown in 1911. It was also in Binswanger's view neither the second edition of the *Einführung in die Probleme der allgemeinen Psychologie* as had been planned in the late 1920s, nor was it a second volume of that work, into which he had put so much. It was much more the independent self-willed result of a debate with Freud and the instruments used by the contemporary philosophers with whom he had constantly hoped to establish methodically the practice of Freud which was convincing to him. Among such thinkers were not only Husserl and Heidegger but also – to mention just two names which were important to him – Theodor Haering, with whom he had friendly contact from 1923,[94] and Martin Buber, whom he met in 1933.[95] The first chapter of the book, which deals with living and friendly togetherness, is unthinkable without Buber's influence: without it the 'comparison there of the nature of love and that of worry'[96] is also possibly not comprehensible, something Binswanger later recognised as a misunderstanding of Heidegger's thinking.

On 23 October in that same year, 1942, Binswanger gave a lecture *Über Daseinserkenntnis* [On the Cognition of Being][97] at the Psychological Association in Berne. During the discussion the psychiatrist Jakob Wyrsch dubbed Binswanger's method 'existential analysis' [*Daseinsanalyse*].[98] Binswanger gratefully adopted this expression and used it from then on to illustrate both the direction of his research and his therapeutic approach and to make it clear that this was thanks to the confluence and blending of psychoanalysis and the phenomenological understanding of existence, but also with the intention of differentiating it from Heidegger's existential analytics [*Daseinsanalytik*].

At the beginning of the last two decades of his life Binswanger made a new philosophical friend, Wilhelm Szilasi, who, like Heidegger, was a student and colleague of Husserl.[99] From May 1947 on Binswanger and Szilasi met almost annually – mostly in Tessin – for discussion and work. Szilasi encouraged Binswanger to study Husserl's later work anew and in more depth, but he also left his mark on another examination of Freud. Probably with the approaching centenary of Freud's birth in mind, in December 1954,[100] Binswanger began writing his *Sigmund Freud: Reminiscences of a Friendship*,[101] in which he quotes extensively from his correspondence with Freud. The reading of Freud's letters out loud in Szilasi's family circle and to their friends stimulated the completion of the manuscript in September/October 1955.[102]

Invited to give a lecture in the centenary year, 1956, Binswanger made a start on '*Mein Weg zu Freud*'[103] in February 1956.[104] He believed that with this lecture he achieved a deeper understanding of Freud's 'naturalism'. Freud had shown, he wrote, 'that we are not here just with our consciousness but also *are "unconsciously" in the world, have a world at our disposal*. [...] He had, to use a word from Wilhelm Szilasi, to whom I must here express my thanks, not only thought of being the subject "as a natural process in combination with other natural processes", but *experienced* and *presented* it in detail'.[105]

Freud would probably have dealt no better with this deepened appreciation than he would the criticism contained in Binswanger's

1936 lecture. But Freud could accept that Binswanger's 'intellectual development' was bound to carry him further and further from Freud's influence,[106] because he was convinced of the honesty of Binswanger's efforts, because he knew that their relationship rested 'on firm motives of a different kind',[107] on participation and support in critical situations in life, and because he respected the incorruptibility of Binswanger's judgement and the honourableness of his fundamental attitudes. It is in keeping with this that Binswanger wrote in his diary after his first visit to Freud's London house[108] in August 1946: 'Freud is indeed my greatest human experience, i.e., my experience of the greatest human being I ever came across.'[109]

The letters below, which are published in full for the first time, were treasured by Binswanger all his life. Only Freud's original letters have survived and even these perhaps not quite completely. Binswanger's letters, on the other hand, of which only two originals have come down to us, probably fell victim to the clearing out of papers that became necessary before Freud's emigration to London.[110] But the carbon copies of Binswanger's typed letters have survived. How fortunate that Freud found Binswanger's handwriting 'atrocious'[111] and 'horrible'[112] and even Binswanger himself thought he had 'poor handwriting'[113] and chose quite early on to have his letters typed. Thus about half of Binswanger's letters are presumed to have survived. Binswanger wrote in his *Sigmund Freud: Reminiscences of a Friendship* that he possessed '101 items in Freud's hand, of which 10 were messages on visiting cards, 8 were postcards and 83 letters. These spanned the period from April 1908 to July 1938.'[114] In fact 114 items remain extant, among them 3 visiting cards, 4 letter-cards (one of them jointly to Binswanger and Paul Häberlin), 12 postcards (some of them picture postcards) and 94 letters. This difference arose in part because one letter or another, when it referred to a patient, would have been kept with that patient's case notes[115] and thus overlooked by Binswanger; but in part it cannot be explained. In the same file in which the correspondence between Freud and Binswanger had originally been kept, together with the letters between Binswanger and Freud's relatives after Freud's death (which appear in the Appendix to this book), there were also two letters from Freud to Alphonse Maeder. They are about a patient of Freud's who was treated by Binswanger and Maeder jointly at the Bellevue in 1910 and, since they contain information helpful to an understanding of the case, they are published here in the context of the letters to Binswanger.

There was a tiresome search for nine letters which had clearly still been in Binswanger's possession when he was writing the *Reminiscences*, but which were no longer in the file in which I had first seen the letters in the late 1970s. Even Anna Freud could give no information about their whereabouts. They did turn up eventually in Freud's house in London. Apparently Binswanger had handed the letters over to Ernst Freud for the preparation of a volume of selected letters which was published in 1960, because three of these letters are published in that edition.[116] Finally in spring 1991 I stumbled upon three handwritten letters from Binswanger and four handwritten letters from Maeder to Freud which were found as copies in the letter-book at the Bellevue Sanatorium[117] and at least conveyed to us an image of what Binswanger's lost letters looked like.[118]

Today the letters are scattered far and wide. The majority of Freud's original letters and Binswanger's carbon copies (174 items) are in the possession of the Bavarian State Library in Munich. The nine letters found in Freud's London house went to the Library of Congress in Washington along with Anna Freud's papers. After Binswanger's death his heirs gave three letters to friends, so today these are in private hands. The letter-card to Binswanger and Häberlin is in the Häberlin Archive in Basle University Library. Finally, the letterbook containing the pressed copies of the Binswanger and Maeder letters is part of the Binswanger Archive in the University Archive in Tübingen and at least 63 items of correspondence from Binswanger to Freud are lost. In the chart in the Appendix, pages 242–7, the surviving and reconstructed letters are listed in chronological order. It enables the changing intensity in the exchange of letters to be clearly followed, although admittedly that is not to be compared with the intensity of the emotional relationship.[119]

———

Right from the start Ludwig Binswanger's children have enthusiastically supported the plan for an unabridged edition of the surviving correspondence between Freud and Binswanger. I remember with gratitude the hospitality afforded me by Trudi and Dr Wolfgang Binswanger when – before the closure of the Bellevue Sanatorium at the end of March 1980 – I established for the first time a transcription of the Freud letters in that same Garden House where Ludwig

Binswanger had once written or drafted most of his letters to Freud. Trudi and Wolfgang Binswanger and equally Dr Hilde Binswanger and Dr Dieter Binswanger patiently answered all the questions that arose in connection with the annotation of the correspondence, but above all they most willingly provided access to the Binswanger family archive. Before her death Anna Freud had, in consultation with Mark Paterson, the Director of Sigmund Freud Copyrights, already given her permission for the publication of these letters of her father's. Dr Kurt R. Eissler, then Director of the Sigmund Freud Archives, supported and promoted the project with all his powers. My thanks in the first place are due to all these people.

Many thanks also to Dr Hannes Maeder (Küsnacht), the son of Alphonse Maeder, who kindly agreed to the publication in this volume of the recently discovered letters from his father to Freud, which do belong within the context of this correspondence.

The Binswanger heirs came to the decision to entrust to the University of Tübingen, as the Binswanger Archive, all the records, documents and correspondence of the former Bellevue archive, together with the so-called doctors' library from the Bellevue and also a large part of the personal papers and Ludwig Binswanger's scientific library. This Binswanger Archive forms a separate part of the Tübingen University Archive and is an invaluable resource for the understanding of the correspondence. I thank Prof. Dr Volker Schäfer, Director of the University Archive, for his support, so generously provided, when I was using this material.

I should like to thank further archives for their willing assistance in clarifying many questions of detail. I was able to use the Häberlin Archive in the manuscripts section of the University Library, Basle; in Geneva Dr Daisy de Saugy guided me through the archive of the Swiss Psychoanalytic Society; in Vienna Prof. Dr Harald Leupold-Löwenthal, Frau Mag. Inge Scholz-Strasser and Dr Manfred Müller enabled me to use the rich holdings of the archive and library of the Sigmund Freud House, and in the Austrian National Library Dr. Eva Irblich provided me with access to the Freud–Ferenczi[120] letters.

I should also like to thank the following individuals for their friendly help and information: Gerhard Biesenbach (Nassau), Prof. Dr Manfred Bleuler (Zürich), Dr Jan Braden (Hamburg), Dr Ernst Falzeder (Salzburg), Prof. Ernst Federn (Vienna), Prof. Dr André Haynal (Geneva), Ludger M. Hermanns (Berlin), Mr Huemer (Register Office in Vienna Town Hall), James H. Hutson (Manuscripts Division, Library of

Congress), Dr Helmut Gröger (Vienna), Dr Eva Laible (Vienna), Dr Helmut Leitner (Vienna), Prof. Dr Peter Merguet (Nassau), Frau Elke Mühlleitner (Vienna), Dr Johannes Reichmayr (Vienna), Prof. Dr Hans H. Walser (Zürich).

Dr Michael Schröter (Berlin) kindly went through the first manuscript of this edition and gave useful advice and discussed it with me in detail. My friends, collaborators and colleagues, Prof. Dr Dietlinde Goltz, Dr Albrecht Hirschmüller, Dr Christfried Tögel, Prof. Dr Burghart Wachinger, Dr Elisabeth van der Waerden, Dr Horst Zehe, and in particular also Frau Ilse Grubrich-Simitis have read drafts of the manuscript in part or as a whole and with their criticism have enriched my knowledge and my insight. I thank them all sincerely.

Gerhard Fichtner

[1] Unpublished letter of 22 November 1912. Johannes (Jaroslaw) Marcinowski (1868–1935) was at the time director of the private sanatorium, Haus Sielbeck, near Eutin, Holstein. Freud praised Marcinowski's institution (1914d, S.E. Vol. XIV, p. 34) as the only private clinic, along with Binswanger's 'Bellevue' at Kreuzlingen, to have opened its doors to psychoanalysis. See Mühlleitner (1992).

[2] See Hirschmüller (1978a), particularly pp. 188–93 in 1989 English edition.

[3] See Freud (1985c).

[4] See the letters of 12 October 1911 and 14 November 1912 to Jung; Freud (1974a).

[5] In the letter of 18 December 1912; Freud (1974a).

[6] See Handlbauer (1990) and *Minutes* (1962–75).

[7] Freud (1892–94a).

[8] Freud (1895d).

[9] See Freud (1974a) p. xv, and also Alexander and Selesnick (1965).

[10] Jones (1953–7), Vol. II, p. 34.

[11] Jung and Riklin (1906a).

[12] Freud (1974a), p. 74.

[13] It is included after this Introduction; see p. xxxi.

[14] See below, letter 3F.

[15] Ludwig Binswanger senior, diary (FAB No. 21), p. 15. In 1852, after the birth of Otto Binswanger, he had all four of his children baptised and regarded this as a 'simple, unfortunately necessary ceremony […], which would enable the children to travel throughout the world without having to disclose to other people what talents and upbringing had shaped them.' (*Ibid.*, p. 25). He himself did not undergo a conversion.

[16] *Ibid.*, p. 3: 'January [1846]. Letters from Griesinger in Tübingen, offer of work in the archive [of psychological medicine].' Griesinger, Wilhelm Roser and Wunderlich had got together to reform medicine in Germany and to put it on a firm basis with the 'psychological method', hence the name of 'Archive'; cf. Sticker (1939–40). Regarding Griesinger, cf. also Walser (1986).

[17] Cf. Albin Beeli: 'Die Emigrantendruckerei Bellevue in Kreuzlingen 1840–1847' [The Bellevue Émigré Printing House at Kreuzlingen 1840-1847], typed manuscript, B.A. 442/364.

[18] Cf. Binswanger's account of his grandfather in (1957e).

[19] Ludwig Binswanger (1957e), p. 16.

[20] Robert Binswanger, 'Das Asyl Bellevue' [The Bellevue Asylum], handwritten MS [circa 1890], Sheet 4, FAB No. 307.

[21] *Ibid.*, sheet 4.

[22] Hirschmüller (1978a), p. 113 in 1989 English edition.

[23] Robert Binswanger, 'Das Asyl Bellevue' [The Bellevue Asylum], sheet 7, FAB No. 307.

[24] *Ibid.*, Sheet 7.

[25] Chap. 13.

[26] Hirschmüller (1978a), pp. 112–14 in 1989 English edition. On the referral of other patients of Breuer's see *ibid.* pp. 183–9.

[27] Hirschmüller (1978a), pp. 145–6 in 1989 English edition.

[28] Ludwig Binswanger, 'Autobiographische Notizen' [autobiographical notes] (FAB), typescript (1950), p.1.

[29] *Ibid.*, p. 2.

[30] *Ibid.*, p. 25a.

[31] *Ibid.*, p. 27.

[32] Cf. Ellenberger (1970), pp. 926–30.

[33] Robert Binswanger, *Tagebuch* [Diary], (FAB), p. 60: 'Above all Joy (Ludwig Binswanger's nickname) [English in the original, so, a bilingual pun, since *Freude* is German for 'joy' – T.R.] is a joy to us because he is healthier, stronger and so fulfilled by his paper (Associations!).'

[34] See note 6 to 51F.

[35] Quoted by Ellenberger (1970), p. 1064.

[36] In the dissertation there are quotations from *The Interpretation of Dreams* (1900a), *The Psychopathology of Everyday Life* (1901b) and 'Fragment of an Analysis of a Case of Hysteria' (1905e); cf. Binswanger (1907–08a), Vol. 10, p. 162, footnote 1; p. 168, footnote 1; p. 176, footnote 1; Vol. 11, p. 88, footnote 2; p.141, p. 150, footnote 1.

[37] Binswanger (1907–08a), Vol. 10, pp. 154, 160.

[38] Cf. Freud's observation in his letter to Jung dated 14 January 1908: 'I received Binswanger's paper today. Of course, I had no difficulty in recognising you as a subject and was delighted with the boy's boldness in disentangling his own muddles', and also the editor's footnote 2; Freud (1974a), p. 109.

[39] The experiments were probably conducted late in 1906. The terminus *post quem* is the end of July 1906, because Binswanger speaks of a 31-year-old colleague (p. 22), and Jung was born on 26 July 1875. The terminus *ante quem* is probably the end of December, because on 8 January 1907 Jung wrote to Freud that he was 'now firmly resolved to come to Vienna during my spring holiday (April)'; cf. Freud (1974a), p. 20. And on 16 April 1907 Jung sent the 'remainder of the manuscript' [the dissertation which had thus by that time already been written] back to Binswanger (unpublished letter of 16 April 1907 from Jung to Binswanger. The fate of Jung's original letter is not known, but a copy is in the possession of the Editor. It will be further cited below).

[40] Binswanger (1907–08a), Vol. 10, p. 166.

[41] *Ibid.*, p. 172.

[42] *Ibid.*

[43] Binswanger (1956c), pp. 2–3; see below, pp. xxxif.

[44] He did not recognise the 'will to power' in Freud until a few years later, but also ventured to mention it in a friendly way. See below, letter 69B.

[45] This is exactly the expression used by supporters of psychoanalysis at that time: on 12.11.1908 Jung wrote to Binswanger naming 'Dr. Stockmayer' who was then working in Jung's laboratory 'by favour of Gaupp from the Tübingen Mental Clinic' with a play on Binswanger's period at the Jena Psychiatric Clinic, 'a hole, a second hole – excuse me – in the German great wall of China'.

[46] Freud (1905e).

[47] Binswanger (1909a) 'An Attempt at Analysis in a Case of Hysteria'.

[48] Unpublished letter, see note 38 above.

[49] The wedding took place on 2 April 1908.

[50] Binswanger (1956c), p. 29 in 1957 English edition.

[51] Binswanger (1911a); because of the patient's central experience of having a heel ripped from her shoe while skating as a child, also referred to in brief as the 'heel analysis'.

[52] Binswanger (1956c), p. 29 in 1957 English edition. If a grouping which is to be found in the Bellevue admission records (B.A. 442/10) can be relied upon, Binswanger conducted altogether 28 psychoanalyses on in-patients between 1909 and 1942, a few of them over many years.

[53] Hence the title of his speech on the occasion of the centenary of Freud's birth: 'Mein Weg zu Freud' [My Way to Freud. (1957b)].

[54] Binswanger (1957b), pp. 207 and 208.

[55] *Ibid.*, p. 208.

[56] Just a few from this circle are named here by way of example, whom Binswanger knew personally and with whom he mostly remained in contact over many years: Otto Friedrich Bollnow, Martin Buber, Ernst Cassirer, Simon Frank, Paul Häberlin, Theodor Haering, Martin Heidegger, Richard Hönigswald, Edmund Husserl, Karl Jaspers, Hans Kunz, Karl Löwith, Max Scheler, Walter Schulz, Eduard Spranger, Wilhelm Szilasi, Leopold Ziegler, Rudolf Borchardt, Leonhard Frank, René Schikkele, Rudolf Alexander Schröder, Henry van der Velde, Ernst Ludwig Kirchner, Edwin Fischer, Wolfgang Fortner, Wilhelm Furtwängler, Walter Gieseking, Werner Jaeger, Wolfgang Schadewaldt, Emil Staiger, Eugen Bleuler, Kurt Goldstein, Roland Kuhn, Eugen Minkowski, Erwin Straus, Viktor von Weizsäcker.

[57] Binswanger (1957b), p. 209, wrongly gave *Max* Liepmann.

[58] Liepmann (1911).

[59] Binswanger (1957b), p. 209.

[60] *Ibid.*

[61] Cf. Binswanger, 'Autobiographische Notizen' (FAB), p. 10: 'But Prof. Haug also embraced the young Kant's critique of pure reason, without comment or explanation, with the result that he was enormously fascinated by the literature, particularly the contradictions of pure reason, but of course without being able to deal with Kant's teaching as such. Since then, L.B. always saw in the critique of pure reason something like a spiritual midwife.'

[62] Binswanger's correspondence with Paul Häberlin (Paul Häberlin Archive, Basle) shows that he was reading Husserl at least from 1913. [Now published: *Paul Häberlin–Ludwig Binswanger Briefwechsel 1908–1960*, Basle, 1997. T.R.]

[63] Binswanger (1922a).

[64] Binswanger described (1959a), p. 64, the train of thought with which he set this book aside as 'the way from Kant to Husserl [...] by way of neo-Kantianism, and here above all Paul Natorp, but also by way of, inter alia, Dilthey, Stumpf, Bergson, Scheler, Pfänder.

[65] Binswanger (1956c), p. 8 in 1957 English edition; in the first manuscript he wrote 'need of metaphysics', see below, p. 234.

[66] *Ibid.*, p. 72 in 1957 English edition (*Freud's Psychology and the Structure of the Personality*).

[67] *Ibid.*, p. 72 in 1957 English edition.

[68] For more detail see Binswanger (1957b), pp. 209–15.

[69] Cf. below, letter 113B with its note 2 and letter 114F.

[70] Cf. below, note 3 to letter 116F.

[71] See Binswanger (1959a), p. 65.

[72] Cf. with the diary entries in note 6 to letter 137B.

[73] The drafts are not in the Binswanger Archive in Tübingen, nor do Binswanger's heirs know what happened to them.

[74] Binswanger (1957b), p. 216.

[75] Binswanger (1926a).

[76] Binswanger (1957b), p. 216.

[77] See Binswanger (1959a), p. 66.

[78] Diary III (FAB), p. 88.

[79] Diary III (FAB), p. 93: 'Reason for journey to F. a lecture by Heidegger at the Kant Society. H. himself disappointing in "build", but otherwise very weighty. After the lecture together with curator Reizler and Heidegger and others.'

[80] Binswanger (1930a).

[81] Binswanger (1959a), p. 68.

[82] Cf. Binswanger (1960a).

[83] Cf. Binswanger (1931–33a).

[84] Cf. Binswanger (1949a).

[85] Much of the sense of this sentence is inevitably lost in the translation, because the double meanings of certain words in the German original do not exist in English. [T.R.]

[86] Binswanger (1957b), p. 217.

[87] 'Our research is anthropological in as much that it also asks what the truth is for man, in so far as it is directed towards the "truth of man". On the other hand, unlike the way the expression anthropology is usually used, it can neither be about an interpretation of man's existence, nor about something like "man's position in the cosmos", nor indeed about anthropological "types".' Binswanger (1942b), p. 18.

[88] Binswanger (1936c).

[89] Binswanger (1957b), p. 217.

[90] Binswanger (1936c), taken from Binswanger (1955a), p. 93.

[91] Binswanger (1936d).

[92] Binswanger (1957b), p. 218.

[93] Binswanger (1942b).

[94] Ludwig Binswanger, Diary II (FAB), p. 185: 29/30. [3.1923] 'Visit from Theodor *Haering* – Tübingen. Read his philosophy of natural science. Very fine man.'

[95] Ludwig Binswanger, Diary IV (FAB), p. 154 ff.: '[beginning of May 1933] *Martin Buber* with me for the day. A really wise man, one of the very few that I know. Very good understanding (about "The Flight of Ideas", one's own and the collective world, space, religion, quotation from the discussion on ego and world in general, found in my particular space [cf. Binswanger (1933a)] a religious "motif" or some background or echo, had come because of that).'

[96] Binswanger (1959b), p. 70.

[97] Typescript of this lecture in the B.A., Tübingen.

[98] Cf. Kuhn (1981), p. 10. In the diary (VIII [FAB], p. 30) the expression *Daseinsanalyse* turns up for the first time on 11.9.1943.

[99] Binswanger, Diary VIII (FAB), p. 90.

[100] Binswanger, Diary X (FAB), p. 115.

[101] Binswanger (1956c).

[102] Binswanger, Diary XI (FAB), p. 10.

[103] Binswanger (1957c) 'My way to Freud'.

[104] Binswanger, Diary XI (FAB), p. 10.

[105] Binswanger (1957b), p. 225.

[106] See below, letter 167F.

[107] See below, letter 140F.

[108] 20 Maresfield Gardens, Hampstead, now the Freud Museum, but in 1946 still the home of Freud's daughter, Anna. [T.R.]

[109] Binswanger, Diary VIII (FAB), p. 126.

[110] Cf. William McGuire's *Introduction to Freud* (1974a), p. xx. [See also note 1 to letter 75aB of 20 October 1912, which turned up after the publication of the German edition of this Correspondence – T.R.].

[111] See below, letter 16F.

[112] See below, letter 41F.

[113] See below, letter 9B.

[114] Binswanger (1956c), p. 21 [in German edn only: the relevant paragraph is inexplicably omitted from the Engl. edn – T.R.]

[115] Albrecht Hirschmüller came across such letters from and to Freud when going through case notes during the course of his work on Josef Breuer. They were then removed from the case files and placed in the Freud correspondence file. But by no means all letters concerning patients were in case notes files.

[116] Freud (1960a), pp. 286–7 (14 April 1912), p. 386 (11/12 April 1929) and p. 286 (8 October 1936).

[117] The name of the addressee is frequently not recorded in the handwritten letters in this letter-book and it is often not recognisable from the salutation either [because of the custom in German at the time of writing 'Dear Professor', 'Dear Doctor', or even 'Dear Friend', the addressee's name was not usually used at all – T.R.], but the letters were clearly identified as being addressed to Freud on the basis of their content. [This seemingly antiquated method of copying – by compressing the original letter and a dampened tissue page of the letter book in a screw press – in fact survived the invention of carbon paper by several decades. T.R.]

[118] Cf. facsimile reproduced on pp. 208–09.

[119] 1908–1914 (7 years): 144 items; 1915–1924 (10 years): 54 items; 1925–1938 (14 years): 46 items.

[120] Since the Editor wrote this Introduction, the Freud–Ferenczi Correspondence has been published in German, English and some other languages: Freud (1992g). [T.R.]

Notes on the Transcription

The following principles have been followed in establishing the text of the Correspondence:

1. Misspelt proper names have been corrected without comment.

2. Abbreviations have been expanded without comment. When the full word intended is in doubt, or where the nature of the abbreviation itself is informative, the additional letters are in square brackets.

Underlining in the manuscript is represented by italics in the printed text. Abbreviations in common use, such as e.g., i.e., etc., have been retained.

3. Where it has been necessary to expand the text for the sake of clarity, the additional letters or words are in square brackets as a matter of principle. This applies also to expansions in the footnotes of Binswanger material which has been published previously.

4. Printed letterheads are reproduced in the form in which they appear in the originals, at least as regards to capital and lower case letters. In the case of Binswanger's carbon copies, the name appears in square brackets.

5. Postscripts are always placed at the end, regardless of where and in what form they appear in the original.

6. Patients' names have been encrypted on principle. The abbreviations of pseudonyms have been chosen in such a way that the same person, and their relationship to their relatives, remain recognisable throughout the book.

7. Comments on individuals appear in the footnotes at the first appearance of their name (cf. Index of Names). In order to facilitate

the reader's understanding of the correspondence, even when it is not read through systematically, extensive references back (and to a certain extent forward) are given. Annotations made to the text by the transcriber are, in this edition, incorporated into the numerical notes of the rest of the editorial apparatus. These not only draw the reader's attention to questionable readings of the manuscript, but also indicate deletions, corrections and alterations, as far as this could be important to the understanding of the text. On the other hand, obvious and minor mistakes which could not be seen as significant have been tacitly corrected. In the case of Binswanger's letters, which have survived in the main only as carbon copies of typed originals, it is, of course, impossible to tell whether a mistake has arisen in dictation, in hearing, or in transcribing.

Ludwig Binswanger

My First Visit to Freud in Vienna
(March 1907)

From *Sigmund Freud; Reminiscences of a Friendship*
(Binswanger, 1956c), pp. 1–4

In the spring of 1906 I passed my state medical examination, and in June of the same year I joined the 'Burghölzli' in Zurich as a trainee physician. During my clinical semesters, when Eugen Bleuler[1] was already doing preliminary work on his *Gruppe der Schizophrenien*,[2] which revolutionised the theory of *dementia praecox*, he had already aroused my admiration by his personality and caused my 'hereditary' love for psychiatry to blossom forth.[3] I can still see him as he was then, scribbling notes at every opportunity on little slips of paper that he drew from his waistcoat pocket. Karl Abraham,[4] my predecessor in the male section of the hospital, was rather reserved by nature, but he too was an influence on his younger colleagues because of his great intelligence and his subtle, often somewhat ironical personality. One of my fellow interns was H.W. Maier,[5] who had been a friend of mine since schooldays. But it was C.G. Jung,[6] then chief physician of the hospital, under whom I planned to write my doctoral thesis, who really fired me with enthusiasm. He kept his students constantly spellbound by his temperament and the wealth of his ideas. In 1906, in collaboration with Riklin,[7] he had published the first volume of his *Diagnostische Assoziationsstudien*[8] and had completed an epoch-making work on the psychology of *dementia praecox*.[9] Jung suggested as a subject for my thesis 'The Psycho-Galvanic Reflex Phenomenon in the Association Test', a subject that proved not only to be more and more fascinating the deeper I went into it but one that brought me into particularly close contact with Jung. Indeed, he was constantly helping me by giving me the benefit of his advice and his knowledge and even by letting me use him as a subject in experiments. But the chief reason I must call my year at the Burghölzli by far the most inspiring year of my psychiatric apprenticeship is that the Burghölzli, even then in 1906, was at the centre of an intellectual movement that had begun in Vienna and which bore the name of psychoanalysis, and could trace its origins to one man: Sigmund Freud. No great amount of imagination is needed to understand with what joy and gratitude I answered 'yes' when Jung one day surprised me by asking whether I would accompany him and his wife on their (first) visit to Freud in Vienna. Our trip took place at the end of February, 1907. If I remember correctly, Herr and Frau Professor Jung[10] stayed barely a week in Vienna, but to my great delight I was able to stay for another week.[11]

The day after our arrival Freud questioned Jung and me about our dreams. I do not recall Jung's dream, but I do recall Freud's interpretation of it, namely, that Jung wished to dethrone him and take his place. I myself dreamed of the entrance to his house at Bergstrasse [*sic*] 19, which was then being remodelled, and of the old chandelier hung there because of the building work. Freud's interpretation of this dream, which I found rather unconvincing – he recalled it thirty years later when my wife and I visited him on the occasion of his eightieth birthday – was that it indicated a wish to marry his eldest daughter[12] but, at the same time, contained the repudiation of this wish, since it actually said that – I remember the interpretation word for word – 'I should not marry into a house with such a shabby chandelier.'

It can easily be seen from these interpretations that an easy-going, friendly atmosphere marked our visit right from the first day. Freud's dislike of all formality and ceremony, his personal charm, simplicity, natural openness and kindness, and not least his humour, allowed no difference to arise. And yet one could not for a moment deny the impression of greatness and dignity that emanated from him. To me it was a pleasure, albeit somewhat sceptical, to see the enthusiasm and confidence with which Freud responded to my teacher Jung, in whom he immediately saw his scientific 'son and heir'. I was present at several conversations between the two, which, needless to say, revolved solely around psychoanalytic problems. Freud's family also received us – and me alone after the departure of the Jungs – with the greatest friendliness. I can still remember a Sunday walk with the whole family on the Cobenzl;[13] Frau Professor was amiability and kindness personified, backed up by her sister, Fräulein Min[n]a Bernays.[14] The children were very well behaved at table, even though here too a completely unconstrained atmosphere prevailed.

The effect that emanated from Freud was strongest during the evenings when I saw him in his study or consulting room. He was then fifty and I twenty-five. What honoured his junior by 25 years was not merely 'the time' Freud devoted to him (he did the same with many others) after a day of hard work and stress, in his quiet, dimly lit study which even then contained important works of ancient and oriental art, but even more the indefatigable, detailed and most instructive and stimulating manner in which he answered the younger man's questions. Freud sat behind his desk, smoking a cigar, his hands resting on the arm of his chair or on the desk; occasionally he would pick up an art object and gaze at it, then keenly yet benevolently scrutinise his visitor, never asserting his superiority and always citing case histories rather than going into theoretical explanations. Sharp and to the point, sparing with gestures, natural and open in his facial expressions, never raising his well-modulated voice – this is Freud as I remember him to this day. His manner of speaking was con-ditioned by his unswerving and passionate devotion to the 'Thing',[15] to the scientific subject and its various implications. At the same time his visitor was repeatedly reminded that the entire edifice of psycho-analytic theory – the tracing of the tangled pathways of the dream, the theories of neuroses, of 'paranoia', of infantile sexuality, and so on – had been erected only through many years of solitary and self-effacing investigation and intellectual labour against the resistance of a scientific world that was not merely 'muffled' but actively hostile and animated by a fanatical will to destroy the new ideas. As to Freud's suffering, he once told me that the ten years of complete isolation and constant attacks had weighed heavily upon him.[16] Only once – I suppose because of his disappointment, indeed crisis, re-peatedly mentioned in his writings, at the untenability of his theory of the infantile sexual trauma as the indispensable 'cause' of hysteria – did he become doubtful of the course his investigations were following, he said, but he weathered this crisis. I remember distinctly what a deep impression these confidences made upon me and what a central role they played in my understanding of Freud's personality and development. For what Dilthey says of man in general, namely, 'What man is, we learn only from his history,' applies also to individuals, and is particularly true of Freud.

Even though I had no complete knowledge at that time of the extent and form the opposition to Freud's theories had taken, nor that more and more new forms of opposition were arising all the time, I nevertheless had depressing (to me) and thoroughly 'eloquent' proof of it when I went to see Breuer[17] to convey to him my father's[18] greetings. I do not recall a spoken remark, but I do remember the very 'eloquent' gestures and facial expressions with which he responded to my naive question about how he stood vis-à-vis Freud since the 'Studies'.[19] His look of downright pity and superiority, as well as the wave of his hand, a dismissal in the full sense of the word, left not the slightest doubt that in his opinion Freud had gone scientifically astray to such an extent that he could no longer be taken seriously, and hence it was better not to talk about him.

I had a distressing experience of an entirely different kind when Freud, after a meeting[20] with not more than six or seven of his followers in his home, took me aside afterward and said, 'So, have you seen the gang now?' This was the second deeply disturbing experience during this first visit, that showed me how alone Freud still felt and yet how keen he could be in his judgement.

[1] Eugen Bleuler (1857–1939), 1898–1927, successor to Auguste Forel, Prof. of Psychiatry in Zurich, and Director of the Cantonal Burghölzli Institute, teacher of Jung and Binswanger, early supporter of psychoanalysis, later increasingly critical. Cf. Freud (1974a), p. 5, note 8; Walser (1970), pp. 27–34; Binswanger (1941a).
[2] Bleuler (1911)
[3] Cf. Introduction, p. vi.
[4] Karl Abraham (1877–1925), intern at the Burghölzli 1904–07, then in neurological practice in Berlin. In contact with Freud from 1907, founded Berlin Psychoanalytic Society 1908, founder member of the committee 1912. Cf. Abraham, Hilda (1976).
[5] Hans Wolfgang Maier (1882–1945), psychiatrist, student of Forel and Aschaffenburg, on the staff at the Burghölzli from 1905; Director of the Burghölzli 1927 (successor to Bleuler); cf. Klaesi (1946). [This sentence is inexplicably omitted from the American edition of Binswanger (1956c) – translator's note].
[6] Carl Gustav Jung (1875–1961), favoured by Freud from 1907 as 'continuer and perfecter' of his work; developed analytical psychology after his break with Freud; cf. Jaffé (1977), Stern (1977) and Brome (1978).
[7] Franz Riklin (1878–1938), intern at the Burghölzli and colleague of Jung in the word-association experiments 1902–04, doctor in the Rheinau Clinic 1904–09. Cf. Freud (1974a), p. 26, note 3, Totentafel (1938) and Ribi (1971).
[8] *Diagnostische Assoziationsstudien: Beiträge zur experimentellen Psychopathologie*, Jung (1906a).
[9] *Über die Psychologie der Dementia praecox: Ein Versuch* (1907).

[10] Emma Jung, née Rauschenbach (1882–1955).

[11] [Binswanger's note] Curiously (or should I say, significantly?) Freud does not mention this visit, either in his 'History of the Psychoanalytic Movement' [1914d] or in his autobiography [1925d]. In the former he reports at that time only the visit of his colleague from Zurich, the refined and distinguished Max Eitingon, then a student, who remained a close associate of Freud all his life. [Eitingon (1881–1943), after first studying natural science, then medicine and philosophy in Leipzig, Halle, Heidelberg, Marburg and Zurich (while there 1906 and 1908 also worked at the Burghölzli), from 1909 (independently from 1910) psychiatrist and neurologist in Berlin, from 1919 directed, with Simmel, the Berlin Psychoanalytic Institute (polyclinic and educational establishment), member of the 'secret committee', emigrated to Palestine 1933, founder of the Psychoanalytic Institute in Jerusalem. Cf. Jones (1943), *Max Eitingon in Memoriam* (1950), Neiser (1978).] According to Freud, this visit took place in January 1907, and 'other visits followed which led to an animated exchange of ideas'. In the same context he explicitly states that his first meeting with Jung took place in Salzburg in the spring of 1908 (*Ges. Schriften*, XI, 161). However, Jung's and my 1907 visit is mentioned in the second volume of Ernest Jones's biography of Freud [Jones, 1953–7, Vol. 2, p. 36]. Furthermore, the author of the paper published in 1906, which Jones ascribes to me [*ibid.*, 2, 37], is Eugen Bleuler. Nor was I later the director of the Kreuzlingen Mental Hospital, but rather of the Private Clinic for Nervous and Mental Patients. The last-mentioned fact is important because subsequently Freud sent patients to this institution for psychoanalytic treatment.

[12] Mathilde Freud (1887–1978).

[13] Cobenzl Palace Hotel on the Kahlenberg, originally the seat of Count Philipp of Cobenzl, a favourite excursion destination of the Viennese.

[14] Minna Bernays (1865–1941), Martha's sister, who lived in the Freud household from 1896.

[15] *Die 'Sache'* in the original: i.e., psychoanalysis

[16] Cf. 'Autobiography' (XI, 160, 168) where he dates his isolation from 1895/6 (his split with Breuer) to 1906/7 (meeting with the Zurich school). Cf. also IV, 411 and 425, as well as Jones I, 365.

[17] Josef Breuer (1842–1925), doctor and physiologist, treated 'Anna O.' whose case was taken up as an archetype of cathartic therapy in *Studies on Hysteria* jointly published with Freud (1895d). Cf. Hirschmüller (1978).

[18] Robert Binswanger (1850–1910), psychiatrist, Director of the Bellevue Sanatorium from 1880 to 1910; cf. Brunner (1911).

[19] Freud (1895d).

[20] This refers to the meeting of 6 March 1907 which was attended by eleven members of the 'Wednesday Society' in addition to Freud himself and the guests Jung and Binswanger. Alfred Adler gave a lecture 'A Psychoanalysis'. Cf. *Minutes*, Vol. I (1962), pp. 138–45 and below, letter 80B.

The Correspondence

1F

Prof. Dr. Sigm. Freud[1]   14 January 1908
                                        IX, Berggasse 19

Many thanks for the First Trick.[2] Looking forward to the Second.

                                               Yours, Freud

[1] Printed visiting card.
[2] This is – as is clear from a note by Binswanger on the back of the visiting card – thanking Binswanger for sending his dissertation (1907–08a); at the same time a play on Wilhelm Busch's *Max und Moritz*, which Freud loved and used as comparisons and illustrations; cf. Jones (1953–7), Vol. II, p. 147, and under 16F. [*Max und Moritz* is a book of children's verse well-known in German-speaking countries. The English translation, *Max and Moritz, A Juvenile History in Seven Tricks*, by Charles T. Brooks, was published in 1871. A.J.P.]

2F

                                              5 January 1909
Prof. Dr. Freud   Vienna IX, Berggasse 19

Dear Dr. Binswanger,
My best wishes to you in your new home.[1] I was very sorry not to have seen you in Zurich,[2] but I had all sorts of pressing tasks. This letter carries what is still a hypothetical question but one that may soon become of practical importance: would your clinic be able to take children (from about eight years onwards) who need psychic[3] treatment of our kind, i.e., do you have nurses whom you feel you could trust yourself to train for this, as the physician himself will not have an easy time with this kind of treatment? I am thinking, for example, of the young lady who, after you had cured her, became a nurse and who could be assumed to have a special interest in this therapy.[4] The analysis of the phobia of a 5-year-old boy[5] published in the first half-volume of our *Jahrbuch* will have drawn your attention to the importance of this type of child therapy.

                                          With kind regards,
                                               Yours, Freud

[1] Reference to Ludwig Binswanger's and Hertha Fanny Buchenberger's (1880–1971) wedding on 2 April 1908.
[2] In September 1908, on his way back from London and Berlin, Freud had visited Jung in Zurich and was Jung's guest in the Burghölzli apartment, but did not on that occasion look up Bleuler who also lived in the Burghölzli; cf. Freud (1974a), pp. 171 and 372.

Ludwig Binswanger's wife, Hertha, née Buchenberger, about 1910.

[3] This interpretation of the abbreviation 'ps' is not certain. Freud usually abbreviated 'psychoanalytic', even then, with the Greek letters ψα. However, the interpretation 'psychotherapeutic' does not fit the context here.

[4] Binswanger's [female] patient 'Irma' who was treated by Binswanger's uncle, Otto B. from February till the end of May 1907 and finally (from 29 May till 20 September) was analysed there by Ludwig Binswanger. In mid-December 1907 Irma took up a nursing post in a hospital, but became ill again in May 1908 and had to give up her nursing career for the time being. From autumn 1909, she worked again as a nurse to a 'mentally ill patient who was not easy to look after'; cf. Binswanger (1909a), especially pp. 353–5, note 1. For the discussion of the case see 16F and 17F.

[5] Freud (1909b).

3F

17 January 1909

Prof. Dr. Freud   Vienna IX, Berggasse 19

Dear Colleague,

I can only say: hurrah![1] So we have a rival for Franz Carl,[2] but one whom you would count among the 3rd generation. You are a young father, and that is a very beautiful thing. Please convey the congratulations of us all to your wife. Incidentally, an announcement in the next few days will reveal that there has been something going on here as well.[3]

My curiosity about the contents of the *Jahrbuch*[4] is also mounting considerably. The prospect you hold out of a visit from you is of course very welcome.[5] We shall discuss your analysis[6] and a host of related matters then.

I am most grateful to you for your information concerning the children requiring treatment. In the meantime, a second case has turned up which might conceivably be sent to your clinic for psychotherapy. It always takes parents a long time to make up their minds. But it is good to know about such things.

Please thank your father[7] for his good wishes. I may perhaps be coming to Constance this autumn and shall be able to make his acquaintance there. I met your uncle at the Viennese Natural Scientists' Congress in 1894,[8] I believe.

Cordially yours,
Freud

[1] Congratulations upon the birth of Binswanger's eldest son, Robert (1909–29) on 2 January 1909.

² This refers to Franz Karl Jung, born on 28 November 1908; cf. Freud (1974a), pp. 184ff. and Ellenberger (1970).
³ Marriage of Freud's eldest daughter, Mathilde, to Robert Hollitscher on 7.2.1909; cf. Jones (1953–7), Vol. II, p. 61.
⁴ The *Jahrbuch für psychoanalytische und psychopathologische Forschungen* was published by Freud and Bleuler, but Jung functioned as an independent editor. The first volume, first half (January 1909) appeared in March 1909.
⁵ Did not take place in that year.
⁶ Reference to Irma's analysis; see note 4 to 2F.
⁷ Otto Binswanger (1852–1929), professor of psychiatry at Jena, where he had treated Friedrich Nietzsche 1889–90 and where Ludwig Binswanger was his assistant for a long time. Cf. Ziehen (1929).
⁸ The 66th conference of the Society of German Natural Scientists and Doctors took place in Vienna 24–28 September 1894. Freud and Lothar Frankl von Hochwart chaired the lectures of the Department of Psychiatry and Neurology. See Wangerin and Taschenberg (1895), pp. 174–202.

4F

28 January 1909
Prof. Dr. Freud   Vienna IX, Berggasse 19

Dear Dr. Binswanger,
Though he is only 23, Herr J. v. T. is already considered to be one of Vienna's most prominent personalities. Because of his pronounced interest in music, ethics and philosophy, and his exceptionally generous donations to cultural causes, he is much liked and respected in intellectual circles.

His father, originally of a refined and kindly disposition, although intellectually undistinguished, contracted syphilis following an unhappy marriage, and then suffered an unending alternation of melancholic and manic episodes, finally dying in December 1908 after a great deal of pain and suffering. His mother, who will be calling on you, is exceptionally unfeminine and has contributed considerably to the aetiology of her son's illness. The brother, Dr. G. v. T., who will be escorting them, is as able as he is intelligent, having successfully surmounted the influences to which he was exposed during his youth.

The underlying causes of J.'s condition are not known to his mother; G. has had to hear about them from me without the patient's knowledge. The patient must not be told about this breach of confidence. He is a homosexual with the usual aetiology, namely flight from libidinous fixation to the mother, which was plainly provoked

6

by her ridiculous infatuation. Also overcompensation through a hyper-moral attitude for a sadistic disposition inherited from the mother; inhibition of sexual activity, so that he believes his many affectionate friendships to be untinged with eroticism. He adopted an abstinent mode of life, which, however, he would secretly interrupt by mastur-bation with homosexual phantasies. The resulting conflict was some-thing he was able to set aside and store up thanks to the cyclothymic disposition he inherited from his father, until, after his father's death, under the unconscious temptation to take his place at the mother's side, he broke down with self-reproach into severe depression.

Hints of suicide and a somewhat furtive and inflexible personality (due to his infantile character) have caused me to break off the psychoanalytic treatment that has been in process for 2 years and to hand him into your care until his depression has passed. At the moment he is not very responsive but should continue with the therapy. I would ask you to let him have his way on the whole, to give him few drugs, to listen to him patiently, to have him carefully watched, to keep him going along the lines I have indicated and to let me have reports from time to time. I am sending him to you because I can talk to you freely about everything.

Please remember me to your father, excuse my breach of profes-sional etiquette[1] on the grounds of personal acquaintanceship and perhaps deal with the case yourself. J. v. T. is at present copying his father's melancholia with a will of his own. His case grants one all sorts of deep insights into the essence of this condition, a subject we shall talk over one day in Vienna.

You can talk freely to Dr. G. about everything. The family phy-sician[2] who will be accompanying (or following) the patient is an ignoramus who has to be brought in for diplomatic reasons, but other-wise *knows nothing about the condition* and its circumstances. Please treat him accordingly.

With kind regards and best wishes to your little family,

Yours, Freud

I have glanced several times at your analysis[3] and shall study it during the next break from work (after the wedding).[4]

---

[1] The referral of the patient should more correctly have been made through the father, as director of the institute.
[2] Cf. note 2 to 5B.

[3] 'Versuch einer Hysterieanalyse', Binswanger (1909a). Cf. above, note 4 to 2F.
[4] Cf. note 3 to 3F.

5B

5 February 1909

Dear Professor Freud,

Since Herr J. v. T. has now been here for a week, I should like to give you a report on him. First, however, our most cordial thanks for your kindness in referring this patient to us.

I kept the patient in bed for the first few days to make observation easier and also because he was still quite listless and tired. His brother, physician and mother were still visiting him at the time, which only tired him more. During this period, the patient was tremendously self-absorbed, brooding about his past and future, about his good and bad character traits, about the bad influence his mother had had upon him, about his current 'neurasthenic' condition, etc. He said he felt he could never get better, that suicide was the only way out, but that he lacked the courage for it. He would recite his complaints, smiling with weary resignation and avoiding one's eyes. Following your advice, I listened to him patiently. We soon became friends and had some good talks about literature, music, etc., with the result that he quickly grew more responsive.

After the fourth day I let him get up and prescribed a fixed plan of treatment, which he follows scrupulously and which greatly interests him. The patient himself seemed to favour a certain measure of polypragmasy. In this connection I bore in mind your request to let him have his way. At first, he wanted to have electric treatment, something I do not normally undertake more than once a year. I accordingly faradised his back for five minutes each morning. Then he asked for permission to continue taking the glycerophosphate[1] Dr. Kauders[2] had prescribed for him. In addition he is having light hydropathic treatment and takes two walks every day. He has been given no drugs so far and will not be getting any either. He is so preoccupied with his treatment that he rarely gets down to the cause of his condition. He looks upon his stay here as a means of getting rid of his 'physical' lethargy. I do not, of course, ever urge him to talk about himself. I believe that I am right in thinking you do not wish me to use psychoanalysis with him here, and there would be no point to it in any case. In the meantime I am trying to keep the patient going along your lines. One day I hope you will tell me more in person about this very interesting case.

I do not take his talk of suicide very seriously, though I have repeatedly enjoined his servant never to leave his side, not even out of doors. The door between his room and that of his servant, who I am told is reliable, is kept open day and night. At my suggestion, the patient advised his mother not to visit him for a week, and never once asked after her during that time. But the mother now visits every day to make sure that nothing terrible has happened (she is staying in the hotel!), that he hasn't got his feet wet, etc. We are quite accustomed to that sort of thing here. She is greatly impressed by her son's cure!

Dr. Kauders tried to draw me out about all sorts of things: the case itself, what I thought of your therapy, etc., but I kept my own counsel. I would, however, point out that he not only knew that the patient had homosexual tendencies, but he was fairly well informed otherwise, by whom I do not know. For the rest, we got along quite well with him. The brother makes a very good impression.

The patient keeps completely aloof from the other patients, and I do not try to discourage this. If you, dear Professor, should have any other ideas on what you think the case requires, please let me know.

[Yours, L. Binswanger]

[1] At that time glycerophosphates were thought to have a tonic effect on the nervous system. Cf. Ewald and Heffter (1911), p. 221.

[2] Felix Kauders (1858–1937 – dates according to I. Fischer, 1938, p. 179) who qualified as a medical doctor on 14 November 1884 (UA Vienna, main doctoral minutes f. 141v) and worked as a junior doctor in the General Hospital from 1885 to 1888 (cf. *Medical Report of the Royal Imperial General Hospital of Vienna for the Year 1885 [–88]*, Vienna 1886 [–90]). In 1909 he was working in general practice in Vienna's first district, at no. 8 Bartensteingasse (as is shown by a visiting card in the patient's case notes).

6F

7 February 1909

Prof. Dr. Freud   Vienna IX, Berggasse 19

Dear Colleague,

Thank you very much for your letter and telegram.[1] The young couple[2] left a few hours ago.

As for J. v. T., I have no further requests. I know that he is in excellent hands. Dr. Kauders is a hypocritical ass. All that he knew before he saw you is what he had cunningly wormed out of the brother the night before he left.

Kind regards to your father. I look forward eagerly to the *Jahrbuch*.[3]

Very cordially yours,

Freud

[1] The telegram has not survived.
[2] Mathilde Freud and Robert Hollitscher; cf. note 3 to 3F.
[3] Cf. note 4 to 3F.

7B

27 February 1909

Dear Professor Freud,

I have not reported to you earlier because no significant change in our patient's condition has occurred. He clings to his illness with unshakable obduracy; but when he is diverted he can be charming, talks animatedly, plays the piano very beautifully, and takes an interest in everything. I consider it a small step forward that recently he let me coax him into coming to supper with me and my wife, that he plays the piano regularly, and that he recently said that he now realises that it is a good thing that he is here. I was very interested to observe how he torments his mother. During her last visit, he talked so much about suicide and about how he had to prepare her for it that she was completely dissolved in tears. I then appealed to his conscience and have temporarily stopped his mother's visits, which were infrequent enough even before that.

Since the patient's complaints are always the same, I hardly think I can tell you anything new. I am very interested in the case, quite apart from my personal interest in the young man. The patient has been saying that he may want to stay on in March.

I must also tell you that I recently gave a lecture on psychoanalysis[1] in Constance to an association of doctors from Baden and Switzerland and that they listened to me with interest. The suggestion came from an ophthalmologist and several general practitioners. A much more appreciative audience than psychiatrists!

[Yours, L. Binswanger]

[1] No reference found. For his spelling of the word 'psychoanalysis', cf. note 6 to 121B.

Bellevue Sanatorium: dining hall.

Bellevue Sanatorium: entrance hall with a view into the reading room
(left) and the entrance to the dining room (right).

8B

Kreuzlingen, 20 March 1909

Dear Professor Freud,

I must tell you that I am not altogether pleased with Herr v. T.'s condition. He tortures himself again and again with the same things, attempting unsuccessfully to put them behind him, and his conversation is unbelievably laborious and monotonous. Last week his main theme was the moral training of children, which he feels ought to take the place of religious instruction. He held forth endlessly on the subject, repeating himself and agonising over the lack of progress in this field, the fact that people are no longer interested in it, etc.; he finds it all quite incredible, completely incomprehensible. For the past week he has talked for half an hour every day about how strange it is that when he was a child he used to take very good dictation but could not write good compositions. He blames himself for not having told you this out of a false sense of shame. On several occasions the patient has made valiant attempts to initiate me further into his case history, which I have found particularly interesting, but he invariably returns to the above-mentioned topics. In addition, he tells me almost daily that he must make his will so that he can then commit suicide in peace; for that reason alone he would not be taking his life *here*. He is convinced that he is never going to get well.

The patient's overt behaviour rather belies his condition, inasmuch as he manages to keep himself busy, plays the piano for quite a long time every day, reads Goethe with pleasure and occasionally seeks out the company of other inmates. Since he is rather inaccessible mentally, I have tried to arouse his interest in gardening and gymnastics and have also tried to persuade him to take his meals at the communal table,[1] where he can sit beside me. I hope I am acting in accordance with your wishes. I do not think it will be long before I shall have talked the patient round, and under the present circumstances distraction seems to be the right thing for him.

A few days ago Dr. Jung was here;[2] I should very much have liked to join him once again on his trip to Vienna,[3] but unfortunately I am so busy right now that I have not even been able to get down to reading the *Jahrbuch*.[4]

With kind regards,

Ever yours, [L. Binswanger]

[1] Patients in the Bellevue Sanatorium who were in a position to do so, took their meals communally with the doctors in a dining hall.
[2] Presumably in conjunction with the visit that Jung had made to Paul Häberlin in March (probably between 17th and 20th); cf. Freud (1974a), p. 214.
[3] Carl Gustav and Emma Jung were in Vienna from 25 to 30 March 1909; cf. Jones Vol. II, pp. 56-7 (there wrongly 25-30 May) and Freud (1974a), p. 215.
[4] Cf. note 4 to 3F.

9B

Kreuzlingen, 13 April 1909

Dear Professor Freud,

Herr G. v. T. will have written to you about his visit here. The patient is determined to stay on until the middle of May, when we shall be able to decide the next step. He constantly dwells on thoughts of death, but I have no fear that he will do anything to himself here. Recently he has developed a taste for reading the death notices in the newspaper in order to discover at what age people die; he has looked up firearms in the encyclopaedia, has been asking about the most reliable method of hastening death, etc., etc. At the moment he is completely taken up with the effect of having had a small boil on his leg lanced. This business has diverted him a little and he declared yesterday that he had had the best day since he has been here. I am very grateful to you for having, with the help of Herr G., persuaded the mother to go to Vienna. She will probably not be leaving until the after-effects of the great operation[1] are over, perhaps at the end of the week.

I have read the analysis of little Hans[2] with immense interest and have learned a great deal from it. I shall soon get down to it once again. As far as the development of my own case[3] is concerned I should like best to send you the manuscript, but dare not do so because of my poor handwriting and also because of the great demands on your valuable time. Is it quite out of the question for you to come over here for a consultation once Herr v. T.'s release has to be considered? My father and I would be very happy indeed to see you. Frau v. T. would be certain to give her consent.

    With kind regards,

Ever yours very sincerely, [L. Binswanger]

[1] Intended ironically.
[2] Freud (1909b).
[3] Binswanger (1909a). The work was published in two parts.

10F

16 April 1909

Prof. Dr. Freud   Vienna IX, Berggasse 19

Dear Dr. Binswanger,

I felt I should write to you today, having yesterday sent a psycho-therapeutic letter in Oppenheim-style[1] to our patient. At the moment there is certainly no alternative to leaving him with you. Dr. G. has sent me a very sensible report on his brother.

For me, a visit to Constance at some point so as to get to know your new clinic and to see your father would undoubtedly be a great pleasure. Just now, however, there would have to be a very clearly expressed need by the party in question to make me agree.[2] I cannot make the journey cheaply, and I know well that rich people are very suspicious and that one can only keep one's authority over them[a] by forgoing every opportunity to earn money.

Your Part I[3] makes an excellent impression on the whole; I would add deservedly so. I should be glad to see the manuscript of Part II, even though you yourself have warned against it. Can the printer read your writing?[4] Although if it is in block capitals like your last letter, I shall be able to as well.

Jung's visit[5] was a great pleasure in more than one respect. I have since been to Venice for three days,[6] but did not have much of a rest. We ought to work until it is impossible to carry on, and take no breaks on the way.

With kind regards,
Yours, Freud

[a] Crossed out in the manuscript: 'Ihnen' (you), replaced by 'ihnen' (them).

[1] A reference to Hermann Oppenheim's (1858–1919) *Psychotherapeutische Briefe* [Psychotherapeutic Letters] (1906). Oppenheim, a psychiatrist and neurologist in Berlin, was director of a private clinic and was at first interested in psychoanalysis, but later became an opponent. See Eugen Bleuler's report on Oppenheim's attack on psychoanalysis at the 4th annual conference of the Society of German Neurologists in Berlin from 6–8 October 1910, Bleuler (1910b). Cf. Arthur Stern (1958).
[2] What is meant here is that the patient's family should ask Freud to visit for a consultation and that they should pay for this.
[3] From Binswanger (1909a).
[4] On Binswanger's handwriting, see Freud's severe verdict in 16F and 41F as well the facsimiles on pp. 208–09.
[5] From 25th to 30th March 1909 in Vienna, cf. note 3 to 8B.

[6] This journey is not mentioned by Jones, nor by Tögel (1989), but turns up as an 'Easter excursion' (so probably from 9–11 or 10–12 April 1909) in Freud's letter to Jung of 16 April 1909; see Freud (1974a), p. 218.

11B

18 April [190]9.

Dear Professor,

As a comment on yesterday's letter[1] from our patient, I should like to let you know that Herr v. T. has fairly suddenly and categorically fixed his departure for the end of this week. I have calmly not stopped him and have indicated to him that his decision is a welcome sign of a return of his former energy. Herr J. [v. T] has in fact made a little progress of late, albeit nothing very significant yet. At any rate he has the feeling that his 'acute depression' has passed and only the 'normal sick sadness' remains. Perhaps you yourself will later establish the source of this sudden upturn. The matter is not clear to me. [The] pat[ient] was previously a little awkward (more in the sense of inaccessible) with me for a time and for a few days did not even want to know about the continuation of the treatment with you. He asked whether he could not now master his illness under his own steam. As you can see, he is now more reasonable again. As the pat[ient] has said that he has given up the suicidal intentions he had in Vienna ('Actually a pity,' he added) and feels he will never get quite well here, we do not think it wise to keep him here. Whether progress can now be made with the analysis, I dare not say. If Herr v. T. *himself* does not change his mind again, and you, Professor, raise no objection, we shall therefore let him return. Particularly in these circumstances a consultation with you here would be very agreeable, but Herr G. v. T. has already told me, you can hardly ever get away. It needs only a word from you and Frau v. T. will agree. I am sorry to let Herr v. T go just when his 'normal' nature is coming a little more to the forefront.

   With kind regards

Yours, Ludwig Binswanger

[1] Not known to have survived.

12F

19 April 1909
Prof. Dr. Freud   Vienna IX, Berggasse 19

Dear Dr. Binswanger,
From the letter I received today from J. v. T., it appears that his depression is over and that he can once again resume his life and his therapy. However, the responsibility of deciding is too great on the basis of his evidence alone. No one but you can decide whether his clinical picture and change of attitude mean he is to be relied on. Please keep him under observation for at least another week. You will then be able to pronounce with certainty.
   Kind regards, yours,

Freud
P.T.O.[1]

P.S. By some chance that has not yet been explained I have mislaid your contribution to Brodmann's Journal,[2] from which I intended to take an example for the third edition of my *Everyday Life*.[3] Could you let me have another copy *by way of loan*?

[1] 'P.T.O.' draws attention to the postscript on the back (small size letter paper).
[2] The dissertation, Binswanger (1907–08a).
[3] Freud did not in fact do this; at least Binswanger's name was not mentioned in the *Psychopathology of Everyday Life* (1901b, 3rd enlarged edition, Berlin: Karger, 1910). Binswanger writes in his *Reminiscences* that Freud had told him verbally that he wanted to use the analysis of the word association 'bös-Öl' ['bad-oil'] (Binswanger 1907–08a) in the book, but had then distanced himself from it because it was 'too complicated'; see Binswanger (1956c), p. 10 in 1957 English edition.

13B

23 April [190]9

Dear Professor,
Owing to the illness of an uncle of mine[1] who has been one of our doctors for 18 years, I am overloaded with work and unfortunately have been unable until today to report on Herr v. T. I have indeed also come to the view that it is better that he should stay here longer, but I wanted to persuade him without arousing his very slight mistrust. Now that he is persuaded from all sides to remain *I* am in a better position and refer particularly to you [?]. Your second letter[2] made him

suspicious, on the other hand in the first he thought he saw an invitation to pull himself up and go home. So now he is *wavering*! I shall make as much use of the situation as possible and let you know what happens. Above all it is better since his mother left; I think he can now make progress before he goes home. At any rate, should he let us keep him at least till the beginning of next week (as I was already convinced when I sent the telegram[3]), then we need have no more worries about suicide, as long as he stays where he is. I do not perceive a 'fundamental change'; everything just seems to me quantitively better.[4] His will to live, to continue the treatment and his studies, is active again. He speaks better, more loudly and clearly, does not let his head drop so much, complains less, but still adheres a bit to certain illusions, e.g. that it would be so difficult for him to make himself understood to people after his return that he would become ill. He will not even be considered halfway well yet, still emphasises his 'sadness' which at least is no longer pushing him towards suicide. I have had a lot of trouble recently denying his stubborn requests for medication. He hopes for everything from bromine and lecithin[5] (!) etc., but gets nothing. In any case I shall not let him travel before Tuesday.

Please hang onto my dissertation. I still have enough copies. I send you the manuscript of the second part[6] with some apprehension after you so kindly expressed your encouragement. Above all I should like to hear of anything in particular you would like to know about in more detail for the theory or for the understanding of the case itself. A lot of it still strikes me as unclear for the reader, such as the analysis of the mirror symptom[7] at the beginning. Anyway, I was a bit depressed when I recently skimmed through it again quickly. I was still in many ways too naive, e.g. to believe that she had not masturbated. I know now how much points to it. Should...[8]

---

[1] Otto von Holst (1861–1910), a brother-in-law of Robert Binswanger, was a doctor at the Bellevue Sanatorium from 1890 till his death.

[2] To the patient.

[3] Not extant.

[4] The words 'everything just' and 'quantitively' are not legible with certainty in the letter book copy.

[5] Bromine preparations were used at that time as tranquillisers and sleeping draughts and were applied widely particularly in psychiatry. Lecithin was prescribed as a means of strengthening and building up in various conditions of weakness; cf. Wolf and Fleischer (1910), pp. 20ff and p. 94.

[6] Of Binswanger (1909a).

[7] Binswanger (1909a), p. 94.

[8] The end of the letter is missing. Presumably inadvertently (or because of private matters in the closing part) not copied by Binswanger, because the pages of the letter book are continuously numbered and no page is missing.

14B

27 April [190]9

Dear Professor,

Herr v. T. leaves here tomorrow (Wednesday) at 2 o'clock and arrives in Vienna at 6.30 on Thursday morning. We can now calmly let him travel! I am very excited how you will judge him; it is certainly easier for you than for me. Since his mother left he is decidedly better, composes his thoughts more clearly, speaks better. Thoughts of death have not disappeared, as you will see, but practically do not now come into consideration. He was already better physically, [but] being confined to his room for a long time, because of the carbuncle on his leg,[1] has left him rather pale.

You see, dear Professor, that I have behaved fairly passively with Herr v. T; do not draw from that any conclusions about my behaviour with other patients. I should be delighted if you are satisfied with the result of his stay here, which I never saw as anything but provisional mental and physical care for the duration of his 'acute depression'.

With kind regards

Yours L. Binswanger

[1] Cf. letter 9B.

15F

2 May 1909

Prof. Dr. Freud   Vienna IX, Berggasse 19

Dear Colleague,

You have done excellent work with J. v. T., gaining his lasting good will, and should it prove impossible to effect a cure, your clinic will always remain the haven he will seek out in difficult times.[1] I found him appreciably more sober, obliging and accessible and shall resume his treatment tomorrow. He has a great deal in him.

Your manuscript,[2] which I could not get down to during the past week, the most strenuous I have ever had to face, will cheer up my evening this Sunday. Let us hope that your hand and my eye will come to terms with each other. I should be very sorry if I had to confess that so paltry a reason prevented me from appreciating your work before it was printed. I am panting a great deal under the work load, am no longer fully satisfied with my corpus and am at present turning out to be quite unproductive. I am already living on my past. What work I can still do must go into the third edition of *Everyday Life* and the second of the 'Theory of Sexuality'[3].

Many thanks for sending me another copy of your thesis. Someone must have carried off the first.

In the hope still of seeing you before America,[4] with sincere regards to your family,

Yours, Freud

[1] J. v. T. received treatment at the Bellevue as an in-patient from 29 January to 28 April 1909, but had to be taken back into the Bellevue in April 1910 and a third time in April 1911; cf. 26F.

[2] Cf. note 3 to 4F.

[3] *Three Essays on the Theory of Sexuality*, 2nd German edition, Leipzig and Vienna, Deuticke, 1910; Freud (1905d).

[4] Freud, Jung and Ferenczi were invited to the 20th anniversary celebrations of Clark University, Worcester, Mass., in September 1909, where Freud and Jung gave lectures and received honorary doctorates; cf. Jones (1953–7), Vol. 2, pp. 59ff. and Freud (1974a), pp. 245–6 and the bibliographic references given there.

16F

17 May 1909

Prof. Dr. Freud   Vienna IX, Berggasse 19

Dear Dr. Binswanger,

You will have your manuscript[1] back within a few days. I have read it carefully, insofar as I could come to terms with your atrocious handwriting, which I finally managed to do. The analysis is as good as any could be without going back to the nuclear infantile complexes and will possibly have a particularly instructive effect precisely because it is incomplete. It is hard to find fault with details, for everything is correct, closely reasoned and put together well.[2] The apportioning of emphasis, in particular, seems to me to be apt. The most important factor is the homosexual component entangled with a displacement to the oral zone. I found that you gainsay my own experiences on just one occasion and it is at this point that I would put my spade in so as to dig down to the buried infantile element. You say that Irma[3] provides an example of non-incestuous object choice. I would say rather that Fräulein Faure[4] is for Irma nothing but a mother substitute in middle life. The proof is no doubt to be found in the attacks, which can only be fully explained by regression to an early infantile stage, and hence also through the phantasies leading up to them. The fact that Irma lost her father so early in her life may well have had a marked influence on the fixation of her homosexuality. The contributory aetiology is frequently observed. The phantasies about the coffin, about being buried alive, about dying with someone else, seem to relieve you of the need for, or else are still lacking in, their final interpretation. Now coffin = womb; being buried alive = life *in utero*. Thus the phantasies show that what is involved here is a return to the womb of the mother, as substitute for whom Fräulein Faure insistently suggests herself. Irma was either a thumb-sucker (which you deny) or else she was once given a surfeit of kisses. The third phantasy, about lying in the grave with someone else, naturally being taken to bed. The question is how many times Fräulein Faure repeated these caresses, which led to the first fixation of the libido, and what share must be *wholly* attributed to care of the infant by the mother. The aetiology must be divided between these two periods. I believe that Fräulein Faure provided a major oral impetus, for she is herself a neurotic whose phantasies are based on the same complexes (Poisoning = pregnancy). On the path to this regression lie the prostitution phantasies, which you have so rightly appreciated. Behind the fear of infection, which is slightly out of context, there is, however, hidden the fear of (and wish for) a child. Pregnancy is an infection (even in biological terms); spermatozoa are amongst the most feared bacteria! (It is to this that overcoat = condom should be traced back.) The staring into the mirror, which stands for the fear of disfigurement, is borne out by the association with the disfigurements of pregnancy. The brooding over what the room [German: *Zimmer*] would look like if it had a skull in it, and the interest in 'what it looks like inside', naturally relate to the inside of a woman [German: *Frauenzimmer*] i.e., to a womb. If a woman jumps out of a window, she not only falls down (which she usually interprets as a straight fall) but she also *bears down*. (Think of little Hans and the falling horses!)

20

Naturally, the blood is part of it as well, which explains the effect of the dream when she heard the scream. It is the sadistic dread of the horrors of childbirth. And so everything would seem to me to lead to the mother complex, along well-laid, indeed along typical, paths. When the hysteric wishes for a child, she identifies with her mother and in the end herself becomes a child in the womb.

You, who know the details of the case so much better than I, who can only infer them from your report, might try to determine whether this key does not also provide a solution to all the other little problems of the analysis. Please feel free to make whatever use you like of these random remarks. I would add a brief survey of the characteristic *methods of suicide* used by men and women. In every case, they are symbolic fulfilments of wishes of a sexual nature (with a negative sign). The woman:

> *drowns herself* – i.e., gives birth
> *jumps out of a window* – bears down
> *poisons herself* – becomes pregnant.

The man *hangs himself* – becomes a penis (pendere)

> *shoots himself* – handles his penis.

Busch put it with prophetic wisdom when he wrote about the hens in *Max und Moritz*:

> Jedes legt noch schnell ein Ei
> Und dann kommt der Tod herbei.
> [Each lays quickly one egg more
> Then they cross to th'other shore.[a]]

Herr v. T. is making quick, though fortunately not too quick, progress and is more tractable than he used to be. He now has the courage to face his parental complexes.

With kind regards and in the hope of hearing that you and your little family are well,

Many kind regards to your father.

Yours, Freud

[a] Tr. C.T. Brooks, published 1871.

[1] Cf. note 3 to 4F.

[2] On this matter, Binswanger says in his *Reminiscences* (1956c) [p. 16 of English edition, 1957]: 'To make somewhat understandable Freud's further discussion of my "Versuch", a discussion which surely is of interest even today, I should relate that a patient Irma was subject to severe hysterical twilight states and periods of excitability, during which she jumped from her bed, shook windows and doors, tried to throw

herself from the window, screamed that she had to dig up corpses in the graveyard and eat them, and passionately bit her own arms, maintaining that she was in her grave and that another woman had come and was biting her. She often contemplated herself in the mirror. In addition to dying and being buried, the themes of hetero-sexuality, homosexuality, and food were the most prominent. Visions of a former housekeeper, Fräulein Faure, also played a leading part in Irma's twilight states. When Irma was still a child, this housekeeper became mentally ill following a light attack of diphtheria; she scratched her throat till it bled, saying that a hole had been made in her windpipe, and screamed and begged that she not be buried before she had died. Irma's mother wrote to us that it took two days before the housekeeper could be confined in an institution. The children had heard the loud speaking and screaming, and Irma, who had conceived a great love for Fräulein Faure, was deeply impressed by all this. When Irma now saw Fräulein Faure appear before her in visions, as she often did, she talked with her. The Fräulein told her how nice she could be and even though she had perhaps spoiled Irma a little, "nevertheless, it was lovely". The Fräulein had the right to love Irma, the patient explained, because she was a girl, and now Irma must give her all the love she had. Fräulein Faure had on occasion rather violently kissed her mouth and eyes when she lay undressed on her bed. (All these statements were made during twilight states.)'

[3] The patient in Binswanger's 'Versuch einer Hysterieanalyse' (1909a). Cf. note 4 to 2F.

[4] The patient's (nursery) nurse in Binswanger (1909a).

17F

25 May 1909

Prof. Dr. Freud   Vienna IX, Berggasse 19

Dear Dr. Binswanger,

I am pleased that you felt able to accept my solutions and thank you, and particularly your wife, for your kind remarks and the renewal of your promise to visit me in Vienna. I have to answer your letter if only because you have asked for my views about the modification of the case history you have compiled. I entirely agree with you that these changes must not be too extensive and could be confined to a few points. It is quite true that the receptiveness of the beginners among the readers would be put to too hard a test and the appeal of the work reduced if you added, or rather included, the infantile ele-ment. What you already offer is enough. It also seems to me that your uncle, who has now given the work the clinical stamp of approval,[1] should not be held responsible for more than he in fact witnessed. Perhaps it would be best, in a short addendum, to point the initiated towards the infantile nuclear problems. To that end you are welcome to make whatever use you choose of the material in my last letter.[2]

As for success, I think this would have been far greater and more lasting had the case been fully resolved but you would have had to spend a *multiple* of the time you actually took to achieve that, i.e., to compel the patient to acknowledge these complexes. As you quite rightly point out, practical considerations are the deciding factor in a clinic. But perhaps your patient's subsequent fate will give you the chance of completing the analysis.[3]

As for your other patient,[4] whose case is highly complicated, I would prefer to discuss matters with you in person. J. v. T. has fully recovered, and for the time being is better than ever before: chastened, trustful and rid of quite a few idiosyncrasies.

With kind regards,
Yours, Freud

[1] Freud uses the Italian expression '*Stampigli*', common in Austria at that time. The work is headed: 'From the psychoanalytic clinic, Jena (Privy Councillor Prof. Dr. O. Binswanger)'.

[2] Binswanger expressly used Freud's comments and thanked him for his clarifications; cf. Binswanger (1909a), p. 337, note 1 and pp. 340ff.

[3] On this point Binswanger noted in (1956c), p. 19 of English edition: 'As regards the patient's subsequent fate, I was able to follow it thanks to her attachment to my wife and myself in the course of long visits to our home and by letters, until her death in her forties as a result of an intercurrent illness. She suffered no relapse despite a most unfortunate and childless marriage with an actor which ended in divorce after a few years, even though at first she had been happy and completely undisturbed in marital intercourse. She endured her immense disappointment just as courageously as she did the very difficult years of the First World War, during which she earned her living as a homeworker and by working in a soldiers' home. She also did various artistic work, including commercial art.'

[4] This is the first report of the analysis of the patient 'Gerda', about which Binswanger first published in 1911 as 'Analyse einer hysterischen Phobie' (1911a) [Analysis of a hysterical phobia], afterwards often referred to as the 'heel analysis'. Cf. note 1 to 58F.

18B

7 November 1909

Dear Professor Freud,

I hear that you have returned from your travels[1] and would like to welcome you back to Europe. I can hardly wait to hear in due course from Dr. Jung about your journey and your impressions.

I am dictating this letter during a spell of enforced leisure due to a fall from a horse. It happened almost four weeks ago now and still the effects refuse to vanish completely. I had spinal concussion and severe contusions on my back. There has been a great deal of time for reading and I have also worked on last summer's analysis, about which I wrote to you once.[2] That case had a successful outcome. The patient is now a happy bride and feels very well. The case has made a most favourable impression on my father and on the patient's family. I have learned an enormous amount from it and for the first time have come to appreciate the infantile element properly. It is precisely because of the emergence of the infantile factor that this analysis forms a good counterpart to Irma's. In respect of the contents, too, there are links between the two cases; I was able above all to apply the information you gave me about Irma very usefully to the new case. For, ultimately, all the boot-heel symptoms reflected the mother complex, and, moreover, the infantile as well as the maternal component. The tearing away of the heel from the boot was a symbol of both the patient's own birth and also of her giving birth to a child. The heel invariably represents the child, the boot the mother. I really cannot imagine in what other way this case, which has been going on for 18 years (from the age of 5), could have been cured. The analysis became a rare pleasure for me towards the end. Apart from this case, I unfortunately had few opportunities to engage in analysis last summer, because my work in the clinic took up a great deal of time (one of the physicians was ill over a long period). At the moment I am supposed to continue work on a case which Frank[3] has long been analysing unsuccessfully. A most unrewarding business; I would a hundred times rather have started from scratch.

I am very much looking forward to reading your contribution in the *Jahrbuch*,[4] first of all because I still know very little about compulsive neurosis, and secondly because I hope to learn from your presentation of the material. The second part of the Irma paper[5] will soon reach you in printed form. I should be very glad if, in due course, you told me quite frankly whether you are satisfied with the way I have handled the interpretations you sent me. I have omitted the analysis of the overcoat only because I felt I lacked the necessary links and that the reader would not be able to make so great a leap.

How is Herr v. T? He sent me a very contented letter in the summer. I hope, dear Professor, that your travels have done you good and that you are not too overburdened with work.

Please remember me to your family.

Ever yours, [L. Binswanger]

24

[1] The trip to Worcester, Mass; cf. 15F.
[2] The 'Gerda' case; cf. 17F and its note 4.
[3] Ludwig Frank (1863–1935), Director of the Münsterlingen Nursing Home 1890–1905, neurologist in Zurich from 1905. Developed, in connection with Breuer's and Freud's 'cathartic' method, a self-psychotherapeutic method. Cf. Walser (1968), p. 515, note 6. Binswanger considered himself to an extent a disciple of Frank; see letter to Frank of 1 April 1927, B.A. 443/37.
[4] 'Notes upon a case of obsessional neurosis' – the 'Rat Man' case, Freud (1909d).
[5] Binswanger (1909a), pp. 319–56.

19F

3 December 1909

Prof. Dr. Freud   Vienna IX, Berggasse 19

Dear Dr. Binswanger,

I have delayed my reply to your letter of 7 November so long that by now I can dispense with commiserations on your accident. I hope that you have fully recovered from the effects of your fall. The reason for my delay was of course something else – at the time the *Jahrbuch* was due from the printers and I wanted to wait until I could read the conclusion of your analysis so as to let you have the opinion you had asked for.[1] Then, as usual, there were weeks of waiting. The *Jahrbuch* finally reached me on 1 October.

Your analysis, quite apart from its diplomatic significance at this juncture,[2] is very valuable and no doubt wholly correct. Its fault, namely that it is so incomplete, becomes a virtue inasmuch as it may encourage beginners in clinics to strive for tangible successes even during short periods of treatment. The disclosure of exceptionally rich phantasies explaining the fits and deliriums is surprising and as yet something quite new in the literature. True, the technique is not the classic one,[3] but I think myself that in a case distinguished by absence states and deliriums it is not possible to make use of any other. The reason the synthesis is not plainly set out must be sought in the gap in the infantile material. You have made full use of my suggestions on this subject. What I meant by 'overcoat' is something that escapes me as well. In short, I can congratulate you with all my heart on this first contribution.

The only thing I took amiss was that with your statement that we only cure the symptoms of hysteria and not the condition,[4] you were quoting Ziehen.[5] In the light of our present knowledge, it is questionable what validity this statement has. In any case, Ziehen has by his loutish behaviour forfeited the right to any mention by us. It is a matter of self-respect. I take it that you noted this passage down before you learned of his well-known pronouncement on my work.[6] Nevertheless I feel there must have been time to remove the phrase at the proof stage.

I might also have wished that your support, of whose staunchness I am so sure, could have been expressed now and again in more forceful and less diplomatic terms.[7]

Herr v. T. is presently suffering a minor depression which stems, in the most instructive way possible, from suppressed rage due to unrequited love. I do not think it will cause any interruption to his life in Vienna. Should there be any dangerous rise in level I shall send him back to you in Constance.

I have not yet finished my work for America[8] and have been particularly taxed of late. December will be an easier month.

With kind regards, and in the hope of learning of your full recovery,

Yours sincerely, Freud

[1] The second half of Volume 1 of the *Jahrbuch* appeared in November 1909; cf. Freud (1974a), p. 621. It contained, among other works, the second part of Binswanger (1909a). Cf. also note 5 to 18B.

[2] This is an indication of how important it was to Freud at this time that psychoanalysis should also have a foothold in (institutionalised) psychiatry.

[3] In this 'course of treatment' ['*Kur*'], which was carried out from 29 May to 20 September 1907, Binswanger used hypnosis even 'for purposes of analysis [...] in the hope of getting it over more quickly, because I was about to go on holiday.' (1909a), p. 307.

[4] Binswanger had described Irma's 'hysterical type of reaction' and written: 'We can cure individual symptoms, but not the hysterical psychopathetical condition itself (Ziehen), the expression of which this type of reaction is.' Binswanger (1909a), p. 334.

[5] Theodor Ziehen (1862–1950), psychiatrist (Utrecht 1900, Halle 1903, Berlin 1904–12), private scholar in Wiesbaden 1912–17, Professor of Philosophy in Halle 1917–30. Cf. Herberhold (1978).

[6] During the discussion following a lecture given on 9 November 1908 by Abraham to Berlin Society for Psychiatry and Nervous Illnesses, Ziehen had said 'What Freud has written is all nonsense'. Cf. Freud (1965a) p. 55.

[7] See also Freud's criticism of Binswanger's work in a letter to Jung of 12 December 1909: 'When questioned by the author, I did not withhold my praise of Binswanger's excellent and effective analysis. But at the same time, in a definitely grumpy mood, I expressed my objection to his utterly superfluous mention of Ziehen and in general accused him of being a little too diplomatic.' Freud (1974a) p. 273.

[8] Preparation of the lectures in Worcester for publication; Freud (1910a).

20F

31 December 1909
Prof. Dr. Freud   Vienna IX, Berggasse 19

Dear Dr. Binswanger,

According to the clock you will be, by the time I reach the middle of this letter, the first to whom I can wish a happy New Year. I am very glad you did not take my candid words amiss; I may have been a little blunt; I am glad to see that no harm was done and even think that I can read more agreement between your lines than in your actual words. I did not object to your independent views, which I deeply respect in everyone, nor to your stopping at your present point of development, but to something different, more fundamental, something to be clarified by analysis, which you will certainly not acknowledge consciously: you unwittingly give the impression of someone in polite society apologising to his peers for having mentioned his association with social inferiors in whom he has discovered all sorts of estimable qualities. You will say 'no', but as you know analysis can be painful on occasion.[1]

Now to the main point: your announcement that you will be coming to see us during the next few weeks is good news indeed. It makes no difference to me what day you choose; I do not expect to be less busy at any particular time. We shall chat in the evening after work and after supper for as long as you can stand it; the day must inevitably be devoted to duty. On Wednesday and Saturday you will give me great pleasure by joining me at our society evenings[2] and taking part in the seminar[3] if you can find nothing better for you, and especially for your wife, to do. We shall be delighted to make her acquaintance. My sister-in-law and my now oldest daughter[4] will endeavour to take her out when you are otherwise occupied. It is a poor programme but only a rogue promises more than he can deliver,[5] and these promises will at least be kept in friendship. (Happy 1910!)

Do please let us know soon when we may expect you. With kind regards, and in anticipation,

Yours, Freud

[1] Cf. note 7 to 19F.
[2] Wednesday evening was reserved for the gathering of the so-called Wednesday Society; cf. *Minutes*, Vols. 1–4 (1962–75).
[3] For the winter semester 1909–10 Freud had announced his 'Lectures on Neurosis

and Psychoanalysis' to be held in the lecture theatre of the Psychiatric Clinic from 7 till 9 on Saturday evenings; cf. Gicklhorn and Gicklhorn (1960), p. 154.

[4] Actually Sophie Freud – i.e., his eldest daughter, Mathilde, had now married and was no longer under the same roof.

[5] German proverb of which Freud was particularly fond: he quotes it again and again. See *Introductory Lectures on Psychoanalysis* (1916–17a), *S.E.*, Vol. XVI, p. 251; letter to Jung of April 1907 (1974a) p. 40; letter to Arnold Zweig of 20 January 1936 (1968a), p. 119.

21F

7 January 1910

Prof. Dr. Freud   Vienna IX, Berggasse 19

Dear Dr. Binswanger,

My letter which crossed yours will have given you the answer *anticipando*[1] that you are equally welcome here at any time. I hope that your wife will be coming with you; you will no doubt have other things to interest you as well during your stay, since my time is so very limited.

Looking forward to seeing you soon.

Yours, Freud

[1] Latin: 'in anticipation'.

22F

12 January 1910

Prof. Dr. Freud   Vienna IX, Berggasse 19

Dear Dr. Binswanger,

In response to your letter, which has just arrived, and in view of the many different visits you threaten to make in Vienna, I would ask you to reserve the whole of the Sunday after your arrival and to take your meals with us despite all the many more glittering temptations you will have. On Saturday I shall be lecturing from 7–9 in the psychiatric lecture theatre of the University (General Hospital).[1] We can discuss everything else on Sunday.

We all look forward very much to meeting your wife.

Kind regards,
Freud

[1] Cf. note 3 to 20F.

Binswanger's Second Visit to Vienna, 15 to 26 January 1910

Binswanger described this visit in his *Reminiscences of a Friendship* (1956c), pp. 4–8 in the 1957 English edition, for which he used a manuscript written down soon after the visit. This manuscript still survives. Binswanger made corrections and deletions to it in preparation for using it in his *Reminiscences*. Because of its freshness and directness, the text of this original manuscript (under the title *Visit to Vienna 15–26 January[1] 1910*), without corrections and deletions, is reproduced in the Appendix to the present volume, pp. 229–34.

[1] Binswanger erroneously gave the month as February in his *Reminiscences*.

23F

17 February 1910

Prof. Dr. Freud   Vienna IX, Berggasse 19

Dear Dr. Binswanger,

Herr v. T. is due to due to start his year's military service in the autumn. It is not too early to take steps to obtain an exemption. We therefore ask you to let us have [an] impressive affidavit,[1] presented with all due pomp and circumstance, concerning his stay at your clinic, in which his heredity should be stressed and everything else painted in the most sombre colours. I shall then send him with it to some of our official psychiatrists.

His condition, incidentally, has greatly deteriorated. I have already initiated moves to send him back to you. His mother's operation (total extirpation[2]) has had a particularly adverse effect. I would ask you to expedite the affidavit and to send it to him direct.

— Young M.[3] has turned out to be a dementia praecox case and his family are unable to afford a clinic.

With kind regards to you, your wife and your father,

Yours cordially,
Freud

[1] Such an affidavit has survived only from the second period as an in-patient from 16 April 1910: 'Herr J. v. T. has been in our sanatorium since the 10th inst. for the second time. The patient is again suffering from melancholic depression, which manifests itself in an explicit inhibition from any expression of will, a slowing down of thought processes and an impoverishment of the content of his thoughts;

additionally in a very subdued mood, self-reproach, anxiety about the future, and huge hypochondriacal notions.

'Alongside this he suffers from great internal unrest, inconstancy and insecurity. The risk of suicide is not ruled out. His physical condition has very much deteriorated. It is predicted that the patient's condition will require him to remain in the sanatorium for several months.'

[2] A disconnection of womb and ovaries.

[3] A patient who clearly had previously been seen at Kreuzlingen.

24F

3 March 1910

Prof. Dr. Freud   Vienna IX, Berggasse 19

Dear Dr. Binswanger,

Although I am in the throes of a fit of writing (a Leonardo study[1]) I must break off to thank you most cordially for embellishing my Japanese corner and for sending me the book[2] in which I am no doubt meant to read the marked passage. I promise to do so as soon as I am over my fit, but in the meantime am unable to fathom how you were able to persuade your uncle[3] to part with the Japanese print since I myself should never have given it up; it is much too fine. Nor do I know why I have deserved such a present but I happily accept it and hope that your generosity has brought you some pleasure too.

v. T. is still carrying on, though in wretched circumstances. He will be exempted from military service.

Kind regards to you and your wife, from my family too.

Yours, Freud

[1] Freud (1910c).

[2] Binswanger had apparently sent Freud a Japanese woodcut and a book, but no further details can be established.

[3] Otto Binswanger.

25B

8 April 1910

Dear Professor Freud,

I had a letter full of dejection from Herr v. T. a few days ago, so that the telegram that came today from his brother was not a complete surprise. I am very sorry about the latest turn of events. The purpose of these lines, dear Professor, is to ask you whether you would agree to my handing the patient over to Dr. Maeder[1] for treatment. My lectures start in a week's time and our clinic is full, so that I am almost stretched to the limit. Should you have any reservations about this, I shall of course try to arrange things so that I can treat Herr v. T. myself. If Dr. Maeder is to take over, however, I shall naturally look in on him frequently, and during the first few days in particular I shall collaborate closely with him. We should be grateful to have your opinion on the danger of suicide.

Herr v. T. will be in the same house as last time, but we cannot offer him the same rooms.

We came back from Nuremberg[2] in very high spirits and are now analysing away for all we are worth. I now also realise how much one can learn from Stekel,[3] provided one has oneself advanced to a certain point.

With kind regards, and regards, too, from my wife and from Maeder,

Yours, [L. Binswanger]

[1] Alphonse E. Maeder (1882–1971), Swiss psychotherapist, was engaged as a doctor at the Bellevue Sanatorium from April to September 1910. After the split between Freud and Jung, he followed Jung. Cf. Freud (1974a), p. 45, note 3, Graber (1962), Bovet (1971) and Rümke (1952).

[2] Second International Psychoanalytic Congress, Nuremberg, 30–31 March 1910, see Jones (1953–57), Vol. II, pp. 75–7.

[3] Wilhelm Stekel (1868–1940), founder member of the Wednesday Society, previously in analysis with Freud; editor (originally in collaboration with Alfred Adler) of the *Zentralblatt* of which Freud was Editor-in-Chief, which he carried out on his own for nearly two years after the split with Freud. Spent his last years in London, where he took his own life. See Freud (1974a), p. 71, note 9, Missriegler (1928) and the obituary, '*Dr. Wilhelm Stekel*', *Psychoanal Rev*, Vol. 27 (1940), p. 506.

26F

9 April 1910
Prof. Dr. Freud   Vienna IX, Berggasse 19

Dear Dr. Binswanger,

So I have had to send J. v. T. back to you after all. When I left, he seemed to be better, but by the time I came back the picture had changed.[1] His apathetic depression had given way to a painful anxiety which makes him a torture to be with for all those around him. In this state, he confessed to consistently practising, almost daily, masturbation with homosexual phantasies, from the effects of which he now expects the worst. Moreover, he is full of justified self-reproach that he had practised deception for so long, feigning a successful sublimation of his libido in friendship. He feels quite wretched physically, asks for exercise [and] rest; I have also promised him probe[2] (or psychrophore[3]) treatment to blunt the masturbation stimulus. He is very *ashamed*, wanted me to keep his masturbation a secret from you and asked that you at least keep it from Dr. Kauders and from his brother (who has been informed by me).

Do not release him in a hurry this time. The prospects of a complete cure are not very favourable.

With kind regards to you, your wife and Dr. Maeder,

Yours, Freud

[1] After taking part in the Second International Psychoanalytic Congress at Nuremberg (30–31 March 1910) Freud, together with Jung spent a further day at Rothenburg-on-Tauber and returned home on 2 April. See Freud (1974a), p. 304.

[2] 'Exploration of the urethra with a straight or curved metal catheter' was described in Rohleder: *Die Masturbation* (1907), p. 317, as an instrumental measure against masturbation. He said its success rate was 'reasonably satisfactory'.

[3] Psychrophore: a catheter with flow and return tubes for flushing out with cold water, recommended towards the end of the nineteenth century by Wilhelm Winternitz for the treatment of seminal emissions, weaknesses of the urethra, etc., see Winternitz (1890), pp. 457–63. See also *Billings Nat. Med. Dict.*, 1890, quoted in *O.E.D.*, 1989.

27F[1]

12 April 1910

Dear Dr. Binswanger,
Of course I have no objections and anticipate that you will have no difficulty in persuading v. T., provided only that you keep M[aeder] well enough informed.[2]

Kind regards, Freud

[1] Postcard.

[2] See above 25B. The treatment of J. v. T. was now delegated to Alphonse Maeder. The following letters between Maeder and Freud arose out of this delegation. Binswanger kept Freud's letters to Maeder together with those addressed to himself. As is clear from the case histories, Freud also wrote to the patient personally during this second period as an in-patient. For example one reads that on 22 May 1910 he was: 'Somewhat excited today about a letter from *Freud*. Before the start of the analysis, the letter contained the warning that he must make a decision about the two courses open to him: man or woman, otherwise he will revert to masturbating.'

28M
[Alphonse Maeder to Freud]

18 April 1910

Dear Professor,

Allow me to tell a little about Herr v. T. He is settling in quickly, despite all statements to the contrary. He is expected to recover physically, demonstrates an enthusiasm for physical activity which easily becomes excessive; one must almost restrain him from physical activity. He works in the garden, goes to the gym, goes for walks, goes through a lot of hydrotherapeutic procedures, craves for Sana-togen[1] ... One of his fears that has become stereotypical is that of 'getting fat', (clearly psychically motivated) he resists every attempt at substantial nourishment – made necessary by his activity, he has lost about 9 kg since his last stay here by the way. It would be very effective suggestively if you were to happen to express a view on it. The following point is not yet cleared up: In the beginning he resisted the psychrophore[2] treatment and we were quite unable to influence him in the matter. Then an earlier occurrence of balanitis[3] came into consideration. Now he was inclined to give his consent. I should appreciate it, respected professor, if you would express your opinion on this. Do you consider it suggestively effective for him; is not the local treatment possibly a new stimulus etc? A word on a postcard will suffice.

The days in Nuremberg[4] have left a deep and strong impression on me; it is to be hoped that such stimulation will be renewed not too seldom. Last autumn I attended the International Congress of Psychology in Geneva,[5] but came home as empty as I had gone. The situation is comparable with the relationship of romanticism and classicism in French literature (XIX), life and the set phrase.

I remain, yours respectfully,
A. Maeder.

Dear Professor,[6]

It is also important that you give the patient some hint about the duration of the treatment. He insists you spoke of only 3–4 weeks. After the experiences last time we must be prepared! I do find an inner improvement in Herr v. T. since last time.

With kind regards,

Yours, L. Binswanger

¹ A lactoprotein preparation manufactured by Sanatogenwerke Bauer & Cie, Berlin, which was prescribed at that time for undernourishment, neurasthenia, hysteria, etc; cf. Wolf and Fleischer (1910), p. 113. [Presumably the same product as that of the same name marketed in Britain from the 1890s as a 'nerve tonic food' and described in advertisements as containing organic phosphorous and protein. It was widely sold, incidentally without prescription, at least until the 1950s. T.R.]

² See note 3 to 26F.

³ Inflammation of the *glans penis*.

⁴ Cf. note 2 to 25B.

⁵ 6th International Congress of Psychology 2–7 August, chaired by Edouard Clapa-rède; cf. Freud (1974a), note 5, p. 245.

⁶ Manuscript P.S. in Binswanger's hand.

29F
[Freud to Alphonse Maeder]

Prof. Dr. Freud

21 April 1910
Vienna IX, Berggasse 19

Dear Doctor ['Maeder' added in Binswanger's hand],

Many thanks for your report on J. v. T. His enthusiasm for physical work is based, as you are aware, on the assumption that he has suf-fered – allegedly excessive – physical damage through masturbation. However, it is desirable that he retain something of that enthusiasm in later life. He only resisted the psychrophore because he doubted whether this method could be applied harmlessly in Bellevue. But now he has learned to trust you. I do not think the probe treatment can do him any harm; rather will it become a masturbation substitute, stop him from masturbating and eliminate the slight organic changes in the *pars prostatica*.¹ Last year he continued to masturbate the whole time he was at the clinic. So please ask him about it!

Whether we can go on leaving him with you depends on whether he becomes used to ps[ychic]² therapy with you. Here he would only be a nuisance to me. Incidentally, I have agreed a minimum period of 4–6 weeks with him.

His obstinacy considerably reduces his chances. He does not want to consider the alternatives open to him. He wants to be neither man nor woman, nor will he settle for guilt-free masturbation; he wants to be completely abstinent, although he might have learned by now that this resolve can only lead to masturbation, which he then hides from me, and which he manages to live with for a while thanks to a heightened manic state; until the crash comes, that is. He is a stone, wrapped in cotton wool.

I shall write to him should you need something in particular, or should he appeal to me.

The after-effects of the 'Nuremberg Reichstag'[3] are making themselves felt to advantage even here.

Please remember me to Dr. and Frau Binswanger. With kind regards,

Yours, Freud

[1] That part of the urethra which is surrounded by the prostate gland.
[2] Cf. note 3 to 2F.
[3] Jocular reference to the 2nd International Psychoanalytic Congress in Nuremberg.

30M
[Alphonse Maeder to Freud]

12 May 1910

Dear Professor,

I should like to inform you a little about Herr v. T's condition. He is gradually recuperating physically, getting stronger. His healthy fresh complexion annoys him; this feeling of well-being strikes him as inappropriate because it contradicts his hypochondriac tendencies. In sport and physical work he is still completely inept and infantile. He goes through the psychrophore treatment without difficulties and, as he says, successfully.

Psychically it can be seen that he has intellectual interest[s] again, he reads relatively a lot, likes discussing it with me; though he gets stuck on the complex points (ethics and denominational questions). Then his stubbornness comes very much to the fore. He has great difficulty coming out of himself. He has a good rapport with nobody here except me. His introversion is very pronounced. His depression changes, it is sometimes less deep, his world-weary expression appears much less often. He can also be diverted more easily. Once he played a Beethoven symphony with Dr. Ludwig[1] with deep musical sensitivity. He has too little spontaneous initiative.

Herr v. T. talks about leaving for Vienna in eight to ten days, which seems decidedly premature. He would certainly accept your opinion. We should be very grateful to you if you would tell him or us your view about it. He is thinking of continuing the treatment with you at the beginning of June.

I remain, Yours faithfully

A. Maeder

Kind regards from the Binswanger family.

[1] Ludwig Binswanger.

31M
[Alphonse Maeder to Freud]

2 June 1910

Dear Professor,

Herr v. T. leaves for Vienna tomorrow. Allow me to bring you up to date about him. The awakening interest in intellectual matters mentioned in my last report has grown much stronger in recent weeks. Music also attracts him again, he wants to hear Wagner in Vienna next week; he will make a start at home with light philosophical works. A glance at the outside world recently let him discover some of the beauty of our lake. Physically he has got decidedly stronger, [even] if he has put on only about three pounds. On the credit side I would also say that he grumbles much less and spontaneously complains less than he did at the beginning.

The two basic characteristics remain which are not good for the prognosis; his isolation in 'la tour d'ivoire' and his stubbornness. He has established contact with nobody but me. Our comfortable rapport was good, but I could have no influence on him with important points if I was of a different opinion. Towards the other people he would rather present himself as slightly hostile, it is very much like a persecution *in nuce*[1] (the brother with his financial control over the patient's spending on philanthropic things, and you yourself, Professor, with your predominance in the sexual field, are both included here). His stubbornness shows itself quite noticeably in the aggravated lack of adaptability and the intransigence. I think that the influences of his milieu upon his ego-feelings have worked strongly in recent years. He still remains undecided about the question of channelling his libido, after receiving your letter he was excited, spoke of total sublimation while going back to Spinoza and Kant. He has certainly moved on a bit since then. At least he sees the possibility of a reasonable choice. I do not know if you knew that Fraülein Tr.[2] was here for a few days. Her presence worked quite well for a while, but I think more by way of a diversion. I had the impression that his attempt at transference misfired. After her departure he was more sorry for himself, grimmer and grumbled more again for a few days. Thus he spoke all the more about the dear [male] friend I., with whom he is to make an excursion on Sunday. His letters have always made him particularly happy. It is significant that the patient has never told me of homosexual tendencies in practice [?] (he touched on all other important points, I believe). The enthusiasm he is now developing for tearing this friend away from his job as an official for some more independent occupation has a distinct character. He probably wants to atone for 'sinful' fantasies. The feeling of guilt with J. v. T. is still very strong; on bad days he distributes to the whole world, himself included, a large load of guilt.

It is also interesting to notice that in matters of everyday life he now shows his ineptitude and puerility, while in discussions on philosophical or aesthetic themes for example his judgement is relatively good and sharp. During the whole treatment I have restricted myself to be as passive as possible in psychic things – I only know what he has volunteered. Only in the matter of choice have I pressed him particularly, to accept a reasoned solution, not an arbitrary one, and asked him not to send a letter he had written to you in anger.

We have used the cold probe[3] until this morning, he has offered no resistance from the first time, on the contrary, he seems at last to regard it as a useful weapon.

The patient will look you up in a few days. You will best be able to see for yourself how he is. – As a person the impression he has made upon me has at times been nice, indeed charming; from the treatment with you he has, I believe, really gained a lot intellectually. If one sees him at a bad moment one has no idea what is hidden beneath all this, may I say, functional nonsense.

I do not know if you have heard anything about the recent conference of south-west German Neurologists and Psychiatrists in Baden-Baden.[4] *Hoche*[5] spoke of Freudism (as Claparède calls the movement) as a psychic epidemic among doctors;[6] and that it was a reaction by doctors against extreme physical therapy in order to attract tired patients.[7] *Laquer*[8] suggested that a discussion should follow because the substance of the paper had been very clear and informative [?] (Everything is reported secondhand, I myself [?] was not there). The first response from the 'deformed creature' was the simultaneous establishment of the *Zentralblatt für Psychoanalyse*,[9] for which I heartily congratulate you.

My professional duties have recently taken me to Friedländer.[10] It was easy to convince oneself that he is an idiot, through and through even.

Our psychiatrists' conference in Herisau[11] (Swiss) comprised more than 25% convinced followers.

I remain yours faithfully, A. Maeder

To this excellent report by colleague Maeder I personally should just like to add my kind regards. M. has dealt with the v. T. case splendidly, as you will be convinced.

Yours ever, L. Binswanger[12]

---

[1] Latin: literally 'in a nut' – in miniature.

[2] An actress whom the patient had supported financially.

[3] Cf. note 3 to 26F.

[4] See 35th Roving Conference of South-west German Neurologists and Psychiatrists 28–29 May 1910 in Baden-Baden, *Arch. Psychiatr. Nervenkh.*, Vol. 47 (1910), pp. 938–89.

[5] Alfred Erich Hoche (1865–1943), Professor of Psychiatry in Freiberg; cf. Binswanger (1944a) and Seidler (1986).

[6] 'Eine psychische Epidemie unter Ärzten' (1910).

[7] 'Pharmacological therapy had already long been discounted here [in nervous conditions], particularly also in sanatoria with astutely varied series of physical treatments it was refused as something hackneyed whose suggestive effect upon patients had been used up.' Hoche (1910), pp. 1009f.

[8] Leopold Laquer (1857–1915), nerve specialist in Frankfurt am Main; cf. Fischer (1962), Vol. 2, pp. 866ff.

[9] *Das Zentralblatt für Psychoanalyse: Medizinische Monatschrift für Seelenkunde* was launched at the 2nd International Psychoanalytic Congress in Nuremberg 30–31 March 1910. The Editor-in-Chief would be Freud, the editors Adler and Stekel, published by J. F. Bergmann in Wiesbaden; cf. Freud (1974a), p. 304.

[10] Adolf Albrecht Friedländer (1870–1949), psychiatrist, at that time director of the Hohe Mark private clinic in the Taunus Mountains, a severe opponent of psychoanalysis who, starting in 1907, had published several critical works about psychoanalysis. Cf. also note 3 to 73F below.

[11] Swiss Psychiatrists Conference, Herisau, Whitsun (15–16 May) 1910. Cf. Freud (1974a), p. 319, note 2a.

[12] Handwritten P.S. by Binswanger.

32F
[To Alphonse Maeder]

9 June 1910

Prof. Dr. Freud   Vienna IX, Berggasse 19

Dear Doctor ['Maeder' added in Binswanger's hand],
I have now talked to Herr v. T. twice and shall continue these talks
twice a week. Whether we shall begin the treatment in the autumn
depends on their outcome. It seems clear to me that he will shortly
be over his melancholy, but he still fails to see that the mood in which
he is caught up is not a normal one. Thus he simply denies that his
slight projection delusion directed against me is due to my making
light of his masturbation rather than strictly interdicting it. Incidentally,
my latitude has not persuaded him to raise the subject of masturbation
during the therapy; had I forbidden him to masturbate we should
certainly have concluded that this ban had made it impossible for him
to own up. The result of my approach is probably an openness about
masturbation phantasies and activities which he is now likely to
maintain. He persists in his resolve to sublimate his libido completely,
but at least he now admits it freely.

Once we have access to his masturbation phantasies we shall have
a chance of influencing him further. However, it is still an open
question whether during the hypomanic phase he can keep the
promises he makes at the end of the melancholic period.

I have five weeks left to the end of this working year.[1]

With kind regards to you and to the Binswangers,

Yours, Freud

[1] Freud used to go on holiday at the end of June or in mid-July.

33F

3 July 1910

Prof. Dr. Freud   Vienna IX, Berggasse 19

Dear Dr. Binswanger,
As I do not know whether Maeder is still with you, I am writing to
tell you directly that J. v. T. is back to normal and much more honest
and reasonable than he was before, a photographically exact repro-
duction of what happened last year.

Having got over the business part, I may, perhaps, be allowed to

39

confess that I do not understand the goings-on in your Zurich circle,[1] and that I have no insight into the motives of the opposition to the International Association.[2] – Surely, those who with Bleuler have refused to join have not altered their views on psychoanalysis? How do you envisage the next Congress, which, after all, can only be attended by members? Why do these dissidents wish to deny themselves any influence on the decisions and actions of psychoanalysts, when they are just as interested in the matter as those others who receive the *Korrespondenzblatt* for 10 francs a year?

With kind regards to you and your wife, I am,

Yours sincerely, Freud

[1] The Zurich Psychoanalytic Association was founded in May 1910, preceded by the Society for Freudian Research, founded in 1907 (chairman Eugen Bleuler). Apparently not all participants in the original group wanted automatically to become members of the International Psychoanalytic Association. Binswanger declared, as reported to Freud by Jung on 17 June 1910, that 'he would accept the vote for president only if all meetings were held in common with non-members', Freud (1974a), p. 329. Freud (in a letter to Jung 19 June 1910) regarded this situation as 'quite untenable'. It was a matter of just two things: 'Two things are involved: to pay 10 francs in dues and put one's name on the list. Why on earth should certain people enjoy all the privileges without meeting these obligations?' Freud (1974a), p. 331. The new body had 19 members to start with; see *Korrespondenzblatt*, No. 1, July 1910, p. 3. Cf. also Walser (1976), pp. 1202–04.

[2] With regard to what follows, see Freud's letter to Jung 5 July 1910: 'Though you have not asked me to, it seemed to me that I might, on my own responsibility, ask Binswanger to throw some light on the extraordinary schizophrenic behaviour of the Zurich people', Freud (1974a), p. 339.

34B

8 July 1910

Dear Professor Freud,

Many thanks for your letter of the 3rd inst. which I have unfortunately been unable to answer until today because my time has been completely taken up with a two-day court case. Maeder, who will be staying here until September,[1] and I were very pleased to receive your good news about J. v. T.

As for your question about what is going on in our Zurich circle, I can tell you very little because the split[2] took place without my knowledge and Bleuler's failure to join the International Association took me completely by surprise. Dr. Jung will no doubt have given you his view of Bleuler's reasons.[3] What I know, too, is what I was told by Dr. Jung; I have never discussed the subject with Bleuler himself because I know that I shall not be able to change his mind in the slightest, the less so as personal complexes stored up for a long time are partly involved. Maier is simply following his leader. The motives of the other dissidents are probably of little concern to us.

What is certain in any case is that Bleuler's and Maier's failure to join in no way reflects the fact that they have changed their attitude to psychoanalysis. Bleuler is continuing to work on his 'Apologia' of psychoanalysis;[4] as far as I can see, it is purely in therapeutic respects that he has grown a little more sceptical, which can hardly be based on personal experience. Since what is involved, therefore, are purely external, personal and not factual differences, I have done all I can to make it possible for Bleuler and Maier to attend our Association as observers. Naturally, we have had to make the same concession to others who are not of particular interest to us otherwise. I have also supported the view that in accordance with local traditions the meetings should continue to be held in Burghölzli. With these two provisos, I accepted the presidency of the Zurich group which had been offered to me.

You also ask, dear Professor, how I envisage the next Congress. I can only say that because of his attitude to the International Association Bleuler cannot expect to be invited and has no right to feel offended if he is not. Whether it is possible to ask him as a guest, I do not know.

It strikes me, dear Professor, that I am able to give you less information than you supposed. However, I am only involved in the goings-on in the Zurich circle to the extent that I am trying to prevent its complete, and publicly recorded, collapse. In that respect I have acted against the intentions of Dr. Jung, i.e., the majority of the Association members shared my view. I do not know whether you, dear Professor, blame me for my 'mediator's role'. In any case I believe I sensed a reproach between the lines of your letter, though I find it difficult to understand why. In view of our customary frankness towards each other, I should be very grateful if you, dear Professor, could let me have your views quite candidly, so that we may under-stand each other. I can see nothing reprehensible in my intervention, as there is provision for members to settle their business between themselves if the occasion demands. Nor do I believe that we have in any way broken the rules of the International Association; on the other hand, I should have considered it most unwise to document my differences with Bleuler in public and so to cause a complete split.

Recently, lying in a wood on a day off, I read your 'Leonardo'[5] with great admiration and pleasure. Of late, whenever time and energy have permitted, I have continued working on my 'heel analysis' and shall be presenting part of it in a lecture[6] in Zurich tomorrow. – With kind regards from my wife and from me to you and your family, and with best wishes for your coming holiday,

Yours cordially, [L. Binswanger]

P.S. Maeder asks to be kindly remembered.

[1] Cf. 25B and its note 1.
[2] Cf. note 1 to 33F.
[3] Jung wrote to Freud on 26 June 1910: 'Actually I could do nothing to oppose the decision. My authority does not extend that far. Except for Riklin all the rest wanted Bleuler and about nine other persons to be present, on the ground that exceptional conditions had to be created for the transition period. At the same time the hope was expressed that these persons would soon think better of it and join. [...] As for my authority, the chairman was always Bleuler; wherever there are resistances he plays them off against me. Binswanger has always had the knack of saying something unpleasant to me and is everybody's friend. Pfister was also in favour of conciliation', Freud (1974a), p. 338.
[4] Eugen Bleuler: 'Die Psychoanalyse Freuds. Verteidigung und kritische Bemerkungen' (1910a) [Freudian Psychoanalysis. Defence and critical remarks].
[5] Freud (1910c).
[6] Part of Binswanger (1911a) as a lecture, but not provable. In his Annual Report of the Association for the year 1910/11 (*Zentralblatt*, Vol. 2, 1911, pp. 233f.), Jung indeed mentions the establishment in July 1910 of the local group in Zurich under the chairmanship of Ludwig Binswanger, but he does not report on the individual activities of the group. Reports on the lectures in the Zurich local group appear for the first time in the *Zentralblatt* Vol. 3 (1912), p. 103.

35F

10 July 1910
Prof. Dr. Freud   Vienna IX, Berggasse 19

Dear Dr. Binswanger,
No, I had no wish to reproach you, nor should I have been entitled to. All I wanted was to form a clearer picture of the events in Zurich, which we cannot make out here, and to call on you, as president of the group, to provide a remedy. By the next Congress everything must surely be settled, as non-members, even a Bleuler, are no use to so

intimate a society. Since that will probably not take place until the autumn of 1911 – because of the Americans – things could easily be put right before then. It remains an odd business, and you should make clear to those gentlemen that the situation is untenable. I assume the personal complexes cannot be directed against you.

At the end of this week I am off to The Hague (Hôtel Wittebrug) and on 1 August I go on to Noordwijk, near Leiden;[1] I badly need the break but am otherwise in good sorts. Hoche's effort has amused me hugely and strikes me as considerable recognition.[2] He obviously finds us a weird lot and that is all to the good. My literary output is making good progress. I have been told that you have declined to take any part in the *Zentralblatt*.[3] I hope this was only because of the clumsy nature of the invitation, for I should not like you to suspect that this Viennese enterprise was a competitor to our Z[urich] one[4] and would, moreover, personally set great store by your name.

With kind regards,

Yours, Freud

Please remember me to your wife and to Maeder.

[1] As a holiday in The Hague, Leiden and Noordwijk from 17 July to 31 August. Cf. Jones (1953–7), Vol. II, pp. 87ff.
[2] The polemic paper mentioned in note 5 to 31M. Freud expressed himself very similarly in a letter to Ferenczi on 3 July 1910, Freud (1992g), Vol. I, p. 185.
[3] Binswanger soon changed his mind about this refusal; regarding his change of opinion see 37B. However, his name does not appear as in the list of collaborators until issue 3 of the *Zentralblatt*; cf. note 9 to 44B.
[4] Namely to the *Jahrbuch für psychoanalytische und psychopathologische Forschungen* which was at that time published by Eugen Bleuler and Freud and edited by C.G. Jung.

36B

12 July 1910

Dear Professor Freud,

Many thanks for your letter of the 10th inst., which I was very pleased to receive. It would indeed have been a most depressing thought had I been forced to assume that you objected strongly to the course of action I took. Your suggestion that I make clear to the gentlemen the untenability of the current state of affairs has already been given practical expression at last Friday's meeting, inasmuch as I have been asked by the society, on a motion by Dr. Jung, to sound Bleuler out before the autumn and if possible persuade him to join. It is true that no personal complexes of the dissidents are directed against me; on the contrary, my appointment as president has kept the circle together so far. I shall, in any case, do my utmost to keep it that way for I should be very sorry indeed if the present split became complete and permanent. I must, however, tell you in complete confidence that I am not yet fully convinced of the untenability of the present position, and that of the Zurich contingent itself no one except Jung and Riklin appears to have taken exception to it. Jung alone repeated at the last meeting that he personally believed any beneficial collaboration with Bleuler along the old lines was impossible and that in any case the conflict between myself, Maeder and other pupils and adherents of you and Jung on the one hand, and Bleuler on the other, would be resolved in the best and simplest way were Bleuler to join the Association. If he does not, and if the meetings were completely severed from Burghölzli, then I should probably have to resign the presidency, since I only assumed it on certain conditions known to you. I am putting this in writing at all events, so that you, dear Professor, will perceive that it would only be done on purely formal grounds and that no personal reasons whatsoever would be involved. It is just that I do not wish to compromise myself.

I shall postpone negotiations with Bleuler for several months because the tension between him and Jung is still too strong; but I shall keep you fully informed.

I have declined to collaborate on the *Zentralblatt* solely because lack of time makes it impossible to contribute regularly, at least for the time being. I am very sorry, dear Professor, that I could not accede to your request. Incidentally, Maeder has written about it to Dr. Stekel on my behalf, and added that I was sympathetic to the cause.

When you go to Noordwijk, you will find my stepmother,[1] sister[2] and three younger brothers[3] there too, enjoying themselves. I am most envious of your being able to take your holiday now. I feel a little overworked myself. My next break will be a spell of military service at the end of August. The number of our patients has increased from 70 to 80 this year for the first time since the clinic was founded. You can see that our involvement with psychoanalysis has done us no harm. The increase in our workload is, however, considerable, although there are 5–6 of us physicians this summer.

My father, incidentally, deplores the action of our opponents[4] as much as we do. Although I have been practising analysis here for 2 years, he has seen no harm come to any patient from the analysis, something the gentlemen in Germany would be hard put to it to explain.

Wishing you and your family a most enjoyable holiday, and with kind regards from my wife and Maeder,

Yours, [L. Binswanger]

[1] Marie-Luise Schlegel, née Meyer-Wolde, widow of Robert Binswanger (died 1941).
[2] Either Anni, married name Hebting, or Bertha, married name Goetz.
[3] Probably Robert (1892–1963) and the stepbrothers Eduard (1898–1959) and Herbert (1900–1975).
[4] That is, the opponents of psychoanalysis.

37B

20 July 1910

Dear Professor Freud,

Following a short analysis with Maeder today, I am able to comply with your wish that I add my name to the list of contributors to the *Zentralblatt*. It struck Maeder last night that my refusal must, after all, be based on a resistance, since you wanted to lay claim not to my time but merely to my name. I became conscious of the fact that this resistance was directed against Stekel, about whose lack of scientific spirit Maeder and I are agreed, although Maeder felt free to join despite this. What I myself had repressed in connection with my resistance was the fact that, when all is said and done, you are at the helm and you have assumed co-responsibility, so that we can safely drop our reservations. It was typical that at the time of my first refusal, transmitted through Maeder, I was not even conscious that you yourself were involved, and that Maeder had subsequently almost to force me to read the names of the editorial board on the covers. As you see, the impression I gained at Nuremberg, where you seemed to be keeping aloof, was quite a lasting one. But now that I am reporting officially as a contributor, I would only beg you to bear in mind my very real lack of time; since, however, you seem mainly concerned to add my name, I have, after overcoming my resistance, no cause to keep my distance from an undertaking to which I am wholly sympathetic. I hope, dear Professor, that you will overlook my complexes and that my belated act of frankness has not come too late.

With kind regards and all good wishes for your holiday,

Yours, [L. Binswanger]

38F

The Hague, 25 July 1910

Prof. Dr. Freud   Vienna IX, Berggasse 19

Dear Dr. Binswanger,

I am very glad to have had fresh proof of the effectiveness of psychoanalysis and of the saying that the analyst should not be alone but
should cultivate the friendship component. As the leader of the Zurich
group your name could not have been missing from the list of contributors to the *Zentralblatt* without feeding rumours of a divergence
between Vienna and Zurich.

I am very comfortable here but looking forward to 1 August when
I shall join my womenfolk in Noordwijk. Kind regards to Frau Gr.[1]

Very sincerely, Your fast recovered, Freud

P.S. The Short Papers: [on the Theory of the Neuroses] first published
in 1906, are now ready for a second edition.[2] That is our answer to
the 'demolitions' of psychoanalysis. However, I have no idea why the
Jahrbuch has still not appeared![3]

[1] Presumably a patient of Freud and Binswanger.
[2] *Sammlung kleiner Schriften zur Neurosenlehre (I) aus den Jahren 1893–1906*,
Leipzig, Vienna: Deuticke, 1906, 2nd edn 1911.
[3] The *Jahrbuch für psychoanalytische und psychopathologische Forschungen*, 2nd
Vol., 1st half, did not appear until August 1910.

39M
[Alphonse Maeder to Freud]

16 August 1910

Dear Professor,

A few days ago Dr. St.[1] of Vienna turned up here. He was staying at
Interlaken with his wife and, feeling bad, came here unannounced.
He intends staying a few weeks in order to build up his physical
strength, wants to tone himself up. I started with an arsenic preparation
(cacodylat. Natr.)[2] and he also took electric baths[3] (with delight even),
works a bit in the garden and goes to the gym. He arrived here with
signs of a slight disapproval of any psychic treatment, says he is not
sure. He says he cannot help himself much at the moment

My rapport with him is very partial; he does not want anyone to get any insight and also in such a short time there is no point. Apart from the compulsive thinking, he seems to have a lot of hypochondria ('il est jaloux de ses richesses').

Perhaps you have particular wishes concerning him; I should be very pleased if you could possibly let us know![4]

The *Jahrbuch* has just arrived. A copious volume.

Dear Professor, I wish you better weather and a thorough recuperation during the last part of your holiday.

Yours ever,
A. Maeder

With kind regards,

Yours ever, L. Binswanger[5]

We are both eagerly studying the *Jahrbuch* just now!

---

[1] This patient was diagnosed at the Bellevue with an anxiety neurosis arising out of an obsessional neurosis.

[2] Arsenic preparations were much used for restoring strength, particularly in cases of neurasthenia and hysteria. Natrium cacodylicum or cacodylanatrium (so-called because of its bad smell) is one such arsenic preparation; cf. Ewald and Heffter (1911), pp. 493ff.

[3] For the effectiveness of electric baths, cf. O. Leichtenstern (1880), especially pp. 244–77.

[4] Vol. 2 (1910), 1st half, appeared August 1910 (cf. Freud, 1974a, p. 621). Included papers by Abraham, Jung, Sadger, Pfister, Freud, Maeder and Riklin and also reviews of other works.

[5] Handwritten P.S. by Binswanger.

40F   Selinunt,[1] 14 September 1910

Sincere greetings!

Freud
Ferenczi[2]

---

[1] Picture postcard: Castelvetrano – Selinunte, Tempio di Ercole (detail).

[2] Sándor Ferenczi (1873–1933), neurologist and psychoanalyst at Budapest, close friend and collaborator of Freud's, founder member of the 'secret committee' and here Freud's travelling companion (regarding which see also next letter). Cf. Harmat (1988) and Haynal (1987).

41F

2 October 1910

Prof. Dr. Freud

Vienna IX, Berggasse 19

Dear Dr. Binswanger,

Many thanks for your father analysis, which certainly needs no apology. Reading more into it is made harder for me by a factor to which I shall be returning. Ferenczi was probably not so happy to be travelling with me as to excite envy.[1] I rather tend to let myself go during holidays and am far from sparkling all the time, and he was most amiable if a little constrained.

I have now written to Bleuler myself asking for enlightenment, since I really[a] do not understand why he dissociates himself from the Association. I do not expect to be able to influence him, but I[b] thought he would after all take offence if I failed to get in direct touch with him.

Frau G. (if that is how she spells her name) was my patient for 6 weeks. She broke off the treatment ostensibly because of the high fees (!), i.e., the treatment was not to the advantage of her husband, who is a dubious fellow. I came to see her during that period as a case badly consumed by passion. When I took her case history, the husband had the effrontery to withhold the fact that when she left a mental home fairly recently (about one and a half years ago) she put a bullet in her skull which is still lodged there. She herself never confessed that *before* this marriage she had done something bad connected with an earlier relationship. *I only heard about it from her family doctor* (discretion). The husband now drags her by her guilty conscience as if by a chain. One ought to take this up with him and she would surely leave her chum in the lurch. The doctor, for whose sake she shot herself, had intercourse with her, of course, probably not without encouragement.

I have not yet seen v. T.; he spent a very blissful summer with his bosom friend, probably highly manic already.

I promised to return to something. It is, dear Doctor, your horrible, schizophrenically repelling handwriting,[2] which is designed to be indecipherable and which is as much a negative complement to your forthright and just character as your father-dreams are a complement to your real behaviour. Can nothing be done about it? Handwriting is, after all, more real than dreams can ever be.

No doubt you will be getting Hitschmann's book.[3] I am very curious about the *Zentralblatt*. And no less about your heel analysis.[4] Even Friedländer praised you recently for your Irma analysis in the *Zeitschrift für Psychologie und Psychologie der Sinnesorgane*.[5] Let us hope it will not spoil you.

Kind regards to you and your wife,

Yours ever,
Freud

[a] Freud wrote 'I'
[b] Freud wrote 'he'

[1] From Leiden Ferenczi accompanied Freud on a journey to Italy and Sicily from 1–26 September. Cf. Jones (1953–7), Vol. II, pp. 89ff. and Tögel (1989), p. 155. Freud's letter of 6 October 1910 to Ferenczi, quoted in full by Jones (pp. 92–3), concerns the difficulties of their being in each other's company so much.
[2] Binswanger's handwriting is indeed readable only with difficulty; see 10F and its note 5.
[3] *Freuds Neurosenlehre* (1911). In a letter to Jung of 25 May 1910 Freud described the book ironically as 'a compendium of my work in ψα – a kind of manual for elementary schools (?)'. Eduard Hitschmann (1871–1957), originally an internist; after 1940 in Boston, Mass. Cf. Freud (1974a) p. 321 and note 3.
[4] Binswanger (1911a).
[5] Friedländer (1910b).

42F

24 October 1910
Prof Dr. Freud   Vienna IX, Berggasse 19

Dear Dr. Binswanger,

I am replying by return, and thank you very much for your beautiful handwriting. I'll be put to shame myself, soon. The required offprint had been despatched together with two others *before* your letter arrived.

As far as Bleuler is concerned, I am having a lively and extensive correspondence with him[1] from which, however, nothing has yet emerged. He appears to be courting us, it is true, is very obliging in several respects, but he still rejects the Association with horror, and that is just what we cannot sacrifice to him even while going out of our way to keep him with us. His arguments are so obscure, imponderable and incomprehensible that I find it hard to make any sense out of him. Since he has expressed the need for a personal discussion I have asked him to meet me in Zurich at Christmas. Needless to say I shall not be going unless the chances of persuading him to join have assumed a more definite form before then. That is all I can tell you and I must leave it to you now to do what you think best in the light of this state of affairs.

The *Zentralblatt* has come out and although it is still a little unpolished I nevertheless hope that it will dispel several misgivings.

With kind regards to you and your wife,

Yours, Freud

---

[1] Only a small part of the correspondence between Freud and Eugen Bleuler has so far been published; see Alexander and Selesnick (1965). Unfortunately it was not possible to gain access to the unpublished part, which could shed light on many details of this Freud–Binswanger correspondence.

43F

6 November 1910

Prof Dr. Freud   Vienna IX, Berggasse 19

Dear Dr. Binswanger,

Many thanks for your kind invitation. I know that it is sincerely and seriously meant as is everything that comes from you. It looks very doubtful, however, that I shall in any case be going to Zurich. Bleuler's last sphinx-like pronouncement was that he would not be replying to my letter for two weeks because he had first to confer with Jung[1] and the tone of his reply might conceivably be modified as a result. That does not sound too promising and we shall probably have no alternative but to make a clean break.

All these personal matters are very unpleasant. I wished I lived closer to Jung so that I could support him in his youthful authority, on which, I believe, a part of our future depends.

Meanwhile I am having problems with my people even in Vienna, which strikes me as being quite uncalled-for. I urgently need my untrammelled energy and enthusiasm for the work. So much wasted effort!

With kind regards to you and your wife,

Yours, Freud

[1] Jung reported to Freud on the matter in a letter of 13 November 1910: 'The discussion with Bleuler took place last Friday evening. [...] He did ask me, though, whether I would advise him to encourage you to come to Zurich. The whole apparatus that is being set in motion to win him over gives him enormous pleasure, so he would be frightfully offended if the negotiations were broken off.' Freud (1974a), p. 370.

44B

29 November 1910

Dear Professor,

Herr Hu., whom you so kindly referred to us, has very quickly settled in here and made the transference to me. He sees the events in Vienna fairly critically, but still shows signs of persecution ideas and keeps on reproaching himself for his daft behaviour which has made him the plaything of society; everyone has made a fool of him and wants to put him to the test. I do not doubt that the man will be capable of work again in a few months' time, whether he can return to Vienna we must consider later. To the family I spoke of two months, but it could indeed last even twice that long. I have installed him in an open house with a private attendant. He still often gets anxious at night, gets out of bed, talks and laughs to himself and talks of suicide. When he does stay in bed completely he allows himself to be influenced for the good for hours at a time. In my opinion it is a clear case of dementia praecox combined with a good intellect, but with an emotional life which has remained infantile. The infantile is what occurs to him first. He seems also to have a strong mother complex, only women he knows to be unattainable stimulate him, for preference he takes up with an archduchess. A homosexual component shows itself clearly. This kind of dementia praecox case particularly interests me. Such phases point particularly clearly to a psychogenic mechanism. I now know several cases who became ill with depression or a confused state in connection with an unhappy love life. It is clear then that the mother complex and the homosexual elements have wrecked the love life and precisely in such cases I clearly saw persecution ideas and homosexuality arising. By the way, in our case here it also has to be taken into account that the woman in question must have been a right little minx.

I am treating Frau G. at the moment while Dr. von Holst[1] is on holiday. I should much rather send her back to you. Her husband is coming at Christmas, then we can talk about it. The only question is whether you would take her on again. She is clearly still completely scatty. Her 65-year-old father has recently married a 25-year-old girl, which has of course hit her enormous father complex very hard. The quest for her father's tenderness occupies her totally. In you she had found her father again, thus still today an extremely strong transference to you, which also radiates a little to me as your disciple. The sado-masochistic element and also the homosexual one seem very strong. I have given her an older nurse because she is impossible to discipline on one's own.—

I am very excited whether you will get anywhere with Bleuler. Jung and Riklin have rescued him from his complexes.[2] He told me he would possibly meet you in Innsbruck, which would unfortunately deprive us of the pleasure of seeing you here. I hope you are enjoying peace in Vienna again; everything is going quite well in Zurich at the moment. The Swiss Psychiatrists held their conference in Berne yesterday,[3] where Bleuler gave a paper on ambivalence, but still very unfinished; Riklin on obsessional neurosis and I on my heel analysis, which met with applause. After the readings, the President (Ris[4]–R[h]einau) declared that the younger generation could reckon on finding a grateful and sympathetic audience for their 'special studies' in the Association.[5]

I like the *Zentralblatt* very much. When one knows Stekel, one forgives his self-publicity,[6] which certainly arises from nothing more than a harmless naivety. I have not yet read Adler's paper,[7] but I always look forward to reading what comes from his pen. Why have I been excluded as a collaborator, are not the stragglers wanted any more?[8] I leave it to you entirely to complain about it or to let the matter rest. I still would like to be on the list, however. Hitschmann's book[9] fills a large gap and is very valuable for practical purposes.

With kindest regards to you and yours from my wife and me,

I remain ever yours [L. Binswanger]

[1] Cf. footnote 1 to 13B.

[2] Cf. Jung's letter to Freud 29 November 1910; Freud (1974a), pp. 374-5.

[3] This letter was probably drafted on 28 November 1910 and not typed by the secretary until the 29th. 'Yesterday' does not tally with the dates of the psychiatrists' conference: the winter conference of Swiss Psychiatrists took place in Berne 26–27 November 1910. Cf. *Korrespondenzblatt* No. 3 (1910), December, p. 5 and Riklin's report in the *Zentralblatt*, Vol. 1 (1911), No. 5–6, pp. 266–9.

[4] Friedrich Ris (1867–1931), psychiatrist and entomologist, student of Forel, Director of the Rheinau Institute 1898–1931. Cf. Bleuler (1931) and Walser (1970), pp. 35–45.

[5] According to Riklin's report in the *Zentralblatt*, Vol. 1 (1911), p. 269, under 'Discussion': 'Chairman Ris welcomed the fact that these burning and acute psychoanalytical questions have succeeded in coming under discussion even here in the Psychiatrists' Society. He considered this a particular advantage for the Society and emphasised that the young forces who bring their work on these subjects here can count on the good wishes of the Society. This verdict of Ris was enthusiastically applauded.'
[6] The *Zentralblatt*, Vol. 1 (1911), Issue 1/2 included three contributions, eleven shorter papers and critiques, as well as a miscellany on 'the positions of authors' by Stekel.
[7] Adler (1910): 'Die psychische Behandlung der Trigeminusneuralgie'.
[8] Binswanger's statement that he was willing to collaborate had come too late for the printing of issue 1/2; cf. 45F.
[9] Hitschmann (1911). Cf. note 3 to 41F.

45F

3 December 1910

Prof Dr. Freud   Vienna IX, Berggasse 19

Dear Dr. Binswanger,

Many thanks for your news about the two patients, though they interest me far less than the other matter you report. I do not want to have Frau G., for I cannot prevail against her dubious husband.

My visit to you will indeed have to be postponed. I am going to suggest to Bleuler that we meet in Munich,[1] which I prefer to dreary Innsbruck and (a secret!), once he has left, it is likely that someone else[2] from Zurich will be arriving. But he is not to know about that. I am pleased as Punch about this little intrigue.

I notice that fate is taking its course and passing control of the clinic into your hands, but assume that Dr. v. Holst is no longer there. Am I wrong?

I have forwarded your objection to the *Zentralblatt*. Sloppiness, of course, the title page was made ready before you had given your consent. The second issue, too, ought to interest you: it contains Jung, Jones[3] and other interesting contributions, apart from a little too much Adler, much as the first had too much Stekel.[4] Caution is called for with Adler's papers; the more intelligence he shows, the greater the danger. His exposition renders everything opaque, but I know that it all boils down to replacing the psychological point of view with the biological and to depreciating the sexual instinct. All this is not as it should be.

Putnam[5] submitted the second of his lectures in favour of psychoanalysis today;[6] resolute and straightforward, full of understanding, *on ne peut pas mieux.* This was well worth a journey and chronic enteritis.[7]

I am now working on Schreber's *Denkwürdigkeiten* [Memoirs of My Nervous Illness][8] and am thus coming to grips with the problem of paranoia, which deeply interests me.

With kind regards to you and your wife, and best wishes to your father,

Yours, Freud

[1] Jung had suggested this to Freud in his letter of 29 November 1910; see Freud (1974a), pp. 374–5.

[2] Namely C.G. Jung. Freud met Bleuler in Munich on 25 December 1910 and Jung came to Munich after Bleuler's departure on Monday 26 December. Freud reported on both meetings in a letter of 29 December to Ferenczi; cf. Jones (1953–7), Vol. 2, p. 158, and the editorial note in Freud (1974a), p. 384.

[3] Ernest Jones (1879–1958), neurologist and psychoanalyst, collaborated with Freud from early on, prompted the setting up of the 'secret committee' around Freud in 1912, and, with his huge Freud biography, established a lasting image of Freud and the development of psychoanalysis. Cf. Winnicott (1958) and the Jones autobiography (1959).

[4] The *Zentralblatt*, Vol. 1 (1911), issue 3 (the first issue was a double one) contained: Jung, C.G.: 'Ein Beitrag zur Psychologie des Gerüchtes' (pp. 81–90), Jung (1910q); Freud, Sigm: 'Über "wilde" Psychoanalyse' (pp. 91–5) – 'Wild Psychoanalysis', Freud (1910k); Jones, Ernest: 'Beitrag zur Symbolik im Alltag' (pp. 96–8); Sadger, J: 'Zum Verständnis der Hypnose und des hysterischen Delirs' (pp. 98–102); Stekel, Wilhelm: 'Zur Symbolik der Mutterleibsphantasie' (p. 102); Adler, Alfred: 'Ein erlogener Traum. Beitrag zum Mechanismus der Lüge in der Neurosis' (pp. 103–08); Stekel, Wilhelm: 'Ein durchsichtiges Beispiel von Verlegen' (p. 109); Stekel, Wilhelm: 'Warum sie den eigenen Namen hassen' (p. 109); Rank, Otto: 'Ein Beispiel von poetischer Verwertung des Versprechens' (pp. 109–10). So Freud described the *one* article and five reviews and critiques by Adler as 'a little too much Adler'.

[5] James Jackson Putnam (1846-1918), Professor of Neurology at Harvard University; took part in the celebrations at Clark University, Worcester, Mass.; was founder (1911) and first president of the American Psychoanalytic Association and revered Freud until he died. Cf. Freud (1974a), p. 271, note 4, and *James Jackson Putnam and Psychoanalysis*, ed. Hale, Nathan, 1971 (Freud 1971a).

[6] 'Personal Experience with Freud's Psychoanalytic Method' (Putnam, 1910b). The first of these lectures ('On the Etiology and Treatment of the Psychoneuroses', Putnam, 1910a) was given before the Canadian Medical Association in Toronto on 1 June 1910 and was translated into German by Freud for publication in the *Zentralblatt* the following year.

[7] Cf. note 6 to 54F.

[8] Cf. Schreber (1903) and Freud (1911c).

46F

9 December 1910

Prof Dr. Freud   Vienna IX, Berggasse 19

Dear Dr. Binswanger,
The few sombre words with which you informed me of your father's[1]
death were more eloquent than any oration. We who were less close
to him will envy him the curtailment of his fruitless suffering and the
quick, kind end; what this death means to his son we shall not try to
guess out of respect and consideration. We know that it was his good
fortune to have been successful in his work and to have left behind
children like you. That is no small achievement.

On behalf of my wife and children I would ask you to convey our
condolences to your entire family.

A heartfelt handshake for yourself.

I still have no further details about the meeting in Munich, since
Bleuler has not yet replied.

As ever, Freud

[1] Robert Binswanger (1850–1910). See page xii of the Introduction.

47F

1 January 1911

Prof Dr. Freud   Vienna IX, Berggasse 19

Dear Dr. Binswanger,
First of all my warmest good wishes on this calendrical occasion to
you, your little family and to the undertaking that now rests in your
hands.[1] Continue to persevere with us and remain in the foremost
ranks of those physicians who do not allow themselves to be deterred
by opposition from paving the way for psychoanalysis in medical
practice.

You are certainly entitled to know how the meeting with Bleuler[2]
turned out. I must tell you that it was favourable beyond expectation.
After his apologia for my psychoanalysis,[3] I could not but be frank
and friendly with him, and he did not make that difficult for me. We
have disposed of all sorts of misunderstandings and have drawn quite
close to each other. In the end I did not speak directly of the
Association, but he expressed himself in such a way that it would have

been unfair to question his intentions. When he had gone, Jung arrived, and as always I was delighted to see him, and realised with pleasure that he, too, wishes to find and to keep the right personal attitude towards Bleuler. So Zurich is likely to thrive now, and a very great deal depends on that, of course.

I was very interested to hear that Strohmayer[4] has joined you. I thought that he was set on a university career. If he stays with you, he will quickly see that there are no grounds for the slight reserve that he still retains. What a very great pity that Maeder was not free![5] He would certainly sooner be with you than with Bircher.[6]

I have handed a paper on paranoia[7] over to Jung and have had a look at his important religious and mythological studies.[8] Our *Jahrbuch* will not be at all bad. I was pleased to learn that your heel analysis was ready.

Good luck then for this new chapter in your life!

Yours cordially,
Freud

[1] Following the death of his father, Binswanger officially took over the direction of the Bellevue Sanatorium on 1 January 1911.

[2] On 25 December 1910; cf. note 2 to 45F.

[3] Bleuler (1910a).

[4] Wilhelm Strohmayer (1874–1936), lecturer, after 1910 Professor of Psychiatry and Neurology in Jena. Cf. Freud (1974a), pp. 127–8, note 3. The planned appointment of Strohmayer to the Bellevue staff did not come about, although he had got to know the Bellevue as early as 1894 and had worked for Uncle Otto Binswanger on the Brunnegg estate as a 'handyman'; see the letter of 28 December 1932 from Strohmayer to L. Binswanger, B.A. 443/40.

[5] Binswanger had tried in vain to get Maeder (as an experienced doctor with an interest in psychoanalysis) to work at the Bellevue, not just as a stand-in, but as a permanent member of staff.

[6] Maximilian Bircher-Benner (1867–1939), doctor and pioneer in natural diet, founder of a private sanatorium (in Hottingen in 1897, after 1904 in Zürichberg). Made contact with Freud as early as 1897. Cf. Bircher (1959).

[7] The Schreber case history (1911c). English title: 'Psycho-Analytic Notes on an Autobiographical Account of a case of Paranoia'.

[8] 'Wandlungen und Symbole der Libido' [Part 1], Jung (1912a).

48B

24 January 1911

Dear Professor Freud,

I have not yet thanked you for your last letter and for the two offprints, and must also express my belated regrets at your son's mishap.[1] I am delighted to see from your letter to Frau G. that a steady recovery is being made. I had a similar experience with my family on New Year's Day when my youngest brother[2] went out in a sleigh and sustained a femoral fracture which is now healing well.

When you, dear Professor, encouraged me to help introduce psychoanalysis into medical practice, you hit upon what is closest to my character and professional interests. I do not yet feel up to engaging in theoretical discussions; in any case my feeling is that I must first accumulate a great deal of personal experience. However, you know full well that I am delighted to give whatever help I can. I have now drafted a circular to medical practitioners in which I mention the change in our administration, and that Strohmayer has joined us, etc., and explain my attitude to analysis in brief, specific terms[3]. I did so the more readily as most other clinics take a most deplorable stand on this issue. Your paper on wild analysis[4] gave me great pleasure. I feel some sympathy for the work on the *Jahrbuch*[5] [...][6] also makes a splendid impression; my father was still looking forward to Bleuler's contribution[7] with the keenest interest.

And so Bleuler was admitted to membership at the last meeting.[8] I am thinking of offering him the chair, not because I am unhappy to continue in the circumstances but because it is probably his due.[9] As for Adler, I had a long talk with Jung about him last time.[10] I share your views and Jung's unreservedly. What I find particularly unattractive is his constant harping on his own discoveries.

I am still somewhat rushed off my feet and that is how it will probably remain until Strohmayer's arrival. I have no real assistance for the treatment of neuroses. A reasonable number of cases takes up a great deal of time, more than I have to devote, and this is true of Frau G. as well. Unfortunately, I can only see her once or twice a week for longer consultations. She then talks extremely well. She has described the Judendorf episode to me at length. She claims that as far as she is aware, she has no other secrets. I am still not sure how long there has been this ardent desire for that kiss. I have never come across so great a degree of eroticism in a woman who is not mentally

Ludwig Binswanger, about 1911.

ill. All the same, her condition borders on the psychotic. She has been known to behave like a maenad. I find it difficult to show her the continuous personal interest she requires. Because of other patients, I am forced to ration my time with her, but in so doing I must avoid the stumbling block of becoming identified with her husband.

[...][11]

unstable and puerile. He will not be able to return to Vienna before the end of February, that is, the end of his holiday, and so he will lose his job. His father is coming here in the near future.

With kind regards to you, dear Professor, and to your family,

Ever yours, [L. Binswanger]

[1] Freud's son, Martin, had broken a thigh bone in a skiing accident on Schneeberg in the Semmering and had to lie on the snow for five hours before he could be rescued. Cf. Jones (1953–7), Vol. 2, pp. 93, 95; and Freud (1974a), p. 386.

[2] Herbert Binswanger.

[3] *Mitteilung an die Herren Aerzte*, Kreuzlingen, February 1911, FA Binswanger, No. 115; cf. note 3 to 51F. Strohmayer was mentioned in the circular (along with Dr. Reese and Dr. Schön, who were actually taken on) only as an 'intern'.

[4] Freud (1910k).

[5] Probably Freud (1910h) – English title: 'A Special Type of Choice of Object made by Men'.

[6] At this point a whole page is missing.

[7] See note 4 to 34B.

[8] Bleuler became a member of the Zurich local group of the International Psychoanalytic Association on 13 January 1911; see *Korrespondenzblatt* No. 4, February 1911. Jung reported his joining in a letter of 18 January 1911; see Freud (1974a), p. 384.

[9] Cf. Jung to Freud (18 January 1911): 'Binswanger will probably cede the presidency to him. I shall confer with Binswanger on this matter', Freud (1974a), p. 384.

[10] Jung was also clearly referring to this conversation in his letter of 18 January 1911 to Freud; see Freud (1974a), p. 385.

[11] A further gap.

49F

30 January 1911

Prof Dr. Freud　　　　　　　　　　　　　　Vienna IX, Berggasse 19

Dear Dr. Binswanger,

Only the most extreme shortage of time can excuse my tardiness in congratulating you on the birth of your daughter.[1] Now you are a father in every respect and have experienced twice over the most remarkable thing life has to offer. May she prosper and bring joy to her admirable mother and to you.

I must protest in retrospect against the notion that by assigning to you the task of introducing psychoanalysis into medical practice I was trying to bar you from scientific work, as you seem to assume in your proudly modest way.

On the contrary, we look to you for many more contributions of the Irma and even more deeply ranging types. I merely tried to convey to you that our method needed certain modifications for institutional application, and these no one could evaluate better than you.

Frau G. has a secret despite her denial. I *suspect* (from a hint by her family physician) that it is connected with a love affair (with a third party) between her two marriages, and might well be the criminal destruction of the fruit of that affair. I leave it to you *whether* and *how* you lead her back to this probably forgotten part of her love life.

My son is getting better; he is due for a fixed dressing within the next few days. I hope your brother is getting better too.

I have been through several particularly wretched weeks that convinced me that the final arteriosclerosis was already upon me, until, quite by accident, I was shown to have been suffering from chronic gas poisoning.[2] Since the replacement of the defective tube, I have been almost transformed and hope to be able to carry on for some time yet.

I am very glad that you are not going along with Adler. It[3] has a paranoic trait and would have had to lead to the destruction of psychoanalysis. The belated denial of sexuality and of the unconscious by the ego unchanged by psychoanalysis. Nevertheless ingenious and instructive.

With kind regards to your whole, now quite considerable, family,

Yours ever, Freud

---

[1] Hilde Binswanger, born 23 January 1911.

[2] The exact circumstances are described in Freud's letter of 17 February to Jung (1974a, pp. 393-4), upon which Jones also based his description of the incident (1953–7, Vol. 2, p. 95).

[3] Adler's thought is meant.

50F

12 February 1911

Prof Dr. Freud

Vienna IX, Berggasse 19

Dear Dr. Binswanger,

I can now read your handwriting very easily! Please do not be cross with me for replying so tardily. I really do have to wait for Sundays and those too sometimes have to be given up.

I am sure you have acted correctly in the Str[ohmayer] affair by maintaining your independence even towards your uncle. Str[ohmayer], incidentally, did not strike me as being a man who is entirely frank or entirely steadfast.[1] Carry on doing your own work and don't let it slip out of your hands.

However, your need is for qualified collaborators now, or else you will quickly wear yourself out with psychoanalysis. A terrible pity about Maeder.[2] Do keep looking for someone else. Ever since Muthmann[3] deserted us so timorously[4] – although he is said to have remained true to himself in his medical practice – our people in Germany only have your clinic to call on, and you cannot possibly analyse everyone who comes to you for analysis. The shortened treatment that will recommend itself to you as suitable for an institution presupposes that one has first acquired, through thorough analyses, a conclusive knowledge of what may happen. With that, it will be possible to shape what you aim for into a more convenient therapeutic set of tools.[5]

My state of health has truly stabilised since the gas-tube business. Work and interest are at a peak. My son is back home in plaster and is learning to get about again.

So Frau G. has by lucky chance forgotten something. I think it is the following: after her divorce she had an affair with an older gentleman, a friend of the family and a father substitute, and was made pregnant by him when she was already engaged to her present husband. It was *this* child she got rid of in a far from innocent fashion and that now cripples her in her attitude towards her – highly dubious – husband. I should tackle her about this man in the middle. She once spoke to me of him in even greater detail.

Putnam writes that he intends to attend the Congress in September.[6] It all augurs extremely well.

I hope that your family, large and small, is well, and my kind regards to you all.

Yours, Freud

[1] Possibly Freud had known Strohmayer personally since the Salzburg Congress (1908), cf. Freud (1974a), p. 128. See also Freud's verdict of Strohmayer in his letter of 26 April 1910 to Jung, *ibid.* p. 312.

[2] Cf. note 5 to 47F.

[3] Arthur Muthmann (1875-1957), psychiatrist, Director of the Bad Nassau Hospital from 1912 to 1918, in 1909 opened a private sanatorium of his own in Freiburg which remained until it was bombed out in 1944. See Amitai and Cremerius (1984); see also note 4 to 107F. The whole sentence probably means that Muthmann had not become a member of the International Psychoanalytic Association; cf. Freud (1974a), pp. 341–2, note 2.

[4] A pun on Muthmann's name (lit. 'courage-man') which is lost in translation.

[5] Binswanger remarked about this in (1956c), p. 29 in the English 1957 edition: 'I no longer know what I strove for in this respect at the time, for I still believed then – particularly after my success with the "heel analysis" – that almost every patient must be analysed. It took ten years of hard work and disappointment before I realised that only a certain number of cases in our clinic were suited to analysis.'

[6] Third International Psychoanalytic Congress in Weimar, 21–22 September 1911. Cf. Putnam (1971), pp. 113ff. (Putnam's letters of 26 January and 6 February 1911).

51F

5 March 1911

Prof. Dr. Freud

Vienna IX, Berggasse 19

Dear Dr. Binswanger,

Thank you for your news. I hope that, given patience, you will get over your problems and that you will not regret having preserved your independence.

I was both hurt to the quick[1] and moved to laughter by your criticism of the footnote to Putnam.[2] It was I, you see, who was the translator, and who was also the author of the short note. But I am not offended; your impression cannot have been entirely without foundation, after all.

Your passage on analysis[3] struck me as being far too fainthearted; but I know there is no credit to be had in beating the big drum, and much more in doing the correct thing and doing it consistently.

I am now president of the Vienna group. Adler and Stekel have stepped down,[4] the first probably because he felt, and rightly so, that no one with his views can be the standard-bearer of our cause. It is admittedly given out that our common ground is the practice of the psychoanalysis method, but in fact what we jointly uphold against the world, namely the appreciation of the libido, is something from which Adler has moved very far. He perpetuates the misunderstandings of the ego which we believed we had overcome.

The relative calm in the literature has not lasted for long. The last *Journal of Abnormal Psychology* is again full of attacks and insults[5] but at least America is joining us in full measure, despite the opposition of individuals. Brill[6] has personally founded a new group in New York.

I must confess that I continue to feel well, aided by a sudden falling off in my practice during the last week to three quarters. This is not likely to last for long.

You are right about Frau G. These are new lies. I do not think I am mistaken about her 'fatherly' friend. It is hard to help this woman. Won't you take the risk of telling her that you have somehow guessed her 'secret'? Her perpetual murderous attempts on herself prove that she has done away with somebody.

With kind regards
Yours, Freud

[1] Cf. Jung's remark to Freud: 'Binswanger had already told me the delicious story (Putnam) before you wrote me about it. I myself noticed nothing, of course, it needed Binswanger's beady eye sharpened by an outsize father complex to spot the joke.' Freud (1974a), p. 417.

[2] Refers to the footnote (1911j) Freud wrote to accompany his translation of Putnam's lecture, 'On the Aetiology and Treatment of the Psychoneuroses', in the *Zentralblatt* Vol. 1 (1911), Issue 4, p. 137: 'J. Putnam is not only one of the most eminent neurologists in America but also a man everywhere greatly respected for his unimpeachable character and high moral standards. Although he has left his youth far behind him, he took his open stand last year in the front rank of the champions of psychoanalysis' (James Strachey's translation in *S.E.*, Vol. XVII, p. 272). Freud apologised to Putnam two months later for having given him a 'character' (letter of 14 May 1911; see Freud 1971a, p. 360). Cf. also Jones (1953–7), Vol. 2, pp. 82–3 and 52F below.

[3] Probably refers to the wording of the circular mentioned in 48B. This prospectus of the Bellevue Sanatorium is dated February 1911 and was clearly sent out by Ludwig Binswanger shortly before that. It says about the therapy: 'In treating the patients I, together with my colleagues, always follow the principles laid down by both my predecessors. Our institution is suited to every requirement that their presence imposes upon facilities and physical therapy. However, we see our chief strength in individualised *psychotherapy*, as we perceive its considerable support meets the needs of patients through physical and mental *activity*. On the basis of my own research and experience, I also consider *psychoanalysis* a suitable and promising therapeutic method for certain types of hysteria, obsessional ideas, phobias, etc. I do not use it, however, without the prerequisites of the moral and intellectual integrity of the patient and the agreement of the referring doctor.' Cf. also 53F.

[4] Adler's opinions were discussed in the Vienna Society on 8 and 22 February 1911, after he had given lectures there on the 4 January and 1 February. At the end of

meeting on 22 February a committee meeting took place in which Adler stood down as President 'on the grounds of the incompatibility of his scientific standing and his standing in the Society'. Stekel (Vice-President) and others stood down likewise in solidarity. Cf. *Minutes*, Vols. 3 (1962), pp. 159–165; Jones (1953–7), Vol. 2, pp. 148–50; Handlbauer (1990).

[5] *The Journal of Abnormal Psychology,* Vol. 5 (1911), No. 6 (February–March) contained: Friedländer A: 'Hysteria and Modern Psychoanalysis' (pp. 297–319); Sidis, Boris: 'Fundamental States in Psychoneurosis' (pp. 320–27); Jones, Ernest: 'Remarks on Dr. Morton Prince's Article "The Mechanism and Interpretation of Dreams" ' (pp. 328–36); Prince, Morton: 'The Mechanism and Interpretation of Dreams – A Reply to Dr. Jones' (pp. 337–53).

[6] Abraham Arden Brill (1874–1948), born in Austria, American psychoanalyst and translator of many of Freud's works, founded the New York Psychoanalytic Society on 12 Feb. 1911; see *Zentralblatt*, Vol. 2, p. 233, and Hale (1971), pp. 317, 527; also 'Abraham Arden Brill' in *Psychoanalytic Pioneers*, (eds.) Alexander, Eisenstein and Grotjahn (1966).

52F

14 March 1911
Prof. Dr. Freud   Vienna IX, Berggasse 19

Dear Dr. Binswanger,

So it is true that politics ruin not only one's character but one's taste as well. I have only just realised in what bad taste it is to issue a certificate of good conduct to a scientific author,[1] something to which I had previously taken no exception. The explanation is that my essay was intended as a counterbalance to the attacks in Berlin and the long heralded article by Friedländer in Morton Prince's journal,[2] that is, it was intended as a means of agitation and not as a scientific contribution at all. That is why I considered it permissible to stress the personal character of the author. Putnam has ordered and received 400 offprints of this lecture of his.

When the empire I founded is orphaned, no one else but Jung must inherit the lot. As you see, my politics follow this aim unremittingly and my attitude to Stekel and Adler fits into the same scheme. Let us hope, then, that you will be spared the option.

On my desk, appreciations alternate with abuse, and good omens with bad. Recently a new continent has reported for the first time. The secretary[3] of the neurological section of the Austral[as]ian Medical Congress in Sydney has revealed that he is a subscriber to the *Jahrbuch* and has asked for an account of 'my doctrines' to be read at a session of the Congress, 'since they are still completely unknown in Australia'.[4] As against that, today I received the splendid reports of the Berlin Congress.[5] And so it goes on.

I wish your young regiment every success and conclude this highly political letter with kind regards,

Yours, Freud

[1] Addendum in Binswanger's hand: 'Putnam'.

[2] The article by Friedländer mentioned in note 5 to 51F, a translation of 'Hysterie und moderne Psychoanalyse' (1910a)

[3] Andrew Davidson (1869–1938), psychiatrist in Sydney, Secretary of the Section of Psychological Medicine and Neurology, Australasian Medical Congress, cf. Freud (1974a), p. 404, note 1.

[4] Freud uses the same quotation in his letter of 14 March 1911 to Jung; see Freud (1974a), p. 405. Freud's paper (1913m) appeared under the title 'On Psycho-Analysis' in *Transactions of the Ninth Session, Australian Medical Congress* (Sydney), Vol. 2 (1913).

[5] Oppenheim and Hoche had launched severe attacks against psychonanalysis at the 4th Annual Meeting of the German Neurologists in Berlin, 6–8 October 1910, on which Abraham reported to Freud in his letter of 18 October 1910; see Freud (1965a), p. 93.

53F

20 April 1911

Prof. Dr. Freud   Vienna IX, Berggasse 19

Dear Dr. Binswanger,

Actually I am not at all unhappy that Oppenheim has borne out my opinion of your prospectus.[1] After all, I did not deliver it gladly.

You are really doing yourself an injustice if you do not add the psychoanalytic complex as a third to the two complexes[2] you mention. Let me know when you again have time to take patients on for analysis; the last ones went to Maeder.

Over Easter I went to Bolzano,[3] where I roasted in the sun. For the moment things seem to be a little quieter in both my practice and in the polemical field. The difficulties in Vienna ought to resolve themselves through a reconciliation with Stekel and our dropping of Adler. The review I am to write of Stekel's dream book[4] for the *Jahrbuch* will therefore be a little more conciliatory, though I shall not swallow any necessary strictures. The lack of ideas and critical acumen in this work, which is otherwise so valuable, annoys me a great deal. He is unteachable, but the decent fellow in him keeps coming through.

The May edition of our *Jahrbuch* will contain all kinds of daring and serious matters written by me. It will be a bold advance to the centre of the enemy position on the paranoia front.[5]

The outcome in the case of Frau G. is very interesting. Just think how often such disturbances occur in analytical cases and then try to make a statistical survey of successes and failures!

I was very sorry about Honegger,[6] too; I had placed great hopes in him, but he was, alas, too abnormal.

With Jung's return,[7] the questions still pending (Congress, American organisation) will probably be quickly settled.

Bleuler continues to be over-correct towards me.

With kind regards and hearty greetings to all your complexes.

Yours, Freud

[1] See note 3 to 51F.

[2] Probably what is meant here is sanatorium work and scientific work; see 55F.

[3] Over Easter Freud made a four-day excursion in the Bolzano and Trento area of the Tyrol (then part of the Austro-Hungarian Empire) to reconnoitre a suitable place for the summer holidays; cf. Jones (1953–7), Vol. 2, p. 101.

[4] Wilhelm Stekel, *Die Sprache des Traumes* (1911) [*The Language of Dreams*]. Freud had in fact already written this review by the end of April and had sent it to Bleuler, but he wanted to tone it down and eventually, in his letter of 16 November 1911, asked Jung to release him from the task, so it was never published; cf. Freud (1974a), pp. 418, 464.

[5] This refers to the presentation of the Schreber case, Freud (1911c) which appeared in the *Jahrbuch* Vol. 3 (1911), pp. 9–69. The first half of this volume did not come out until August 1911; see Freud (1974a), p. 621.

[6] Johann Jakob Honegger, Jnr. (1885–1911), psychiatrist, disciple of Jung, trainee at the Burghölzli, intern in Territet (near Montreux) and at the Rheinau Institute. He took his own life on 28 March 1911. Cf. Walser (1973) and the mentions here and there in Freud (1974a).

[7] From a 16-day holiday trip to the south of France from 5 April 1911; cf. Freud (1974a), p. 408.

54F

2 May 1911

Prof. Dr. Freud   Vienna IX, Berggasse 19

Dear Dr. Binswanger,

It grieves me to have to confess that my enjoyment of your detailed letter, received today, was spoilt by my inability to read it. It is true I can guess your complexes, but I cannot work out what your attitude is towards them, just as sometimes happens in analysis.

And so I shall reply as best I can. I know nothing about Stuttgart.[1] Jung has not yet written to me. I hope that at least the personal reception was better[2]. – I had hardly seen anything of J. v. T. this season before he fell ill; since then, a little at a time. I am not responsible for Kauders[3] and for whatever mischief he may have caused; I believe he has had him consult all sorts of other people. J. [v. T.] clung on this time for longer than he usually does. Perhaps he now realises that sublimated homosexual friendship won't do for him either. He has had his bosom friend with him for the whole year and naturally he failed once again to cope with his sensuality and its expression by masturbation. Intellectually, he is rapidly going downhill.

I count on seeing you in September, above all at the Congress.[4] If you do not turn up, I shall be so put out that I shan't come to see you in Constance. I am not yet sure how much time I shall have to spend in Zurich – probably the week *following* the Congress.[5]

In July I am off to Karlsbad and then on to Oberbozen and Ritten [Renon].[6] In Karlsbad I hope to put down in writing all sorts of things that are now beginning to take shape, all pointing towards libido theory.[7]

Kindest regards to you, your wife and your children,

Yours, Freud

---

[1] The annual meeting of the German Psychiatry Society, which Jung and Binswanger had attended, had taken place in Stuttgart from 21 to 22 April 1911. Jung reported on the proceedings to Freud, who was eager for news, on 8 May 1911; see Freud (1974a), p. 621.

[2] i.e., better than the reception of psychoanalysis.

[3] Cf. note 2 to 5B.

[4] The 3rd International Psychoanalytic Congress, Weimar 21–22 September 1911, which Binswanger did in fact attend.

[5] Cf. the announcement of the Zurich visit in Freud's letter of 15 June 1911 to Jung, where he was still planning the visit for 22–27 September; see Freud (1974a), p. 429. But in the end Freud went to Küsnacht from 16 to 19 September; cf. *ibid.*, p. 443 and also Jones (1953–7), Vol. 2, p. 101.

[6] Freud left for Karlsbad on 9 July 1911 in order to cure his 'American colitis', as he wrote to Jones, and then followed the family, (not to Oberbozen, but) to Klobenstein on the Ritten (in the Dolomites). From there he went on alone to Zurich on 15 September. See Jones (1953–7), Vol. 2, p. 101, and Freud (1974a), p. 443.

[7] Freud is probably referring to his first thoughts about 'The Horror of Incest', i.e., the first of the three discourses which formed *Totem and Taboo* (1912–13a). In a letter to Jung of 20 August 1911, Freud wrote from Klobenstein that he had 'been working in a field where you will be surprised to meet me' (Freud 1974a, p. 438). The editor of *The Freud–Jung Letters* was certainly correct in indicating that this

referred to 'The Horror of Incest', because Freud had already written to Ferenczi on 11 August 1911: 'I am totally totem and taboo' (Freud 1992g, Vol. 2, p. 300). But it could also have been about the first considerations of 'The Uncanny' (1919h), because Freud wrote on 28 May 1911 (again to Ferenczi): 'Various themes, all of a non-medical nature, have arisen and are recommending themselves for the days of solitude in Karlsbad, as is the case with the uncanny and tragic guilt.' (*Ibid.*, p. 286). Cf. also the last paragraph of 61F.

55F

8 May 1911
Prof. Dr. Freud   Vienna IX, Berggasse 19

Dear Dr. Binswanger,

On the contrary! Like all fathers I am weak and blind and therefore proud of such a son, so I am reluctant to reproach him. I am quite certain about your psychoanalytic complex, I just think that if you were to reflect on which side to lay the main emphasis of your conscious preference, you would decide for psychoanalysis rather than the clinical complex, for the latter is so safely secured in the unconscious that it has no need of reinforcement.

I have recently referred several Moors (guess why we call them that in psychoanalytic jargon![1]) to Maeder. At the first opportunity I shall try to send you a good case for psychoanalysis, if I can still muster the necessary authority, which I am decidedly losing in Vienna although it is still standing up to all 'demolitions' abroad.

If you see Jung, please ask him why he has not written to me since the middle of April. He has probably been fairly busy, anyway.

I am already counting the days to 9 July, when I am expected in Karlsbad. In view of the fact that I reached the age of 55 a few days ago, I ought to be allowed to be tired on occasion, but my complexes tell me that I should not. Complexes can harry and hound one.

v. T. is a stone wrapped in cotton wool, as I may have written to you before. I do not think there will be a happy ending. Moreover his homosexuality is due to receive the scheduled aggravation from the loss of his mother (carcinoma), of which, however, he is not aware and should not be told until the diagnosis has been confirmed.

With regards to you and your family, very cordially,

Your old
Freud

[1] See Freud's clarification in the next letter.

56F

28 May 1911

Prof. Dr. Freud

Vienna IX, Berggasse 19

Dear Dr. Binswanger,

It is without doubt a friend's job to stand up to the gloomy thoughts that creep up on an ageing man and send them packing. Nor do I complain. Most of the time I, too, believe that I have started something that will keep people occupied in perpetuity; sometimes I am filled with deep dissatisfaction about the extent and depth of its influence and faint doubts about the future arise. In truth there is nothing for which man's disposition befits him less than occupying himself with psychoanalysis.

The Moors come from an old joke, well known to us, in which psychoanalysis is called an impossible task.[1] And not without some justification, once we rise above the level recognised by internal medicine. I often console myself with the thought that if we accomplish so little therapeutically, at least we learn why it is not possible to accomplish more. Our therapy strikes me as being the only rational one in this sense.

I still have 6 weeks of the most arduous toil ahead of me before I can go to Karlsbad. As you know, the Congress will be held on 21–22 September and it is fairly certain that I shall spend the week after that in Zurich. So I shall be able to stop off in Constance then and see your family.[2] I am delighted to hear that you are all well and that you are satisfied with your assistant. Is it true what I hear about Stockmayer[3] joining you? He seems to be a less problematical character than his half-namesake[4] from Jena.

Your contributions to the *Zentralblatt*[5] will be highly welcome. I am now busy trying to get rid of Adler so as to be left with Stekel alone. I shall have much more influence on the paper then.

With kind regards,
Yours, Freud

---

[1] [In German, *Mohrenwäsche*: literally 'Moor-washing'. A.J.P.]. According to the editors of the German edition of Freud 1974a [p. 132, note 1], the expression could be a reference to Jeremiah 13, 23 – 'Can the Ethiopian change his skin, or the leopard his spots?' [In the English edition, p. 119, the expression is simply translated as 'attempting the impossible', with no note on the German terminology. T.R.] In any case the expression should be compared with its first appearance in *Studies on Hysteria* (Freud 1895d), *G.W.*, Vol. 1, p. 262; *S.E.* Vol. II, p. 263, which, in the original

German, also characterised the predominant futility of psychoanalysis as '*Danaiden-arbeit*'. ['Work of the Danaids', or daughters of Danaus, who in Greek mythology were condemned eternally to pour water into bottomless vessels. In James Strachey's English translation this became 'a Sisyphean task' – an allusion to Sisyphus whose task in Hades was to roll a stone uphill which at once rolled down again – and *Mohrenwäsche* is not translated, but since it is tautologous in the context, there is no loss of meaning. T.R.] Jones's explanation (1953–7, Vol. 1, p. 166) is therefore scarcely relevant: 'The consultation hour was at noon, and for some time patients were referred to as "negroes". This strange appellation came from a cartoon in the *Fliegende Blätter* depicting a yawning lion muttering, "Twelve o'clock and no negro".'

[2] This visit did not take place; see 59F below.

[3] Jung wrote to Freud on 8 May 1911: 'It will interest you that Stockmayer is taking up a post in Binswanger's sanatorium.' Freud (1974a), p. 420. – Wolf Stockmayer (1881–1933) intern under Gaupp at the University Nerve Clinic, Tübingen, with Binswanger 1911–12, analyst in Berlin in 1913 (cf. B.A. 443/34), after war service became an analytical psychologist in Stuttgart. He is often mentioned in *The Freud–Jung Letters*; see Freud (1974a).

[4] Wilhelm Strohmayer; cf. note 4 to 47F.

[5] On the future fate of this journal, see 78F and 79F below.

57B

15 June 1911

Dear Professor Freud,

Your last letter gave me great pleasure. As I wrote to you once before, I cannot picture you as an ageing man. I imagine this is because my father, who as you know lived into his sixties, never struck me as being an ageing man. I can see him now, with all his undiminished mental vigour and enterprising spirit. In short, I have the feeling that a man is not yet old at 60, let alone at 55.

I thought of you today while analysing a patient's dream. She had dreamt that I had moved away and was devoting all my time to analysis (mainly, of course, to hers) in a foreign city. Material: I was much more suited to being an analyst than to being the director of a clinic; I must be much more interested in the first occupation for it is so much more demanding. 'How can anyone allow his energies to be so dissipated, and turn the main matter into a side issue? What a waste! How can you devote yourself to anything else when you could be doing something so important, when you belong to this new movement, a great cause for which you have such a special talent?' – You said something like that to me once, too, and, like the patient, you have a personal interest in making such comment. But both you and my patient know perfectly well that you are addressing a strong complex in me. My emotions have no trouble in opting for three quarters analysis and one quarter clinic. In reality it is the exact reverse. With time, however, it may perhaps be possible to strike an even balance between the two. I am not at all the kind of person who has to do everything himself, and I unload as much as I can on to my colleagues. I know very well that I cannot pride myself on any success unless it has been arrived at by way of analysis, and that every cure leaves me unsatisfied unless it is an analytic one.

Now for 'sundries'.

Whenever I read Stekel's *Dream Language* [Die Sprache des Traums][1] I invariably get a slightly bad conscience, because although inwardly I rail horribly against the man, I have on the other hand also learned something from him, namely to use a bit more impudence in my interpretations, for without that, truly, you get nowhere.

Stockmayer is coming here in October, unfortunately for no more than six months; he can't manage more and besides Dr. Schön[2] is coming back after that. He is in Jena now and intends to study with Bleuler and Jung during the winter. I am delighted to have turned him from a sceptic into a believer.

v. T. is about to leave. He is in a terrible state, torturing himself and hoping to skin the hide off me. His inhibitions have not yet gone but certain manic impulses have begun to stir in him: he wants to get back to living his life, his friend is calling; but on the other hand he still feels unable to make up his mind, it takes him two weeks to write to his friend, he keeps wavering between him and death (suicide). His stay here was a perfect copy of the last one, except that when he came here this time it was at a slightly later phase in his cycle. He will have a good summer again. Nevertheless I dispute that he has regressed psychically; I believe that he shows signs of inhibition rather than of loss of function, to put it in official psychiatrist's language. How exactly did you imagine his further relationship with his friend? Shouldn't the friend be initiated to a certain extent and the good J. kept a little bit further away from him? He intends to leave Vienna and to join him in Mödling as soon as possible. I too believe that his mother's death will drive him still further into the friend's arms. He has, incidentally, once again made himself at home here very quickly; only from afar does our clinic seem to him like a prison or a grave.

Did Hu.[3] ever look you up?

My wife and I are very much looking forward to seeing you here in September. But first Weimar.[4]

With kind regards from my wife and me to you and your family.

Yours, [L. Binswanger]

[1] Stekel (1911).

[2] Ewald Schön (1884–...). Cf. Jung's remark in his letter of 22 March 1912 to Freud: 'Burghölzli gets sillier every day. I was all the more astonished that Binswanger sent his assistant there for training...' Freud (1974a), p. 496. Schön had completed his dissertation in Jena under the supervision of Otto Binswanger and qualified as medical doctor on 23 April 1909 (UA Jena, L No. 280, sheet 226/1–2). He worked in Kreuzlingen from 1910 (apart from the interruption in Jena and Zurich mentioned here) until the outbreak of World War I and then again from 1 February 1919 until October 1920; cf. Binswanger's letter of 17 February 1919 to Wolf Stockmayer (B.A. 443/36) and the entry of 21 October 1920 in Ludwig Binswanger's visitors' book (in the possession of Trudi and Wolfgang Binswanger). Thereafter he worked as a neurologist in Constance.

[3] A patient whom Freud had referred to the Bellevue Sanatorium for in-patient treatment and who was treated there from 20 November 1910 until 10 May 1911. Cf. 44B.

[4] Cf. note 4 to 54F.

58F

Klobenstein am Ritten [Collalbo], Tyrol
Hotel Post, 23 August 1911

Dear Dr. Binswanger,

I have only just received the *Jahrbuch* and read your 'heel analysis',[1] with which you have succeeded splendidly. The incompleteness of the analysis of the *masculine* aspect must have rendered your account much more difficult, yet a very convincing impression remains. In matters of classification I am entirely on your side.

I do not believe for a moment that this is the last offering we can expect from you. Despite your obligations to the clinic, you will go on with your work, of that I have no doubt.

I am exempted from further discussion by our forthcoming meeting.[2] I hope that all goes very well with you, your wife and children, clinic and affairs. I have been here since the end of July and am planning to stay until 10 September. After a brief stopover in Merano, I shall go straight to Zurich on 15 September.[3]

Kind regards from,
Yours ever, Freud

[1] 'Analyse einer hysterische Phobie' (1911a). In this work Binswanger reports on his patient 'Gerda' who underwent treatment in the Bellevue Sanatorium from 20 February till 11 August 1911 and was analysed by Binswanger. 'It is about a 21-year-old girl who, when she was 4 years old, got her heel stuck in a skate. Since then she has suffered from a terrible anxiety and – if she cannot run away – suffers a syncopated hysterical attack as soon as she notices that anyone has a split opening up between heel and boot, or when anyone takes their heel in their hand, or even just talks about the heel.' Binswanger (1956c). [This is a new translation, the one on p. 34 of the 1957 English edition (1956c) being inaccurate and incomplete – T.R.]
[2] At the Congress in Weimar.
[3] Cf. notes 5 and 6 to 54F.

59F

Klobenstein 10 September 1911

Dear Dr. Binswanger,

I know of no better way of celebrating the second anniversary of the doctorate[1] I received at Worcester than by answering your letter. First of all many thanks for having been so very kind as to have it copied out (your wife's handwriting?). My next response was going to be to tell you that I would be visiting you in Constance to discuss your project[2] with you *after* the Congress. But then I received a letter from my 79-year-old (!) brother[3] in England with the news that the younger of my two old brothers (76 years old)[4] had died, and with the very understandable hope that he would see me again this autumn. And so I have decided to go on to England, Holland, Belgium or wherever he would like to meet me, after the Congress, and my visit to you, for which I had already made so many preparations, has had to be called off. There is not enough time *before* the Congress, for I cannot leave here before the 15th or be in Zurich before the 16th and on the 20th we shall be back on the train.[5] In Zurich itself, however, there will be a great many things to discuss, and I believe Putnam will be waiting for me there as well.

That is why I shall delay no longer in saying that your project seems very suitable to me. All of us consider you a connecting link with orthodox psychiatry, whose obduracy none of us indeed wishes to reinforce. Your past, your family associations and your inclinations all point you towards such a mediator's role. Very few of those with a traditional training have had your opportunities for judging and comparing. Your circumspection and honesty of intent entitle you to implement your plan. But I would just like to point out that a certain tendency to tread softly – as shown in your prospectus – is best avoided.

Should you substitute me for Wernicke[6] in your train of thought, you must surely bear in mind that Wernicke has a far greater right to recognition, being already dead. Nor should you forget that he was in the agreeable position of encountering dispassionate apathy, while it has been my lot to 'disturb the peace of this world'.[7] However, as far as your writing is concerned, no doubt, personalities will take second place to content and the relationships of the theories.

I have not read L.'s[8] essay on Wernicke. Wernicke always seemed to me an interesting example of the poverty of scientific thinking. He was a brain anatomist and could not stop himself dissecting the soul into serial sections as he did the brain. His great aphasia discovery[9] has led him to introduce the schema of a-, hypo- and hyper- or cortical, sub- and transcortical, into all his writings and to apply it in even the most inappropriate cases. But in so judging him, I am measuring him by a high standard; I know very well that with others, whose names resound throughout the world, the question of scientific thought never arises at all.

Our plans have had to be changed on account of the hot weather, so that we are no longer making for Merano but will go our separate ways when we leave here. I am having to deal with rather a lot of illness in my family right now. Inevitable, with the increase in numbers.

The *Jahrbuch*,[10] in which Jung, in particular, has distinguished himself, will at long last have reached you by now. I expect to find my special offprints[11] in Weimar, and shall distribute them there.

The frequency of crucifixes [*Herrgötter*] here in the Tyrol, where they are more numerous than the edible boletus [*Herrenpilze*][12] used to be until recently, has persuaded me to make a study of the psychology of religion,[13] something of which may see the light of day in years to come. Following publication I shall probably not be allowed back to the Tyrol.

With kind regards to you and your little family, and looking forward to meeting you in a few days' time,

As ever, Freud

---

[1] At the closing ceremony of the 20th anniversary celebrations at Clark University, Worcester, on 11 September 1909 Freud and Jung were awarded the title Honorary Doctor of Laws (LL.D.). Cf. Freud (1974a), p. 246 and Jones (1953–7), p. 63.

[2] In April (not in summer as Binswanger himself writes)) 1911, Binswanger had heard, at the annual meeting of the German Psychiatry Society in Stuttgart, a 'very impressive lecture' by Hugo Liepmann on 'The Influence of Wernicke on Clinical Psychiatry', cf. Liepmann (1911), and he had planned a 'parallel paper' with the title 'The Significance of Freud for Clinical Psychiatry' but in the event had to admit that he 'was completely lacking in the necessary scientific and philosophical background for such a task'; see Binswanger (1956c), p. 35 in the 1957 English edition. The work did not come out until 1936; see Binswanger (1936c). Indeed the project gradually changed. Thus not only the 1920 paper came about (1920a), but also the *Einführung* [Introduction] (1922a) the planned second volume of which, however, was never published.

[3] Emanuel Freud (1833–1914).

[4] Philipp Freud (1834–1911), died 29 August.

[5] Freud could not travel before the 15th September because on the 14th he was to celebrate his silver wedding. In the end he stayed in Zurich from the 16th to the 18th September and presumably travelled on to Weimar with Jung, Mrs. Jung and Putnam on the 19th; cf. Freud (1974a), p. 489.

[6] Carl Wernicke (1848–1905), Professor of Psychiatry in Berlin, Breslau and Halle; cf. Lanczik (1988).

[7] Possibly an allusion to Matthew 10.34 (and parallels): 'Think not that I am come to send peace on earth; I came not to send peace, but a sword.' It is also possibly (in vague recollection of the biblical quotation?) a modification of the Hebbel quotation in 'On the History of the Psycho-Analytic Movement': 'disturbed the sleep of the world', Freud (1914d), *S.E.*, Vol. XIV, p. 21.

[8] Hugo Liepmann, 'Über Wernickes Einfluss auf klinische Psychiatrie' (1911) [On Wernicke's influence upon clinical psychiatry].

[9] Wernicke had published the work *Der aphasische Symptomenkomplex. Eine psychologische Studie auf anatomischer Basis* [The complex of symptoms in aphasia. An anatomically based psychological study] in 1874, which Freud had had a good look at in his 'On the interpretation of the aphasias; A critical study' (1891b). Cf. Eggert (1977).

[10] The *Jahrbuch für psychoanalytische und psychopathologische Forschungen*, Vol. 3 (1911), part 1, which appeared in August 1911, contained the following by Jung: 'Wandlungen und Symbole der Libido' [Part 1] (pp. 120–227), a debate with Morton Prince (pp. 309–28) and a review of a Bleuler paper (pp. 469–74).

[11] Of 'Formulations regarding the Two Principles in Mental Function' (1911b) and 'Psycho-Analytic Notes on an Autobiographical Account of a case of Paranoia' [The Schreber case] (1911c).

[12] Mushrooms, not '*Herrenpilger*' [pilgrims], as Binswanger read it (1956c), p. 36 in the 1957 English edition. Freud was an avid collector of mushrooms when he was on holiday.

[13] This refers to his work on *Totem and Taboo* (1912–13a); cf. also his intimation to Jung in his letter of 1 September 1911, 'my work in these last few weeks has dealt with the same theme as yours, to wit, the origin of religion' (1974a) p. 441, and note 7 to 54F above.

60F

23 November 1911

Prof. Dr. Freud   Vienna IX, Berggasse 19

Dear Dr. Binswanger,
How kind of you to think of me in your military prison.[1] I gave myself
time until I knew that you were at liberty again and back at home.

Your decision to go back to the work you had given up is very
welcome news. I was disappointed when you declined my offer so
soon after I gave you my support. Not that I looked for a practical
result from your efforts; I believe one generation will have to pass
before the next can heed your exhortations; but I think it worthwhile
for you and reassuring for us that you should be writing like that. If
you now believe that we of the Psychoanalytic Association are only
good for cultural fertiliser, and will have to die out first, then that,
too, does not trouble my egoism. I shall have gone by then anyway,
and as far as the intellectual goal is concerned, I need merely honour
the achievement, not the means to it. But I don't really share your
view and consider your prognosis heretical. Perhaps you are merely
justifying your own slight reservations about the Association. I have
the impression that we are in a phase of quiet progress along a gentle
incline, to be followed by a more impetuous spurt, the Association
being a large part of the driving force.

I have been told nothing at all about the frictions in Zurich.[2] I am
left in peace at the moment in Vienna, though I was certainly not
impartial. Everything would be perfect, except that as a result of the
bitter smear campaign my practice is not large enough to keep my
colleagues well supplied. I shall console myself with the fact that, as
I know from experience, patients do not start sounding the alarm in
the autumn until the weather has turned bad. This year, November
has been unusually fine.

J. v. T. remains completely unmoved in his mania by his mother's
death. We expect that he will soon be paying for this with an exceptionally severe attack, and he himself is aware of this.

It is good to hear that your little family is getting on so well. Please
give them all my kind regards, and greetings to you, too,

from yours,
Freud

---

[1] Binswanger was apparently called up for annual reservist exercises, which was
normal practice in Switzerland.

² Jung reported on these 'frictions' in his letter of 24 November 1911 to Freud; see Freud (1974a), pp. 466–7. In this connection Bleuler announced his resignation from the Zurich Psychoanalytic Society and notified Freud of this on 28 November; see *ibid*. p. 468.

61F

26 December 1911

Prof. Dr. Freud   Vienna IX, Berggasse 19

Dear Dr. Binswanger,

I hasten to reply to your kind Christmas greetings, the only ones from our circle as it happens, and reciprocate with my best wishes for 1912 to you, your family and your clinic. I am quite sure you will live to see the recognition of psychoanalysis and that you will then be glad to have been among the rebels in your youth. Don't worry about me; I really have no wish to grow *that old*.

I should very much like to accept your wife's kind offer of hospitality some day, but as you know this is the time when I have to earn money to pay for all the holiday extravagances.

The goings-on in Zurich are annoying, but I know Bleuler too well to blame Jung for them. Things went no better with Breuer either; I was only too willing to be grateful but he did not want me to be.

Minor chores here,¹ and unfortunately no time for the greater things that have been nagging me since the summer.²

Happy New Year!
Yours cordially,
Freud

Regards to Stockmayer. Isn't there a good precedent for the 'shackling'?³

I have been asked (purely formally) to recommend a Viennese patient, brought to you by Dr. Sam. Kohn,⁴ and do so herewith.

¹ On the same day he wrote to Ferenczi: 'These days I have been writing without the proper mood: On Types of Onset of Neurosis (*Zentralblatt*) [1912c], On the Universal Tendency to Debasement in the Sphere of Love (*Jahrbuch*)' [1912d] – Freud (1992g), p. 322.
² Cf. note 7 to 54F.
³ Possibly Binswanger had reported a case to Freud where there was no avoiding the physical restraint of the patient.
⁴ Freud had probably mixed up the name, because there is a letter (7 December 1911)

with the relevant case notes from a Dr. *Edmund* Kohn, Landesgerichtstrasse 12, Vienna. This doctor was born in Königswart Spa (Marienbad district) in 1863 and died in Vienna in 1929 (information kindly provided by Mr. Huemer, Vienna City Council). At the same time there were two doctors by the name of Samuel Kohn. The one Freud knew and possibly confused with Edmund Kohn is perhaps Samuel Kohn (1853–1923); cf. Fischer (1938), p. 151. The year of death given by Fischer cannot be confirmed by the Jewish cultural authority in Vienna nor in the register of residents in the new Vienna town hall. See also *Internat. klin. Wschr.* 3 (1889), p. 676, and *Wiener klin. Wschr.* 4 (1891), p. 347.

62B

5 March 1912

Dear Professor Freud,

At the moment I am enjoying a spell of involuntary leisure following an attack of appendicitis which is now subsiding but will probably call for the removal of the trouble-maker in a few months' time.[1] You are often in my thoughts, but particularly this past week, for personal as well as for scientific reasons. I would have written earlier had I any progress in my work to report.[2] No matter how much thought I devote to it, however, little practical headway is made, and even today I still doubt whether anything will come of it and whether there is the slightest chance of relating the psychoanalytical method to clinical psychiatry in such a way that something new will emerge. Jung has already stated the gist of the matter in his *Inhalt der Psychose*[3] [The Content of the Psychoses]. Even so, I have no regrets about continuing to pursue this theme since it defines the basis of my own attitude and obliges me to read much that I should otherwise have neglected.

I was very interested in Kronfeld's paper,[4] which unfortunately no one appears to be inclined to challenge. It shows clearly how, by relying on 'logic' alone, one's view can be obstructed, and broad, fertile and cultivated fields overlooked. His account of your doctrine seems very good to me; it is probably the best from the other camp. His impertinent judgements and condemnations from the platform of pure logic should no doubt be put down to his youth. After all these clinical surveys, I myself thirst for living material; and I can have it for the asking. – The new year has begun quite well. My colleagues have settled down to the work so well that I can confine myself to the role of director and take on just the isolated case, which I then treat by analysis. I have much more peace and quiet than I did last year, when I was still feeling my way into my role and responsibilities.

In January I spent a week with Bonhoeffer[5] in Breslau, where I was very well received and saw much that I found instructive. Bonhoeffer, at any rate, is not hostile to analysis and at least acknowledges the justification of and need for this line of research, which is saying quite a lot for a Prussian professor. I recently sent him my 'heel analysis' and am waiting to see how he reacts to it. He himself is a sincere, upright character. I am glad he is going to Berlin. Afterwards, my wife and I spent a week in Dresden with friends, where I was terribly lazy. Unfortunately I have not been to Zurich more than once since Christmas as a result of that trip and my present illness, but hope to be able now to go back there again on a regular basis. In the Zurich press campaign, it was Forel who annoyed me most by his underhand conduct.[6] I found your articles in the *Zentralblatt*[7] particularly valuable and hope that you will publish many more soon.

Stockmayer is very hard at work and has already done wonders with Dr. W.,[8] if mainly by relying on transference and education. The patient still lives in our closed house, but otherwise takes his meals and mixes with our neurotic patients.

Dresden did my wife a great deal of good as well. At the moment she is completely occupied with our son, who, to crown it all, is down with a severe case of enteritis.

How are things over there, and especially with you? I look forward to hearing from you soon. With kind regards, dear Professor,

Yours,

[L. Binswanger]

[1] The appendectomy was carried out on 18 March 1912; cf. Binswanger's letter to Karl Bonhoeffer of 14 May 1912, B.A. 443/37.

[2] In the meantime, the plan to write a paper on 'The Significance of Freud for Clinical Psychiatry' (see note 2 to 59F above) had developed into a plan for a conceptual and methodical study of the principles of the relationship between psychiatry and psychoanalysis. However, only the first part of this was ever published – under the title *Einführung in die Probleme der allgemeinen Psychologie* – and that not till 1922; see Binswanger (1922a).

[3] Jung (1908).

[4] 'Über die psychologischen Theorien Freuds und verwandte Anschauungen' (1911) ['On Freud's psychoanalytic theories and related ideas']. Arthur Kronfeld (1886–1941), intern at the Psychiatric Clinic in Heidelberg 1909–13, after 1913 in Berlin, lecturer (Privatdozent] from 1927. See Kittel (1986).

[5] Karl Bonhoeffer (1868–1948), Professor of Psychiatry in Heidelberg, Breslau and Berlin; cf. Stertz (1970). Binswanger had met him while a student in Heidelberg in 1904, (1956c), p. 38 in the 1957 English edition. In letters which have survived, Binswanger asked if he might visit Bonhoeffer in Breslau from 20 to 25 January,

together with his friend Hans Wolfgang Maier. A month later he congratulated
Bonhoeffer on his appointment in Berlin. Cf. B.A. 443/34.

[6] On 2 January 1912 the *Neue Zürcher Zeitung* reported on a lecture by the Zurich
neurologist Max Kesselring 'On the Theory and Practice of the Viennese Psychologist
Freud' which had been given before the Zurich branch of the Kepler Bund. The report
instigated a polemic correspondence with contributions from, among others, Forel,
Jung and F.M. (Fritz Marti). Forel's letter of 25 January expressed regret that Breuer's
successful study of cathartic therapy had been distorted by Freud. According to Dr.
Ludwig Frank in Zurich, psychoanalysis ought to be studied seriously. Cf. the detailed
account of the controversy in Ellenberger (1970).

[7] Freud (1911b) and (1911c).

[8] A patient of Ferenczi, Freud and Binswanger. He was diagnosed in the Bellevue as
suffering from 'degenerative melancholy with hysterical characteristics'.

63F

15 March 1912

Prof. Dr. Freud   Vienna IX, Berggasse 19

Dear Dr. Binswanger,

What an unpleasant surprise that you should be facing an appendectomy. Let us hope that you will recover from it as well as my youngest
daughter did.[1] But it won't be for months yet, will it?

I have no idea why Kronfeld's essay has made so great an impression in some places.[2] I found nothing praiseworthy in it except for
its decent bourgeois tone. The assurance with which he refutes psychoanalysis *a priori* is no greater than that with which any philosopher
of any school dismisses all other schools. His objection to the inter-
ference of experience is a wretched sophism, and an impertinence
besides. I hope that feelings will die down on this topic as well.

And so we are to lose our dear Geheim-Rat [privy councillor]
Ziehen[3] from Berlin. But why? Do you know anything about it? He
must surely be younger than I am.

It upsets me that you have got no further with your work, for now
my worry is that it will never be done at all and then your fate will
be to retire [*zurückziehen*] from the battlefield, something which you
are even less entitled to do than Ziehen. (I could easily have made a
condensation joke[4] here.)

Meanwhile, you will have received two more special offprints[5] from
me, routine stuff, nothing out of the ordinary. Good things do not
prosper with such application and such fruitful expectations. I commend our *Imago*,[6] which should be ready in a couple of weeks or so,
to your attention. I am now working on an essay on the 'taboo' of

the primitives,[7] which is intended to smuggle psychoanalysis into ethnopsychology. In the Association, things have been lively but peaceful ever since the Adler plague[8] was eradicated.

As luck would have it, there is little to say about our state of health, which is satisfactory on the whole. I hope that I will hear nothing but good of you and yours too, and that I may ignore the faviform enteritis.

Kind regards to your wife and to Stockmayer,

As ever,
Freud

[1] Neither Peters (1979) nor Young-Bruehl (1988) mention Anna Freud's having an appendectomy.
[2] To Jung, Freud wrote on 14 May 1912: 'None of the recent critiques has made more impression than Kronfeld's (on me, I am sorry to say, none).' Freud (1974a), p. 504.
[3] Cf. notes 5 and 6 to 19F.
[4] See Freud (1905c), *S.E.*, Vol. VIII, particularly pp. 25–33 and 40–41.
[5] Presumably 'The Handling of Dream-Interpretation in Psycho-Analysis' (1911e), and 'The Dynamics of Transference' (1912b).
[6] The full title of the journal was *Imago. Zeitschrift für Anwendung der Psychoanalysis auf die Geisteswissenschaften* [Journal for the Application of Psychoanalysis in the Arts]. Vol. 1, No. 1 (1912) appeared on 28 March 1912 (Freud to Putnam 28 March 1912; see Freud, 1971a, p. 137).
[7] He is referring to part II of *Totem and Taboo*, which appeared in *Imago* in two instalments under the title: 'Taboo and Emotional Ambivalence' (*S.E.* Vol. XIII, pp. 18–74).
[8] Cf. note 4 to 51F.

64F

2 April 1912
Prof. Dr. Freud   Vienna IX, Berggasse 19

Dear Dr. Binswanger,
I am writing today just to welcome you home after your operation,[1] and to thank your wife for kindly letting me know about it. I shall spare you any serious chitchat today. The main thing is that you are safe and well again.

Kind regards,

Yours,
Freud

[1] Cf. 62B above and its note 1.

65F

14 April 1912

Prof. Dr. Freud

Vienna IX, Berggasse 19

Dear Dr. Binswanger,

An old man like me, who should not complain (and has decided not to complain) if his life comes to an end in a few years, feels especially aggrieved when one of his flourishing young friends, one of those who is meant to continue his own life, informs me that his life is in danger.[1] On thinking it over, however, I gradually collected myself and remembered that in spite of the existing suspicions all the odds are in your favour and that you have only been reminded a little more conspicuously of the precariousness in which we all live and which we are so ready to forget.

But you will not forget it just now, and life, as you say, will hold a special and enhanced charm for you. As for the rest, we will be hoping for the best, something our present-day knowledge permits us to do without self-deception. I shall, of course, keep the secret, as you have asked me to, proud of the privilege you have granted. But it goes without saying that I would like to see you as soon as this is possible without disturbing you. Perhaps at Whitsun? I trust you will let me know if this would suit you. I am pleased to hear that the plan for your paper[2] preoccupies you more than ever, and I will now answer your other questions, which bear witness to your interest in everything that goes on in our circle.

I too, no longer consider Bjerre's case as a hysteria,[3] but it would seem to prove clearly the importance of homosexuality. The patient escapes paranoia so long as she can invest a part of her libido in the man, succumbs to it when she is completely dependent on the woman, and is cured by the restoration of her relationship with the man. Since Bjerre omitted to provide an elementary analysis of sexuality, he has had to fill the gap in comprehension with rather too much rhetoric.

Silberer[4] has a sensitive mind with a strong penchant for the occult, which he came upon on his way to psychoanalysis and has only used psychoanalysis to further his favourite interest. On a personal level he is not part of the Vienna group at all. He is a convinced Christian and well-to-do, his father a conservative provincial civil servant, sportsman and aviator.

Jung is to start a course of lectures at Fordham University in New York on 10 September, in English this time.[5] Because he has to do his military service before then, the only date available for the Congress is the middle of August, a date to which I am opposed for health reasons and because of holiday plans; so that this year's Congress will probably not take place.[6] I think that would be no loss, every other year would be better. I am no longer so happy with Jung as I had hoped – I beg you to be discreet about this. He busies himself with the interests of the Society, where they do not damage his own, too little. He buries himself completely in his own work and hardly ever turns up at our committee meetings, so that the various groups do not get to hear from each other. Probably what is behind this is that he is playing out his father complex against me,[7] for which I have certainly provided no cause, and if one pursued the matter one would probably find the influence of a woman,[8] not his wife. But, I beg you, keep this to yourself, I hope for a harmless conclusion to the whole disturbance.

I have concerned myself very little with the individual great men[9] whom you mention. Nor have I taken much interest in the whole species. It has always seemed to me that ruthlessness and arrogant self-confidence constitute the indispensable condition for what, when it succeeds, strikes us as greatness; and I also believe that one ought to differentiate between greatness of achievement and greatness of personality.

Dr. S. of Merano is an excellent man and dear friend. The woman whom you mention is his stepdaughter, of a rather different ilk. I know both her and her mother and have always found that with all their kindness and charm these women lack something like a moral backbone. They are as though in a permanent state of erotic intoxication. But it is very possible that the grim experience of her marriage has brought out a more serious side in the young woman, and I would be very pleased to hear that under your guidance she had turned into a useful person.

Imago has just appeared;[10] I hope that my second essay (on taboo[11]) in the third number will be more interesting than the first.

And now I send you and your dear nurse my warmest wishes for your recovery and for the maintenance of your excellent, manly and courageous spirits.[12]

Yours ever, Freud

[1] In the second half of March 1912 Binswanger underwent surgery not only on his appendix but also for a testicular tumour, so he feared at that time that he did not have long to live. See Binswanger (1956c), pp. 39–40.

[2] Binswanger (1922a).

[3] Bjerre (1911). Cf. this also with Chauzard and de la Payonne-Lidbom (1988). In the letter of 12 February 1912 to Poul Bjerre published there Freud still preferred to consider it an 'hysteria in the form of paranoia'. On Poul Bjerre (1876–1964), a Stockholm neurologist who had introduced Lou Andreas-Salomé to psychoanalysis, see Freud (1966a), p. 212, and *Minutes*, Vol. 3 (1974), p. 101. N.B. There is a pertinent note (1) in the German edition, *Protokolle* (p. 102), which does not appear in the *Minutes*.

[4] Herbert Silberer (1882–1922), Viennese psychoanalyst, member of the Vienna Society from 1910, committed suicide. On Herbert S. and his father Victor (1862–1924), cf. Nitzschke (1988). pp. 9–70.

[5] Jung reported to Freud in his letter of 22 March 1912 that he had been invited to give a course of lectures at Fordham University commencing 10 September, Freud (1974a), p. 496. Freud and Jung had given lectures in German in Worcester in 1909 (*ibid*. pp. 245–6).

[6] Freud to Jung (24 March 1912): 'Besides, I have the impression that there is no need for a congress this year. [...] I think your trip provides excellent justification for skipping the congress.' Freud (1974a), p. 497.

[7] Freud had already mentioned 'a lack of understanding in dealing with your father-complexes' to Jung on 31 December 1911. Freud (1974a), p. 476.

[8] Possibly Antonia Wolff (1888–1953); cf. Eissler (1982), p. 93. – but perhaps also the patient Frau Gi. who was in treatment with Freud at least from 1910 to 1914, cf. 107F.

[9] Reference not clear.

[10] Vol. 1, No. 1 (1912), published 28 March 1912; cf. note 6 to 63F.

[11] Cf. note 7 to 63F.

[12] About two-thirds of this letter was published in Freud (1960a), pp. 286–7 and those portions of it are here in the same translation by Tania and James Stern.

66F

16[1] May 1912

Prof. Dr. Freud

Vienna IX, Berggasse 19

Dear Dr. Binswanger,

You could not know why I stopped writing so abruptly. Here is the explanation: my 77-year-old mother[2] came down with a severe neuritis brachialis (herpes zoster), which meant that it was impossible for me to say whether or not I would be able to visit you over Whitsun. And so I did not know what to write. Today I am able to say that there is no need for me to be detained here and that I would be most pleased to appear on your visitors' list for Whitsun. I shall be leaving on Friday the 24th, and will be with you on Saturday. Should I come to Bellevue or would you prefer to meet somewhere else? Depending on what you decide, I shall let you know the time of my arrival.

I am bringing nothing with me except perhaps for a photograph,[3] which you will be able to compare with the original. I say perhaps, because I do not yet know how the attempt to wrest its likeness from the light has turned out. In exchange, I shall listen with particular attention to what you have to tell me about your work. We shall also talk about everything else that is on our mind, Bleuler, Jung and the general state of the world.

Today I received an amusing collection of printing errors from Dr. D., a patient of Stockmayer's from Moscow.[4] He is in Munich at present, wants to have a meeting with me, and if you decide on Bellevue and are agreeable, I shall grant his request and ask him to meet me there – for an hour, as he writes.

With kind regards to you and your wife and my best wishes for your well-being,

Yours, Freud

[1] Corrected from 17.

[2] Amalie Freud, née Nathanson (1835–1930).

[3] Perhaps no. 213 in Freud, Ernst (1976), p. 197.

[4] The patient was analysed in the Bellevue by Stockmayer (cf. note 3 to 56F). On the other hand, in a letter of the same date to Ferenczi: 'Today I received a funny collection of typographical errors from a docent in physics, which Maeder admits to having produced.' (Freud 1992g, Vol. 1, p. 372).

67B

18 May 1912
Bellevue, Constance

Dear Professor Freud,

Alarmed to have heard nothing more from you, I fear that you might be ill, or else, as I hope, that you are indeed still coming here at Whitsun and that you are dispensing with written discussions in anticipation of verbal ones. I hope very much that the second supposition is correct, and would merely ask you to let me know roughly when you will be arriving so that I can make myself available. My wife and I look forward to your visit with enormous pleasure.

Yours cordially, [L. Binswanger]

Freud's Visit to Kreuzlingen 25 to 28 May 1912

This visit played a particular role in the growing estrangement between Freud and Jung. Jung was not at all pleased with Freud that he did not take the opportunity of being in Kreuzlingen to visit him also (cf. Jung's letter of 8 June 1912 to Freud; Freud 1974a, p. 509) and later described Freud's behaviour as the 'Kreuzlingen gesture' (see 71F). Freud and Jung discussed the incident at a conference of presidents of psychoanalytic societies in Munich on 24 November 1912 (cf. 81F and its note 2) during a two-hour walk before lunch and they became reconciled. Jung had to admit that he had not been in Zurich at all on the weekend of the visit and therefore Freud's announcement of the visit (on a postcard which was not delivered; see Freud 1974a, p. 509, note 3) had not arrived in time (cf. detailed report in Freud's letter of 26 November 1912 to Ferenczi, Freud 1992g, Vol. 1, pp. 433–5). The visit to Kreuzlingen was particularly important to Freud because he feared for Binswanger's life.

Binswanger made no notes about this visit. He reported on it for the first time, from memory, in his *Reminiscences*; the text is in the Appendix, p. 235. Also given in the Appendix is a passage from a letter in which Freud tells Ferenczi about the visit (p. 236).

68F

14 June 1912

Prof. Dr. Freud

Vienna IX, Berggasse 19

Dear Dr. Binswanger,

Just imagine this curious fruit of my visit to you: I could read your letter without difficulty, although I am not at all sure that it was more clearly written than the previous letters.

Many thanks for your personal news and that of your work. Please do not trouble to thank me when Heller[1] sends you a book[2] which should remind you of our conversation about the green stones.[3] But he (H.) is so slow that it will certainly be quite a time yet before he gets round to it.

Jung reproached me for not going to Zurich and said the reason for for my staying away was my dissatisfaction with his new libido theory.[4] He did not say, however, why it did not occur to him to come over here himself. I had certainly done enough travelling and could not, as your guest, reduce my stay by half.

In these last four weeks my judgement as well as the amount I take on winds steadily down. But I shall not be sorry when the 14th July comes round again, which historic day[5] also means a bit of freedom for me. I had a silly idea[6] a few days ago out of which something might come, a private amusement like the Leonardo.[7]

A thick book by Rank[8] about incest in literature[9] has just had its final corrections; it will, I hope, make a strong impression.

Jones arrived here today. Perhaps his sick wife[10] will decide to have preliminary psychoanalytic treatment.

I send you my kindest regards and please remember me to your wife and the lady at Brunnegg.[11]

Yours truly, Freud

[1] Hugo Heller (1870–1923), bookseller and publisher in Vienna. He published both of the first two issues of *Schriften zur angewandten Seelenkunde* (Issue 1: Freud 1907a, Issue 2: Riklin, 1908). See also Freud (1906f).

[2] Victor Hugo, *Notre-Dame de Paris*. It is no longer possible to determine with any certainty the edition that Freud chose.

[3] Presumably what is meant here are the green glass beads with which Esmeralda's amulet is decorated in Hugo's novel.

[4] Jung to Freud, 8 June 1912: 'The fact that you felt no need to see me during your visit to Kreuzlingen must, I suppose, be attributed to your displeasure at my development of the libido theory.' Freud (1974a), p. 509.

[5] He is referring to the fall of the Bastille. Direct references to the French Revolution are rare with Freud; see also Elrod (1989).

[6] The first mention of 'The Theme of the Three Caskets', Freud (1913f). See 70F.

[7] *Leonardo da Vinci – a Memory of his Childhood*, Freud (1910c).

[8] Otto Rank (1884–1939), originally Rosenfeld, 1906–15 Secretary and Minutes Secretary of the Vienna Psychoanalytic Association, founder member of the 'committee'. In the early 1920s he began to turn away from classical psychoanalysis, and from 1935 lived in the USA. Cf. Taft (1958) and Lieberman (1985).

[9] *Das Inzest-Motiv in Dichtung und Sage*, Vienna 1912. Not published in English until 1992: *The Incest Theme in Literature and Legend. Fundamentals of a Psychology of Literary Creation*, Johns Hopkins Univ. Press, Baltimore, MD.

[10] Loe Kann, with whom Jones lived from 1905 till 1912. Although not officially married to him, she took his name and he spoke of her (as Freud also does here) as his wife. As a result of repeated operations for kidney stones she had developed an addiction to morphine. Jones confirmed in his autobiography that she had a 'psychoneurotic constitution' (1959, p. 139). After 1912 she was in treatment with Freud. Later she married the novelist Herbert Jones. See Jones (1959), pp. 139f, p. 197, and Freud (1960a), pp. 305, 467.

[11] Binswanger's stepmother, Marie-Luise Binswanger, who lived on the castle-like Brunnegg estate near Kreuzlingen which she had inherited from Binswanger's grandfather, Ludwig Binswanger. She received Freud there during his visit to Kreuzlingen.

69B

Constance, 29 June 1912

Dear Professor Freud,

I was particularly glad to hear that you were able to read my letter without difficulty, for it showed that you had given up some of your resistances against me. I have always found that my wife and other women close to me could make out my handwriting with ease from the very outset. That is why I thought that all that was needed to read my hand was a positive transference. Perhaps this is going a bit too far, and since this letter is going to be fairly long I had best use the typewriter all the same.

While I happen to be on the subject of analysing you, I must also tell you how struck I was, on re-reading *The Interpretation of Dreams*, by your enormous will to power, or more specifically to dominate people: the fact that you wanted to study law first and that government ministers play an important role in life is probably all part of the same thing. You are a born ruler and the fact that you have diverted this ruling passion into the psychic control of individuals is a particularly successful sublimation. It is not true[1] to say, however, that this passion to control mankind is reflected in all your scientific work. How closely the instinct is bound up with your father complex is again easily gathered from *The Interpretation of Dreams*.

Heller is clearly deserving of your opinion, for the book has not yet turned up. I shall gladly dispense with the thanks, but will permit myself to wonder why it is that you have so great an aversion to expressions of gratitude. I have noticed this on many occasions, *inter alia* from a remark by Frau G. that you were cross with her on one occasion only: when she thanked you.

I was in Zurich two weeks ago; Jung was very cool towards me. I felt that his talk against analysis by laymen, which he hurled[2] at Pfister,[3] was a sign of his resistance to you. Although I agreed with him largely on matters of fact, his words nevertheless showed me how changeable he is under the influence of affects. Having helped to make poor Pfister feel guilty, he ought not to have left him in such distress.[4]

Adler's *Neurotic Constitution*[5] has reached me. I have only read the preface, the introduction and the conclusion, and am quite dumbfounded at the outrageous nonsense he perpetrates. His pigheadedness is incredible; I often fail to understand him at all. His objections to [what he calls] your fundamental errors are so astonishing that I now fully realise why you got rid of him. What he proposes, namely the alleged final purpose of neurosis, can be seen at a cursory glance to be untenable. Only complexes and resistances can have led him on to so futile a path, given his intimate knowledge of analysis. On the one hand, he expresses his resistance against you with some perfidy; on the other, his identification with you is evident in every phrase. I hope I am not mistaken in believing that *this* disappointment has not affected you too deeply.

I am very well; I have been very busy and am getting more and more work, but have had occasion to reflect further about my own 'work'.[6] At the moment, that consists mainly of classifying the material in accordance with your suggestions.

Our lady from Merano[7] is already head over heels in love with one of the doctors; our matron has already properly pronounced a diagnosis of hypomania, adding: 'We've had the likes of her as patients before.' I think she is too big a child for us.

I recently spent a day in Berlin and called on Oppenheim, who was so stiff and condescending that I very quickly took my leave again. There were several patients on whom I had to give him reports.

I am eagerly looking forward to hearing about your new idea, and hope that you keep your strength up until the close of term.

With kind regards from my wife and myself to you and your family, I am, dear Professor,

Yours ever, [L. Binswanger]

---

[1] Possibly Binswanger had dictated 'Is it not...?'

[2] On 14 June a discussion took place in the Zurich local group following a seminar paper by Pfister in which Binswanger presumably took part; see *Korrespondenzblatt* 3 (1910), p. 103.

[3] Oskar Pfister (1873–1956), Protestant pastor and psychoanalyst in Zurich; cf. Hoffer (1958b), Bori (1990) and Zulliger (1966); Lück and Mühlleitner (1993), p. 174, as well as his correspondence with Freud (1963a).

[4] There is an allusion here to Goethe, the Harpist's song in *Wilhelm Meister's Apprenticeship*, 2, 13, which is largely lost in translation:
'You lead us on; by you incited, / A wretched mortal will transgress, / And then you leave him comfortless; / For every earthly wrong's requited.' [1983 transl. by Michael Hamburger].

[5] *The Neurotic Constitution*, Adler (1912). Cf. Freud (1974a), p. 511.

[6] Binswanger (1922a).

[7] Binswanger's colleague, step-daughter of Dr. S.; see 65F.

70F

4 July 1912
Prof. Dr. Freud   Vienna IX, Berggasse 19

Dear Dr. Binswanger,
The contributions to my self-analysis that you have lavished on me took me quite by surprise, and I hope to learn something from them. I dare not contradict you about the will to power – but know nothing about it. I have long suspected that not only the repressed but also the dominant aspect of our life, the essence of our ego, is unconscious though not inaccessible to the conscious.[1] I deduce this from the fact that the conscious is only a sense organ, directed towards the outer world, so that it is attached at all times to a part of the ego which is not perceived.

If you are right about the will to power, then the displacement to my psychic sphere took place because I lacked all means needed for attaining the more direct aims: strength, beauty, money, etc.

My motive for refusing expressions of thanks is more obvious to me. This trait has already been brought to my attention. In most cases it has roughly the significance of Schiller's 'I want no thanks, dear lady'.[2] In other words, since the age of 14 I have had to strive to provide financial support for those I love: mother and sisters, later wife and children, and today, of course, the entire libido of the old man is expended on handing out money. So there are motives enough for inhibiting claims to love based on such gifts. This also applies to the dream used as a paradigm in my short essay 'On Dreams' in the Grenzfragen.[3]

Anyway, thank you for finding me so interesting.

You have certainly coined the right word for Adler. Since I have not received the book I am taking the excessive personal liberty of not reading it. Unfortunately Jung is implicated by association. You know that I do not share your view about the medical monopoly of psychoanalysis. But to side against Pfister in this way is especially cruel. Everything I hear about Jung and the goings-on in Zurich adds up to the same impression.[4] I don't know if you have already heard that I have had Pfister in Vienna for a week.[5] My grand patient,[6] who made his acquaintance last summer, allowed him to help her wean herself of an addiction.

Jones is here at the moment; I am preparing his very intelligent and very sick wife for later treatment, and Oberholzer has been having treatment [*Kur*] himself for some weeks.[7]

Rank has published a fat tome on the incest problem, and I expect a great deal from it. He is a decent man and has a good head on him.

Did I really write something to you about a new idea? It was a mere trifle about what the caskets in *The Merchant of Venice*, the *Judgement of Paris* and the opening scene of *Lear*[8] have in common. It is all finished with now; it would make a nice subject for a chat while walking beside the lake, but is not important enough to write about.

I am very glad to hear that you are getting on so well in your work. Please remember me to your wife and to all the pleasant people in and around Bellevue.

Yours cordially,
Freud

[1] An early indication of a train of thought which Freud did not discuss in detail until much later, eg. in (1920g), (1923b) and lecture 31 in (1933a).

[2] Verse at the end of the ballad 'Der Handschuh' [The Glove].

[3] *On Dreams*, first published in issue 8 of a serial publication *Grenzfragen des Nerven- und Seelenlebens*. The dream is described in *S.E.* Vol.V, p. 637, its interpretation on pp. 637–41.

[4] Freud wrote on the same day to Ferenczi: '[…] Everything that comes from Zurich or reports about it speaks of a bad situation there. Oberholzer, Pfister, Binswanger are meeting under the sign of Jung's rebellion, which makes the future very uncertain […]' Freud (1992g), pp. 388–9.

[5] Not mentioned by Jones. Even in the correspondence with Pfister, to whom Freud actually wrote on a letter on 4 July 1912, there is no indication of this visit. On the other hand in his letter to Ferenczi of 23 June 1912 he writes: 'The news here is the presence of Pfister and Jones, both of whom also participated in the evening on the Konstantinhügel. Pfister was asked by my grand patient to help for a week with a withdrawal process.' Freud (1992g), p. 386.

[6] Presumably an expression alluding to grandfather–grandchild, because this is about a patient who had been put in touch with him through disciples of his. See also 'My Grand-Patient, My Chief Tormentor', *Psychoanalytic Quarterly*, 1994/2.

[7] Emil Oberholzer (1883–1958), psychiatrist and psychoanalyst, member of the Zurich local group, after the dissolution of which in 1919 he, together with his wife Mira, née Gincburg (1887–1949), and Pfister founded the Swiss Society for Psychoanalysis. Increasingly in conflict with Pfister and critical about lay analysts, he founded the Society for Medical Psychoanalysis in 1928. Freud opted for the old group. With the emigration of the Oberholzers to the USA in 1938, the new group lost its signifi- cance. Cf. Walser (1976), and Meerwein (1979).

[8] Freud (1913f).

71F

Karlsbad, 22 July 1912

Prof. Dr. Freud   Vienna IX, Berggasse 19

Dear Dr. Binswanger,

As an accompaniment to the book that has at long last been sent off today, I am including a copy of a letter from Jung[1] that arrived yesterday (five weeks after mine to him):

> Dear Professor Freud,
> Until now I didn't know what to say to your last letter. Now I can only say: I understand the Kreuzlingen gesture. Whether your policy is the right one will become apparent from the success or failure of my future work. I have always kept my distance, and this will guard against any imitation of Adler's disloyalty.
>   Yours sincerely, J.

Despite its obscurity is this not a letter of virtual resignation?[2] You will be the best judge as to what the 'Kreuzlingen gesture' is supposed to mean.

With kind regards,

Yours, Freud

---

[1] Jung's letter dated 18 July 1912; see Freud (1974a), p. 511. Trans. R.F.C. Hull.
[2] Apparently Binswanger had confirmed Freud's view (in a letter which has not survived); cf. Freud's letter of 28 July 1912 to Ferenczi, Freud (1992g), pp. 398–9.

72F

Karlsbad, 29 July 1912

Prof. Dr. Freud   Vienna IX, Berggasse 19

Dear Dr. Binswanger,

So Jung's letter has made the same impression on both of us. Don't worry, I shall do nothing that might incite a breach; I should much prefer to keep personal matters quite separate from business. Fortunately you are completely wrong in your assumption that I am suffering in any way from his behaviour. I am not at all hurt. Warned by earlier experiences and proud of my resilience, I withdrew my libido from him months ago at the first signs, and now I feel no sense of loss. This time it is easier for me, too, because I can fill the gaps that have appeared with people like you, Ferenczi, Rank, Sachs,[1] Abraham, Jones, Brill and others.

What you write about Maeder has affected me strangely.[2] What shallow experiences they must have had to retain the least doubts about the infantile complexes! And how far they must have strayed from the understanding of the unconscious, which is our pride, if, like our most fatuous opponents, they seek to seize upon racial differences. There is only one serious thing about it all: Semites and Aryans (or anti-Semites), whom I wanted to unite in the service of psycho-analysis, have separated once again like oil and water.

Since then I have also received an essay by Riklin (haven't I written about him yet?) called 'Oedipus and psychoanalysis'[3] in *Glauben und Wissen* together with a pacifying letter telling me not to worry, Zurich was working hard and not at all paranoically. The essay is fine, but conciliatory to the point of obscurity and insincerity, which is not even clever. The new tone in it does not please me at all. I did not mince my words in my reply, though I was polite enough.

I am very well indeed here in Karlsbad; I am equipped for all battles. I hope that you, for your part, are not over-exerting yourself, but are still finding time to continue your work, the beginning of which I still think of frequently.

With kind regards to you and Frau Hertha,

Yours ever,
Freud

[1] Hanns Sachs (1881–1947), lawyer in Vienna, member of the Vienna Society from 1910, editor jointly with Rank of the journal *Eros und Psyche* (later *Imago*) from 1912, founder member of the committee, from 1920 psychoanalyst in Berlin, emigrated to Boston, Mass. in 1932, established *American Imago* 1944. Cf. Sachs (1944), Deutsch (1946–47), Moellenhoff (1966) and Mühlleitner (1992).

[2] What Binswanger had written is underlined by Freud's letter of 28 July 1912 to Ferenczi: 'I gather the true content from Binswanger's report about a conversation with Maeder, who was with him for a visit. They are now doubting the influence of infantile complexes and are already on the point of appealing to racial difference in order to explain the theoretical disparity. Those must be pretty shallow experiences to make such doubts possible.' Freud (1992g), p. 399.

[3] According to Grinstein, this appeared in *Wissen und Leben*, Vol. 5 (1912).

73F

Bolzano, 2 September 1912
Prof. Dr. Freud   Vienna IX, Berggasse 19

Dear Dr. Binswanger,

Having arrived here following a wonderful stay in Karersee, only occasionally interrupted by cold weather, news has now reached me that my eldest daughter[1] has recently fallen ill, so that I am going to have to return to Vienna and probably to write off the rest of my holiday. I have already cancelled a visit to Jones in London planned for 8 September.

Since I've owed you a letter for some time, I am writing to you now, before I am once again distracted by Viennese impressions. I cannot quite make out to what extent you see an excuse for Jung's behaviour – if it is so mistaken that it needs one – in his productive phase. Perhaps I fail to make you out because I am not being productive myself at present.

Karlsbad did me quite a lot of good but was otherwise quite taxing. I hope that you, your wife and your children are well and that your work is in full flow.

A Berlin lawyer[2] has asked me to substantiate the remark about Friedländer[3] I made at a party in your mother's house in favour of one of Friedländer's adversaries at the court of honour. But I dislike that sort of thing and am saying nothing.

With kind regards to you and your family,

Yours ever,
Freud

---

[1] Mathilde Freud was taken ill in Vienna while Freud was on holiday in Bolzano, so that Freud (together with Ferenczi) returned to Vienna; see the report of the illness in Jones (1953–7) Vol. 2, p. 106.

[2] Leopold Sternau, see note 3.

[3] On Friedländer, see note 10 to 31M. On 30 May 1910 Freud reported in detail to Jung on Friedländer's notable visit to Freud on 28 May that year (Freud 1974a, pp. 322–4). From then on Freud was convinced '(There is no need for discretion) that he is a liar, rogue and ignoramus'. (Freud to Abraham, 5 June 1910, Freud 1965a, p. 89). During his visit to Kreuzlingen Freud had described Friedländer as a 'swine' (see 93F). When Friedländer raised the matter of Freud's obviously negative opinion in a letter of 1 August 1913, Freud answered him on 4 August: 'I am in receipt of your letter and can clarify two points for you:

'a) When you came to see me that time in Vienna I received you as a colleague and a professional opponent. I did not know the details of your previous history in

Vienna. I only heard about these from your former high school and university colleagues when I mentioned the remarkable impression your visit had made.

'b) When the lawyer, Dr. S., asked me to let him know the information against you that I had been using, I remained silent and only when he renewed his request did I reply that I did not wish to say anything. Of course it was the combination with the professional opposition which made me [Freud actually wrote 'also', not 'me' – 'auch' for 'mich', which does not make sense, of course, and must be a slip of the pen] keep quiet. *The same motive* ought to have stopped me mentioning the matter to Binswanger.

'Incidentally neither your success in the official investigation nor the impertinently threatening tone of your letter improve my opinion of you.'

Transcriptions of both these letters, together with a further letter from Friedländer (26 August 1913) and Freud (3 September 1913) were sent to Binswanger by Friedländer's lawyer, Leopold Sternau. (See B.A. Tübingen 443/1.) From 95F we learn that one of the reproaches against Friedländer was that he was a cheat. It is similarly clear from a letter from Freud to Ferenczi on 5 August 1913: 'Another recent adventure is an impertinent letter from the confidence man Friedländer, whose integrity has been certified by a tribunal, and who wants to sue me because of a statement I made about him to Binswanger. I hope my sources won't leave me in the lurch. You can imagine how much I would *otherwise* make of this affair.' (Freud 1992g, Vol. 1, p. 505.)

74F

Rome, 22 September 1912

Prof. Dr. Freud   Vienna IX, Berggasse 19

Dear Dr. Binswanger,

I was tempted by a line in your letter to send a telegram to Constance: [I] too am in 'Italy'![1] Come and see me at the Hotel Eden, Via Ludovisi. The reason I held back was due only in part to the realisation that my company would not be relaxing but strenuous for you; the more pressing reason was that I was in a very poor state myself. I have been through several weeks of wretched health, with the diagnosis uncertain as ever. If one may judge *ex juvantibus*,[2] after Karlsbad I was suddenly unable to tolerate my normal smoking and the drinking that was added to it in the Tyrol. So I suppose my heart rebelled; everyone will attribute that to psychic influences, but please don't blame Jung too much. Anyway, I am recuperating here after various relapses and now feel, having all but forsworn the noble Roman wine as well, that I am on the road back to my former self. I am very happy in Rome, as I am in fact each time I come here, and this time particularly so.

My coming on this trip[3] means of course that my daughter's health has greatly improved; according to reports she is making further progress. Ferenczi insisted on accompanying me at this trying time. We leave here on the 28th.

Jones has told me quite a lot about the Congress[4] and the Zurich discussions. The reproaches of our Zurich colleagues were justified inasmuch as I have indeed always spoiled Jung, which has done him no good. I am quite prepared to take whatever steps may lead to an outward reconciliation; inwardly nothing in me will change. I have finally seen the paper;[5] it is very controversial but provides no grounds whatsoever for personal conflict, any more than his earlier errors. (I consider the new view to be mistaken as well.) The whole thing can be dealt with quite calmly.

I hope that your beautiful Buon Retiro,[6] which I remember very well, and our peerless Italy, have been kind to you and have helped your work to flourish. May you have many more fine days during the rest of your holiday here and enjoy them fully with your dear wife. While I am writing this I cannot help smiling at the thought that I could meet you on the Corso tomorrow. But for you Italy probably does not include Rome.

Yours cordially, Freud

[1] Reference to 'I too am in Arcadia', the motto with which Goethe headed his *Italienischer Reise*. Freud stayed in Rome, together with Ferenczi, from 15 September 1912, after he had been on holiday in Bolzano and San Christoforo; cf. Jones (1953–7), Vol. 2, pp. 106–09. No details are known about the duration and route of Binswanger's Italian trip, because Binswanger's diaries do not start until 1916. But cf. letter 75F, from which we learn that Binswanger went, among other places, to Milan and Venice, but not, however, to Rome; see 75aB and 95F below.

[2] The doctor can arrive at a diagnosis from the medicaments which have helped (*ex iuvantibus medicamentis*).

[3] Cf. 73F.

[4] Third International Congress for Medical Psychology and Psychotherapy in Zurich on 8 and 9 September 1912, chaired by Bleuler. Cf. Jones (1953–7), Vol. 2, p. 106, who wrongly describes it as the 'Second' Congress, and Freud (1974a), p. 513.

[5] On 10 September 1912 Emma Jung – Jung himself was in America – sent Freud the offprint of part 2 of the 'Wandlungen und Symbole der Libido' (1912c). Cf. Freud (1974a), p. 514.

[6] Schlössli Wolfsberg ob Ermatigen. In Binswanger's time there was a small *pension* there, to which he was fond of withdrawing to work in peace.

Sigmund Freud, circa 1912, on the balcony of Berggasse 19, Vienna.

75F

15 October 1912
Prof. Dr. Freud   Vienna IX, Berggasse 19

Dear Dr. Binswanger,
You will surely have returned home by now, with the summer behind
you like a beautiful dream. That is true of me too; not everything in
the dream was beautiful, but the last scene in Rome certainly was.

When your letter from Milan arrived, I had already bought my
ticket for the sleeper, so was unable to change anything and resigned
myself to missing you in Venice. I hope you greatly enjoyed both it
and your wife's response to the beauty of Italy.

Everything at home is fine now, myself included. I am working
extremely well already, and the refreshed state in which I have
returned has inspired several more literary projects.[1] The 'Points of
Agreement'[2] for *Imago* must be made ready, and all sorts of other
matters requiring my attention are bound to crop up at the same time.

I do not want to withhold from you a piece of news that is both
surprising and gratifying. Kraus[3] in Berlin, who is about to publish a
new textbook of internal medicine in 10 volumes, has offered me
hysteria and obsessional neurosis.[4] I have accepted and have thus lived
to see psychoanalysis being made official in Berlin.

Your own work[5] should really be finished this year. It is perhaps
the most propitious moment for it.

I hear occasionally from Maeder and Riklin and leave them in no
doubt in my replies as to my critical attitude.

With kind regards and in the hope of receiving more good news
from you soon.

Yours ever,
Freud

---

[1] 'The Moses of Michelangelo' (1914b); cf. Jones (1953–7), Vol. 2. pp. 407–10.

[2] Freud was working at this time on the third part of *Totem and Taboo. Some points
of agreement between the mental lives of savages and neurotics* was published in
Imago under the title 'Animismus, Magie und Allmacht der Gedanken' ['Animism,
Magic and the Omnipotence of Thoughts'] (1912–13a).

[3] Friedrich Kraus (1858–1936), Professor of Medicine and Director of the Medical
Clinic at the Charité in Berlin. Cf. Wollheim (1958).

[4] There was much to-ing and fro-ing about these articles, because a second author
was also asked to contribute articles under the same catchwords. The episode turns
up in the correspondences with Abraham, Ferenczi and Jung and is described in detail

in Jones (1953–7), Vol. 2, pp. 278–80. In the end, no contributions from Freud were
included in the 11-volume work (Kraus and Brugsch, 1919–27).
[5] Binswanger (1922a).

75aB

Nagelshausen, 20 October 1912[1]

Dear Professor,

I have come out again for Sunday, bringing my work with me, this
time to relations nearby.[2] I am letting that work wait for now, so that
I can reply to your last letter at leisure. I was extremely delighted by
the news about Kraus-Berlin, partly because of the satisfaction for
you personally and for our whole thing, but equally because I
anticipate an extraordinary pleasure in finding the field of hysteria
and obsessional neurosis summarised in handbook or textbook form
edited for once by your pen.[3] How much time have you got for it?
May I take this opportunity to wish you luck! – I am glad that things
are going well for you at home and that you are still feeling the benefit
of your holiday, both of which I can say for myself too. I do not know
whether my work[4] will be finished this year; it would not be impossible if it continues to be as relatively quiet at the clinic as it has been
since I came back. Your encouragement is very supportive anyway.
By the way, on looking more closely, I had to change quite a lot of
what I read aloud to you,[5] purely with regard to content. The psychiatric part, which I have dealt with on its own, is ready; now I am on
the description of psychoanalysis and its relationship to Part 1. I am
really enjoying it. – I have read your work on taboos[6] with great
interest and was delighted by the broadening of our horizon which
you have thus made possible for us. I was also highly delighted once
again with your paper on impotence.[7] Nos. I and II of your 'Conditions'[8] etc. are so interesting and so important for practitioners, that
I am looking forward to No. III. I have read Jung's remarks on the
libido theory[9] as well. It is certainly commendable that he goes further
into the problem that you brought up in the 'Schreber'[10] and tries to
find a solution to it. But it is a bit laborious and in my opinion goes
too far into the biological on the one hand and the philosophical on
the other. I admit that I found the attempt as such interesting, but
expect a real solution by another route. Though I also share his
misgivings about Abraham,[11] I think the solution must be found,
without having to look too far afield and without going beyond the

bounds of actual psychoanalytical research. What do you think? – In addition, I have read a rather weak paper by Sadger on pathographics and psychographics,[12] and in the Swiss *Korrespondenzblatt*,[13] Riklin's paper on psychoanalysis, which is very suitable for that journal. Do you know Bertschinger's paper on the aetiology of neuroses and psychoses in the *Allgemeinen Zeitschrift für Psychiatrie*?[14] Very neatly put together for practitioners. I am dying to read Abraham's analysis of an Egyptian which you told us about.[15] The latest volume of the *Jahrbuch*[16] is very impressive and promises much; in brief, *ça marche*.

By the way, have you any idea where I should publish my work? My first choice would be for Bonhoeffer ([new editor of the] *Ziehensche Zeitschrift*[17]) to bring it out, where the work is read more by psychiatrists, at whom indeed it is largely aimed, but thought also of the *Jahrbuch*, possibly with a special supplementary edition. Wonder, of course, whether B. would take it anyway, possibly via Bleuler.[18]

We very much enjoyed Venice and by studying Burckhardt's *Cicerone*,[19] which I love, I really benefited from it and learned to 'see'. But next time, Rome!

I am just wondering when I shall see you again; it looks as if it will not be until the summer!

With kind regards, I remain, dear Professor,

Yours, L. Binswanger

[1] This is one of only two handwritten letters from Binswanger to Freud which have survived. It was discovered by the Editor only after some reorganisation of the files in the Library of Congress and after the publication of the German edition of the Correspondence. Presumably it went to Washington with Anna Freud's papers. Presumably also, it was mixed up with some other correspondence when in 1938 many letters were destroyed before Freud's emigration, and only turned up again during sorting work at the Library of Congress. Anna Freud was quite unaware of the survival of *any* of Binswanger's original letters.

[2] Adolf Meyer-Wolde, brother of Binswanger's stepmother Marie-Luise Binswanger, lived in Nagelhausen, not far from Kreuzlingen.

[3] See 75F, note. 4.

[4] Binswanger (1922a).

[5] See Appendix (p. 235) for report on Freud's visit to Kreuzlingen from 25 to 28 May 1912.

[6] Freud (1912–13a).

[7] Freud (1912d).

[8] Freud had published the paper 'On the Universal Tendency to Debasement in the Sphere of Love' (1912d) as No. 2 of 'Contributions to the Psychology of Love'. The paper 'A Special Type of Choice of Object made by Men' (1910h) formed No. 1,

'The Taboo of Virginity' (1918a), which did not appear until 1918, was No. 3 of these 'Contributions'. The 1912 work mentions the 'conditions' ('Bedingungen') of psychical impotence. Perhaps therefore Binswanger mistakenly wrote 'Bedingungen' instead of 'Beiträge' ('Contributions').

[9] Jung (1911a) and especially Jung (1912c).

[10] Freud (1911c).

[11] This surely refers to Jung's criticism of Abraham's opinion that 'the schizophrenic symptomatology is produced by the withdrawal of sexual libido from the outside world'. Jung (1912a), quoted in *C.W.*, vol. 4, para. 277.

[12] I[sidor] Sadger, 'Von der Pathographie zur Psychographie.' In: *Imago*, Vol. 1 (1912), pp. 158–75.

[13] Franz Riklin, 'Über Psychoanalyse.' In: *Korr. bl. schweiz. Ärzte*, Vol. 42 (1912), pp. 1015–26.

[14] H. Bertschinger, 'Über Gelegenheitsursachen gewisser Neurosen und Psychosen.' In: *Allg. Zschr. Psychiatr.*, Vol. 60 (1912), pp. 588–617.

[15] Karl Abraham, 'Amenhotep IV. (Echnaton). Psychoanalytische Beiträge zum Verständnis seiner Persönlichkeit und des monotheistischen Aton-Kultes.' In: *Imago*, Vol. 1 (1912), pp. 334–60.

[16] *Jahrbuch für psychoanalytische und psychopathologische Forschungen*, Vol. 4 (1912).

[17] The *Monatschrift für Psychiatrie und Neurologie*, Vol. 1 (1897), from 1912 published by Karl Bonhoeffer.

[18] See p. xxxiv, Note. 1.

[19] Jakob Burckhardt: *Der Cicerone. Eine Anleitung zur Genuss der Kunstwerke Italiens*, [A guide to the enjoyment of the art of Italy] first published in Basel 1855, was available at this time in its 10th enlarged and corrected edition (revised by Wilhelm Bode and C. v. Fabriczy, Leipzig 1909–10).

76F

Prof. Dr. Freud

20 October 1912
Vienna IX, Berggasse 19

Dear Dr. Binswanger,

I have just been reminded to report to you on a lady, Frau F.,[1] who was sent to your clinic last month on my advice. I saw the case in the spring; on the basis of her physical symptoms I diagnosed Basedow's [Graves'] disease and, from her psychic symptoms, erotomania (paranoia), and considered the outlook to be very unfavourable. In the meantime you will no doubt have learned much more about the patient. I should be particularly pleased, of course, if I knew that you yourself were treating the patient, not one of your assistants.

The case, and her husband, fully deserve your interest. She is asking for a divorce, but I do not think she means to carry it through. The whole drama – that she no longer loves her husband, that she is in love with another man and wants a divorce so as to marry him – is a false front, not to be taken seriously. The reality – that she is as attached to her husband as ever – shines through unmistakably. If our assumption is correct, this woman, who has always been sexually abnormal, must be suffering from a disturbance on the homosexual plane, an acute aggravation of a previously latent, but constitutionally overwhelming, component. I could not pursue this line of investigation. You may follow it now, but do not allow yourself to be put off by any failures at the outset. It may be that she can be reached in this way; but not, of course, through her false front.

Maeder recently asked for a discussion with me, to which I agreed; whether things will improve as a result, I cannot tell. I was quite severe, though certainly not rude, for which there was no cause. Riklin's attitude, by contrast, is full of equivocation. As for Jung, Brill wrote to me that he is planning to stay in America for a few months.

With kind regards to you and your wife,

Yours ever, Freud

---

[1] This patient received treatment in the Bellevue from 5 September to 20 December 1912. She was diagnosed there as having Graves' disease (goitre) and a psychopathic tendency, but it was questionable whether she was psychotic. Before that the patient had been in treatment in the Mariagrün Sanatorium near Graz from November 1911 to spring 1912. She consulted Freud shortly after Whitsun 1912.

77B

24 October 1912

Dear Professor Freud,

Many thanks for your report on Frau F. I had already been asked by one of my colleagues in Italy[1] if you had written to me about the case as the husband has alleged, but did not want to bother you with an enquiry since I was not sure how interested you were in the case. Graves' and erotomania were diagnosed by us here as well and we also suspected 'dementia praecox'. The transformation this woman has endured is indeed too striking to be explained without assuming a psychosis. I am grateful for your indication of a homosexual component, which is perhaps corroborated by the fact that during her earlier attacks of hysteria the patient identified herself completely with her sister-in-law. Here the heterosexual component is very much to the forefront in every way. Since the colleague who received her in my absence is about to go on leave, I shall have an opportunity of making closer personal contact with her. The patient is giving us no trouble at all, but is, of course, quite unshakable in her ideas and plans for the future.

I am, with kind regards, dear Professor Freud,

Yours [L. Binswanger]

[1] Cf. note 1 to 74F.

78F

28 October 1912

Prof. Dr. Freud   Vienna IX, Berggasse 19

Dear Dr. Binswanger,

Many thanks for your information about Frau F. I think you would do well to pursue the trail of her identification with her sister-in-law – of which I know nothing – by analytical methods. Herr F. drew my attention to the fact that his wife could only be persuaded to go to the clinic on the pretext that she would receive treatment for Graves' disease, so it would be wise to allay any suspicions by a make-believe treatment for that condition.

For the rest, I have to tell you that I have got rid of Stekel.[1] I have left him the *Zentralblatt* and am about to establish a new journal myself. All my friends will shortly be withdrawing their names from his masthead. I would ask you too not to send any contributions over which you have any influence to the *Zentralblatt* but to reserve them for my new journal.

With kind regards to you and your family,

Yours ever, Freud

[1] A disagreement had arisen between Freud and Stekel early in 1912. As a defence against Jung's diverging views, Freud wanted to set up a 'review board' for the *Zentralblatt* (Reitler, Hitschmann, Tausk, Federn, Ferenczi) which in particular was to review the *Jahrbuch* from Freud's point of view (letter of 17 October 1912 from Freud to Ferenczi, 1992g, p. 411.). But Stekel declared he would never concede to having Dr. Tausk write in *his* journal (letter of 27 October 1912 from Freud to Ferenczi, 1992g, p. 418). Because Bergmann, the publisher, did not agree to Stekel's dismissal as editor, Freud founded the *Internationale Zeitschrift für ärtzliche Psychoanalyse*. Cf. the somewhat imprecise presentation in Jones (1953–7), Vol. 2, p. 109. Stekel's departure from the Association was announced on 6 November 1912; see *Protokolle*, Vol. 4, p. 108 and note 2. [In the Engl. edn., *Minutes*, Vol. 4, p. 113, the relevant words 'Stekel resigned' are missing, as also is note 2 – T.R.] Cf. also *On the History of the Psycho-Analytic Movement*, S.E. Vol. XIV, p. 47.

79F

3 November 1912
Prof. Dr. Freud   Vienna IX, Berggasse 19

Dear Dr. Binswanger,

Here is the information you asked for. The reason for the parting of
the ways with Stekel was not scientific but his personal arrogance.[1]
He refused to accept contributions from a member[2] who had seriously
offended him some time ago, on the grounds that the *Zentralblatt* was
'his paper'. When I pointed out that it was, after all, the official journal
of the Association and I myself something like its editor, he refused
to back down. I then asked the publisher what he would do in case
of a difference between me and Stekel and when I received no clear-
cut reply and also realised that there were secret agreements between
Bergmann and Stekel, which explained his presumption, I withdrew
and left the paper to him. The split was ostensibly a friendly one; but
with someone of his character you can imagine how long this position
will last. I am very glad about it all, however; he was always a trial
and lately quite insufferable – his petty jealousies knew no bounds
and his exaggerated opinion of himself verged on the grotesque.

I immediately began negotiations to establish a new journal, and
believe that Ferenczi,[3] one of our best people, can probably be persuaded to become the editor. I shall, of course, take all my friends
with me. You will shortly be asked in a circular to remove your name
from the *Zentralblatt* and to lend it to our new journal. Needless to
say you would have my full support if you took the first step even
earlier.[4]

I have received all your letters. I did not reply to your question
because it was not pressing. Your work[5] will make an impact wherever
it appears. I would prefer to have it in one of our journals, but much
will depend on the length it attains.

I am overwhelmed with work. With kindest regards to you and your
wife,

Yours ever,
Freud

[1] Freud wrote in exactly the same words to Abraham on 3 November 1912; cf. Freud
(1965a) p.125.
[2] Victor Tausk; see note 1 to 78F; also Roazen (1973).
[3] Freud, Rank and Jones undertook the editing; see Jones (1953–7), Vol. 2, p. 155.

[4] In a letter of 6 November 1912 to Stekel, Binswanger withdrew his name from the list of collaborators in the *Zentralblatt*; cf. B.A. 443/34.
[5] Still that same project which led to the publications of (1920a), (1922a) and (1936c).

80B

Constance, 6 November 1912

Dear Professor Freud,

Many thanks for your information. I am glad that you have made a *tabula rasa* and am surprised at only one thing, that you – forgive me – have taken so long to see through your Viennese pupils. Something must have held you back from acknowledging your innermost convictions to yourself or to others, for I remember very well that you said after a meeting, on my very first visit to Vienna: Did you ever see such a gang?[1] Perhaps it was said half tongue-in-cheek, but at the time it took me aback and caused me great concern, for I realised even then that there was a gulf between you and them and that you must be affected deeply by it. That is why I have always been so amazed at the tenacity with which you stuck to them, until they went too far.

I have already written to Stekel. I shall of course support your journal as much as I am able. But I hope, because of the way we now stand towards each other, that I am entitled to express a wish which is close to my heart, or, should you think that too presumptuous, at least to ask a question: wouldn't it be possible for you to be both editor and publisher at the same time, or do you absolutely have to have a separate editor? From everything I have heard from you about Ferenczi I am sure that he means a great deal to you both as a person and as a pupil, and I am sure, too, he deserves it. But however much I value some of his scientific contributions, in my view he still lacks the kind of scientific and critical perspective that I – perhaps unjustifiably – expect from someone who takes on the editorship of a journal published by you. Now that I am devoting myself so intensely to your kind of research, I have come to realise that I can follow you in almost every respect, whereas Ferenczi's contributions seem to me, now and then, to be lacking in the high seriousness that distinguishes your entire work in its every detail. I venture to say that not only Ferenczi, but no one else of our company, can measure up to you. Hence it is my dearest wish to see you alone at the head of the journal, if need be surrounded with a number of collaborators. But I believe that, since you have created your main work by your own effort, you ought also to find great satisfaction in running a journal that bears none but your personal imprint. Leaving everything else aside, a journal run by you alone is bound to gain in authority among scientific and other readers; if not, it can only lose in impact.

I hope, dear Professor, that you will take these comments in the spirit in which they are offered and as springing solely from my great admiration for your personal contribution and for your life's work. And please do not think that my suggestion involves any sort of selfish consideration for I shall serve as collaborator whether or not Ferenczi is the editor, if only for your sake. Please let me know soon what you think about this.

With kind regards,

Yours ever, [L. Binswanger]

[1] Cf. the report on Binswanger's first visit to Freud in Vienna, above pp. xxxi–xxxv.

81F

28 November 1912

Prof. Dr. Freud · Vienna IX, Berggasse 19

Dear Dr. Binswanger,

I know of no possible reason why I should be cross.[1] My silence was due to over-preoccupation with the latest business.

The Council of Munich[2] passed off splendidly, thanks to the great affability of our colleagues, those from Zurich included. The new journal will be a replacement for the *Zentralblatt* in every way.

Jung was very pleasant, and in one hour of private conversation with him I was able to convince him that there was scant justification for his complaint against me. The 'Kreuzlingen gesture'[3] which he had been blaming me for turned out to be based on an incredible symptomatic action on his part, which would produce good material verbally. I think everything will be all right now. The theoretical differences remain only until they can be cleared up by discussions in papers and at the Congress.

I am indeed absolutely delighted to have exchanged Stekel for the Zurich contingent, but am still very tired from the exertions of the past weeks.

With kind regards and in the hope of hearing from you soon,

Yours ever, Freud

[1] Binswanger had probably written again after 6 November 1912 and asked if Freud was angry with him.

[2] A conference of the presidents of the psychoanalytic associations took place in Munich on 24 November 1912 which is reported in Jones (1953–7), p. 155 (there wrongly recorded as 24 September) and p. 164, and also in Freud (1974a), pp. 521–2. Freud's suggestion of the establishment of a new journal was accepted, the theme of the next congress decided upon.

[3] Cf. p. 86 and 71F.

82F

16 December 1912

Prof. Dr. Freud   Vienna IX, Berggasse 19

Dear Dr. Binswanger,

I'm sure you possess splendid courage of the kind a man should have. You work and you create[1] and you deserve that both your efforts should flourish. You are right to ignore the uncertainty still hanging over you[2] just as we frivolous ones ignore our uncertainties.

I am prepared to be declared a candidate for eternity on the strength of my mishap in Munich.[3] Stekel wrote the other day that my behaviour already displayed a 'hipocritical trait' (sic!). They can all hardly wait for it, but I can give them the same answer as did Mark Twain in similar circumstances: 'Reports of my death grossly exaggerated.'[4]

Indeed, I am working – at last – on the third of the 'Points of Agreement'[5] for *Imago* which is meant to clear the way for the fourth,[6] to which I am very much looking forward.

My daughter[7] is very well. I have heard from Bleuler. He has even threatened to ask me for special clarifications, which I am quite prepared to give him. He is always suddenly pretending not to understand this or that.

Our journal[8] has gone to the printers and will come out in January.

With regard to Frau F., I must ask you for a few explanatory lines. Her husband has written to me enclosing two letters from Dr. Haymann[9] denying that she is psychotic.[10] However, I was quite unable to extract anything concrete from the diplomatic phrases of these letters. I promised the husband a reply after approaching you.

Kind regards to you, your wife and your children. Your *son* is indeed bearing out our earlier interpretations of his behaviour.

Yours, Freud

[1] Presumably Binswanger had told Freud that his wife was pregnant again. See note 2 to 87F.
[2] Cf. note 1 to 65F.
[3] Freud fainted at the end of lunch. Cf. note 2 to 81F.
[4] While Mark Twain was on a European lecture tour, a rumour appeared in the American press that he was dead. Several friends immediately telegraphed his London address to find if the rumour was true. Twain himself telegraphed back: 'Reports of my death greatly exaggerated.' Cf. the use of this anecdote in 'On the History of the Psycho-Analytic Movement' Freud (1914d), *S.E.* Vol. XIV, p. 35.
[5] See note 3 to 75F.
[6] 'The Return of Totemism in Childhood.' See 89F and its note 3.
[7] Mathilde Hollitscher; cf. 73F and 74F.
[8] *Internationale Zeitschrift für ärtzliche Psychoanalyse.*
[9] Hermann Haymann (1879–1955), psychiatrist, worked as an intern in the Bellevue Sanatorium 1910–21 (with an interruption brought about by World War I), later as a neurologist in Badenweiler, had to emigrate in 1938 via Nice to the USA and lived the rest of his life in New York; B.A. 443/34–443/48 and 443/59.
[10] Cf. note 1 to 76F.

83B

19 December 1912

Dear Professor Freud,

To come first to the F. case, it is indeed, as Dr. Haymann wrote in his letter of 20 November, imposible to determine a psychosis in this patient. At first we suspected – and this mainly under the influence of the husband's account – a form of dementia praecox, but that suspicion has not been confirmed in any way. We feel, however, that we cannot completely exclude the possibility of there having been a touch of hebephrenia, but, as I have said, we are lacking in clear clinical and psychological signs to diagnose that condition with certainty. To our mind, Frau F. is, apart from her Graves' disease, a simple psychopath who just wants in her obstinate way to translate into practice the ideal of life she has constructed over the years, without appreciating the obstacles reality has placed in her path. Nor can we find any evidence of erotomania, the less so as her love for the gentleman in question has here taken second place to the divorce from her husband. The way in which Frau F.'s idea of a divorce has developed strikes us as being explicable in normal psychological terms. Frau F. married her husband, almost twice her age, when she was 17, without love and at the behest of her family, especially her mother. She had absolutely no understanding of marriage, but hoped that in due course the ideals she had nurtured in her teens would turn into reality. Instead, as she developed a woman's intellect, she discovered an ever wider gulf between her and her husband, for which the husband plainly had no feeling at all, but from which the wife has now been suffering for years. Outwardly she gave no signs of all this, so that her husband thought she was perfectly happy and believed he was doing quite enough by looking after her as a father looks after his child. No kind of inner bond resembling an intimate friendship, which Frau F. had always wanted for herself, was ever established; instead her husband constantly practised a more or less overt form of tutelage. This is what Frau F. eventually came to realise. A contributory factor, no doubt, was her reading of modern texts on the nature of women, marriage, etc. Simultaneously with an ideal conception of marriage and of the role of women she developed a pronounced sense of truthfulness, and so one day she came to the conclusion that continuing with the comedy she had been playing was an intolerable lie towards both herself and her husband. For her husband, who until then had obviously had no inkling of her inner development, this was a bolt from the blue and he could find no other explanation for what had happened than the alternatives of either sick or wicked. In reality the wife had done nothing that could be interpreted as wickedness for, honest and truthful as she was in her psychopathologically exaggerated way, she had never had any furtive relations with the other man whom she admittedly saw in a most favourable light. As soon as she realised what was happening, she told her husband. And so the husband had really had no choice but to pronounce her sick.

It may well be, dear Professor, that our interpretation does not seem clear enough to you. We have indeed found it difficult to form a clear picture of Frau F. and to put this picture into words. Above all, however, I believe that if we are to understand Frau F. at all then we must ignore a great deal of what we have learned about her from her husband. The husband could never see beyond external appearances, and our own experiences with him are such that we must deny him any deeper understanding of his wife. Certainly, he always believed that he had done his duty by her. With his somewhat autocratic character, he seems to be one of those men who cannot grasp that they are unable to satisfy their wives. We have also noticed in his correspondence with us that he cannot understand any opinion he does not share.

Our view is largely based, as you see, on information supplied by the wife herself, which is of course bound to be unsatisfactory. We nevertheless believe that we can rely on her information to a certain extent and are in any case quite sure that a measure of scepticism towards the husband would not be out of place, for the reasons mentioned earlier. Unfortunately, I was unable to find out very much more by analytical means because Frau F. *deliberately* closes up at a certain point, something I do not necessarily consider a sign of dementia praecox.

I heard about your fainting fit in Munich and was a little worried about it; Zurich seems to have come up with some psychogenic interpretation. Please tell me in due course what you feel about it. I cannot really worry too much, having seen you looking so fit and youthful at Whitsun. It was good news indeed to hear that you are being so active and I only hope that you are not taking on too much. I am eagerly looking forward to the new journal. My work has been interrupted by a stay of several days in Munich, where we met some old acquaintances. That is why I was unfortunately not able to see Seif.[1] Since then I have been preparing a lecture on hysteria[2] which I am due to deliver tomorrow to our cantonal medical association.

I wish you, dear Professor, a very happy Christmas. Enjoy the triumph of having shaken off the generation of vipers for this year.

My wife joins me in sending you kind regards.

[L. Binswanger]

[1] Leonhard Seif (1866–1949), neurologist in Munich, founded the Munich Psychoanalytic Society in 1911 and followed Adler after his break with Freud. Cf. Fabricius (1973).

[2] Not traceable.

84F

1 January 1913

Prof. Dr. Freud

Vienna IX, Berggasse 19

Dear Dr. Binswanger,

Best wishes for the New Year. May it bring you the end of our fears.[1]

Many thanks for your note about the F. case. You were right to think that I would not be deeply impressed by it. After all, it merely concerns her overt behaviour. Characteristically, she keeps all her deeper motives from her doctors. Even if her motivation of her rejection of her husband were correct, the way she reacts is still characteristic of erotomania. The 'simple' psychopathy is probably not so simple after all.

My dizzy turn in Munich was undoubtedly caused by psychogenic factors with some somatic reinforcements (a week of much travail, a sleepless night, something very like migraine, the daily round). I have already had several such attacks, each time similarly reinforced, often by a drop of alcohol, for which I have no head. Among the psychic factors there is the fact that I have had similar reactions in the same place in Munich on two previous occasions, six and four years ago. It seems unjustified even with the most stringent evaluation to put a more serious interpretation on the incident, for instance cardiac insufficiency. Repressed feelings, this time against Jung, as earlier against one of his predecessors,[2] are naturally all-important.

The agreement reached in Munich will hardly last for long. Jung's attitude precludes that. I should gladly dispense with any kind of personal relationship with him and merely maintain the official links. I did not, incidentally, know what it was about my visit to Kreuzlingen that had upset him so much. He told me there straight out that he had assumed that I was conspiring against him with his enemies, you and Häberlin![3] I would beg you to help slow down the development of the rift by exercising strict discretion about everything concerning him and me. With kind regards to you and your wife,

Yours ever,
Freud

[1] Cf. note 1 to 65F.
[2] He is referring to Wilhelm Fliess; cf. *The Complete Letters of Sigmund Freud to Wilhelm Fliess; 1887–1904* (Freud 1985c). See also Jones (1953–7), Vol. 1, p. 348.
[3] Paul Häberlin (1878–1960), educationist and philosopher, to begin with seminar director at Kreuzlingen, private lecturer in Basle 1908, Professor of Philosophy in Bern 1914 and in Basle from 1922. In May 1913 together with Binswanger visited Freud in Vienna, at first open-minded about psychoanalysis, later increasingly critical. Cf. Kamm (1977–81) and Häberlin (1997).

85B

26 January 1913 a.m.[1]

Professor & Frau Freud
Berggasse 19, Vienna IX

Many congratulations to you and your daughter.[2]

Dr. & Frau Binswanger

[1] Probably a carbon copy of a draft telegram.
[2] Sophie Freud and Max Halberstadt from Hamburg were married on 14 January 1913; cf. Jones (1953–7), Vol. 2, p. 111.

86F

20 February 1913

Prof. Dr. Freud   Vienna IX, Berggasse 19

Dear Dr. Binswanger,

Letter-writing is truly no way to communicate for those who have something to say to each other. For three weeks, I have agonised over my reply to your last comprehensive letter, but precisely because it so called for a reply I could not get down to it and had to wait for this evening when, shivering slightly with influenza, I am incapable of any other work. As you will readily understand, my tasks have mounted up all the more since my recent travels, so that for the most part each day is a struggle for existence.

You are right, I am sure, in your view of the homosexual choice of object, and perhaps even more than you imagine. Even in the most normal people the object represents a bisexual wish fulfilment and will constantly be transposed from man to woman and vice versa. The matter has long since ceased to be as simple as the homosexual spokesmen make it out to be.

The problem of counter-transference, which you touch upon, is – technically – among the most intricate in psychoanalysis.[1] Theoretically I believe it is much easier to solve. What we give to the patient should, however, be a spontaneous affect, but measured out consciously at all times, to a greater or lesser extent according to need. In certain circumstances a great deal, but never from one's own unconscious. I would look upon that as the formula. One must, therefore, always recognise one's counter-transference and overcome it, for not till then is one free oneself. To give someone too little because one loves him too much is unfair to the patient and a technical error. This is all far from easy, and perhaps one has to be older for it, too.

Castration phantasies are extremely frequent in women, though not to be sought behind every vomiting fit, of course. For example, everything that is correct in Adler's assumptions may be reduced to penis envy and fear of castration.

I can see that I am not even up to letter-writing today. So let me conclude with the hope that you, your wife and all your children are very well, something I would, of course, like to have confirmed.

Yours cordially,
Freud

[1] Possibly this discussion arose from Binswanger's reading Freud's work 'The Dynamics of Transference' (1912b). In Freud's work the concept of 'counter-transference' first appeared in the paper 'The Future Prospects of Psycho-Analytic Therapy' (1910d).

87F

25 February 1913

Prof. Dr. Freud   Vienna IX, Berggsse 19

Dear Dr. Binswanger,

I am not going to wait until I have influenza again or until I have finished the work I have started for *Scientia*,[1] but will congratulate you without delay on the birth of your second son[2] and on your all enjoying such good health. Soon we shall have finally banished our worry,[3] and then we shall also see the completion of your work.[4] I have already written the introduction to Pfister's book.[5] Not that I am offering to write one for you. No reason for that; after all, my turn did not come until after a long period of incubation.

Your regret that psychoanalysis is in such a shambles now is something I prefer to keep at bay. I believe that you are too much under the sway of Jung and his influence in Zurich. This carries very little weight with me. If, as is very likely, it turns out that Jung is on the wrong track with his innovations, you will soon see how little influence he and Zurich have on the vigorous development of psychoanalysis. The Zurich group has an exaggerated opinion of its own importance for which I am largely to blame myself. Jung has become so completely superfluous to me personally in so short a time that I can scarcely imagine myself back in the old situation. His scientific errors do not compensate for his unpleasant qualities.

I must decline your invitation for Easter with many thanks. I can only spare four days during which I want to fetch my little daughter from Merano.[6] Otherwise I am really overworked, but my being ill played little part in that as I did not have to lose even one hour of consultation as a result of it.

Be happy and work hard.

With kindest regards to the heroic lady of the house,

Yours ever,
Freud

[1] 'The Claims of Psycho-Analysis to Scientific Interest' (1913j).

[2] Ludwig Adolf Binswanger (14 Feb. 1913–6 Feb. 1978), psychiatrist and psycho-therapist. Cf. *In memoriam Ludwig A. Binswanger* (1978).
[3] Cf. note 1 to 65F.
[4] Binswanger (1922a).
[5] Preface to Oskar Pfister: *Die psychoanalytische Methode* (Freud 1913b).
[6] Freud met his daughter Anna in Bolzano on 22 March 1913, and over four days they travelled together to Venice via Verona and made the return journey via Trieste; cf. Jones (1953–7), Vol. 2, p. 111.

88F

27 March 1913

Prof. Dr. Freud   Vienna IX, Berggasse 19

Dear Dr. Binswanger,

Agreed. You and Häberlin will come to see me in April, your stay to include a Sunday. I do not in the least mind which one. I am very much looking forward to the pleasant company.[1] One ought to meet from time to time. Letters are no substitute. The return of my Whitsun visit ('the Kreuzlingen gesture')[2] is a nice idea of yours. How much happier things are with you now, though, than they were then![3]

In the meantime, I have experienced so much outwardly and inwardly that you will not find it difficult to account for finding me aged. At times I am sure the core is still good; at others I doubt even that. The distortions of my psychoanalysis do not, of course, leave me unconcerned. I tell myself then that I cannot be held responsible for its future destiny and that the many enemies among its 'followers' might yet fail to reduce it *ad absurdum* altogether.

My wife will unfortunately be away when you come; she has promised to visit our newly-married daughter[4] in Hamburg. But my sister-in-law will be our hostess and will express our regret that our hospitality is no match for that of Bellevue and Brun[n]egg (?)

Meanwhile, I send greetings to you and to your whole, now very considerable, family, from,

Yours ever, Freud

P.S. Could you perhaps bring your work along with you? Many thanks for the promised contribution.[5] We have become used to expecting *nothing* from the Swiss for our journal.

[1] Cf. Häberlin (1997), p. 110.
[2] Cf. p. 86 and 71F.

[3] Cf. note 1 to 65F.
[4] Sophie Halberstadt; cf. 85B.
[5] Binswanger (1913a), cf. also note 2 to 89F.

89F

Vienna, 21 April 1913[1]

Dear Dr. Binswanger,

Many thanks for your truly informative, clear and excellent review![2]
It was additionally welcome as a sign of your participation in the
journal. – I am working feverishly on totemism[3] so as to have a little
more free time when you come.

Kind regards,

Yours, Freud

[1] Postcard, postmarked 22 April 1913.
[2] Ludwig Binswanger, 'Bemerkungen zu der Arbeit Jaspers: Kausale und "verständliche" Zusammenhänge zwischen Schicksal und Psychose bei der Dementia praecox
(Schizophrenie)' (1913a). ['Remarks upon Jasper's Work: Causal and "Understandable" Correlations between Fate and Psychosis in Dementia Praecox (Schizophrenia)'].
[3] Part 4 of *Totem and Taboo*: 'The Return of Totemism in Childhood.' ['Die infantile
Wiederkehr des Totemismus'] appeared in *Imago* Vol. 2 (913), pp. 357–408 (probably
in the November after the work on it had been completed on 12 May. Cf. Freud's
letter to Ferenczi 13 May 1913; Freud (1992g), Vol. 1, pp. 485–6.

90F
[To Ludwig Binswanger and Paul Häberlin][1]

[16 May 1913]

Dear Guests,

The barbaric conditions of our existence and the decline of hospitality
are particularly significant to me at the moment, because I am inviting
you to spend the day in my house from 10 a.m. on *Sunday*. – I can
see you only briefly on Saturday and offer you nothing. I am free
from 2 till 3 but otherwise not, and the evening, being the last of the
week, is unacceptable. – Would you like to let me know by telephone
or otherwise whether I may come to see you, meet you somewhere,
or expect you here, after 2 on Saturday. – I hope you had a good
journey[2] and add best wishes from my wife and family.

Freud

[1] Letter-card in the Häberlin Archive, Basle, Switzerland. The card was sent to the guests at their hotel. From this and from the dates of the Breslau Congress mentioned by Binswanger (see editorial note after this letter) the date of the letter can be established.
[2] From Breslau to Vienna. Cf. the following editorial note.

Binswanger's Third Visit to Vienna (in the company of Paul Häberlin), 17 to 18 May 1913

Binswanger wrote in his book (1956c, p. 9 in 1957 English edition) that he had 'only a few recollections' of this visit. He also gave the date wrongly as April. As can be seen from Freud's letter, the visit must have taken place on the weekend 17–18 May. This is also confirmed by Binswanger's letter of 30 March 1913 to Häberlin: 'Freud is very much looking forward to the "pleasant company". Question: Can you really not come to Vienna in mid-May? I have a congress in Breslau on 15–16 May, so it would actually be mad to go to Vienna before that instead of leaving it till May when I can go straight from Breslau! We would then meet in Vienna on the 17th (Saturday) and then see Freud together on the Sunday (18 May) after Whitsun, which falls on 11–12 May. However, you would be my guest from Basle rail station!'[1] All Binswanger could report about this visit was what Häberlin recalled for him in his letter of 10 June 1954.[2]

[1] Häberlin (1997), p. 110.
[2] Cf. Appendix pp. 236–7.

91B

Constance, 24 July 1913

Dear Professor Freud,

Along with your latest two papers,[1] which came yesterday but of which I have so far read only the challenging, shorter one, I have also come into possession of your Marienbad address.[2] I am glad to know that you are a long way from Vienna and free of the pressures of all your vast work. Let us hope the weather will not spoil your stay; it is atrocious here and we were lucky that the rainy period did not set in until we were about to leave Wolfsberg.[3] I worked hard even there, so hard by my standards that I have not returned to my job fully refreshed. Lest my book drag on for yet another year,[4] however, I am trying to work on it here as well as best I can, although it is an uphill struggle. I have revised everything again except for the first part, i.e., the outline of clinical psychiatry, and have nearly finished the chapter on natural science and psychology and on psychology and psycho-analysis. However I have still to write the main chapter, on clinical psychiatry and psychoanalysis,[5] but it will cause fewer problems since I will not need to familiarise myself with the material while I write.

Do you still remember our talk about the cause of the separation of and contrast between libido and ego during a walk beside the lake when you were here? I pointed out at the time that conditions also existed in which libido and ego joined together and in which the separation could no longer be maintained. You then mentioned two points that had caused you to introduce that separation and which, to the best of my knowledge, you have not put in writing. The first was, if I remember rightly, that, as you said, the separation must follow from the observation that, when the libido had taken pathological control of a function of innervation as a case in point you mentioned, I believe, the function of walking the ego could not exert any influence on that function. Do you remember? – The second point, however, I have forgotten and I should be very grateful if you could prod my memory. I presuppose, of course, that you feel like doing so at the moment; if you do not want to be bothered now, the reply can wait until we meet in Munich.[6] I am working again just now on the description of libido theory, which is why I cast my mind back to that conversation.

The other day I started Jung's American lectures[7] in the *Jahrbuch* but have not yet been able to discover much that is new. When Pfister's new book[8] came out I was afraid at first that he might have anticipated me in many things which, luckily, I find not to be the case. The structure of the book seems very good, but to me the treatment of the case material is less satisfying.

Incidentally, have you read Thomas Mann's short novel, *Death in Venice*,[9] which, if you have not, I would recommend for your spare time? It describes, with rare skill and unusual truthfulness, the links between delight in travel, Eros and the longing for death in an ageing homosexual.

Wolfsberg has done my family a great deal of good. I hope that one day you will get to know our third offspring,[10] who is flourishing. The eldest[11] is fortunately growing a little less dependent on his mother and becoming appreciably more active. – Häberlin was here recently, and we were happy to refresh our memories of our trip to Vienna.

Please remember me to all your family, or at least those of them who are at home. With kind regards, dear Professor, from myself and my wife,

Yours [L. Binswanger]

---

[1] Titles not determinable with certainty. Most likely (and available in Binswanger's collection of offprints): 'The Theme of the Three Caskets' (1913f) and the third part of *Totem and Taboo* – 'Animism, Magic and the Omnipotence of Thoughts' (1912–13a).

[2] Freud stayed at the Villa Taube in Marienbad, along with his wife, sister-in-law and daughter Anna, from 13 July till 10 August; cf. Jones (1953–7), Vol. 2, p. 112.

[3] See note 6 to 74F.

[4] Once again, this concerns Binswanger's plan for a book which did not become a reality until 1922; see Binswanger (1922a).

[5] In the book that appeared in 1922 there is no longer such an arrangement of chapters, but much more a comparison of 'the non-natural scientific portrayal of the psychic' (chapter 3) with 'the scientific portrayal of the individual' (chapter 4).

[6] 4th International Psychoanalytic Congress, Munich, 7–8 September 1913. Cf. report of the congress in Jones (1953–7), Vol. 2, pp. 113–16 and pp. 168–169.

[7] 'Versuch einer Darstellung der psychoanalytische Theorie. Neun Vorlesungen gehalten in New-York im September 1912', *Jb. psychoanal. psychopathol. Forsch.*, Vol. 5 (1913), pp. 307–441; Jung (1913a).

[8] *Die psychoanalytische Methode*, Leipzig, 1913.

[9] At that time Mann's novella aroused a lot of interest in psychiatric and sexological circles. Cf., e.g., Numa Praetorius (pseudonym for Magnus Hirschfeld) (1917/18).

[10] Cf. note 2 to 87F.

[11] Robert Binswanger.

92F

Prof. Dr. Freud

Marienbad, 27 July 1913
Vienna IX, Berggasse 19

Dear Dr. Binswanger,

Until two days ago I would sadly have joined in your complaint about the weather; I hope that it has now improved for you as well.

I am feeling so agreeably feeble-minded that I find myself unable to recall exactly the point you raised. Wasn't it something about – apart from the conditions of organ paralysis – the state of being in love and the 'end of the world'?

I was delighted to hear the good news about your family and your work. Do try to persevere in good health for a little while longer so that we may both feel liberated.

You will have to tell me more about the totem book in due course.[1] You probably realise that it is a great step forward and that much will follow from it.

We have been having a very enjoyable time here with our regained daughter and son-in-law from Hamburg.[2] Alas, all enjoyable times pass so quickly and time spent working lasts so long. I often wish I were a pensioner and could leave the work to others. But what man alive will pension me off?

Our Congress will be very interesting, at least from a personal point of view. Could you not bring Häberlin along? Perhaps his appointment will have come through by then.[3]

Kind regards to you, your wife and your family,

Yours ever,
Freud

[1] Binswanger wrote about this in (1956c), p. 54 in the 1957 English edition: 'Even though he was gratified by the approval I had voiced in an earlier letter, he perhaps sensed certain reservations on my part, but these applied only to the assumption of a primal horde and what went with it, which I regarded as too "speculative".'
[2] There is no mention of the presence of Sophie and Max Halberstadt in Marienbad in Jones (1953–7), Vol. 2, p. 111.
[3] In June 1913 Häberlin had the prospect of appointment to a newly created chair in psychology and education at Heidelberg. When this fell through at the beginning of 1914 he accepted the appointment as Professor of Philosophy with special consideration of psychology and education at Berne. See Kamm (1977–81), Vol. 1, pp. 313–18.

93F

Marienbad, 7 August 1913
Vienna IX, Berggasse 19

Prof. Dr. Freud

Dear Dr. Binswanger,
Before you reproach me as I usually reproach you, I must mention a touch of rheumatism in my right arm which has turned writing into a feat of gymnastics.

I am of course very pleased with the impression my work on totemism has made on you, and even more with the dwindling of the misgivings you mention. Soon we shall have been weaned from writing altogether.

I am naturally sorry that that lovely Whitsun evening in 1912 should have left such an unpleasant aftertaste with your aunt.[1] But she had the choice, after all, of taking up my offer and made her own decision. That wretch, Friedländer, will have told you a pack of lies; he cannot help himself for he is incapable of speaking the truth. Up to now he has [not] sued me; I'm told I can safely expect him to; I don't think my informants have been deceiving me. One day before your letter arrived, he sent me a characteristic letter, impudent and hypocritical, to which I have replied. I drew attention to the fact that despite the opposing lawyer's request, I provided no evidence against him, only because, of course, it might be misinterpreted as resulting from our so-called scientific dispute. '*The same reason,*' I continued, 'ought also to have stopped me from making that comment at Binswanger's.' I was being really hard on myself here! 'For the rest neither your success in the official inquiry,[2] nor the impertinent, threatening tone of your letter, has been able to change my opinion of you for the better.'

I hope he won't twist my words round. I am telling him frankly: I know that you are a swine, but since you are considered to be my 'opponent' I should not have 'said' so.

Incidentally, supposing he does sue, do you really think I'll be able to keep quiet about where and when I made my remark? Wouldn't that be too indulgent? True, I should not be able to avoid giving the facts, but that wouldn't do you much harm.

Kind regards and I look forward to our meeting in Munich!

Yours, Freud

[1] On the dispute with Friedländer and the letters mentioned here, see note 3 to 73F.
[2] In this regard, cf. the remark in Freud's letter of 5 August 1913 to Ferenczi; see note 3 to 73F.

94F

7 December 1913
Prof. Dr. Freud   Vienna IX, Berggasse 19

Dear Dr. Binswanger,
I was very glad to have good news of you after so long an interval – good news about your health, your family and your clinic. It is annoying that your work is not progressing, since that means it is in

danger of missing its moment. Were it in existence right now, I would gladly have invited you to contribute it to the new *Jahrbuch* (July '14).[1]

In the peace that has now descended we are making a good recovery from the impressions of Munich.[2] I shall soon be continuing with the 'shuffling off' of the Zurich contingent which I started there, when they gave themselves out as my adherents and continuators. I have now taken over the *Jahrbuch* and intend to maintain a high level. Abraham and Hitschmann will be the editors.[3]

The Friedländer farce has come to a grotesque conclusion. He informed me indirectly that he would be sending copies of our correspondence to you and to your esteemed aunt in Bremen. I am curious to know if he actually does so. Anyone hearing of this threat would certainly gain the impression that my two replies were humble billets-doux. But they consisted of the choicest insults in tersest language! Could he have misunderstood that?

Apart from the spadework needed to prepare for all sorts of later publications, I am engaged on revised editions, and especially on the fourth of the *Interpretation of Dreams*.[4] My family is completely disintegrating. One of my sons is now studying in Munich,[5] another[6] has become a doctor of law and will probably be going to Berlin, the third[7] will leave us for good as an engineer within a year. Then I shall be left with just one daughter,[8] the one with whom Häberlin spoke. But they are all a cheerful and hardworking lot.

With many kind regards, especially to your wife,

Yours ever,
Freud

[1] Did not in fact come out until September 1914; cf. 103F.

[2] Cf. note 6 to 91B.

[3] The announcement of the removal of Eugen Bleuler as Editor-in-Chief and C.G. Jung as Editor of the *Jahrbuch für Psychoanalyse und psychopathologische Forschungen* and Bleuler's replacement by Freud and the appointment of Abraham and Hitschmann as Editors was published in the *Jahrbuch* Vol. 5 (1913), p. 757, and is reprinted in Freud (1974a), p. 550.

[4] 4th, enlarged and revised edition, Leipzig and Vienna, 1914.

[5] Ernst Freud (1892–1970).

[6] Jean Martin Freud (1889–1967).

[7] Oliver Freud (1891–1969).

[8] Anna Freud (1895–1982). Cf. Peters (1979), Young-Bruehl (1988) and Coles (1992).

95F

8 March 1914

Prof. Dr. Freud

Vienna IX, Berggasse 19

Dear Dr. Binswanger,

I am very glad to hear that you are well, and am sure that soon you will feel no more uncertain of life than anyone else.[1] That your family is flourishing into the bargain is not only very good news but also redounds without question to the credit of your wife!

It was very pleasing, too, to hear that you have, after all, drawn closer to Shakespeare.[2] It often puzzles me why humanity needs so many new writers. I am very much looking forward to hearing your views on Rome next year. It is generally accepted that the first impression is disappointing, not to say harrowing.

So far this year has brought me a great deal of work which has only now begun to slacken. It is a pity that your theoretical work is not making any progress. We really could have done with it for the first volume of the new *Jahrbuch*.[3] In the event, that contains two contributions from me, an essay entitled 'On Narcissism: an Introduction'[4] and another 'On the History of the Psychoanalytic Movement',[5] which I hope will clarify the relations with Jung. You are unlikely to have missed Jelgersma's[6] rectorial address in Leiden.

Everyone in my family is well. My wife left yesterday for Hamburg, where we are expecting a rise in status in the near future, in other words elevation to the rank of grandparents.[7]

I am very pleased about Häberlin's appointment.[8] If you should see him, please convey my congratulations. I have little hope, however, that he will turn out to be an active champion of psychoanalysis.

Recently one of Friedländer's colleagues again confirmed that he was demoted for cheating at tarok while he was a voluntary cadet medical officer. Perhaps you will now appreciate my reluctance to have any kind of contact with the wretch.

With kind regards to you and your wife,

Yours, Freud

[1] Cf. note 1 to 65F.

[2] Shakespeare lectures are still often mentioned in Binswanger's diaries after 1916.

[3] The *Jahrbuch* now had the new title *Jahrbuch der Psychoanalyse*, but continued the volume numbering with Vol. 6 (1914), although it ceased publication after that because of the war.

[4] Freud (1914c).

[5] Freud (1914d).

[6] Gerbrandus Jelgersma, *Ongeweten Geestesleven* (1914) [Unconscious Intellectual Life], a lecture given at the 339th anniversary of the University of Leiden on 9 February 1914.

[7] Ernst Halberstadt (now W. Ernest Freud), son of Sophie and Max Halberstadt and Freud's first grandchild, was born on 11 March 1914.

[8] See note 3 to 92F.

96F

12 June 1914

Prof. Dr. Freud   Vienna IX, Berggasse 19

Dear Dr. Binswanger,

Heartiest congratulations on your fourth offspring,[1] and regrets only that I cannot decipher your letter well enough to allay your anxieties,[2] which glimmer faintly through. It would seem, however, that you have gone back on your own prognosis.

I was also very pleased to hear about your lecture,[3] but could not understand why you had it printed by Alzheimer[4] (?) instead of supporting our journal with a contribution for once.

What are we doing? We are preparing the new *Jahrbuch*, the appearance of which will, I hope, enable a clean break with the Swiss.[5] My contribution for Kraus[6] will be done in the summer, at Seis-am-Schlern where we plan to go after Karlsbad. At the end of September, after the Congress,[7] I shall be giving a lecture in Leiden.[8]

Kind regards to you and to all your family, now no longer small. I hope to hear good news from you before long.

Yours, Freud

[1] Wolfgang Binswanger, b. 8 June 1914.

[2] Cf. note 1 to 65F.

[3] 'Current psychological issues within clinical psychiatry', given as a lecture at the 50th conference of the Society of Swiss Psychiatrists held at the Bellevue on 2 June 1914, (1914b).

[4] Alois Alzheimer (1864–1915), psychiatrist and discoverer of the brain disease named after him, founded with M. Lewandowsky the *Zeitschrift für die gesamte Neurologie und Psychiatrie* and with others edited this journal from 1910 to 1915. Binswanger had offered him his lecture on 9 June 1914 and heard that it had been accepted on 21 July; cf. B.A. 443/34.

[5] Vol. 6 (1914). It contained no contributions from Swiss analysts and above all brought out the polemic paper that Freud had completed in February 1914, 'On the History of the Psychoanalytic Movement' (1914d). Cf. also 97F.

[6] See note 3 to 75F.

[7] The next Psychoanalytic Congress should actually have been held in Dresden on 20 September; see Jones (1953–7), Vol. 2, p. 194. An announcement then appeared in the *Korrespondenzblatt* of the *Internat. Zschr. ärztl. Psychoanal.*, Vol. 2 (1914), p. 483, that, because of events in the outer world, the Congress had had to be post-poned indefinitely.

[8] At the invitation of Jelgersma, Freud was to have given a lecture at the University of Leiden on 24 September 1914. The outbreak of war put an end to this plan. Instead he spent 12 days, from 16 September, with his daughter Sophie in Hamburg. Cf. Jones (1953–7), Vol. 2, p. 195.

97F

19 June 1914

Prof. Dr. Freud   Vienna IX, Berggasse 19

Dear Dr. Binswanger,

I was not really as 'indignant' as you think. I explained things to myself in much the same way as you did in your letter. It is only that I believe that psychiatrists will also be reading the journal and I am very reluctant to dispense with your contributions. Perhaps I seemed irate because I was uneasy, being unable to make out from your letter, or for that matter from the second, whether you were simply being 'peevish' or had some reason for concern.

Vol. VI of the *Jahrbuch* is ready now and due to appear in about 3 weeks' time. For that issue, therefore, your kind offer has come too late, but in the next *Jahrbuch*[1] we shall have as much space as you need. We don't want to leave you out any longer.

You will soon be receiving some printed material from me.[2] I am anxious to hear what effect[3] it has. Let me have news of you.

Very cordially yours, Freud

[1] No further issues appeared.
[2] Freud (1914d); cf. 99B.
[3] 'reaction' deleted, replaced by 'effect'.

98B

Constance, 22 June 1914

Dear Professor Freud,

Many thanks for your letter of 19 June. I should be grateful if you would let me know, in due course, when *approximately* the next issue of the *Jahrbuch* is due to appear. – I am very much looking forward to your promised work.

I have been back in harness, which I am still finding rather hard going, since the 18th. I am neither peevish nor is there any cause for concern; it was probably no more than a case of nicotine poisoning[1] with cerebral and cardiac symptoms. I still suffer a little from giddiness and get tired very easily, but feel better back at work than if I were doing nothing at all.

With kind regards, and in unchanging affection, I am, dear Professor,

Yours, [L. Binswanger]

[1] In Ludwig Binswanger's diary (II, pp. 5–8) under the date 12 June 1917 there is a dramatic report of renewed nicotine poisoning: 'First acute nicotine poisoning for three years. Vascular character more clearly expressed than last time.'

99B

Constance, 27 June 1914

Dear Professor Freud,

Many thanks for your offprint.[1] I found the paper so interesting that I read it through in one gulp the very first evening, the interest being of such a high order that I was spurred on, now by the content, now by your deadly aim. I can find no fault with it whatever, for the work is, in every respect, the product of your whole personality and as such of the utmost importance for your future biographers. I was particularly pleased with the blows you dealt out; but above all I was delighted to see how much the whole work is suffused with an unbroken vigour. May you be granted that for a very long time to come.

With kind regards,

Ever yours, [L. Binswanger]

[1] 'On the History of the Psychoanalytic Movement' (1914d).

100B

Constance, 22 July 1914

Dear Professor Freud,

You will have heard that the Zurich group has decided to withdraw from the International Psychoanalytic Association by a vote of 15 to 1.[1] Whether that one vote was mine I do not know because I was not present at that particular meeting, although I did tell Maeder over the telephone beforehand that I would vote against a separation. I can accept neither the latent nor the manifest reasons for a break. And I find it particularly amusing that the frightful spectre of the threat to independent research was used as a scapegoat even here. I cannot join, or make further contributions to, the new independent association and am willing to join the Vienna or Berlin group if you advise me to do so; I don't know how you see the future standing of the International Association yourself, now that Jung has so belied your hopes. Your history of the analytic movement is being recognised and admired, especially by independent minds.

With kind regards,

Ever yours, [L. Binswanger]

1 See *Internat. Zschr. ärztl. Psychoanal.*, Vol. 2 (1914), p. 483: 'On 10 July the Zurich local group decided by 15 votes to 1 to leave the Association.' Cf. also Freud (1974a), p. 552.

101F

Prof. Dr. Freud

Karlsbad, 25 July 1914
Vienna IX, Berggasse 19

Dear Dr. Binswanger,

How extremely comical that you, of all the Zurich people, should have refused me the favour for the sake of which I wrote the history of the psychoanalysis movement![1] And what luck that you should have so little influence in Zurich! I am dying to hear officially that we are rid of the 'independents'.

There is, of course, nothing against your changing over to another group. And you won't be the only one, I know.

The Congress will debate the continued existence of the International Psychoanalytic Association, for that item has been put on the agenda.[2] I think that it will be possible to demonstrate the need for it, and that Jung's defection will pale into insignificance as a mere episode.

Why don't you tell me how you are? Or am I meant to take your silence as an *optimum signum*? I am very willing to do so, and would like from now on to feel light-heartedly optimistic on this point.

With kind regards to you both, and to your flock of children,

Yours, Freud

From 4 August at Pension Edelweiss, Seis-am-Schlern, Tyrol.[3]

[1] Freud had expected that Binswanger, as well as Pfister, would resign and join the Vienna group, which did then happen; see 102B. Cf. also Freud's remark to Ferenczi in a letter of 17 July 1914: 'A letter from Pfister the day before yesterday unexpectedly contains the assurance that he considers himself with us and is prepared to enter the Viennese group, if the Zurichers bring about the *exit that they are planning*. So there is the first piece of news, and it is good.' Freud (1992g), Vol. 2, p. 2.

[2] The debate did not take place because of the cancellation of the Congress; see note 7 to 96F.

[3] This holiday did not take place because of the war; cf. 105F.

102B

28 July 1914

Dear Professor Freud,

I should like herewith to submit my application for membership of the Vienna group.[1] I have chosen this group since I believe that through joining it I can most easily demonstrate my respect and admiration for you, as well as my adherence to you. I am looking forward to seeing you in Dresden.[2] You are right to take my silence for an *optimum signum*: any danger is in fact far from my mind.

My wife joins me in sending kind regards and in wishing you a very good holiday.

Ever yours, [L. Binswanger]

[1] His joining is announced in *Internat. Zschr. ärztl. Psychoanal.*, Vol. 3 (1915), p. 184.

[2] See note 7 to 96F.

103F

29 September 1914

Prof. Dr. Freud   Vienna IX, Berggasse 19

Dear Dr. Binswanger,

I gladly comply with the admonition enclosed with your last interest. communication. (Incidentally, don't I know the anonymous author, L.B?)[1] However, I cannot really tell you anything other than you will have guessed yourself: that we are entirely under the influence of the events, are bracing ourselves with difficulty to continue our work, and anticipate a quite extraordinary falling off in our practice. My eldest son is a volunteer in the army,[2] still in the Tyrol, my daughter[3] has returned from England with the Austrian diplomatic party.

Our journals will continue to appear, somewhat reduced and delayed; the *Jahrbuch* has long been ready but has not yet been distributed by Deuticke. We intend to hold the first meeting of the Society on 7 October. May I take that opportunity to announce, as agreed, that you are joining us?[4]

I was in Berlin and Hamburg[5] last week and came back a little more optimistic. I hope to hear nothing but good news soon from you, your wife and your flock of promising children.

Very cordially yours, Freud

[1] Binswanger had apparently sent Freud his work: 'Klinischer Beitrag zur Lehre vom Verhältnisblödsinn (Bleuler)' [A clinical contribution to the theory of pseudo-dementia], *Zschr. P*(1914a), which he had published under the pseudonym 'Lothar Buchner', probably out of consideration for his teacher, Bleuler.

[2] Martin Freud had volunteered and become a gunner and was training in Salzburg and Mühlau bei Innsbruck; see Jones (1953–7), Vol. 2, p. 194, and Freud's letter of 23 August 1914 to Ferenczi, Freud (1992g), Vol. 2, p. 13.

[3] Anna Freud, who had been in England since 18 July, travelled back to Vienna via Gibraltar and Genoa under the protection of the Austrian diplomatic corps; see Jones (1953–7), Vol. 2, p. 194.

[4] Cf. *Protokolle*, Vol. 4 (1981), p. 257 – Binswanger's name appears only in the 1981 German edition, with a note to the effect that only one line of minutes has survived. [In *Minutes*, Vol. 4 (1975), p. 266 the note reads: 'The minutes of this meeting are missing.' T.R.]

[5] Freud had been staying with his daughter Sophie Halberstadt in Hamburg since 16 September, and on the return journey had spent five hours with Abraham in Berlin. Cf. Jones (1953–7), Vol. 2, p. 195.

104F

10 January 1915

Prof. Dr. Freud Vienna IX, Berggasse 19

Dear Dr. Binswanger,

Best wishes for the New Year from me, too. I am glad you do not need them as badly as others do these days.

One's love of travel, and the opportunities for it, are blighted indeed; it will no doubt be a long time before the next entry in your visitors' book.[1]

I am happy to supply all the information you ask for: two of my sons are in the army,[2] both still training as gunners in provincial towns. My son-in-law in Hamburg has been called up and is waiting to be sent for training. My middle son's[3] turn will come in the spring.

The Society meets every other week, quietly and not very productively.[4] Rank and Reik[5] alone seem to be working hard; the first has been exempted, the second, newly married, joins up this week. Our journals for the current year are slowly being completed. The last issue of the *Zeitschrift*[6] should be out within the next few days, and so should the last-but-one issue of *Imago*.[7] Deuticke will probably not be publishing the *Jahrbuch*[8] in 1915.

I am productive and listless by turns. A long case history,[9] the most detailed so far, is finished and awaits being put to use. Occasionally I busy myself with a kind of synthesis of psychoanalytic theories,[10] but I am not making much progress. Practice, needless to say, is negligible.

There is the very occasional, isolated sign that interest in psychoanalysis has not yet died out in the world. For instance, I recently received an Italian translation of the five lectures,[11] prepared by Prof. Bianchini[12] of Naples, and my Berlin publishers inform me that a Swedish translation of *Everyday Life*[13] is in preparation.

We hear as little from your neighbours as you do. Pfister still writes from time to time, but I find every one of his letters annoying.[14] So much for our news.

Many thanks to your wife for her kind regards, and may your present good state of health continue.

Yours, Freud

---

[1] Freud had written in the visitors' book: 'Sigm. Freud / Whitsun 1912 (for the first time)'.

[2] Martin and Ernst. Martin Freud was posted to the Galician front on 20 January 1915; see letter to Abraham of 25 Jan. 1915, Freud (1965a) pp. 209–10.

[3] Oliver Freud was still finishing his education as an engineer. He was engaged in engineering work throughout the war, constructing tunnels and barracks; see Jones (1953–7), p. 201.

[4] Until the beginning of the war these meetings had taken place weekly, apart from holiday periods, but from 7 October 1914 they became fortnightly. Cf. *Minutes*, Vol. 4 (1975).

[5] Theodor Reik (1888–1969), after studying psychology, literature, philosophy and religion, underwent a training analysis with Karl Abraham. (Lay-)training analyst at the psychoanalytic institutes in Vienna and Berlin. Fled to Holland in 1934, emigrated to New York in 1938. Cf. Reik (1956), Eidelberg (1970) and Sherman (1970).

[6] *Internat. Zschr. ärztl. Psychoanal.*, Vol. 2 (1914), No. 6.

[7] *Imago*, Vol. 3 (1914), No. 5.

[8] Cf. note 3 to 95F.

[9] 'From the History of an Infantile Neurosis', [The 'Wolf Man' case]; Freud (1918b); see Jones (1953–7), Vol. 2, pp. 306–12, esp. pp. 312–13.

[10] A planned series of twelve metapsychological works, of which only five were published in Freud's lifetime. See Jones (1953–7), Vol. 2, pp. 208–09 and from recent years the Introduction by Ilse Grubrich-Simitis to her edition of the rediscovered manuscript of 'Overview of the Transference Neurosis' (Freud 1985a). Cf. also note 8 to 109F.

[11] *Cinque Conferenze sulla Psicoanalisi*, translated by Marco Levi Bianchini, Nocera Superiore, 1915. Translation of Freud (1910a).

[12] Marco Levi Bianchini (1875–1961), at that time Professor of Psychiatry in Naples, translated Freud's writings into Italian for the first time and founded the first Italian psychoanalytic society in 1925; cf. *L'Italia nella Psicoanalisi* (1989), pp. 97–103. See also Freud's letter to Ferenczi of 30 October 1914 (1992g), Vol. 3, p. 22: 'An Italian Levi Bianchini, Associate Professor in Naples and director of the "Manicomio", wants to publish an international psychiatric library and begin with a translation of my "Five Lectures". He also offers an exchange of journals. Accepted.'

[13] Grinstein's Bibliography (1977, p. 76) lists only a Swedish translation from 1924.

[14] Neither letters from Pfister to Freud nor from Freud to Pfister from the period 11 March 1913 to 9 October 1918 are still extant; see Freud (1963a) p. 61.

105F

1 April 1915

Prof. Dr. Freud   Vienna IX, Berggasse 19

Dear Dr. Binswanger,

I am delighted by your good news and also by the fact that you still find my articles worthy of praise and of use to you. I have nothing directly bad to report; my son in Galicia[1] is well, on the whole, the other son[2] is still doing his military training in Klagenfurt, the third[3] has even been exempted, but worry and tension are understandably so great that little prevails against them. Fortunately I have roused myself to some modest efforts,[4] the results of which you will find in the *Zeitschrift* and in *Imago*. I am also preparing something that seems not unimportant, namely a characterisation of the unconscious[5] intended to render it intelligible, and also an explanation of melancholia[6] based on narcissism. The eight months of the war weigh upon us like a bad dream. My wife and sister-in-law miss the summer holiday they forwent in 1914; I myself cannot boast that I feel refreshed by having my work load reduced to a third. However, we are planning to make up for it all in the summer of 1915 and have been thinking of many nice places, including Lake Constance, in which case I shall be seeking your advice. Still, all such decisions depend on one's fatherland and family permitting, and that is something no one can vouchsafe in advance. In reality we live only from one day to the next; all the rest is phantasy.

Kind regards to you, your wife and your little ones. I recently exchanged letters with Häberlin[7] and shall today be sending you the offprint you asked for.

Yours very sincerely,
Freud

[1] Martin Freud, see note 2 to 104F.

[2] Ernst Freud.

[3] Oliver Freud.

[4] 'Observations on Transference Love' (1915a), 'Thoughts for the Times on War and Death' (1915b), 'Instincts and their Vicissitudes' (1915c). According to letters to Abraham, the first of these works was already in print by 18 February 1915, (1965a), p. 211 (N.B., in the English edition the expression 'im Druck' has been mistranslated as 'at the printer's', rather than 'in print', even though the sentence continues: '[…] which I am sending you'); on the second he wrote on 4 March 1915, *ibid*. p. 213; he began the third on 15 March 1915, *ibid*. p. 214.

[5] 'The Unconscious' (1915e).

[6] 'Mourning and Melancholia' (1916–17g).

[7] As a joint editor (with Gonzague de Reynold) of the *Internationalen Rundschau*, which had been founded in 1914 by Karl Brockhausen and Ludo Moritz Hartmann, Paul Häberlin had invited Freud to collaborate on the journal. Freud's reply declining the offer is published in Kamm (1977–81), Vol. 1, p. 387 and again in Häberlin (1997), p. 357. The original is in the Häberlin Archive, U.B. Basle.

106B

19 April 1915

Dear Professor Freud,

Frau Gi. from D. has been telephoning me from Zurich at intervals since January, saying that she wants to come here unless I will go to see her in Zurich. She asked me a long time ago to consult you about her, but I did not want to bother you since I thought that she would never in the end make up her mind to come to us. She does not want analysis nor could I take her on at this moment. Since she has repeated her request and claims that she is ill and insists on my coming to Zurich in the near future, I have promised to write to you. As far as I can make out she seems to be a most difficult case of obsessional neurosis. I also know that she is 'an Evidential Dream'.[1]

Many thanks for your last letter. I should also be glad for a word on how your son is doing. Should you come anywhere near Lake Constance, I would be entirely at your disposal, and would also be happy to find you somewhere to stay.

With kind regards,

Yours, [L. Binswanger]

[1] Namely, the patient in 'The Evidential Dream' (Freud 1913a).

107F

24 April 1915

Prof. Dr. Freud   Vienna IX, Berggasse 19

Dear Dr. Binswanger,

By chance I sent you an offprint[1] yesterday. I am replying to your letter without delay. I should be very glad to supply you with information about Frau Gi., but what is it you want to know? There is a great deal to say about that patient. She is a case of obsessional neurosis of the severest kind who was *nearly* analysed to the end, has proved incurable and has resisted all efforts because of particularly unpropitious extreme circumstances and is supposedly still dependent on me. In fact, however, she has been running away from me ever since I let her into the real secret of her illness. Analytically useless to anyone. She is pulling the wool over Pfister's eyes. A need for association, friendship with people whom she knows to be with me, because in the quarrel with Zurich she sided with me and was herself one of the objects of Jung's professional laxity. *You* are probably meant as a substitute for Pfister.

Her character has been maintained until a short time ago; she has a pleasant, over-considerate, shrewd and distinguished personality. Her demands on household and clinic are absurdly involved, and will not, I believe, be reduced despite the war. For years, she was the leading figure in the Nassau clinic[2] (Poensgen,[3] Muthmann[4]): her juvenile tendency to change is becoming more pronounced (Muthmann – Pfister – Binswanger), while her affection is given to a succession of fathers (Poensgen – Freud).[5] Strives for friendship and incorporation into a family. I do not know the latest changes but she seems to have altered a great deal during the past year, in which I have hardly seen her. Her husband – the bone of contention – shows enormous patience and tenderness towards her, but seems to be ill now; suspicion of arterio-sclerosis?, metasyphilis? She is waiting, of course, for his end, but will never admit it.

Do have a look at the patient by all means. I don't know why she is paying court to you but can see no reason either why you should not take her on.

She has played a considerable part in my writings: Evidential Dream,[6] Disposition to Obsessional Neurosis;[7] she is also a daughter who wants to help her father, like Joan of Arc. In short, one could never be done with telling her story.

Kind regards,

Yours, Freud

P.S. The news is good of my sons – thank you.

[1] Probably 'Thoughts for the Times on War and Death' (1915b) because Freud also wrote to Abraham on 4 May 1915: 'It was very gratifying of you to like even the "Thoughts of the Times" '; Freud (1965a), p. 221.

[2] The Kurhaus Bad Nassau was founded in Nassau on the Lahn in 1856 by Dr. Emil Haupt as an 'institute for electricity, therapeutic gymnastics, pine needle baths and cold water baths' (see Haupt 1858 and Laehr 1907, p. 146), and from 1885 to 1910 remained as a hydrotherapy establishment under the direction of Dr. Eugen Poensgen. After 1922 his son, Fritz Poensgen (1885–1935) took over together with a Dr. Fleischmann. (For this information I am grateful to Gerhard Biesenbach, Nassau/Lahn.) At the beginning of the 20th century the clinic predominantly recommended itself for 'nervous complaints' excluding mental illnesses; cf. Neumann (1905). The building was totally destroyed in an air raid in March 1945.

[3] Eugen Poensgen (1855–1925). Cf. also the previous note.

[4] Arthur Muthmann (cf. note 3 to 50F) was engaged as an intern in Dr. Eugen Poensgen's clinic from 1902 to 1907 and took over the management from 1912 till the end of World War I; cf. Amitai and Cremerius (1984), p. 743.

[5] The patient was being treated not only by Freud, Pfister, Binswanger, Poensgen and Muthmann, but also by Jung and Pierre Janet. Even Eugen Bleuler was consulted. On 8 November 1916 Pfister wrote to Binswanger: 'You were the first to understand how to set the patient's stubbornness against the strength of the stronger will in such a way that an escape was impossible. Prof. Freud writes to me, and these were his actual words: "I am very pleased with the change in Frau Gi. I had written in my last letter that the only thing is to let yourself be forced. But she could not have done it on her own. Binswanger had a lot to do with it [...]".' Cf. B.A. 443/35.

[6] Cf. note 1 to 106B.

[7] Cf. 'The Disposition to Obsessional Neurosis', Freud (1913i).

108B

Kreuzlingen (Thurgau), 18 May 1915

Dear Professor Freud,

Many thanks for your letter concerning Frau Gi. I hope to have further details from you one day in person. At the end of April I went to see her in Zurich for a consultation. She wanted to discuss whether there was any point in her coming here. I told her quite frankly what she could expect here and what she could not. A few days ago she wrote to me saying she could not come for financial (?) reasons. I had told her what you had said about her coming here. She still has a strong transference to you, speaks very well and affectionately of you, and wanted to make sure, above all, that I was still your follower. What she told me of Jung's remarks during his short treatment of her astonished me, particularly as she strikes one as being credible. Frau Gi. still displayed her old safety-first system during my visit. She has been living in a few small rooms in a Zurich hotel since the beginning of the war, and now wants to move to a hotel above the town for the summer.

Many thanks for your two offprints.[1] And your remarks on transference-love have my fullest approval. Let us hope you continue to have good news from your son. People in your part of the world will be breathing a sigh of relief about the victory in Galicia. Here we live in the sort of peace you must find it hard to imagine. On Sunday I took my wife and our eldest boy for a marvellous walking tour into the Säntis mountains, and while there nurtured the hope that one day, should you come to Lake Constance, I might be able to show you round the small Appenzell Canton.

With kind regards and many good wishes,

Yours, [L. Binswanger]

[1] Most probably 'Remembering, Repeating and Working Through'(1914g) and 'Observations on Transference Love' (1915a), although neither work is still in Binswanger's offprint collection.

109F

Prof. Dr. Freud

17 December 1915
Vienna IX, Berggasse 19

Dear Dr. Binswanger,

I am answering your kind letter by return of post, gratified by your interest in my news even in these times.

Well, my two sons were for a time involved in heavy fighting, but are both still alive, uninjured, decorated, and at present down south in the mountains. Last month the older one spent a ten-day leave with us, gladdening us with his appearance and good spirits.[1] My son-in-law[2] from Hamburg is now in training as a gunner. My middle son, the engineer, who is working on the construction of a tunnel of strategic importance,[3] is coming to Vienna tomorrow and a day later will take his bride back with him.[4]

Our Society still meets, although not so often,[5] having shed all unreliable elements. The number of those who can contribute anything to the literature is naturally small, since they are all helping with the war in one way or another. The publisher has promised continued publication of our *Zeitschrift* and of *Imago*. It is, of course, impossible to keep to schedules. Rank should be going to Kracow soon; Sachs joined up but was discharged as unfit for service.[6]

I do not wish to paint too rosy a picture of my own position, but there has been an unmistakable improvement in my practice during this second year of the war, and I have several things ready for when the war is over. Among them is the series of essays, the first of which you have seen in the *Zeitschrift*.[7] In all, twelve are almost ready. They will be called 'Preliminaries to a Metapsychology'.[8] My lectures for beginners,[9] which I had to repeat this year,[10] will probably be published before peace is signed. Heller will bring them out in three parts.

And now, please give my kind regards to your wife and your little family, and let me hear from you again soon.

Yours, Freud

Do you still think back, sometimes, to the worry that I shared with you, and that must now be considered vanquished?

[1] As can be seen from Freud's letter of 23 November 1915 to Ferenczi, Martin had a ten-day leave in Vienna at the end of November; Freud (1992g), Vol. 2, p. 89.

[2] Max Halberstadt was called up for training in the artillery on 8 December 1915; see Freud to Ferenczi 6 December 1915; Freud (1992g), Vol. 2, p. 94.

[3] Under the Jablunka pass in the Carpathians in Eastern Silesia; see Jones (1953–7), Vol. 2, p. 229.

[4] This first marriage of Oliver's took place in Vienna on Saturday 18 December 1915 and was to last only until the end of May 1916 when he was divorced in Vienna. This becomes clear from letters from Freud to Ferenczi 17 and 24 December 1915 and of 13 and 29 April 1916; Freud (1992g), Vol. 2, pp. 97, 98, 124 and 126 respectively. However, there is no record of this marriage either in the Viennese Jewish community, or in the entries for Oliver Freud in the residence register held in the Vienna new town hall (there only his second marriage to Henny Fuchs is recorded, which took place in Berlin on 10 April 1923).

[5] Fortnightly until the meeting on 12 May 1915, which is recorded as the final meeting in the attendance register. Up to the end of the year no more minutes exist, so it is not clear whether meetings took place during this period; cf. *Minutes*, Vol. 4, 1975.

[6] Rank was conscripted in June 1915. Sachs was called up in August, but was released again after twelve weeks of training in Linz. See Jones (1953–7), Vol. 2, p. 203.

[7] Cf. Freud (1915c), (1915d) and (1915e).

[8] Also in the letter of 4 May 1915 Freud called it 'Abhandlungen zur Vorbereitung der Metapsychologie' ['Introductory Papers on Metapsychology']. See Freud (1965a), p. 221. Cf. also note 10 to 104F.

[9] *Introductory Lectures on Psycho-Analysis* (1916–17a).

[10] Cf. Gicklhorn and Gicklhorn (1960), p. 190 ('of 11 actual audience, 9 women'). The diagram given there – plate 12 – (overview of all the lectures) falsely lists the lecture in W.S. 1915–16 as 'heralded, not read'.

110F

7 May 1916
IX, Berggasse 19

Prof. Dr. Sigm. Freud,[1]

Many thanks to my Lake Constance friends.[2]

[1] Visiting card.

[2] The wording indicates that Binswanger together with his wife or indeed with the patient Gi. (cf. 131F and 136F) had congratulated him on his 60th birthday.

111F

25 December 1916
Prof. Dr. Freud   Vienna IX, Berggasse 19

Dear Dr. Binswanger,

Little as these times are conducive to the writing of letters, I was still very pleased to hear, after so long a silence, that you are well,[1] that it can be taken that our fears[2] are now disposed of, that your wife and children are flourishing and that your interests have not deviated from analysis. – In return, I can report that we are keeping our end up, that the intervals between the publication of our journals grow longer, and that everything is ready for the re-establishment of relations when friends return after peace has been signed.

Parts 1 and 2 of my lectures have appeared;[3] several things are in preparation or appearing bit by bit in the journals. Of the contributors, however, Sachs is the only one who still has free time, and he gives me energetic support.

My three sons are in the army. I am glad to say that they are doing well. Two of them are artillery officers, decorated, and in fine fettle; the third has only recently joined the sappers – up till now his presence has been deemed indispensable in the construction of a military tunnel.

For the rest, we must just wait.

Very cordially yours,
Freud

[1] Binswanger was posted to Lucerne on military medical service from mid-October to the end of November 1916 and had very much enjoyed this time and the opportunities for reading and going to concerts; cf. Diary I, pp. 58–90. The diary does not mention the contact by correspondence with Freud.
[2] Cf. note 1 to 65F.
[3] (1916–17a) No. 1: Parapraxes (Lectures 1–4, *S.E.*, Vol. XV, pp. 15–79), published Leipzig and Vienna 1916; No. 2: Dreams (Lectures 5–15, *S.E.*, Vol. XV, pp. 83–239), published Leipzig and Vienna 1916; see Grinstein (1977), p. 98, no. 244.

112F

8 May 1917[1]

Many thanks for your telegram.[2] So I have heard from you at last, and hope that all is well with your family.

Freud

[1] Postcard.
[2] Obviously for Freud's birthday.

[Addition in Binswanger's handwriting:
'received Kreuzlingen 14/5/17']

113B

Kreuzlingen, Switzerland, 10 August 1917

Dear Professor Freud,

I have been telling you for years about the work I am writing on psychoanalysis,[1] and I even read you some of it when you stayed here. Lest you should imagine that that was all there was to it, I propose sending you a chapter of the manuscript very shortly. The work is divided into two parts: the first, of 200 typewritten pages, is almost completed and deals with general psychological problems such as the definition of the psyche, the basic concepts of psychology, the various scientific methods of dealing with psychic phenomena, etc., all based on historical examples. This is followed, as the second part, by an appreciation and examination of psychoanalysis, that is, of the latter's purely psychological aspect. You will be receiving the first chapter [of the second part].[2] You can imagine how particularly delighted I am that you are interested in the book, and if the material appeals to you, and you should wish to add some personal comments, I shall of course be most grateful to you; that is not, however, the main reason for my sending it to you. I assume that the second part will also run to at least 200 typewritten pages and I would prefer to publish the whole as a self-contained book. I am sending you a *copy* of the typescript so that there is no rush about sending it back; because of censorship it will in any case take a long time to and fro.

I should be very glad to have a brief note letting me know when you are hoping to publish Part III of the Lectures on Psychoanalysis.

With kind regards,

Ever yours, [L. Binswanger]

---

[1] Only the first part of this work was published (under the title *Einführung in die Probleme der allgemeinen Psychologie* [Introduction to the Problems of General Psychology], Berlin, 1922). Although part 2 was already flourishing in 1922, it was never finished. The manuscript appears not to have come down to us: Binswanger's heirs know nothing of its whereabouts. Cf. note 2 to 59F.

[2] Should probably read: 'of the second part ... ' because Binswanger wrote in his diary under the date 14–18 August: 'Chapter I of the second part finished and sent to Freud. Chapter II begun in my head.'

114F

Csorbató (Tatra), 20 August 1917[1]

Dear Dr. Binswanger,
I received the first chapter of Part II today and read it at once and, on this first, preliminary, reading, with great interest. It is very instructive for me and very creditable, but I am uneasy about one thing. What are you proposing to do about the unconscious, or rather, how will you manage without the unconscious? Has the philosophical devil finally got you in his clutches?[2] Reassure me. I did not receive a letter.

Very cordially yours, Freud

[1] Postcard.
[2] Binswanger wrote on the matter (1956c), p. 64 in 1957 English edition: 'Unfortunately I cannot find a copy of my answer to this question. Needless to say, I have never "managed without the unconscious," either in psychotherapeutic practice, which is indeed impossible without using Freud's concept of the unconscious, or in "theory". But after I turned to phenomenology and existential analysis, I conceived the unconscious in a different way. The problems it presented became broader and deeper, as it became less defined as merely the opposite of the "conscious", whereas in psychoanalysis it is still seen largely in terms of this simple opposition. Heidegger's existential analysis, as contrasted to Sartre's takes as its point of departure not consciousness, but existence conceived as being-in-the-world; accordingly, the opposition in question recedes into the background in favour of a description of the various phenomenologically demonstrable modes and structures of being-in-the-world.'

115F

Csorbató, 21 August 1917[1]

Dear Dr. Binswanger,
Your letter came today. I am longing to see what comes next, but shall do my best to reserve my comments until I have seen it all, and even then I shall exercise a respectful reticence. Publication in book form does seem to me the best thing. Part III of the Lectures[2] has been in the bookshops for more than two months.

Kind regards,

Yours, Freud

[1] Postcard.
[2] (1916–17a), part 3: General Theory of the Neurosis (Lectures 16–28), Leipzig and Vienna, 1917. See Grinstein (1977), p. 98, no. 244.

Binswanger's four oldest children (about 1917); left to right:

Ludwig A., b. 1913; Hilde, b. 1911; Wolfgang, b. 1914; Robert, b. 1909.

116F

21 April 1918

Prof. Dr. Freud   Vienna IX, Berggasse 19

Dear Dr. Binswanger,

Special thanks for your kind letter at a time that is driving us towards pauperisation and isolation! Congratulations to you and your wife on your new child, whom you call the fourth son.[1] Am I mistaken in thinking that you also have a daughter? In which case he would be a son *and* the fourth child.[2]

I am very glad to hear that you are so busily engaged in your work,[3] and that it is making such good progress. With the impatience of an old man who is no longer quite sure of the length of his days, I should have liked to see your book already completed. But I have always felt such impatience, even in the old days. It is true that recently it has seemed as if German science may be readier now to take to analysis. Perhaps its truth is gradually being recognised, with the exception, of course, of the Oedipus complex, for which a special latency period and the passing of a generation is required.

Meanwhile we have not been entirely idle here. Help from outside has, admittedly, come only from the Dutch, who, as you know, have founded a new local group.[4] I hope you are receiving the *Zeitschrift* and *Imago* regularly if rarely. It hasn't been possible to send you special offprints because of the restrictions. My writings since 1914 are about to be published by Heller in Vienna as the fourth volume of the *Sammlung*.[5]

I would love to spend a summer at Lake Constance near you, but cannot consider it while my sons are in the army. One of them is at home with a minor lung complaint,[6] the other two are in Italy and Bessarabia, still unharmed. When peace comes, I shall remind you of your promise to come here. That will put an end to a long period of privation. Let us look forward to it!

With kind regards to you and your large family,

Yours, Freud

[1] Johannes Binswanger (1918–1926).

[2] He was in fact the fourth son and (including the daughter) the fifth child.

[3] In March Binswanger wrote in his diary (II, p. 28): 'Third chapter of part 2. End of chapter 2 left aside, beginning of chapter 3 done three times. First version: concept of conscience according to Lipps and appreciation of the objectivity of Freud; second

version: the concept of personality; third: ego trinity stays, but the total ego will be reworked as soon as possible.' On 25 April (Diary II, p. 29): 'Chapter 3 finished, 116 manuscript pages, the longest of the second part. The work is my support again, or better, my *target*.'

[4] On 31 March 1917, shortly before his death on 19 May, Johann Stärcke had informed Freud of the establishment of the 'Nederlandsche Vereeniging voor Psychoanalyse' [Dutch Psychoanalytic Society] in Holland as a 'department' of the International Psychoanalytic Association; see: 'Gründung einer neuen Ortsgruppe der Internationalen Psychoanalytischen Vereinigung in Holland' [Establishment of a new local group of the International Psychoanalytic Association in Holland], *Internat. Zschr. ärztl. Psychoanal.*, Vol. 4 (1916/17), p. 217.

[5] *Sammlung kleiner Schriften zur Neurosenlehre* [collection of shorter writings on the theory of neuroses from the years 1893–1906], Vol. 4, Leipzig and Vienna: Heller 1918. The first three volumes from 1906 to 1913 had appeared with Deuticke. See also Jones (1953–7), Vol. 2, p. 230.

[6] On Ernst Freud's tuberculosis, see Jones (1953–7), Vol. 2, p. 230.

117F

2 January 1919

Prof. Dr. Freud   Vienna IX, Berggasse 19

Dear Dr. Binswanger,

Although I gained much satisfaction from your last two letters with their news that you are well, that your family is thriving and that your great work[1] is making progress, I failed to reply to them. The catastrophe with its attendant tensions and worries, the general upheaval, and the anxiety about one of my sons[2] who was missing – we have finally heard that he is a prisoner-of-war in a hospital in the Abruzzi – caused me to lose all interest in letter-writing. The New Year gives me the chance to make good this neglect. The old year will not easily be surpassed in horror.

Our psychoanalysis is the only thing to have flourished. The Budapest Congress[3] turned out splendidly and brought me a considerable endowment,[4] the proceeds of which Rank and I are using to set up a psychoanalytic publishing house,[5] to ensure the regular appearance of our two journals and to bring out psychoanalytical books. The sixth edition of *Everyday Life*[6] will be the first of these. Others are in preparation.

I even have enough money left over for two small psychoanalysis prizes.[7] The first have already been awarded to Abraham (earliest stages of the libido 1916),[8] Simmel (war neuroses)[9] and Reik (puberty rites among savages)[10] These prizes are to be awarded annually, and perhaps I shall live to see the day when I can similarly honour your work.

Conditions here, as you in Switzerland must know, are very bad, but the city is calm, the people patient and flight impossible for very many reasons. Dr. Sachs is suffering from a tuberculous catarrh and is staying at the Hotel Eisenlohr in Davos-Platz. He would certainly be very pleased if you were to take some notice of his presence there and to ask after him.[11]

I hope to learn from your early reply that you have forgiven my long silence

With kind regards

Yours, Freud

[1] The diary entries about the progress of the work after 25 April 1918 (II, pp. 29–40) say:

'29 April 1918: looked through chapter III. The total ego.

'18 August. Reworking of chapter 4 of part 2. Kant's substance and form, Plato's "desire for pleasures" and "aiming for excellence". Science and life on the same root here!

'11 November. Starting chapter 5 of my work. Beginning (Wundt's apperception) already done, but it will have to be done again. The unconscious must go into it now. Studied *Cassirer*, *Stadler*, decided progress in getting into *Kant*. Before that Interpretation of Dreams VII [chapter], *Breuer* and the new essays gone through by *Freud*.' [For information on Wundt, see note 12 to 147B. T.R.]

[2] Martin Freud; see Jones (1953–7), Vol. 2, p. 228.

[3] The 5th International Psychoanalytic Congress, Budapest, 28–29 September 1918.

[4] Anton von Freund (1880–1920), Dr. phil., a rich brewer in Budapest, had made an endowment for the benefit of psychoanalysis out of gratitude for his treatment by Freud; cf. Jones (1953–7), Vol. 2, p. 221.

[5] For the early days of the International Psychoanalytical Publishing House, see Jones (1953–7), Vol. 3, pp. 32–8.

[6] *On the Psychopathology of Everyday Life*, 6th enlarged edition, Leipzig and Vienna: Internationaler Psychoanalytischer Verlag, 1919.

[7] See Freud (1919c).

[8] Abraham (1916/17).

[9] Simmel (1918).

[10] Reik (1915/16).

[11] There is no mention in Binswanger's diary of contact between him and Hanns Sachs.

118F

Vienna, 13 February 1919[1]

Transmit soonest five hundred lire to Doctor Martin Freud tenente[2] prisoner-of-war Genova San Benigno inferiore explanatory letter follows

Prof. Freud

[1] Telegram.
[2] Lieutenant.

119F

16 February 1919

Prof. Dr. Freud   Vienna IX, Berggasse 19

Dear Dr. Binswanger,

Please accept my cordial thanks for your speedy assistance. My son was taken prisoner with his entire corps towards the end of October, one of the 300,000 who, according to Austrian claims, were cut off after the ceasefire had been agreed. It was a very long time before we received news of him and learned where they were keeping him, and it was not until the day before yesterday that he acknowledged receipt of the first of our letters to reach him. In his last letter he also asked for money because Genoa is very expensive. He lost all his luggage and other belongings during the capture. Unfortunately, francs and lire are completely unobtainable here, the banks make great difficulties and the transfer of money from Vienna seems to be as difficult as it is uncertain. That is why I decided to turn to you.

It is very likely that Dr. Rank will be going to Switzerland in the next few weeks to further the interests of our publishing house.[1] He will have a Swiss franc bank account at his disposal and will be able to repay my debt to you. If his visit should be unexpectedly delayed, I feel sure you will extend my credit for a little longer.

Our general situation is pretty wretched and the individual comes in for his share of it. Psychoanalysis is the only thing that is doing well. With the help of the Budapest endowment we have embarked on various matters. I hear that a new group is being formed in your country too,[2] hope that you have a hand in it, and should consider it most satisfactory if you took on its direction.

My correspondence with Jones has begun again;[3] he reports great advances in England. Our friend Putnam in Boston has unfortunately died.[4]

With kind regards to you, your wife and all your children,

Yours ever,

Freud

[1] At that time Rank was, along with Freud, Ferenczi and von Freund, one of the directors of the International Psychoanalytical Publishing House that had been founded in January 1919; cf. Jones (1953–7), Vol. 3, p. 32. The journey took place in March 1919; cf. Freud's letters of 3 February, 9 and 31 March 1919 to Ferenczi (1992g), Vol. 2, pp. 208–9, 213 and 220–1. See also note 12 to 121B.
[2] See note 7 to 70F.
[3] See Freud's letters of 15 January 1919 and 18 February 1919 to Jones printed in (1953–7), Vol. 2, pp. 231 and 284–5, also in Freud (1993e), pp. 329–30 and 333–5.
[4] Putnam died 4 November 1918 and Jones informed Freud of this in a letter of 31 December 1918; see Jones (1953–7), Vol. 2, p. 227, and Freud (1993e), p. 327. Cf. also Freud's obituary of Putnam (1919b).

120F

25 December 1919

Prof. Dr. Freud   Vienna IX, Berggasse 19

Dear Dr. Binswanger,

Your welcome largesse was a sign of life and of your continued interest in our fate after a long interval. Thank you very much! But I would like to hear more about you, your family, your great work which has been too long in preparation,[1] your attitude to analysis, etc.

My prisoner-of-war, whom I was able to provide with money thanks to you, is back home and has entered into the more comfortable bondage of a marriage for love.[2] It seems to be turning out well.

I have meanwhile accumulated a sum of money in London and can pay you from there if you would be kind enough to let me know how many Swiss francs you spent at the time. Five hundred lire are no longer what they were a year ago, and there is little reason to expect the [Austrian] Krone to improve.

With kind regards and best wishes for 1920 to you and your family,

Yours, Freud

[1] The diary (II, pp. 50–7) reports on Binswanger's progress with his work on the *Introduction* (1922a) during 1919:

'19 February. Have begun work (self-awareness) [...]

'5 [March] Fifth chapter finished (Transcendental Self-Awareness), "second revolution" in Germany.

'20 July. I have been working on the *Brentano* extract which has been a great help to me. [...] now about to start *Husserl*. What will become of the book? I only know that I shall write it. It will have the same edges and corners that I have and it will be in my image.

'12 August. *Husserl* extract finished.

'3–16 September. Davos – Clavadel. Lipps extract for Part I written. New impulse to publish Part I on its own.

'7 October. Since Clavadel, Natorp (V, Ch. VI), now Ch. II of first part.

'12 November. Ch. II of the first part separated from first chapter containing in particular the creativity from [?] *Bergson*; now the context and the unity of psychology.'

[2] Martin Freud married Esti Drucker on 7 December 1919; see Jones (1953–7), Vol. 3, p. 8; cf. also Freud's postcard of 8 December 1919 to Sam Freud: 'Martin was married yesterday, a courageous deed in these times.' Freud (1996g).

121B

7 January 1920

Dear Professor Freud,

It was very good to have a sign of life from you and to hear that the food parcel arrived safely. I am only too happy to give you detailed news of myself. Please forgive the typewriter, but I know that deciphering my hand gives you no pleasure.

First, best wishes on your son's marriage. I am glad that you are able to give so good a report of it, and beg you to convey my best wishes to your son as well.

I paid 400 francs for the 500 lire at the time. I would ask you once again not to worry on my account about when to repay me.

I shall start with my family. My wife is well except for attacks of sciatica. She took a cure in the summer. We then spent a very pleasant time in the mountains. I sent you a postcard while we were there but do not know if it reached you. For the past two years, as I wrote to you earlier, we have been living in a spacious house[1] of our own which, together with the five children and her duties in the clinic, keeps my wife fully occupied. Of the children, the eldest, whom you probably remember, is at present receiving Latin lessons from his father;[2] in other respects, too, he is a great joy to me. He has the right mixture of fun, independence and boyishness with an integrity and perception in keeping with his age. The youngest, who will soon be two, is very healthy and mentally alert; our daughter and the other two boys too give us much pleasure.

The clinic is still not nearly as busy as it used to be in pre-war days. Germans and Austrians, of course, are very rare; on top of that we have lost many of our permanent inmates because of foreign currency problems, and since costs have risen horrendously we are still working at a loss. Nor can we see any improvement in the next few years. Because my brother[3] and I are the owners but have invested only a very small proportion of our private means in the clinic, the remainder coming from the rest of the family, the situation is by no means simple and we depend on the good will of the family creditors.[4] That, of course, leads to all sorts of problems which, however, we have always managed to overcome so far.

My work is making as good progress as I would wish.[5] I can understand why you speak of it as having been too long in preparation. But the field has grown wider as I worked; I have come to realise more and more that I cannot give what I would consider a fair and necessary account of psychoanalysis[6] exclusively in its own terms, but only in terms of the main problems of psychology. Much as you immersed yourself in the history of the psychology of dreams, so I have immersed myself in the history of psychology, particularly in modern times, the better to do justice to basic psychoanalytical ideas in an historical sense as well. The result, a first volume entitled *Einführung in die Probleme der Allgemeinen Psychologie*[7] [Introduction to the Problems of General Psychology] has progressed so far that it will be ready for printing in the summer, while psychoanalysis will not be dealt with until the second volume.[8] Though the work is maturing very slowly and though I do not like to defer its impact on the outside world, it is nevertheless of great importance to my own intellectual development. I feel greatly stimulated and fortified by the magnitude of the task, by having to reflect and by the increase in my knowledge; throughout the war it, together with my family, was my greatest support.

You ask about my attitude to psychoanalysis. In brief, it remains what you have always known it to be; in therapeutic practice I use it exclusively, now as before, only in such cases as strike me as particularly suited to it; as a basis of understanding patients, by contrast, it probably serves me in every single case. At the moment I am particularly interested in the study of an incipient case of insane jealousy, and I daily regret the fact that I cannot discuss it with you. Little though you have written on the subject of jealousy, that little seems infinitely more worthwhile to me than what is normally said on the subject.[9] I hope somehow to have a chance of talking it over with you, for jealousy, in its normal as well as in its psychopathological aspects, seems to be able to throw the clearest light on psychic life. I have made not the slightest change of direction from Freud to Jung or Adler, and I probably never shall. In the present circumstances, I cannot attend the Zurich psychoanalytic meetings; I am merely kept informed about what is happening there. I am in constant touch with Bleuler and Maier,[10] but no longer with Jung.[11]

It was a great pleasure at the time to see Jones, Sachs and Rank.[12] Please give my regards to the last two. Kind regards to all your family as well, but especially to you, dear Professor. It would make me so very glad if you could come over here for just a couple of weeks during the summer. I have a large, very quiet guest room, in which you would be able to work very well. You could not give my wife and me greater pleasure than by paying us a visit.

Ever yours, [L. Binswanger]

[1] The so-called Garden House was built within the grounds of the Bellevue Sanatorium in 1916–17. The family moved in on 21 October 1917; see diary II, p. 17.

[2] Cf. diary II, p. 56: '30 August [1919]. Böbi's first Latin lesson.'

[3] Otto Binswanger (1882–1968), Dr. phil., Dr. med., first studied agriculture and then from 1908 was administrator of the Bellevue Sanatorium and the family estate at Brunnegg; President of Association of Swiss Hospitals 1936–56; see 'Dr. Otto Binswanger 85 years old', *Thurgauer Volksfreund* (journal), 20 June 1967.

[4] For this reason a public company was formed in 1922 to support the Bellevue Sanatorium, although the major holding remained in the family.

[5] Cf. note 1 to 120F.

[6] Binswanger here omitted the 'o' from *Psychoanalyse*, as he often did in the early days, but later always used the 'o' as in current usage. [The German spelling was much debated around 1921 and *Psychoanalyse* officially settled upon. Curiously the French settled upon omitting the 'o' and for the English Strachey and Jones favoured a hyphen – psycho-analysis – but this has tended to be dropped in recent years. T.R.]

[7] Published by Springer Verlag, Berlin, 1922.

[8] Never published.

[9] See the remarks on delusions of jealousy in the Schreber case (Freud 1911c); first dealt with thoroughly as a major theme in Freud (1922b).

[10] See the extensive correspondence with Eugen Bleuler and Hans Wolfgang Maier in the B.A., Tübingen.

[11] Jung's letters to Binswanger were once in the possession of the family but are no longer to be found. They run from 3 January 1907 to 13 November 1911. After that there is just one letter from Jung dated 21 December 1939.

[12] Ernest Jones met Otto Rank in Switzerland in March 1919 to plan a London branch of the International Psychoanalytic Publishing House. [Jones was already insisting to Freud in his letter of 31 December 1918 that an official organ in English was badly

needed (Freud 1993e, p.327–8). Jones wrote two letters to Freud from Switzerland: 17 and 25 March 1919, (*ibid*, pp. 336–9) from the second of which it becomes clear that he met Binswanger at a meeting of the Swiss Society on 24 March. See also his letter of 2 April after his return to London, summarising the trip (*ibid*, pp. 339–40). T.R.] Cf. also Jones (1953–7), Vol. 3, pp. 37–8.

122F

14 March 1920

Prof. Dr. Freud　　　　　　　　　　　　　Vienna IX, Berggasse 19

Dear Dr. Binswanger,

When your admonitory postcard[1] came yesterday, I had to ask myself: was your full and friendly letter of 7 January really left unanswered? Yes, it was, and the explanation is to be found in the sad events of that month. First, day after day, I was affected by the gradual failing of a dear friend,[2] whose name you will discover from an obituary in the *Zeitschrift*, 1920, No. 1. When I tell you that your own fate gave me hope for him for a year and a half, you will find it easy to understand why I could not write to *you* in particular. He underwent the same operation as you,[3] but did not escape a relapse. We buried him on 22 January. That same evening we received an alarming telegram from our son-in-law Halberstadt in Hamburg. My daughter Sophie, aged 26, mother of two boys, had come down with influenza; she died in the morning of 25 January after a four-day illness. At that time, no trains were running so that we could not even go there. My wife, deeply distressed, is preparing for the journey now, but the recent disturbances in Germany make it doubtful if she will actually be able to go.

We have all been under a great strain ever since, something that has also affected my ability to work. Neither of us has been able to come to terms with the monstrous fact that children may die before their parents. In the summer – and this is my answer to your kind invitation – we want to be somewhere with the two orphans and the inconsolable husband, whom we have loved as a son for 7 years. If it is possible!

You will know about the gravity of all the other circumstances here. I have a great deal to do, but poverty is not held at bay. Because there is no sense in waiting for the exchange rate of the crown to improve, I have instructed a firm in Amsterdam to settle my debt to you. All the post is so slow now. It should have happened long ago.

With kind regards and best wishes for you and your thriving family

Yours truly, Freud

[1] Has not survived.
[2] 'Dr. Anton von Freund †', Freud (1920).
[3] Cf. note 1 to 65F.

Sixth International Psychoanalytic Congress,
8 to 11 September 1920 in The Hague

The first congress after World War I for which, according to Jones (1953–7, Vol. 3, pp. 26–7), a neutral country seemed the obvious choice, gave Binswanger an opportunity to meet Freud again. He described his participation in this congress in his diary:

'5 September [1920]. Went to The Hague in the morning. Afternoon at Ophuijsen's with Ferenczi, Jones, Reik etc., also there for dinner.

'6 September. Morning in Leiden, hideous town, had to take the trouble to seek out the few attractions [...]

'7 September. [...] Greeted Freud, he was slimmer and paler, but had the same expression. Then Maurits-Huis [...]

'9 September. Two days' stressful doings at the congress. Lectures from 9.30 till 1 and 3 till 7. A fantastically busy and attentive company! Many lectures instructive, many one-sidedly narrowly analytical. Freud spoke today about dreams.[1] He still has the old magic. At 9 this evening another private session which I skipped in order to be fresh for my lecture tomorrow. Fortunately I was on first and got a whole hour.

'10 September. Lecture[2] too difficult even here, but audience's attention good. An hour. Freud found it "very clear". Afterwards ate with Freud and daughter [Anna], was particularly nice. Tomorrow last full day [...]. This evening official dinner.' (Tagebuch II, pp. 84-8)

[1] 'Supplements to the Theory of Dreams' (1920f).
[2] The lecture was entitled 'Psychoanalysis and Clinical Psychiatry' (Binswanger 1920a). Binswanger had already given this lecture at Reichenau on 18 August 1920 and had sensed that it was too difficult for his audience. Cf. Diary II, p. 80.

123B

20 June 1921

Dear Professor Freud,

I have not been in touch since Holland[1] because I did not want to 'catch your eye' until my book was more or less ready. This is now the case.[2] At the same time I have a request. You told me in The Hague[3] it was my fault that Switzerland had fallen so far behind in the psychoanalytic movement. That reproach I had to swallow. However, I need not feel too despondent, because my conduct has been due not to laziness or to a wasted opportunity, but to my complete (inner and outer) unsuitability for the task. Still, what I was unable to do about the 'outer' development of the psychoanalytic movement, I think I am able to contribute towards its inner development. Above all I would like in a small way to put it on record that your scientific life's work, along with that of Bleuler, has given the most powerful impetus to my own scientific work and thought, and that I cherish the greatest admiration for it. I am therefore asking you for permission to dedicate my book to you and to Bleuler, in the following words: 'To my teachers Eugen Bleuler and Siegmund [sic] Freud.' I would add that this book, entitled *Einführung in die Probleme der allgemeinen Psychologie*, does not as yet concern itself with psychoanalysis and mentions your name but rarely. Its sole purpose is to examine the foundations of psychology up to that point, and in such a way that in the next volume an account of psychoanalysis can follow naturally. It would give me pleasure to include your two names in my book, which I would refer to in some form in the preface[4] in order to demonstrate that the scientific impetus exerted by teacher on pupil is in no way confined to the teacher's particular field of research, but, far beyond that, provides an impetus to scientific work in general. I can safely say that without the interest in psychiatry which I acquired through you and Bleuler, I should not have written this book, since my heart belongs to psychiatry, to which I shall always return, not least by the detour of this book. I have not yet written to Bleuler, because I shall include any dedication only if I have your consent.

How have you been since Holland? Are you still unable to make up your mind to pay a visit to Switzerland? I extend my invitation again, in my wife's name as well, despite all previous failures. We are both going to the Engadine for two weeks; during the second half of August we intend to take the children on a walking tour of the Black Forest.[5]

With kind regards,

Ever yours, [L. Binswanger]

[1] Sixth International Psychoanalytic Congress, The Hague, 8–11 Sept. 1920. On the proceedings at this congress, see Jones (1953–7), Vol. 3, pp. 28–30.

² On 23 June 1921 Binswanger wrote in his diary (II, p. 111): 'Finished my book today, Thursday at 4.45 in the afternoon.' On 26 July (pp. 114ff.) he went on: 'In the later sections only minor changes needed, only the very last on the psychological individual extended. Thus finished today and so now *really* finished.'

³ Corrected from 'Amsterdam'.

⁴ 'This book stems from the author's endeavours to achieve clarity about the conceptual basis of what the psychiatrist perceives, considers and does at the "sickbed", from a psychological and psychotherapeutic point of view. It is dedicated in gratitude to the two researchers through whose life's work we have experienced such a large growth in the psychiatrist's psychological knowledge and treatment in the last two decades.' Binswanger (1922a), p. v.

⁵ Even after that the plans changed a little. From 25 June to 6 July Binswanger and his wife and a family with whom they were friends went on a tour of the mountains in the area around Avers, Maloja, Sils Maria and Pontresina (Swiss Alps). In mid-August his wife went to Niedernau with their sons, while Binswanger himself went with his son Robert on a longer journey, with mountain tours on the Altman and Säntis, to Arosa, Frauenkirch, over the Sertig Pass to Piz Kesch and to Celerina. See diary II, pp. 111–18.

124F

Prof. Dr. Freud

23 June 1921
Vienna IX, Berggasse 19

Dear Dr. Binswanger,

I hasten to reply that I accept your dedication with thanks. I shall be proud to have you acknowledge yourself publicly as my pupil. I nearly added that I am also proud to find my name and Bleuler's mentioned together in this context. But I cannot deny that Bleuler's coming to a full stop in exploring the depths of the psyche and his incorrigible ambivalence have resulted in his being considerably lowered in my esteem.

Needless to say I am eagerly looking forward to your book and should tell you straightaway that from 15 July to 15 August it can reach me at Villa Wassing, Badgastein. But how much more pleased I will be to see the second volume!

Many thanks once more for your kind invitation; the four of us are still unable to travel to Switzerland.

Please give your wife our kind regards. By now you must have a considerable number of children romping about.

As ever,
Freud

125B

15 September 1921

Dear Professor Freud,

I have not yet thanked you for your kind acceptance of my dedication because I wanted to be able to let you know what was finally happening to my book at the same time. That I can now do, since Springer in Berlin have had a look at the manuscript and have at once declared themselves willing to publish it.[1] They estimate it will run to 500 pages and have offered what for a 'beginner' are most advantageous terms. I don't think, however, that the book can be printed this year, but hope it will come out during the first few months of next year.

May I take this opportunity of commending to you my colleague, Prinzhorn,[2] who will be calling on you very soon? He has a fresh mind, unburdened by prejudice, is very receptive if not very deep, has an artist's love of independence and strong dislike of all authority, is, as far as I can tell, trustworthy, and has a difficult marriage. I treated his wife some years ago for a grave psychosis. He did a good job of setting up the Heidelberg museum for the artistic works of mental patients.[3]

I am not sure if you are back in Vienna but hope in any case that you have had a good holiday. Your latest book[4] has been on my desk for several days and I am very much looking forward to reading it.

With kind regards, ever yours, [L. Binswanger]

[1] Diary II, p. 115: 'Manuscript sent to Springer on the 10th [August], after [I had] asked him on 26 July and he at once agreed.' And p. 118: '19 September agreement with Springer about my book.'

[2] Hans Prinzhorn (1886–1933), psychiatrist who became widely known for his work on the 'paintings of the mentally ill'. Cf. Jarchov (1980) and Geinitz (1986/87).

[3] Binswanger had seen the 'Exhibition of paintings and sculpture by mental patients' in the Heidelberg Psychiatric Clinic on 13 September 1920 on his way back from the congress in Leiden and wrote of an 'overpowering impression', see diary II, p. 91. Prinzhorn then visited the Bellevue in October and December 1920; *ibid.*, p. 96, and visitors' book, p. 50.

[4] *Group Psychology and the Analysis of the Ego*, Vienna (1921e) was published at the beginning of August 1921; see Jones (1953–7), Vol. 3, p. 45.

126F

3 November 1921

Prof. Dr. Freud   Vienna IX, Berggasse 19

Dear Dr. Binswanger,

On my return to Vienna five weeks ago I was very glad to learn from your letter that you, your wife and your flock of children are all well.

Dr. Prinzhorn gave us a most interesting lecture,[1] in which, however, he kept off the subject of analysis. He personally made a good impression.

I am glad that despite my great age you give me hope of living to see the first volume of your work. Let us hope that the second does not put my stamina to too hard a test.

Your excellent clinic accommodates at present – as well as my old patient Gi. – someone in whom I am interested both because of his perceptive writings and also because he is the cousin of one of my closest women friends (formerly a patient): Prof. V. of I. May I ask you what is wrong with him and if you think he will ever be able to return to his work?

With kind regards,
Yours, Freud

[1] Lecture held in the Vienna Psychoanalytic Society, 12 October 1921 'On mental patients who draw and primitives', author's abstract in *Internat. Zschr. Psychoanal.*, Vol. 7 (1921), p. 529.

127B

Kreuzlingen, [8] November 1921

Dear Professor Freud,

It is always a particular pleasure to set eyes on your handwriting and to hear your news.

Professor V. displayed anxiety and obsessional symptoms even in childhood, had pronounced delusional ideas in his student days, was never free from obsessional fears, obsessional acts, etc., from which his literary output, too, suffered severely. In 1918, this was the basis of a grave psychosis, no doubt triggered off by his approaching old age, the material, until then elaborated more or less neurotically, now being given psychotic expression. In addition, there was intense psychomotor excitation, which continues to be present, even though subject to strong fluctuations. He is in our closed section here, but is usually calm enough in the afternoons to be allowed to receive visitors, to join us for tea, to go on excursions, etc. He is still so dominated by his fears and precautions, which clearly border on compulsion and delusion, that, though his formal logic is quite un-impaired, there can be no question of his engaging in scholarly activity. True, he takes an interest in everything, still has excellent judgement of men and the world and a remarkable memory; but he can keep his mind fixed on scholarly subjects for short periods only. I believe that, with time, the psychomotor excitation will continue to decrease slowly, but I do not think that there will a restoration of the status quo prior to his acute psychosis, or a resumption of academic work. I would ask you, of course, to be sure to keep me covered when you pass on these details. Have you read his Luther? It is a terrible pity that he will probably never again be able to draw on his vast store of knowledge or to use his immense library.

Frau Gi. turned up voluntarily this time, unless it was under the pressure of financial circumstances, since her husband believes he can no longer afford to allow her her former level of luxury and she wants to try to learn here how to do without one or two things. She has asked us not to constrain her as we did the last time but to leave her to her own initiative, and I was pleased to agree to this. However, the results bore out my doubts, for in the six weeks she has been with us she has achieved nothing of importance by her own initiative, merely leading me up the garden path which, as I have said, is only what I expected. Her husband is here at present and we are still thinking about what method we are going to use.

The contract with Springer for my book is ready.[1] The manuscript will be ready for the printers very soon and I hope that the book may still appear this winter. Before it does, however, I must point out that apart from the preface it will hold little interest for you, with the possible exception of the conclusion, which amounts to a psychology of the individual but without going to deeply into the empirico-psychological element. I shall then proceed to my next task without delay, and very much hope that your stamina will prevail over my tardiness and chronic lack of time.

I have probably already told you that there are just two of us doc-tors here now, and that my practice has picked up once again.

With kind regards,

Ever yours, [L. Binswanger]

[1] In addition to the contract of 30 October–3 November 1921, the B.A. holds the whole of Binswanger's correspondence with the Julius Springer Verlag, Berlin; cf. B.A. 443/79.

128F

Vienna, 24 November 1921[1]

Dear Dr. Binswanger,

Many thanks for your kindness in supplying the details concerning V. It was quite predictable that Frau Gi. would achieve nothing 'by her own efforts'. Your book will interest me all the same, and apart from that I am very much looking forward to the long life you have promised me. Very cordially yours,

Freud

[1] Postcard.

129B

22 April 1922
Constance, P.O. Box 83

Dear Professor Freud,

Herr Gi. has repeatedly begged me to ask you whether you think his wife could be given psychoanalytic treatment with any hope of success, and where in your opinion the best point of attack would be. Although I still clearly recall your views on the entire case, I would nevertheless like to execute my commission faithfully. I am not quite clear about Herr Gi.'s true motives. I have told him that I should be happy to continue the analytic work with his wife insofar as her condition permits, but that – after you had done what was humanly possible – the main emphasis must now be laid on her education, with which, in fact, we have already made quite appreciable outward progress. Frau Gi. is to stay on for some time; however, a return to Germany for financial reasons, possibly to Muthmann, has been mooted.

I hope to be able to send you my book in June. Last week I took on the slave labour of preparing the index.[1] Should you agree that I am trying to reach in a conceptual way the same goal that you have approached so closely along the empirical path, namely laying the foundations for a psychological interpretation of man, then I should be very glad indeed. It goes without saying that the empiricist must pave the way, but I should be glad if you in particular appreciated (as, for example, Bleuler does not) that 'work on the concept'[2] is important even for empirical research.

With kind regards,

Ever yours, [L. Binswanger]

[1] '16 April [1922] Index completed after strenuous work from 28 March until today, Easter Sunday, 16 April.' (Diary II, p. 125).
[2] Binswanger had placed a quote from Hegel at the front of his *Allgemeine Psychologie* (1922a) [General Psychology]: 'True thoughts and scientific insight are only to be won through the labour of the Notion.' (Hegel: *Phenomenology of Spirit*, transl. H.V. Miller, Oxford, 1977, p. 43).

130F

27 April 1922
Prof. Dr. Freud   Vienna IX, Berggasse 19

Dear Dr. Binswanger,
Regarding Frau Gi., my opinion is that in her case it is probable that nothing will be accomplished except by a combination of analysis and prohibition (counter-compulsion).[1] I regret very much that, at the time, I could only avail myself of the first; the second can only be imposed in an institution.[2]

I have, surely, never belittled your efforts; yet it is a pity that this volume is to be no more than an introduction.

With kind regards to you, your wife, your flock of children, and also to Frau Gi.,

Yours ever, Freud

[1] This concept also in Freud (1919a), *S.E.* Vol. XVII, p. 166.
[2] On this point Binswanger writes in (1956c), p. 70 in the 1957 English edition: 'This "opinion" is all the more interesting because to my knowledge it stands alone and Freud has not expressed it elsewhere. Once again, as happened so often, Freud proved to be much more "tolerant" than many of his adherents who regard such "a combination" as a professional error. I learned this personally in connection with the case (described in my lecture on psychotherapy) [...] of a hysterical *singultus* coupled with loud screams which I treated by a combination of analysis and "counter-compulsion". Here action was required, and urgently so – it took the form of seizing the patient by the neck – if the patient who up until then had defied all treatment was not to remain master of the situation this time too.'

131F

Vienna, 8 May 1922[1]

May the Kreuzlingen local group,[2] whom I thank most cordially for their telegram on the occasion of my 66th birthday, prosper and grow; may its female members be ever favoured with rapid improvement and may its male members produce work with the speed of greased lightning!

These are the friendly wishes of

Yours, Freud

[Addition in the hand of Binswanger, who apparently forwarded the postcard to the patient, for whom it was also intended: 'Kind regards from Lake Geneva and best wishes for the sponge and soap!! Are you taking the air as well? My wife sends her best wishes and so does her sister. Cordially and fraternally, your Dr. and bath superintendent.']

[1] Postcard.
[2] Meant jocularly. The card is addressed jointly to Binswanger and the patient Frau Gi.

Seventh International Psychoanalytic Congress, Berlin, 25 to 27 September 1922

Binswanger wrote in his diary only very briefly on his participation in this congress:

'23 September went to Berlin for the 7th International Psychoanalytic Congress. 24–28 September *Berlin*. Congress not on the same level as the last one in The Hague. Since then even greater material and personal distance from psychoanalysis. But respect for Freud remains the same. Took Butz [the second son, Ludwig] with me to the lectures.' (Diary II, p. 147.)

132B

Kreuzlingen, 31 January 1923

Dear Professor Freud,

Having allowed the first day of the New Year to pass without writing to you, I would at least like to make sure that this does not happen with the first month. I have been thinking of you a great deal, partly because now that I have done the necessary spadework, the idea of my book on psychoanalysis[1] is gradually taking clearer shape, but partly for purely personal reasons. Towards the end of the year, I dreamt that I had invited you to come here for a consultation. When I woke up, I discovered that this pious wish had just one real component, namely that the patient in question was well-endowed with foreign currency whereas all the other attributes (age, nature of the psychosis) were absent. Reality turned out to be all the more grotesque in relation to my dream in that the patient's family, as I heard today, have asked Kraepelin,[2] who is at present in Switzerland, to look at the patient.

I was very sorry to hear from Frau Dr. Oberholzer[3] that your family has suffered another grievous loss.[4] My own family has so far been spared all ills and we are still expanding. At the end of September our fifth son[5] was born and has been distinguishing himself by being especially vigorous and healthy. My wife is still breast-feeding him and is well even though she does feel that she has expended most of her strength on her children. But despite everything she still devotes much of her time to our patients. On the other hand, I recently heard to my sorrow that my stepmother,[6] whom you once met, is suffering from advanced intestinal cancer. Her operation could only be considered a palliative one. My stepmother is not yet 50, was married for the second time to a much younger man[7] two years ago, and has only just attained her full intellectual development and maturity.

You have never written to me about my book, something, however, that neither upsets nor grieves me. I had to expect that my whole approach would strike you as 'philosophically' alien, or even completely repugnant, because it pays scant regard to empirical experience. I hope you know me well enough to appreciate that my personal friendship for you is in no way affected by what you make of the book. True, I wished to have your name in it, but simply because I wanted, in my first major scientific contribution, to proclaim myself your pupil and thus to express my gratitude to you. For the rest, I am very much looking forward to your new book.

Since Berlin, Frau. Gi. has granted me slightly deeper glimpses into her neurosis, but I hardly believe that since she left you she has elaborated and grasped essentially new aspects of herself. Mostly she seems to be ruminating about the analysis she had with you and everything still revolves around her husband. At all events, she now manages more easily, when one takes some interest in her, to make some concessions to reality. For instance, her attitude towards her husband has slightly improved, and the husband is very satisfied. Her chief motive, however, seems to be the wish to make an effort while her husband is still alive, ostensibly to give him pleasure but in reality, no doubt, in anticipation of the self-reproaches that are bound to appear after his death. The fact, moreover, that her complaints against her husband are the same old ones was fairly obvious. The husband, incidentally, is still enjoying the best of health.

I hope, dear Professor, to hear from you one day soon. Please give my regards to your wife and to anyone else in your family who might remember me. My wife joins me in sending you kind regards.

Ever yours, [L. Binswanger]

[1] The planned Part Two of *Einführung in die Probleme der allgemeinen Psychologie* [Introduction to the Problems of General Psychology] which never appeared; cf. also note 2 to 113B. In the diary (II, pp. 151–3) Binswanger says about it: '7 January. [...] Reading *Dilthey*, more of Hegel's youth which I find ever more gripping, especially since I have read a lot of the New Testament. The character of Jesus becomes apparent to me for the first time in the Bible. Read *Schleiermacher's* monologues and shorter writings, very strong impression from the law of nature and moral law. – Have begun *Krueger's* boring Development Psychology. Have yet to read *Kant's* "Inquiry concerning the Distinctness of the Principles of Theology and Morality" [1764c].

'From all this, the idea of a work about the principles (?) of psychoanalysis has become clearer, or: the philosophy of psychoanalysis combined with *Einführung in die allgemeinen Psychologie* [Introduction to General Psychology].

'28 January. "Critique of psychoanalysis"? Very much attracted by Cassirer again. Read in the third volume of his cognition problem with *Hegel, Schelling, Fries, Schopenhauer* very profitably. Schelling has for the first time stepped out of the darkness that surrounded him. Got closer to Hegel [...].'

[2] Emil Kraepelin (1856–1926) Prof. of Psychiatry in Dorpat (1886–91), Heidelberg (1891–1903) and Munich (1903–22), creator of a modern psychological nosology. The visit to Switzerland is not mentioned in Kraepelin's *Lebenserinnerungen* (1983). Binswanger recorded a meeting with Kraepelin a year later in his diary (III, p. 190): '16 April [1924] *Kraepelin* last week for a consultation. Very strong impression of his vitality and his medical and clinical energy.'

[3] Cf. note 7 to 70F.

[4] This probably refers to the suicide of Freud's niece, Cäcilie ('Mausi') Graf, the daughter of his sister Rosa. Freud was specially fond of this his 'best niece' and was 'deeply shaken' by the tragedy, as he wrote to Jones on 24 August 1922; see Jones (1953–7), Vol. 3, p. 91; Freud (1993e), p. 499, and his assessment of Mausi's predicament in Freud (1996g), in his letter of 22 August 1922 to Sam Freud.

[5] Dieter Binswanger, born 29 August 1922.

[6] Marie-Luise, née Meyer-Wolde, died 1941. Cf. Diary II, p. 154: '28 January. [...] *Mamis* illness very unsettled' and p. 155: '12 February. Mami had been quite given

up on the 8th, but now the abscess has been lanced she has revived. Schlegel [her husband] here today.'
[7] Ernst Schlegel.

133F

7 February 1923
Prof. Dr. Freud   Vienna IX, Berggasse 19

Dear Dr. Binswanger,

Before I reply to your kind letter of the day before yesterday, I would like to dispose of a professional matter, which is one of the reasons for my writing.

I am currently treating a very distinguished American, N. To. from S. Francisco, a retired businessman with slight sexual inhibitions. The man we are sending to you is his older brother, whom I know only from his brother's reports and from the cousin who is looking after him. He is said to be a confirmed homosexual, obstinate, intractable and to suffer from the gravest guilt feelings after every sexual encounter. The enclosed letter from Dr. Deutsch[1] will show you to what extent his organic complaints are mere excuses or are being used as such.

Since he is unmistakably sinking ever deeper into hypochondria, dissipation and a compulsion for tormenting those relatives who are at his mercy, I have suggested separating him from his cousin, a selfless, simple and kindly lady, and handing him over to you for care and psychic guidance. The intention is not, of course, to try to redress his perversions – that would be hopeless – but to find some way of reconciling him with life on a homosexual basis and hence to find a possible *modus vivendi* for him. Since he is very rich even by American standards, you have a free hand to do everything you can for him. Above all, keep a firm hold on him, since otherwise his guilt feelings and sadism will lead him to a bad end.

The good news about your family – good except for that about your stepmother – gave me much pleasure. Unfortunately I can see few prospects of visiting you again in the near future since a consultation trip to Bellevue would not easily make up for what would be lost here. So don't count on it too much.

Your book[2] has impressed me greatly – but has, admittedly, also been a disappointment for it is not what you have repeatedly led me to expect in correspondence. I anticipated that you would be building a bridge between clinical psychiatry and psychoanalysis which you would then cross in a second volume. The dedication is no doubt a vestige of your earlier intention and in any case does me great honour. I console myself with the thought that Bleuler has no closer links with the contents than I have myself.[3]

With kind regards to you, your wife and your children,

Yours, Freud

[1] Felix Deutsch (1884–1964) intern and psychoanalyst, had treated the patient for a 'pseudo-angina pectoris' and considered the attacks to be of psychogenetic origin. For Deutsch's biography see Murphy (1964).

[2] The copy of Binswanger's book (1922a) with the author's manuscript dedication of 16 August 1922 still exists in Freud's library in the Freud Museum, London. (Information kindly supplied by Michael Molnar.)

[3] In fact Binswanger wrote in his diary (II, p. 135) under the date 24/25 June 1922: 'Depressed by Bleuler's inability to acknowledge my book which I had given him at the second proof stage.'

134B

Kreuzlingen, 23 February 1923

Dear Professor Freud,

Many thanks for your letter and for the referral of Herr To. I was very glad that everything had been so well contrived on your side and that the patient was handed over expressly to me. On the second day of his stay here he produced a severe and doubtless psychogenic attack of asthma. When he realised, however, that he was impressing no one, he displayed no further acute symptoms of any severity. I have assigned a nurse to him; he is given oxygen baths, which have a favourable effect on his pulse, bromide, mild soporifics, etc., and is already getting used to a regular way of life, with walks, drives, etc. I get on well with him personally and he has caused us no real problems so far. The only thing I would still like to hear from you or his brother is what I am expected to do if he suddenly decides to leave. So far, it is true, there have been no indications of that, but it could well happen one day. It would be a good thing, perhaps, if I received official instructions from his brother (which I should only communicate to the patient in an emergency) not to let him go before I had notified you. It would thus be possible to gain time.

My psychiatric-clinical view of the case is that, apart from his inversion, he is a man with a hypomanic[1] constitution who, on the

163

basis of his own statements, has had very brief attacks of deep depression, first ten and then again three years ago, and who is now in a state between mania and depression. In addition he has the usual pronounced hysterical traits. His hypochondriac ideas can well be described as hypochondriac delusions. My diagnosis implies that I believe the prognosis is wholly favourable, although I am not of course able to say anything about the duration of the present phase of the illness.

May I ask you to thank his brother on my behalf for sending me the X-rays, etc.?

What you say about my book is what I expected. I hope that I shall still be able to show you at the very least fragments of that part of the work that is more closely concerned with the empirical aspects and also with the bridge between psychiatry and psychoanalysis.

With kind regards to you and your family,

Ever yours, [L. Binswanger]

[1] Corrected from 'hypochondrischer' – hypochondriac.

135B

Kreuzlingen, 28 March 1923

Dear Professor Freud,

The To. case did not turn out as any of us expected. Breathing and cardiac action became gradually more impaired, so much so that we were left in no doubt that there was an organic cause. In the middle of the month large quantities of blood in the sputum with corresponding pulmonary symptoms suggested a pulmonary infarct associated with bronchial pneumonia. Cardiac action became sluggish. The former nephritis flared up again, there were deliria that quickly led to a comatose state to which the patient succumbed on the 26th inst. I had called the relatives to the sickbed just as soon as we were certain about the organic symptoms. They took it very well and greatly facilitated our task. A postmortem has fully confirmed the clinical diagnoses. Large organised thrombi were discovered in the heart.

One coronary artery was severely constricted and atheromatous. The major arteries of the base of the brain were badly sclerosed. It now appears, therefore, that neither the patient's depressive nor his hysterical symptoms during the past few months were purely psychogenic, but represented his specific reactions to incipient physical deterioration. As soon as I had reached that opinion, I called in a specialist for internal medicine who took over the physical treatment. Perhaps you will be so kind as to forward this report to Dr. Deutsch, for whom it will be of some interest.

With kind regards,

Ever yours, [L. Binswanger]

136F

10 May 1923[1]
Vienna

Many thanks to Ludwig and Gi.[2] from the now 67-year-old Fr[eud]

[1] Postcard. Postmarked 11 May 1923.
[2] Freud used the first name of the patient, who at that time was again undergoing in-patient treatment at the Bellevue. Presumably she and Binswanger had written jointly to Freud on his birthday.

137B

Kreuzlingen, 27 August 1923

Dear Professor Freud

I only recently came into possession of the fifth volume of your *Sammlung kleiner Schriften*[1] [Collected Short Papers], and having just finished reading the History of an Infantile Neurosis[2] I feel impelled to send you a few lines about it at once, since it has made so very great an impression upon me. I admire your perspicacity all over again and the incredible intellectual work underlying the actual analysis (which is not even reported in full) and your account of it. Above all, however, I would like to put on record that you are the first person to place the discussion[3] (with Jung and Adler) on a truly scientific basis and to test the various theoretical views against the individual empirical fact. The ideas of the others have always struck me as being more in the nature of sudden fancies or intellectual hobbyhorses than the results of true scientific investigations. I found the case itself of the utmost interest and I must say that I could raise almost no objection, even in respect of the time factor. What you have to say about the primal scene in general as well as in this particular case, and about the differences in approach, has helped me a great deal. The whole problem of the *primal scene*, i.e., the convergence of all the analytic threads to an original point, is of the greatest importance even in methodological respects, and I was most pleasantly impressed by the careful and yet 'inviting' way in which you proceed from ontogenesis to the phylogenetic instinct.

My heel analysis,[4] which I have once again brought out for the purpose of a lecture before our Thurgau-Baden Psychiatric Society,[5] has convinced me of the accuracy of reports by adults about their infantile neurosis. That analysis, incomplete though it is, has helped greatly to prepare me for your case. Conversely, I am sorry that my heel analysis should have been put to so little theoretical use in psychiatric literature. It also makes an interesting counterpart and parallel to your case, if only because it concerns a fully developed infantile neurosis which, however, has continued almost unchanged into adult life but in which it is fairly easy to distinguish what was pre-formed in childhood and what was added later.

Your work has once again aroused my longing to see you, and I would like once again to invite you to visit me if ever you are any-where nearby. Your daughter, whose style is no longer distinguishable from her father's, would be most welcome here, too. I fear, however, that as with Mohammed and the mountain, I shall simply have to go to Vienna myself one day, if you will still have me, that is. It wouldn't be before next year, however. In the autumn I shall probably be going to Madrid, where I have excellent psychological and psychiatric connections and the opportunity to make my psychoanalytic views known in lectures and in writing.[6] In any case, I am again drawing closer to psychoanalysis because in my next volume[7] I shall be attempting to link your psychology and what theoretical insights I have accumulated since, thus implementing the original plan first conceived during your visit here and for which, at the time, I still lacked the necessary theoretical knowledge. My Introduction is, after all, nothing but a detour, as the preface makes clear.[8]

My family is very well. The three big ones are at present by the North Sea.[9] The youngest, who will be one in the near future, gives us pleasure anew each day with his health and 'intellect'. The more I observe my children, or one might say the more I see of them, the more I come to agree with you that it is impossible to attribute to them a psychic life and 'unconscious ideas' at too early a stage.

With the kindest regards from my wife and myself,

Ever yours, [L. Binswanger]

[1] *Sammlung kleiner Schriften zur Neurosenlehre*, 5th printing, Leipzig, Vienna and Zurich: International Psychoanalytic Publishing House, 1922.

[2] Freud (1918b) ['The Wolf Man']. Was published in the 4th printing of *Sammlung kleiner Schriften zur Neurosenlehre* in any case.

[3] Corrected from 'controversy'.

[4] Binswanger (1911a).

[5] Lecture on 8 September 1923; cf. Larese (1965), p. 27. The diary entry (II, p. 168) under this date says: 'Lecture on psychoanalysis at Seehof.'

[6] On 18 October 1923 Binswanger gave a Spanish lecture in the Real Academia de Medicina in Madrid entitled 'Introduction to Medical Psychoanalysis' for which he took his heel analysis as the focal point. Ludwig Binswanger, 'Introducción a la psicoanalisis médica' (1924a). Binswanger noted in his diary (II, p. 175): 'Benevolent astonishment at the Gerda case.' – While he was in Madrid he learnt from Eitingon, whom he met there by chance, of Freud's cancer and the operation on his jaw which was carried out, according to Pichler's case notes, on 26 September 1923. (Jones 1953–7, Vol. 3, pp. 497ff.) See Binswanger (1956c), p. 71 in the 1957 English edition.

[7] In 1923 there is more in the diary (II, pp. 158–66) about the development of 'part two' of the *allgemeine Psychologie*:

'4 April. Meeting in the Insel Hotel [Constance] with *Pfänder* of Munich who, by his appreciation and discussion, encouraged me to continue my work (methodological synopsis of the individual psychology so far). [...].

'23 April. [...] Reading *Spranger* (with mixed feelings), Kuno Fischer's *Hegel* (phenomenology) and *Leibniz* (on monadology). Hegel and Leibniz are now in the forefront as far as I am concerned. In my thoughts always onto my next book. Read carefully through the chapter on *Freud* in my manuscript. It is a start, only this foundation needs more depth. [...].

'10 August. Met *Husserl* on the Reichenau. Disappointed with the "philosopher", no genius, too academic, pleasantly surprised by the man himself. He does not in fact make a sharp enough distinction between the psychological and the transcendental. – Parallels to Freud: the man, the work, late recognition, school. Freud the wittier, H. the greater thinker.

'15 August. *Husserl's* visit in the Garden House. Lecture on the nature of phenomenology. Ph. as consistent subjectivism which objectivity allows to emerge spontaneously. Relation to *Descartes*, whose basic teachings I am only now getting to grips with. (Learning more through Cassirer.) Relation to Kant: unity of the norm as constituent element of the object. Beyond Kant: mathematics as an *example*, not a borderline area vis-à-vis applied sciences, breaking down of barriers Kant has put up; free rein for the other sciences. Looking for "typology" in the latter. Husserl's a priori unlike Kant's *a priori* not the general case. Problems in Husserl's a priori and the absolute. [...]

'On Sunday, 12 August, "Preface" to the new book written! [never published]'

[8] It was not in the Preface that Binswanger tried to clarify this, but in the Introduction originally planned as a preface to (1922a): 'In carrying out our psychiatric task we actually distance ourselves more and more from concrete reality, from the psychological individual, and thus our path divides in two different directions: one leads to the concept of the mind, the mental context of function, or the mental organism; the other leads to the concept of a neurophysiological context and so to the brain or

cerebral cortex. It is now valid to make the observation that neither the function concept nor the organism concept, nor the mental nor the cerebral physiological, have anything directly to do with the concrete reality known as the psychological individual. Both provide "diversions" with the aim of clarification and alteration of the concrete reality, diversions on the way from individual to individual.' Binswanger (1922a), pp. 1–2. Even in this Introduction, however, Binswanger does not spell it out clearly that this book was seen as the first part of an account, the later part of which would deal with psychoanalysis in depth. In the additional Preface (1922a) it simply says: 'This book stems from the author's endeavours to achieve clarity about the conceptual basis of what the psychiatrist perceives, considers and does at the "sickbed", from a psychological and psychotherapeutic point of view.' *ibid*, p. v. Cf. also note 2 to 142B.

[9] Robert, Ludwig and Hilde Binswanger were on the North Sea coast until 7 September 1923; see Diary II, p. 168 (7 Sept. 1923).

138F

Eden Hotel, Rome, 3 September 1923[1]

Dear Dr. Binswanger,
Your letter reached me here today and I was most gratified by what you had to say. My daughter who is with me, also sends you her thanks.[2]
   With many kind regards to you and your large family,

Yours, Freud

[1] Postcard.

[2] On this Rome trip before the two major operations on his cancer on 4 and 11 October 1923 see Jones (1953–7), Vol. 3, p. 103.

139B
[to Anna Freud]

Kreuzlingen, 19 November 1923

Dear Fräulein Freud,
In Madrid I heard from Dr. Eitingon that your father had had an operation on his jaw.[1] As long as everything [has] gone well and he is no longer in any danger, then this news has reawakened my long cherished wish to visit him again in Vienna. The admiration and love I feel for your father has not diminished over the years, but has increased. But I know that from his standpoint there is a certain disappointment that I have not taken a more active or leading role in

the psychoanalytic movement. I therefore direct my request to you, so that a refusal will be easier if a visit is not convenient for your father for personal or health reasons. If your father would be pleased for me to visit him, then I would ask him to fix a time himself. I can always set a couple of days aside during the winter until mid-March. In any case I should be very grateful if you would be so kind as to write me a few lines at once about his condition.

In old comradeship,

Yours ever,
[L. Binswanger]

[1] For the development of Freud's cancer, see Jones (1953–7), Vol. 3, pp. 94–102.

140F

24 November 1923[1]
Prof. Dr. Freud   Vienna IX, Berggasse 19

Dear Dr. Binswanger,

My daughter has passed to me for an answer the letter about me she has received from you. Its contents gave me great pleasure. What you say is indeed right. I should be even more pleased if you had maintained your leading position in Switzerland or could have placed your institution more exclusively in the service of analysis. But our relationship is based on firm motives of a different kind and is independent of such objections. So I should be very pleased to see you here again. It is out of the question at the moment, of course. I am convalescing slowly and the treatment I am receiving drains me of all strength.[2] But if all goes well, it could well be that what today would be a burden to me will, towards the spring, be a pleasure.

With warm thanks for your offer,

Yours, Freud

[1] Typewritten letter. [Freud bought an Underwood typewriter in about October 1923, but he seems never to have really taken to it. Examples of typewritten letters exist in diminishing number over the years 1924–7, after which there are very few indeed. T.R.]
[2] Cf. the detailed case history in Jones (1953–7), Vol. 3, pp. 497ff. See also Romm (1983).

141B

Kreuzlingen, 3 January 1924

Dear Professor Freud,

I do not normally send New Year letters but I cannot refrain from putting in an appearance this year, so crucial for your convalescence, in order to send you my best wishes. At the same time I want to express my cordial thanks for your reply to the letter I sent to your daughter. Although it offered me no prospect of seeing you in the near future, it nevertheless gave me great pleasure because you so frankly testified not only to what has kept us apart in recent times but also to the personal bonds between us. It was one of the greatest pleasures I had towards the end of the year. I need hardly say, after everything we have already gone through together in this respect,[1] how much I wish you a complete recovery. And should it really be granted to me to see you in the spring, I should be a happy man, though of course even then my visit should be in no way a burden to you. You know me well enough to realise that I should be not in the least offended if you had to put me off even longer. I shall be going to Rome[2] with my wife from the middle of March to the middle of April, and an opportunity will probably not arise before that. But should we meet once again, I would hope to make it clearer to you what precisely I intended with my book and to what extent it was essential groundwork for me. I feel that although I have had a great deal of appreciation, with few exceptions my intentions have been more or less misunderstood; above all, nothing was further from my mind than a 'philosophical neutralisation' of psychoanalysis.

Please do not take up your time and energy in replying to these lines; I am sustained by the sentiments you expressed in your last letter and that is enough for me. My wife, who also wishes you a speedy full recovery, sends you her kindest regards. I myself remain, in old affection and friendship,

Yours, [L. Binswanger]

[1] Binswanger was certainly also thinking here about his own operation on a tumour; cf. note 1 to 65F.

[2] On 17 April 1924 Binswanger drove with his wife, via Milan and Florence, to Rome in order to give a lecture on 3 May in the Palazzo Giustiniani on 'Modern psychology and psychiatry' (Binswanger 1925a). From there they made a detour to Naples from 6–9 May, returning home on 14 May. (See diary II, pp. 1912–20 and III, p. 1.)

142B

Kreuzlingen, 11 April 1924

Dear Professor Freud,

I regret very much that I shall not be able to attend the Salzburg Congress[1] since next week we are due to leave for Rome, after which I am expected back here by a specific date. I should very much have liked to see you in Salzburg, but would like even more to meet you in Vienna. I still hope that will be possible one day. At the moment I am so deep in the preparation of the theoretical part of my next book, which will be devoted in the main to psychoanalysis, that I keep conversing with you in spirit.[2] But quite apart from that, I often long to be with you.

With kindest regards to you, your wife and your daughter Anna,

As always, yours, [L.Binswanger]

[1] The 8th International Psychoanalytic Congress, Salzburg, 21–23 April 1924. Freud also was unable to attend this congress owing to an attack of influenza; see Jones (1953–7), Vol. 3, pp. 69ff. and pp. 106ff.

[2] Binswanger wrote about this in his *Reminiscences*: 'I still have my very extensive, unpublished, manuscripts recording these "conversations". Since they bear witness to my continually coming to grips with Freud's intellectual world, perhaps I may briefly refer to them. Entitled "Freud's Psychology and the Structure of Personality", they deal first with the definition of the psychic in Freud, that is to say, with its "meaningfulness". It is generally known that Freud interprets "meaning" [*Sinn*] as "significance, intent, tendency, and place within a chain of psychic connections". I analysed all these terms in detail on the basis of my *Probleme der allgemeinen Psychologie* [Problems of General Psychology] and followed this with a lengthy discussion of Freud's description of the psychic life, which centres around the theory of the psychic conflict and the psychic agencies, i.e., in a personification and dramatisation of the life of the psyche, and which has never before been carried out so systematically and so penetratingly. [...]

'I have not published any of these manuscripts and the "second volume" on psychoanalysis never appeared because, as I have said before, my study of Husserl's phenomenology (and later Heidegger's ontology) soon led me beyond the method I had followed in my investigations. This method has been confined largely to the conceptual and the methodological plane, so that I could not go to the roots of Freud's conception and theories of the psyche and of human nature. This I did only in my papers [Binswanger (1936c) and (1936d)] written on the occasion of Freud's eightieth birthday; today, however, I no longer regard his naturalism, which is brought to the fore in these papers, as something merely negative.' Binswanger (1956c), pp. 72–3 in the 1957 English edition.

143B

Kreuzlingen, 27 August 1924

Dear Professor Freud,

I was delighted with your paper on masochism[1] and should be most grateful if you could let me have an offprint of it and, if possible, of some of the preceding short papers, too, if you still have enough copies. Since I possess almost all your earlier papers in the form of offprints, I am anxious to add the most recent ones. Needless to say, I have all your major works. I often long to see you and to discuss matters with you, but I assume that a visit would still be a burden to you, and for that reason I shall not bother you.

Everything is well with us, and our six are healthy. The youngest is now the same age as the oldest was when last you saw him. The latter has done very well in throwing off his ties to his mother[2] and has become an independent and strapping young fellow. He is already in the Obersekunda.[3] The clinic has suddenly become very busy again this year, because the Germans have been allowed to come back. I have had a young assistant from Berlin[4] since April, very capable analytically. All my mental efforts are now dedicated to my next book,[5] in which I intend to apply what general psychological knowledge I have gleaned to psychoanalysis. That will probably be the main work of my life. Once psychoanalysis has held one in its grip, it never lets go again; depending on predisposition, one surrenders to it practically or theoretically, unable to deny that it has become one's life work.

With kind regards from my wife and myself,

Ever yours, [L.Binswanger]

[1] 'The Economic Problem of Masochism' (1924c).

[2] Cf. the report of Freud's visit to Kreuzlingen, in the Appendix, p. 235 ('mother-fixation') and 91B with its note 11.

[3] The seventh year in a German secondary school. [A.J.P.]

[4] This refers to Clemens E. Benda (1898–1974), who was an assistant doctor at the Bellevue from 1924–28. Cf. the obituary in the *New York Times*, 25 April 1975, p. 38. See also Binswanger (1957e), p. 35, and diary II, p. 188: '16 April [1924] Dr. *Benda* appointed end of March, very gifted psychologically and philosophically, good doctor, very stimulating for me, finally one with whom contact is possible without a great deal of words. Appears reliable person, very critical, but with complete and genuine passion for all matters of the mind.'

[5] Cf. this with the entry in diary III, p. 1:

'6 June [Binswanger erroneously wrote May] [1924]. This evening […] the introduction to my new book drafted, leading off with the relationship of the particular and the general and the moment of individuation in psychology.'

144F

Semmering, 10 September 1924[1]
Prof. Dr. Freud   Vienna IX, Berggasse 19

Dear Dr. Binswanger,
I should gladly have granted your modest wish, but the *Zeitschrift*
no longer issues offprints and so I have none. I am delighted to hear
of your family's progress. My own health is not bad and a meeting
no longer out of the question, as it was only a few months ago.

Very cordially yours,
Freud

[1] Typewritten letter.

145B

Kreuzlingen, 12 January 1925

Dear Professor Freud,
For some time now I have been wanting to quote to you a passage
from a short work Herder wrote in 1778. It could serve as a motto
for your life's work and I shall perhaps put it at the beginning of the
book on psychoanalysis on which I am working at this moment. The
piece which I am no longer able to withhold from you is found in
one of Herder's works that also anticipates many other psychoanalytic
insights, namely his *Vom Erkennen und Empfinden der menschlichen
Seele: Bemerkungen und Träume* [On the Recognition and Perception
of the Human Soul: Observations and Dreams]. It goes as follows:
   'The greatest truths, like the most wicked lies, the most sublime
knowledge and the most hideous mistakes of a people, generally grow
from seed corns that are not recognised as such; they are activated
by influences that are often taken for the very opposite of what they
are. The physician, therefore, who wants to cure ills should seek their
foundations; yet when he seeks them there the child or the sick century
will not thank him for it. If he delves down to our cherished illness
and merely tries to spin a web of health over it – who is greater and
more welcome than he is! He is the pillar of all knowledge and all
glory. But should he reach for our hearts, for the cherished emotions
and foibles which make us feel so good – away with him, that betrayer
of mankind, that murderer of our greatest truths and joys! We wanted
to be his allies, and be of service to him up there among the treetops,

but, ingrate that he is, he prefers to grub around the roots and rip away at the smooth bark – how ungrateful!'[1]

I have read *Der Untergang des Ödipuskomplexes*[2] with great pleasure. I don't know why I should have received so many insights from those few pages which, if anything, sum up what is fairly well known. If it is not too much trouble, I should be very glad if you could send me just one line, but I do not expect it.

My wife and I send you and all your family our kind regards. In unchanging affection and gratitude,

Yours, [L. Binswanger]

[1] *Johann Gottfried von Herders sämmtliche Werke* [collected works], Zur Philosophie von Geschichte [on the philosophy of history], Part 9, Stuttgart, Tübingen, Cotta 1828, pp. 61f. Binswanger possessed this edition and had, as can be seen from the markings in his copy, gone through Herder's writing thoroughly. For access to the volume I am grateful for the kindness of Wolfgang and Trudi Binswanger. [A substantial selection of Herder's writings on the philosophy of history is published in English as *Reflections on the Philosophy of the History of Mankind*, ed. Frank E. Manuel, Chicago and London, 1968. T.R.]

[2] 'The Dissolution of the Oedipus Complex', Freud (1924d).

146F

27 January 1925[1]

Prof. Dr. Freud   Vienna IX, Berggasse 19

Dear Dr. Binswanger,

Many thanks for your sign of life of the 12th inst., that is, your letter with the Herder quotation. A multitude of distractions prevented me from getting down to writing a reply last week. I am of course delighted to hear that you continue to read my straggling little publications with pleasure. The next few issues of the *Zeitschrift* will have some more. But then there will be a long pause, for I am working on a revision of *The Interpretation of Dreams* for the Collected Works.[2] Perhaps there will be nothing else after that.

I take it that you, your wife and your family, now so numerous, are all well, although you did not mention them this time.

With kind regards,

Yours, Freud

[1] Typewritten letter.

[2] '*Gesamtausgabe*' – properly called the *Gesammelte Schriften*, Leipzig, Vienna and Zurich: Internationaler Psychoanalytischer Verlag, Vol. 2 (1925), pp. 1–543, and Vol. 3 (1925), pp. 1–185.

147B

Kreuzlingen, 15 February 1925

Dear Professor Freud,

Your letter, as always, has given me great pleasure. The news that you intend revising *The Interpretation of Dreams* for the Collected Works in person is very welcome, for that book holds the same central position among your works as *The Critique of Pure Reason* holds among Kant's. One is loath to see a stranger's hand in works of this sort. Incidentally, I have not yet congratulated you on your Collected Works. I think it is very well done and worthy of you in every respect, both in its appearance and in the way the material has been arranged![1]

You ask after my family. Everyone is well, thank God. None of our six children has so far given us the least cause for worry and we sometimes wonder how long this can go on, surrounded as we are here by the misfortunes of others. I consider myself especially favoured by fate because my oldest son is showing the same interest in the Greeks and in philosophy[2] as I have had since early youth. And though I continue to be his mentor and teacher in these fields, my lack of mathematical and astronomical aptitude and education affords my son opportunity enough to triumph over his *father* and to restore the necessary equilibrium.

I should like, if I may, to ask you a few questions that have arisen from my work and which you must answer or not depending on your mood, free time and state of health. I am content simply to put them to you.

I have long been impressed by your remark that the analyst's unconscious must be as passive towards the analysand as the telephone receiver is to the transmitting plate,[3] etc. I fully understand this pronouncement as a technical principle, but I have always wondered on what 'capacity' or intellectual faculty you think that this type of 'understanding' is really based. The reply: 'on the unconscious itself', would be circular and no real answer. You have to postulate a uniform intellectual disposition, equal in all people, and assume that, provided this disposition functions without personal strains (affective inhibitions), understanding will come about by itself. Now it is precisely in this 'by itself' that my problem lies. Far more interesting to me than making a successful interpretation and learning something new about someone else's unconscious is the problem of what it is that *enables* me to make the interpretation in the first place. One person

175

will reply: experience; but your technological analogy shows that you do not take so simple a view of the problem. After all, one has to ask how that kind of experience is possible, how it comes about. Am I right in thinking that you have thought no further about the problem and have been only too happy to leave it to the philosophers? But quite apart from the fact that it is not really a 'philosophical' problem, the 'student of human nature' must be concerned to find an answer to that problem, for either he must, on purely rationalist grounds, postulate the existence of a general 'organisation of reason' common to every man, or else he must end up with a mystical or at least romantic conception of man's intellectual intercourse. The problem strikes me as being of some practical importance, because I believe that psychoanalytic interpretation and understanding[4] are, in principle and historically, highly significant extensions and reinforcements of the so-called hermeneutic interpretation and exegesis as practised and investigated at length, especially by Schleiermacher[5] and Dilthey.[6]

In respect of the contrast between rationality and romanticism: I had never before felt the intensity of that contrast *in your work* so much as I did during a recent reading of your Moses of Michelangelo.[7] Only those can understand *your* character to any extent who can feel the force of that contrast in you. Anyone who can let Moses affect him in that way, who experiences Michelangelo, Shakespeare, Goethe, Leonardo[8] (as an artistic genius) as 'congenially' as every quotation and every comment of yours betrays that you do, and anyone who, on the other hand, can only attain full enjoyment of a work of art when he can explain 'rationally' whence the dimensions of that effect are derived, anyone, moreover, who understands the human soul so profoundly and at the same time knows how to combine its manifestations into so rational a scientific system – must have combined 'feeling and reason' not only quantitatively but also qualitatively to a most astonishing degree. The greater mystery for me in all this is that the tremendous weight of the rational element in you should go hand in hand with so large an amount of 'feeling' and I sometimes wonder whether you would have become the 'rationalist' you are had you come up against another trend than the current materialist rationalism, the materialism of natural science no less than the philosophical variety in the widest sense of the term. In fact, did David Friedrich Strauss[9] or Feuerbach[10] influence you at all in your youth?

I am also very interested in your attitude to *Fechner*.[11] Apart from Wundt,[12] towards whom I feel as negatively as you do,[13] he is practically the only recent psychologist you quote. Have you read his paper on the Greatest Good[14] in which the problem of pleasure and pain looms large, or have you only read his *Psychophysics*?[15] What I am concerned with is not the biographical and historical detail, because my work does not impinge upon that, or at most secondarily, but the 'consensus of minds' even, or indeed precisely, *without* personal knowledge and influence.

Well, now, dear Professor, you must blame a Sunday morning for my detaining you so long and perhaps boring you. By way of an apology, I can only offer you complete freedom not only in answering but also in reading this letter. I remain, whether you reply to the whole, to part, or to nothing at all, and in the sincere hope that these lines find you in reasonable health,

Yours in unfailing affection, [L. Binswanger]

[1] A set of Freud's *Gesammelte Schriften*, much annotated in Binswanger's hand, is held in the B.A., Tübingen.

[2] Cf. the diary entry (III, p. 7 and pp. 9ff.):

'22 September. [...] Reading *Phaedo* with Bobi this holiday, Greek, great pleasure. [...] – 25 November 1924 [...] Bobi has finished *Phaedo*. He is reading about it in Natorp [Paul Natorp (1854–1924), German philosopher and socio-educationist, neo-Kantian, joint founder with Hermann Cohen (1842–1918) of the Marburg school] with understanding. [...] – 1925 [January] *Gorgias* since Christmas [1924] with Bobi.'

[3] In 'Recommendations to Physicians Practising Psycho-Analysis' (1912e), *S.E.* Vol. XII, pp. 115–16, Freud wrote: 'Just as the patient must relate everything that his self-observation can detect, and keep back all the logical and affective objections that seek to induce him to make a selection from among them, so the doctor must put himself in a position to make use of everything he is told for the purposes of interpretation and of recognising the concealed unconscious material without substituting a censorship of his own for the selection that the patient has forgone. To put it in a formula: he must turn his own unconscious like a receptive organ towards the transmitting unconscious of the patient. He must adjust himself to the patient as a telephone receiver is adjusted to the transmitting microphone. Just as the receiver converts back into sound waves the electric oscillations in the telephone line which were set up by sound waves, so the doctor's unconscious is able, from the derivatives of the unconscious which are communicated to him, to reconstruct that unconscious, which has determined the patient's free associations.'

[4] Cf. 'Erfahren, Verstehen, Deuten in der Psychoanalyse', ['Experience, Understanding and Interpretation in Psychoanalysis'], Binswanger (1926a).

[5] Friedrich Schleiermacher (1768–1834), Protestant theologian and philosopher whose philological influence with his *Hermeneutik* [hermeneutics] as a 'synthetic theory of understanding' continues through Dilthey down to the philosophy and theology of today. [A summary of Schleiermacher's psychology can be found in Richard E. Palmer: *Hermeneutics*, Evanston, 1968, pp. 84–97. T.R.]

[6] Wilhelm Dilthey (1833–1911), philosopher, strove for an 'empirical science of mental phenomena'. Influential in the history of psychology with his *Ideen über eine*

beschriebende und zergliedernde Psychologie [Ideas on a descriptive and analytical psychology] (1894; cf. Bollnow [1967]).

On his own studies of Schleiermacher and Dilthey, Binswanger wrote in his diary as early as 1924 (III, pp. 5–7): '1 September [...] read a lot of *Dilthey*, vols. 5 and 6 recently published. Very important! *Dilthey* and *Freud*, two poles of a psychology which does not even exist yet. From *Dilthey* and *Häberlin* back to *Schleiermacher* who now stirs me afresh. Here are the basic requirements for my work. [...]

'16 September. Read Schleiermacher's psychology with the feeling that I am on kindred and secure ground. His paper on *Hermeneutik* [...] makes me certain that my book on psychoanalysis must begin with hermeneutics, must be tied in with it. This view had already dawned upon me through [reading] *Dilthey's* paper on hermeneutics and *Warburg's* work on Sassetti. I should reduce the contents of the book down to the programme of comparing *Dilthey* and *Freud*. But with Schleiermacher everything clearer, simpler, indeed deeper than with Dilthey.'

[7] Freud (1914b).

[8] Binswanger wrote 'Lionardo'.

[9] David Friedrich Strauss (1808–74), Protestant theologian, founder of a radical Bible criticism with his *Leben Jesu* [Life of Jesus], and, under the influence of Hegel, an advocate of speculative theology; cf. Barth (1948).

[10] Ludwig Feuerbach (1804–72), philosopher, developed a radical assessment of theology and religion through his criticism of Hegel's concept of "absolute spirit"; cf. Braun (1971).

[11] Gustav Theodor Fechner (1801–87), after studying medicine, became a physicist, psychologist and philosopher, influential especially through his attempt at a *psychophysics*; cf. Jaynes (1971).

[12] Wilhelm Wundt (1832–1920), after studying medicine, became a psychologist and philosopher, founder of the first institute for experimental psychology in Leipzig (1879); cf. Boring (1950). He is often described as the 'father of psychology'.

[13] Freud in no way perceived Wundt negatively, although Wundt's explanations of dream and taboo seemed to him to be inadequate. Certainly there is a sarcastic remark about Wundt in 'Little Hans': 'As a matter of fact, he [little Hans] was behaving no worse than a philosopher of the school of Wundt. In the view of that school, consciousness is the invariable characteristic of what is mental, just as in the view of little Hans a widdler is the indispensable criterion of what is animate.' Freud (1909b), *S.E.*, Vol. X, pp. 11–12, note 3.

[14] Fechner (1846).

[15] Fechner (1860–89).

148F

22 February 1925[1]

Prof. Dr. Freud   Vienna IX, Berggasse 19

Dear Dr. Binswanger,

Of course I am happy to answer your scientific and personal questions. The statement that the unconscious of the analysand must be seized with one's own unconscious, that we must so to speak hold out the unconscious ear as a receiver, was one I made in an unassuming and rationalistic sense, although I grant that important problems are concealed behind that formulation. I simply meant that one must eschew the conscious intensification of certain expectations and so set up in oneself the same state one requires of the analysand. All ambiguities disappear once you assume that, in the sentence in question, the unconscious is meant purely descriptively. In a more systematic formulation, unconscious must be replaced with preconscious. There is no need to go into the deeper problems here.

I have read several other works by Fechner besides the *Psychophysics* but not his 'Über das Höchste Gut', in which the pleasure-pain problem is said to play such a great role. I should be most interested to find that I had come close to his views even though I have not been directly influenced by him.

It is true that when I was young I read David Friedrich Strauss and Feuerbach with pleasure and enthusiasm.[2] However, it would seem that their influence has not been an enduring one.

I was very glad to have good news of your family. Cordially yours,

Freud

[1] Typewritten letter.
[2] On Freud's interest in Fechner and his reading of Strauss and Feuerbach see *Letters of Sigmund Freud to Eduard Silberstein,* Freud (1989a).

149B

Kreuzlingen, 4 May 1925

Dear Professor Freud,
I have heard in a roundabout way via Pastor Pfister and Frau Gi. that you have now fully recovered, so it is with particularly great pleasure that I congratulate you on your birthday. My hopes, too, are renewed that I shall see you again, be it in Vienna or on one of your trips or at a congress.

Many thanks for your kind reply to my questions.
With every good wish from my wife and myself,

Yours,
[L. Binswanger]

150F
Prof. Dr. Sigm. Freud[1]

Vienna IX, Berggasse 19

Many thanks to you and Frau Gi. It looks as if I am going to last a bit longer yet.

Yours, Freud

10 May 1925

[1] Visiting card.

151B

Kreuzlingen, 4 May 1926

Dear Professor Freud,
From your latest book, *Inhibitions, Symptoms and Anxiety*,[1] which absorbed me during my spring break on the shores of Lake Lugano, I can see that, having recovered your physical strength, you continue to pursue your chief scientific problems with youthful intellectual vigour and critical acumen, to substantiate them afresh and to defend them against the unsustainable distortions of others. And so it is with particular happiness that I congratulate you, dear Professor, on behalf of my wife and myself, on the occasion of your 70th birthday. On this day, when you are being feted throughout the world and are receiving felicitations from all corners of the globe, I shall spare you my wishes and reflections and simply express my feelings of gratitude and affection, and once again my pleasure that fate should have granted me this opportunity of congratulating you on your 70th birthday.

Your life, though always on the ascendant, has repeatedly been dealt heavy blows. And so I should just like to tell you that I deeply lament the wound fate has inflicted upon you in the death, at so early an age, of Karl Abraham.[2] Abraham was one of the few who fully understood the libido theory and applied it correctly, and one of the few to have developed it clinically with lasting results. Since I witnessed all the stages in the development of your relationship with Jung, I realise only too clearly what it must mean to you to have lost your scientific heir for the second or third time.

180

I have not given up the hope of seeing you face to face once more. For the moment, I conclude with my very best wishes for a happy birthday spent among your family, which I celebrate with you in spirit.

As always, yours, [L. Binswanger]

[1] Freud (1926d).
[2] Karl Abraham died on 25 December 1925; see Jones (1953–7), Vol. 3, pp. 122–3, and Freud's obituary (1926b).

152F

21 May 1926[1]

Prof. Dr. Freud   Vienna IX, Berggasse 19

Dear Dr. Binswanger,
In the concert of voices raised on my seventieth birthday yours could not be absent. Despite the fact that we have met so few times, we have shared many important experiences and you have always remained loyal to me and to my cause. I too shall not abandon the hope of seeing you and your charming wife again, but you will have to come to Vienna for I have given up travelling.

You are quite right about what Abraham's death meant to me. But if one lives as long as I have, one cannot always avoid surviving others.

Still, psychoanalysis is not my private property and will continue to exist even after I am no longer able to shape its fate. With kind regards,

Yours, Freud

[1] Typewritten letter.

153B

Kreuzlingen, 7 October 1926

Dear Professor Freud,
The new psychoanalytic Almanac[1] arrived a few days ago. I do not know to whom I owe the honour of being represented in it,[2] but I am certainly very glad to appear once again publicly in such company,

particularly of course in yours. The inclusion of my little essay in this collection pleases me all the more as psychoanalysis has, until now, been opposed for the most part to theoretical discussions and standards not inherent in it but brought in 'from outside'. But as you know, I myself feel the need to examine psychoanalytic theories in the light of general methodological criteria and to determine their place in man's intellectual development, which is precisely what I have tried tentatively to do in this essay. I hope that I shall be able to discuss the subject at greater length in the second edition of my General Psychology,[3] which, I am pleased to say, is already in hand. *You* will not take it amiss that in it I reach conclusions which in many questions of principle differ from those of the psychoanalytic 'school', since you have once again shown in your book on anxiety[4] how remorselessly you 'expose' your own intellectual children once they have ceased to be compatible with your more advanced views. My own differences are not in respect of therapy as such, but concern the application of certain results obtained in practical psychoanalysis to mental life in general. It was thus that I made a critical comment at the Groningen Congress during the discussion of Jones's lecture on the psychology of religion,[5] but I could see that he did not understand what I meant. How often I find myself conversing with you in my mind about these questions, noting your disagreement but occasionally also – I will not say your approval, but your attentive ear! I will make no attempt as yet to trouble and tire you with all these things in person. To my delight, however, the next Congress of the German Association for Neurology is to be held in Vienna[6] (September 1927); I shall see you then as often as you will allow me.

Now for something personal: at a time when my life was under the gravest threat,[7] you stood by me in a way that, apart from all other ties, binds me to you for ever. And though my own life has not been threatened since, one of my children, a lovely eight-year-old boy, who showed promise of becoming a strong personality, died quite unexpectedly after a fourteen-day illness and great suffering on 31 May.[8] It was tubercular meningitis with no preliminary symptoms. He was our fifth child, quite different from all the others, and especially dear to us because of his delicacy of spirit. I could not bring myself to let you know of the boy's death with a printed announcement, nor did I feel up to writing, particularly to you. But now I have done it. I know that you have had a similar experience and it is perhaps harder still to lose a grown-up child. My wife, who from the first days of his life had given this child a particularly large share of her maternal love and care, and who was particularly fond of him, did not make the blow I suffered more difficult to bear but has helped me by her total acceptance of the inevitable. I need hardly tell you that she has not yet fully recovered her spirits and that she will probably never get over the blow. Even if something *in* us does not die for good yet something *of* us does and can never be replaced. As regards the other children, too, our sense of triumphant security has now vanished, and naturally our sharpened vigilance finds things to worry about here and there.

I expect no letter from you, dear Professor, but a line from you would give me and my wife more pleasure than anything else.

With fond affection,

As always, yours, [L. Binswanger]

N.B. I did not dictate this letter but wrote it out by hand and had it transcribed for you.

---

[1] *Almanach für das Jahr 1927* (Almanac for 1927), ed. A.J. Storfer, Vienna: International Psychoanalytischer Verlag [1926].

[2] Ludwig Binswanger, 'Erfahren, Verstehen, Deuten in der Psychoanalyse' ['Experience, Understanding and Interpretation in Psychoanalysis'] (1926a).

[3] In spite of extensive revision, this second edition was never published.

[4] *Inhibitions, Symptom and Anxiety* (1926d).

[5] At the International Psychology Congress held in Groningen from 6 to 11 September 1926, Ernest Jones gave a lecture with the title: 'The Psychology of Religion'; see *VIIIth International Congress of Psychology [...] Proceedings and Papers*, Groningen 1927, pp. 99–105. At the same congress Binswanger gave his paper: 'Verstehen und Erklären in der Psychologie' [Understanding and explanation in psychology], *ibid.*, pp. 117–23. Discussions are not included in the published congress proceedings. Even in the diary, Binswanger simply wrote (III, p. 63): 'During the discussion I spoke about the psychology of language (Bühler), the psychology of religion (Jones) and gestalt psychology.'

[6] See note 4 to 155B.

[7] Cf. note 1 to 65F.

[8] Johannes Binswanger (1918–26). The acute illness began on 15 May; there are detailed entries in the diary (III, pp. 46–54) about the course of the illness and his death.

154F

15 October 1926

Prof. Dr. Freud   Vienna IX, Berggasse 19

Dear Dr. Binswanger,

How could I fail to write to you, not words of superfluous condolence, but from an inner urge only, since your letter has roused a memory in me – absurd, for it has never been asleep. You are right, I lost a beloved daughter when she was 27 years old,[1] but I bore that loss remarkably well. It happened in 1920, when we were crushed by the misery of war, and after years of having to steel ourselves against the news that we had lost a son, or even three sons. Thus we had become resigned to what fate held in store. Two years later, however, I brought the younger child of this daughter, a little fellow of 3 or 4, to Vienna, where my childless eldest daughter took him in, and this child died – in June '23 – from an acute miliary tuberculosis. He was far advanced intellectually, so much so that the consultant took that into account when the diagnosis was still uncertain. For me, that child took the place of all my children and other grandchildren, and since then, since Heinele's[2] death, I have no longer cared for my grandchildren, but find no enjoyment in life either. This is also the secret of my indifference – it has been called courage – towards the threat to my own life.

My fate bears some resemblance to your own, indeed, in that I too have suffered no recurrence of the neoplasm. In the other respect I hope that you will escape the resemblance. You are young enough to overcome your loss; as for me I no longer have to.

Should you come to Vienna in September '27, and I am still alive, I won't be in Vienna but on the Semmering,[3] as in recent years. So come and see me there.[4]

With kind regards to you and your wife,

Yours, Freud

[1] Cf. 122F.
[2] Heinz Rudolf Halberstadt, nicknamed Heinele, 1 January 1919–19 June 1923; cf. Jones (1953–7), Vol. 3, pp. 21, 96.
[3] A mountain (4577 feet) 60 miles south-west of Vienna.
[4] Cf. the editorial note which follows 160F and the Appendix, pp. 237–8.

155B

Kreuzlingen, 29 November 1926

Dear Professor Freud,

At yesterday's meeting of the Swiss Psychiatric Society in Zurich, I, as the current president, proposed that you be made an honorary member[1] in the place of the late Professor Kraepelin,[2] adding that though it was a disgrace that we had not done so long ago, it were better done late than never. My motion received unanimous approval and you will be notified of your appointment within the next few days. I would just add that I know perfectly well that such an honour would have given you pleasure a generation or even twenty years ago, but that such things no longer make any impression at all upon you. The pleasure and honour are thus ours rather than yours.

But perhaps giving pleasure to others, and to me in particular, will not leave you indifferent even today!

I gather that the German psychiatrists will be arriving in Vienna as early as April.[3] But they have so little to offer that I shall probably wait until September and join the neurologists instead.[4]

With kind regards,

As always, yours [L. Binswanger]

[1] The copy of Binswanger's official invitation to Freud of the same date, as President of the Swiss Society for Psychiatry, has also survived in the Binswanger Archive (B.A. 443/90, 85):
'Kreuzlingen and Lausanne, 29th November 1926.

Dear Professor Freud,

The Swiss Society for Psychiatry decided at its meeting yesterday to appoint you as honorary member in place of the deceased Prof. Emil Kraepelin. We ask you please to see this decision as a sign that Swiss psychiatrists, some of whom were among the very first to find their way into your teachings, also today still place a high value on your contribution to psychiatric knowledge, and they ask you kindly to accept this, the highest professional honour available to them, as a mark of their gratitude.

We are delighted to be the bearers of this decision and remain, with respect

Yours faithfully,

President   Secretary'

[2] Emil Kraepelin had died on 7 October 1926. When he was offered honorary membership, he turned it down. There is, however, in the Binswanger Archive, a draft of a greetings telegram which Binswanger, as President of the Swiss Society for Psychiatry, sent to Kraepelin as honorary member on 15 February 1926. There is also Kraepelin's letter of thanks of 25 February 1926; see B.A. 443/90, 85. Regarding Binswanger's proposal, cf. Binswanger (1927b).

[3] The annual conference of the German Association for Psychiatry did not actually take place in Vienna until 13–14 September 1927; see *Zbl. ges. Neurol. Psychiatr.* Vol. 48 (1928), pp. 468–512.

[4] The 17th annual conference of the Society of German Psychiatrists, Vienna, 15–17 September 1927; see *Zbl. ges. Neurol. Psychiatr.* Vol. 47 (1927), pp. 767–844.

156F

4 December 1926

Prof. Dr. Freud   Vienna IX, Berggasse 19

Dear Dr. Binswanger,

I thank you. You are right, the honour as such leaves me cold, but not insensible to its symptomatic value as evidence of the steady waning of resistance among psychiatrists.

Twenty, let alone thirty, years ago, recognition such as this of analysis, then still in its babyhood,[1] would scarcely have made sense. I neither expected nor felt the lack of anything of the sort at the time.

When I get the official document I shall of course reply with a formal letter of thanks.[2]

Very cordially yours,
Freud

[1] 'In its babyhood' = '*babyhaft*' in the original. [A.J.P.]
[2] Not known if extant.

157B

Kreuzlingen, 11 July 1927

Dear Professor Freud,

The dates of the Vienna Congress are 13–17 September. Would it suit you if I came to see you on the Semmering beforehand? I freely confess that visiting you is the main purpose of my trip to Vienna and that I am only combining it with the Congress because then the Clinic bears the costs! Nor do I have to be there from the beginning. Please choose a day for me.

I need not tell you, who are always in my thoughts, how much I look forward to seeing you again.

With kind regards,

Yours, [L. Binswanger]

158F

15 July 1927
Prof. Dr. Freud   Vienna IX, Berggasse 19

Dear Dr. Binswanger,
I need not tell you how delighted I shall be to see you again, no matter
when you come, whether in the first half of September or the second.
However, I must add that no matter when you come you will have to
share my time with others. In August I shall be free of both patients
and visitors, but in September both will return. Immediately after our
Congress in Innsbruck,[1] on 1–3 September, Jones, Ferenczi, Laforgue[2]
and others have announced that they shall be coming here for longer
or shorter stays.[3] I am no longer as efficient as I used to be and my
ability to speak and to listen has suffered considerably since the
operation. But I hope you will not be put off.
  With kind regards to you and your family,

Yours, Freud

[1] 10th International Psychoanalytic Congress.
[2] René Laforgue (1894–1962), Alsatian – bilingual in French and German, psychiatrist
and psychoanalyst, founder of the French psychoanalytic movement and first President
of the Société psychanalytique de Paris. Cf. Freud (1977h), Bourgignon 'La correspondance entre Freud et Laforgue', *Nouv. Rev. Psychanal.*, Vol. 15 (1977), pp. 233–
314; the correspondence is extensively quoted in English translation in Bertin (1982).
Cf. also Elisabeth Roudinesco, 'René Laforgue und Matthias Heinrich Göring',
Psyche, Vol. 42 (1988), pp. 1041–80 and Mühlleitner (1992).
[3] See Jones (1953–7), Vol. 3, p. 145.

159B

Kreuzlingen, 25 July 1927

Dear Professor Freud,
Many thanks! I cannot think what would put me off from coming to
see you, certainly not the visit of the gentlemen you mentioned, all
of whom I know personally. I shall come between 10 and 13 September, if that suits you. Perhaps your daughter or someone else would
have the kindness to send me a postcard to let me know, in due course,
where on the Semmering you may be found, and where your visitors
usually stay.

I have just returned from Lucerne, where I held a five-day psychological lecture course[1] with Bleuler and Häberlin. I was delighted to find that my lectures on dreams were very well received. I hope to send you these lectures in printed form before the end of the year.[2] Bleuler was very pleased with the letter you sent him following his article in the *Neue Zürcher Zeitung*;[3] Häberlin is very sorry that he will not be able to come to Vienna this time. I am tremendously looking forward to seeing you, even if only for a short time. I find it impossible to believe that it is 21 years since we first met.

With kind regards,

Yours, [L. Binswanger]

[1] The first meeting of the Stiftung Lucerna (a charitable foundation, its founding benefactor and president the banker Emil Sidler-Brunner, 1844–1928) took place in Lucerne from 18 to 22 July with 'courses in psychology'. The foundation had set itself the aim of 'promoting scientific work in the field of psychology and aiding the dissemination of culturally important research results in this area of knowledge [...].' (From the programme of the meeting.) Eugen Bleuler (Zurich) spoke on 'Affectpsychologie' [affect psychology], Pierre Buvet (Geneva) on 'La psychologie et l'école aux États-Unis' [psychology and the American school], Paul Häberlin (Basle) 'Zur Charakterkunde' [on the science of character], and Binswanger on 'Auffassung und Deutung des Traumes in alter und neuer Zeit' [Perception and interpretation of dreams in ancient and modern times]; cf. Kamm (1977–81), vol. 1, p. 48, and Sneessens (1966), no. 135. In the diary (III, p. 75), it says: '23 August. Back today from the *Lucerna lectures* which worked out *very* well, with Hertha, who was there from beginning to end. [...] For me a great experience and a step forward.'
[2] Binswanger (1928e).
[3] Probably E. Bleuler, 'Zu Siegmund [sic] Freuds siebzigstem Geburtstag [For Freud's seventieth birthday]', *Neue Zürcher Zeitung*, 6 May 1926, morning edn., pp. 1f. It is clear from this article that Bleuler first became aware of Freud's name in 1891, as a result of Freud's paper on aphasia (1891b) and that the tribute was put together at very short notice: 'The significance of the day having come to my attention only at the eleventh hour, I cannot do justice here to the greatness of Freudian achievement.'

160F

Semmering, 28 July 1927[1]

Dear Dr. Binswanger,

Five paces from our Villa Schüler is the Südbahnhotel,[2] which will meet all requirements.

Until we meet again!

Yours, Freud

[1] Postcard.

[2] The Südbahnhotel has the appearance of a large palace and is a built in an historic style, making it appear older than it actually is. According to Baedeker's *Austria* (30th edn., Leipzig 1926), it boasted more than 400 beds in 350 rooms, but today [1992] it is standing empty. It is indeed scarcely more than 100 metres from the Villa Schüler with its view of the Rax. Cf. Kos (1984), pp. 152–4.

Binswanger's Fourth Visit to Freud on the Semmering, 16 to 17 September 1927

Binswanger first described this visit in his paper 'Freud und die Verfassung der klinischen Psychiatrie' (1936) and then in his *Reminiscences* (1956c, pp. 79–83 in the English edition, 1957). Both reports are based on diary entries, whose original text appears in the Appendix, pp. 237–8.

161B

Kreuzlingen, 24 September 1927

Dear Professor Freud,

Although you were unable to satisfy my 'religious needs' I was tremendously pleased with my visit to you; 'pleased' is putting it mildly since the visit was a great event in my life, in purely personal as well as in 'spiritual' respects. Above all! I was of course delighted to find you so vigorous and youthful, and I only hope that your vigour did not mislead me into tiring you too much. I recall every word of our conversations, and I have learned much that will help me to deepen and round off my understanding of your theories and of your personality. I very much hope for an occasional repeat of our contact, and that next time I shall be able to bring my son[1] with me. But first, I hope to be able to send you my little book on the Changes in the Conception and Interpretation of Dreams,[2] as a small token of my gratitude; it will not, however, be appearing before Christmas at the earliest.

My wife was very sorry that she did not come with me and she sends you and your ladies her most cordial regards.

Despite the after-effects of my 'flu, I went back to Vienna from the Semmering rested and rejuvenated, and it is the best testimony to your unbroken vitality and spirit that you can impart so much vigour to others.

I was also very glad to make the acquaintance of the Princess,[3] and would ask you to tell her that she would give me great pleasure if she called on us during one of her visits to Switzerland. With her keen interest in psychopathology and her eager receptivity in general, there are one or two things here that may perhaps interest her.

In cordial friendship and affection as ever,

Yours, [L. Binswanger]

[1] The eldest son, Robert, in whom Freud took a particular interest after 1912, and who decided at that time – to his father's delight – upon a career in psychiatry (162B).
[2] Binswanger (1928e).
[3] Marie Bonaparte (1882–1962), patient and disciple of Freud; cf. Bertin (1982).

162B

Kreuzlingen, 21 February 1928

Dear Professor Freud,

I have been meaning to write and wish you a happy New Year since the beginning of January, but kept postponing it because I did not want to do so empty-handed. Now I am having to do just that, because the printing of my last book has been delayed and I cannot keep you waiting any longer for a sign of life. I hope that you received the letter I wrote on my return from Vienna and that the winter has so far been kind to you. The memory of my visit is still most vivid, and I am very glad to have seen you and spoken to you again. From the writings which I now hope to be able to send to you by spring, you will be able to see that you continue to be my starting-point, and I am sure you will not hold it against me that I cannot follow you in every one of your trains of thought. Despite that, or perhaps precisely because of it, I always feel that I am your pupil. My little Dream Book is almost ready for the printer; two lectures[1] will appear in March and April. Should you then be inclined to drop me a few lines, I would be very pleased, but I would not be cross if you did not. At present, the clinic is exceedingly busy and I have to devote all my spare time to the second edition of my *General Psychology*; everything else is being kept at arm's length. All is well with my family, though the youngest[2] sometimes worries me because of his marked physical and intellectual resemblance to his dead older brother.[3] My eldest[4] has now definitely decided in favour of psychiatry.

190

Oberholzer's defection[5] will not have surprised you, any more than it did me. Such incidents cannot have concerned you for quite some time now. I have, of course, read the Future of 'your' Illusion with keen interest in the light of our conversation and would have been very glad to thrash matters out with you once or several times again, even at the risk of having you overestimate my religious needs even more than you do. Will Switzerland really never see you again? The connections to Zurich and Lake Constance are excellent now; if you leave Vienna in the evening you arrive in Rorschach at 1.00 p.m. by taking the Vienna–St. Gallen express and the Vienna–Feldkirch wagon-lit, and can be here, one hour's drive by car from Rorschach, by 2.30 in the afternoon.

I must once again thank you for allowing me to call on you on the Semmering, and would ask you to remember me to your wife, sister-in-law, daughter and also to Frau Prof. Schaxel[6] when you see her, and remain, with many kind regards,

Ever yours, [L. Binswanger]

[1] One of them is probably the lecture of 22 January 1927 'Über Alkoholismus' ['On Alcoholism'] which was published in a very much extended form in the *Neue Deutsche Klinik* (1928a). The other is probably on 'Lebensfunktion und innere Lebensgeschichte' ['Life functions and inner life histories'], a lecture which was probably delivered the first time in Berlin in December 1927 (Diary III, p. 85), Binswanger (1928c).

[2] Dieter Binswanger.

[3] Johannes Binswanger.

[4] Robert Binswanger.

[5] This is a reference to the establishment by Emil Oberholzer of the *Gesellschaft für ärztliche Psychoanalyse* [Society for Medical Psychoanalysis] (an indication of the adoption of a position opposed to lay analysis and against Oskar Pfister); cf. note 7 to 70F.

[6] Hedwig Schaxel-Hoffer (1888–1961), psychoanalyst, married first the Professor of Zoology and General Biology, Julius Schaxel (1887–1943); and secondly the psychoanalyst Willi Hoffer (1897–1967); cf. Rosenfeld (1962).

163F

26 February 1928
Prof. Dr. Freud   Vienna IX, Berggasse 19

Dear Dr. Binswanger,

It appears certain that I shall not be seeing Switzerland again, no. I am already aware that Constance lies on Lake Constance and proclaimed this fact publicly not long ago.[1] The garden of Villa Schüler on the Semmering is ready to receive you whenever you feel the need to have a discussion with your old friend.

I am glad to hear that all is well with you.

Very cordially yours, Freud

[1] In *The Future of an Illusion* Freud writes by way of illustration of 'teachings': 'We are told that the town of Constance lies on the Bodensee [the German name for what in English is called Lake Constance]. A student song adds: "if you don't believe it, go and see." I happen to have been there and can confirm the fact that that lovely town lies on the shore of a wide stretch of water which all those who live round it call the Bodensee.' (1927c) *S.E.*, Vol. XXI, p. 25.

164F

2 April 1928
Prof. Dr. Freud   Vienna IX, Berggasse 19

Dear Dr. Binswanger,

I have received your short dream book and have read it through without stopping. It is splendid and very characteristic of you. I have found all your qualities confirmed in it, the respectable ones no less than those that are less to my taste, your thoroughness, your tendency to agree with people, your cool head, and finally your correctness in face of the real object.

I was sorry to learn that I had missed so many important sources in my review of the dream literature.[1] No one had drawn my attention to them; moreover, even as it was, I found it difficult to study so many authors, instead of the object. I obviously lack the scholar's nature and can admire your scholarship without envy.

You will perhaps be surprised to hear that I have not read the analysis of myself carried out by Michaelis[2] whom you praise so highly. To analyse somebody [in public] who is still alive is hardly admissible, let alone polite. I shall leave aside the question of whether failure to send the victim the result of the autopsy aggravates or mitigates the incivility. I was not curious, since this Michaelis does not know me. I must say that our clinical analyses presuppose greater familiarity with the object.

Your concluding words[3] amused rather than annoyed me. So you, too, have a God. No doubt one who has been philosophically distilled. Now, I have always been quite temperate, almost abstinent, but have had a decent respect for a proper drinker (e.g. G. Keller,[4] Böcklin[5]). Those who manage to get intoxicated on a non-alcoholic drink, however, have always struck me as being a bit comical.

With kind regards,

Your old friend, Freud

[1] Cf. chapter 1 of *The Interpretation of Dreams* (Freud 1900a), *S.E.*, Vol. IV, pp. 1–95 and the Bibliographies A and B 5, *ibid.*, Vol. V, pp. 687–713.

[2] Michaelis (1925). Binswanger had written about this publication in his Dream Book: 'Michaelis [...] had however quite correctly observed, when he pointed to great discrepancies between the man and the work, a sign that even Freud was not privileged fully to seize his own transcendental self.' Binswanger (1928e), p. 66, note 1.

[3] The last sentence in Binswanger's book reads: 'Indeed, we shall not demand a metaphysics of the dream: that would be too pedantic an understanding of our concept, but, if it drives us anywhere, it is to postulate and to foresee a metaphysics of the spirit, and where can that lead us but to the idea of God?' Binswanger (1928e), p. 110.

[4] Gottfried Keller's alcoholism was mentioned during a discussion in the Wednesday Society about a review by Victor Tausk 'Über das alkoholische Beschäftigungsdelir' [On alcoholic occupational delirium] (31 March 1915); see *Minutes*, Vol. 4 (1975), pp. 288–9. Cf. also Hitschmann (1919), p. 52.

[5] The alcoholism of Arnold Böcklin, whose pictures Freud much admired, had already been mentioned by Freud in 'On the Universal Tendency to Debasement in the Sphere of Love', (1912d), *S.E.*, Vol. XI, p. 188.

165B

Kreuzlingen, 23 April 1928

Dear Professor Freud,

I am today again sending you some printed material, without doubt the last for some time to come, since I will be fully occupied in the future with the second edition of the *General Psychology*. Your criticism is always welcome even when it is not flattering, and that is why I was pleased with your last letter; I prefer rebukes, rejection or ridicule from you to the praises of anyone else. You will not hold it against me if I have enough self-confidence to believe that you do not perhaps judge me correctly in every respect!

I met Michaelis in December in Berlin; an unassuming little fellow. I asked him if he had sent you his book but he said that he would not have thought that very tactful. I honestly believe that one can be of two minds on the matter, in all good faith. I have no reason whatsoever to defend him, have no closer links with him, but do think that he has performed the task he has set himself competently and tactfully. What he has done, after all, is not a real psychoanalysis in our sense, and you will simply have to accept that great minds are likely to be dissected by smaller fry.

With kind regards,

Ever yours, [L. Binswanger]

166B

Kreuzlingen, 7 January 1929

Dear Professor Freud,

I am not writing to you at the beginning of the year to bother you with New Year greetings, but to tell you how often I have thought of you this past year and how much I am with you in spirit. Don't hold it against me if I also take the opportunity to wish you all the best for 1929. You have long since attained philosophical calm, and removed from the hustle and bustle of the world, so that all I need wish you is your continued well-being, in the hope that since I last saw you your health has indeed remained good. As far as I know you have no cause to worry about your family, since I hear nothing but good of your sons, know nothing but good about your daughter, and Frau Professor also seemed very well when I saw her. I too have little cause for complaint as far as health matters are concerned. The children are all doing very well. Little Johannes[1] continues to dwell in spirit in our midst. The eldest[2] is already in his fourth term of studying medicine, and despite marked talents in the fields of mathematics and physics, could not be dissuaded from remaining true to the family psychiatric tradition. My responsibilities in the clinic have if anything been increasing with time, as they are recognised more and more clearly and our limitations felt ever more keenly. However, I have very good assistants at present, including a married couple, friends of mine,[3] both of them psychiatrists and Bleuler's pupils. The new edition of my *General Psychology* takes up a great deal of my time because I believe I owe it to myself to do a thorough revision of the work, still rather callow and too theoretical and didactic, and above all to bring it into greater accord with psychiatric and psychoanalytical practice. My development has been the very opposite of that of so many others, inasmuch as, with growing experience, I have become if anything less theoretical and turn more and more to practice.

194

With best wishes once again to you and your entire family, and with kind regards from my wife and myself, I remain, dear Professor Freud,

Ever yours, [L. Binswanger]

[1] Cf. note 8 to 153B.
[2] Cf. Binswanger's report on Freud's visit to Kreuzlingen, in the Appendix, p. 235 and note 14.
[3] Ernest Wenger (1888–1932) and Martha Wenger (1890–1955); cf. obituaries by Binswanger (1932a) and (1956a).

167F

11 January 1929
Prof. Dr. Freud   Vienna IX, Berggasse 19

Dear Dr. Binswanger,

Many thanks for your New Year letter with its welcome news! Unlike so many other people, you have not allowed your intellectual development, which you have increasingly removed from my influence, to destroy our personal relationship, and you have no idea how much good such refinement does for a person – in spite of that indifference you admire that comes with age.

I am happy to confirm your assumption that I am not at present dogged by any health concerns in the family. Even my almost 94-year-old mother is in fine fettle, and this stops me doing things an old man ought to be free to do. From a financial point of view, the family has not recovered from the harm done by the Great War. With declining powers, I still have to earn enough to support a number of younger people. Among my seven grandchildren is many a charming characteristic which ensures I cannot forget the one lost in 1923.[1]

We do not want to spend this summer on the Semmering again, but do not know where to go. Our symbiosis with an American family[2] (without husband), whose children my daughter is bringing up with a firm hand analytically, is getting more and more established, so our needs for the summer are shared. Our two dogs, the faithful Wolf and the gentle Pekinese Lun Yug, are the latest additions to the family.

Sincere regards to you, your dear wife and the optimistic throng of children and all the best for 1929, whether I see you agan this year or not.

Yours, Freud

[1] Cf. note 2 to 154F.
[2] Dorothy Burlingham (1891–1979), close friend of Anna Freud; cf. 'In memoriam Dorothy Burlingham, 1891–1979', *Psychoanal. Study Child*, Vol. 35 (1980), pp. ix–xxii, and Burlingham (1989).

168F

11 April 1929
Prof. Dr. Freud   Vienna IX, Berggasse 19

Dear Dr. Binswanger
I do not remember whether it was in 1912 or 1913 that I came to see you and found you so full of courage[1] that you won forever a high place in my esteem. The years since then have, as you know, left me a fairly decrepit old man. I am no longer able to make the trip to come and take your hand.

12 April 1929
My daughter who died would have been thirty-six today. Yesterday I nearly made a serious mistake. I started to read your letter, discovered several kind words I should have been sorry to miss, but was unable to piece together a single sentence, and the further I went the more puzzling your characters became. I considered returning the letter to you with some jocular expression of indignation and the request that you have it copied and sent back to me. Then my sister-in-law came to my aid and told me the shocking news the rest of the letter contained.[2] And I realised why, this time, you had preferred not to dictate it to a typist.

We know that the acute sorrow we feel after such a loss will run its course, but also that we will remain inconsolable, and will never find a substitute. No matter what may come to take its place, even should it fill that place completely, it yet remains something else. And that is how it should be. It is the only way of perpetuating a love that we do not want to abandon.

I would ask you please to remember me kindly to your wife.

In unchanging friendship,
Your old Freud

[1] Cf. note 1 to 65F and the editorial remarks after 67B.
[2] Binswanger had told Freud of the death of his eldest son, Robert, just 20 years old; cf. Binswanger (1956c), p. 84 in the 1957 English edition. Under the date 6 April 1929 he wrote in his diary: 'the most painful day in my life so far.' (Diary III, p. 94).

169B

Kreuzlingen, 3 May 1929

Dear Professor Freud,

As I have done each year for many years past,[1] I send you my very best wishes for 6 May, this time with special gratitude and joy that you are still with us, and with the special wish that you may long continue to be so. In my present state the mere thought of your existence lends me support and spurs me on to persevere and to continue my work. You may find that selfish of me, and could reply with justification that you have achieved and existed enough and that you ought now to be granted your rest. But what I saw of you eighteen months ago on the Semmering leads me to think that life still has quite a few things to offer you. And I believe that the knowledge that you can be a stay and comfort to your friends in need and in darkness is not the least merit attaching to your existence. And so today I repeat my thanks for everything you have given me through your work and in your person for a quarter-century, including your words of sympathy on the death of my eldest son.

I wish you above all a very good summer on the Semmering, your own good health and the health of all your dear ones. My wife, who stands so bravely by my side, joins me in sending you greetings.

Ever yours, [L. Binswanger]

[1] The first occasion for which there is evidence is 1916, cf. 110F.

170F

12 May 1929[1]

Prof. Dr. Freud

Vienna IX, Berggasse 19

Dear Dr. Binswanger,

I thank both you and your wife most sincerely. It is unnecessary to use a great many words to do so. Although it is true that I have enjoyed many a good thing in my life, on the whole it has been hard. I have been only too willing to become fond of others, as I am of you, for instance, but many people have made that impossible.

This year we are not going to the Semmering but have rented a place in Berchtesgaden (Schneewinkellehen) where we intend to go on 15 June.[2]

Very cordially yours, Freud

[1] Lettercard.
[2] Freud and his family were in Schneewinkl near Berchtesgaden from 18 June until 14 September, cf. Jones (1953–7), Vol. 3, p. 155, and Ferenczi's letter of 12 September 1929 (1992g), Vol. 3, p. 371.

171B

27 December 1929

Dear Professor Freud,

As always at the end of a year, I take the opportunity of telling you how very much you have been in my thoughts this year again, and to wish you a very happy New Year. Wherein that happiness lies for you is easily stated. Those who are wise need little more than good health and the health of their dear ones. May the coming year grant you this happiness.

I hope you had a good summer in Berchtesgaden. I learned from the relatives of a patient with whom both of us are concerned that you made a trip to Berlin.[1] The fact that you agreed to go for a consultation struck me as a good omen.

The loss of my eldest son has spurred me on to greater productivity and greater diligence. Since he is no longer there to carry on my practical and scientific work, my feeling is that I have to work for him now as well and in that way best continue his existence. My wife has most admirably concentrated all her energy on the upbringing and well-being of our other children and in this way has remained busy and well.

With kindest regards to you, your dear wife, your daughter, your sister-in-law and your sons,

[Yours, L. Binswanger]

[1] After the holiday in Berchtesgaden Freud went for a consultation with Prof. Hermann Schröder in Tegel, a suburb of Berlin (cf. Simon, 1972), where he stayed from 19 September until 20 October at least, as is apparent from the letters Freud wrote from Tegel to Stefan Zweig (19 September; 1987c); Abel de Castro (26 September; 1977i); Smith Ely Jelliffe (12 October, 1983a) and Theodor Reik (20 October; 1956l). Cf. Schultz and Hermanns (1990), where the duration of the visit is given as 15 September to 20 October 1929.

172F

1 January 1930[1]

Prof. Dr. Freud

Vienna IX, Berggasse 19

Many thanks for your kind letter, and a happy New Year to you and your family. I rejoice at the strength and dignity with which you face life's burdens.

Yours,
Freud

[1] Letter-card.

173B

4 May 1931

Dear Professor Freud,

I know you are no lover of birthday congratulations; all the same you will have to understand that I am unable to keep silent on your seventy-fifth, and wish to send you my warm greetings. I converse with no one in spirit more than I do with you, be it in everyday life or at my desk. So I feel compelled on an occasion such as this to emerge just once from my silence and to tell you how grateful I am to you for everything you have given me personally and scientifically. I only hope that you have no physical complaints, that you continue to work, and at the kind of work that interests you. A few years ago on the Semmering I found you so full of zest that I can only hope that your health has stayed at the same level since then.

I myself recently celebrated my fiftieth birthday,[1] or rather I did not celebrate it since I went to Italy that day with my daughter.[2] The children who have remained to us give us a great deal of pleasure. I hope that you, too, have had no further sorrow in your family.

My wife joins me in my congratulations and in sending you kind regards,

Ever yours, [L. Binswanger]

[1] '13 April [1931] My 50th birthday. My friends wish me a good second half century. I take this wish as read, I feel so young and full of plans, thus beginning a second life with Bobi *in* me. Pain is part of a full life!' (Diary IV, p. 74).
[2] Binswanger went with his daughter, Hilde, to Siena, Orvieto, Perugia, Assisi, Bologna and Milan from 13 to 24 April. See Diary IV, pp. 74–80.

Sigmund Freud, circa 1931.

174F

Vienna, May 1931[1]

Thank you for your kind message on the occasion of my seventy-fifth birthday.

[added in Freud's hand] 'and as ever warmest good wishes for the well-being of you and your family.'

Freud

[1] Preprinted postcard.

175B

13 April 1932

Dear Professor Freud,
On Thursday, 21st of this month, I am due to deliver a lecture[1] in Vienna at the Academic Society for Medical Psychology.[2] My daughter, who is studying political economics in Munich, will accompany me. You can imagine how much pleasure it would give me if I could see you once again, bringing my daughter with me. I should be very grateful to you if you could let me have a note at the Hotel Regina on the 20th or 21st saying whether and when I could come to see you on the 22nd or the 23rd. I had always wanted you to meet my eldest son, whom you saw here when he was still a little boy.[3] But you would enjoy meeting my daughter, too.

With kind regards, as always,

Yours, [L. Binswanger]

[1] "Über Klinik und existenziale Anthropologie. Thema, exemplifiziert an der "Ideenflucht, Traum und Ermüdungsoptimismus", [On the clinic and existential anthropology. Topic, exemplified by 'the Flight of Ideas', dream and the optimism of fatigue] cf. Larese (1965), p. 28, there with the wrong date of 21 April 1931. Cf. also Binswanger's letter of 7 April 1932 to Oswald Schwarz, B.A. 443/40. Binswanger was invited to give this lecture on 2 September 1931 by the Academic Society for Medical Psychology, which was run by medical students; see B.A. 443/40.
[2] The lecture was originally planned for 10 March 1932, as is shown in the Society's programme for the winter semester 1931/32 held in the B.A. (443/40). There it still says 'Subject to be advised'.
[3] See the report on Freud's visit to Kreuzlingen in the Appendix, pp. 235.

Binswanger's Fifth Visit to Freud in Vienna,
22 to 23 April 1932

Binswanger reported on this visit in his *Reminiscences* (1956c, p. 88 in the English edition, 1957), based on diary notes, whose original text appears in the Appendix, p. 239.

176F

Vienna, 5 June 1933[1]

Dear Dr. Binswanger,

How useful a postmark turns out to be.[2] Otherwise I should not have been able to tell *where* all is well with you and your family. I trust that you are enjoying your holiday to the full and that you are glad to have a native country. All my family, who remember your visit with pleasure, send you their kind regards, as does your old

Freud

[1] Postcard, postmarked 6 June 1933, addressed to: Herrn Dr. L. Binswanger, Bödele bei Dornbirn, Vorarlberg [Austria].

[2] Binswanger was on holiday in Bödele bei Dornbirn from 15 May until 10 June 1933, accompanied for some of the time by his sons Wolfgang and Dieter and by his wife Hertha; Diary IV, pp. 153–73. He continued working there on the second edition of his *Einführung in die Probleme der allgemeinen Psychologie*, which was never published.

177B
[To Anna Freud]

12 July 1934

Dear Fräulein Freud,

If you are coming to Switzerland, and would like to use our home to prepare yourself for the coming exertions of the Congress,[1] or to rest after it, my wife and I would like to take this early opportunity to invite you to stay with us. I shall never forget your father's visit to us and should be very glad to welcome you too.

If any of the colleagues attending the Congress wish to call on me or be shown round our clinic, I shall, of course, be happy to be of service. Perhaps you would be so kind as to convey my invitation verbally at the Congress. Should several colleagues come here at the same time, it might then be possible to have a discussion on the subject of 'Psychoanalysis in a Sanatorium'. I would rather not speak on the subject at the Congress, since it could be taken for advertising.

I hope to take a short holiday at the end of August or the beginning of September, so should be most grateful if you could let me know by the end of this month or the beginning of August if you would like to come here for a while and, if so, whether you prefer to come before or after the Congress.

Please give my kindest regards to your father and tell him that I have been up to my neck in work since May, even though my legs do not yet allow me to walk for more than 20 minutes at a time.[2] Please also remember me to your mother and aunt.

In the hope of being able to welcome you here, I remain, with the kindest regards from my wife and myself,

Yours very sincerely, [L. Binswanger]

[1] The 13th International Psychoanalytic Congress, Lucerne, 27–31 August 1934. Cf. Gidal and Friedrich (1990).
[2] Early in 1934 Binswanger had suffered a prolonged attack of phlebitis, following influenza. Cf. Diary IV, pp. 196–8.

178AF
[Anna Freud to Ludwig Binswanger]

23 July 1934[1]

Anna Freud   Vienna IX, Berggasse 19

Dear Dr. Binswanger,
Thank you very much for your letter and kind invitation, which I much appreciated. I should very much like to visit you, the more so as my father has so often spoken of his visit to Kreuzlingen, but unfortunately it is out of the question. My absence from Vienna for the Congress must be as brief as possible. My father, although well, needs me for so many things that leaving here is always difficult for me. I shall be departing from Vienna just before the Congress and will return as quickly as possible. I know that you will understand and will not take my refusal amiss.

Shall I see you at the Congress?[2] I take it that you will be attending.
With kind regards and many thanks,

Yours, Anna Freud

¹ Typed letter.

[1] Typed letter.

[2] Binswanger did indeed take part in the congress; cf. Gidal and Friedrich (1990), No. 101.

179B
[To Anna Freud]

28 July 1934

Dear Fräulein Freud,

Much though my wife and I regret that we shall not be able to have you with us, I fully understand and respect your wish to return to your father as soon as possible. Naturally, I shall be seeing you in Lucerne. I am very much looking forward to it.

With kind regards to you, your father and all your family,

Yours, [L. Binswanger]

180B

30 March 1936

Dear Professor Freud,

The Academic Society for Medical Psychology in Vienna has asked me to deliver an address on *7 May* in honour of your eightieth birthday.[1] I have accepted with great pleasure; I regard being permitted to speak and pay tribute to you in your native city on so festive an occasion as a high point in our old friendship. I read through our whole correspondence once again a short while ago and was reminded how much suffering and joy – it was more suffering than joy – we have shared. You stood by me, in any case, during the three most distressing events of my life – my illness, and the deaths of my two sons – more staunchly and warmly than all but a few of my friends. These are things one can never hope to repay in one's lifetime.

The reason for this letter is now, however, a very special one. I wish to ask your permission to quote, in my address in Vienna and in an essay[2] I am writing about you for a journal, a few recollections of my conversations with you, or one or two verbatim passages from a letter of yours. At first I did not want to bother you at all with such a request, since I anticipate your agreement. However, you yourself are so meticulous and correct when you quote others that I felt it was best to ask you beforehand. No reply means that you agree.

I shall probably not be arriving in Vienna until late on 6 May or on the morning of the seventh, and do not want to disturb you on your birthday in any case. If, however, I could see you for just a moment on the *8th* I should be, of course, absolutely delighted. Perhaps your daughter would be so kind as to let me know. I shall again be staying in the hotel near the votive church, the name of which escapes me for the moment.[3]

The other day I read your last *Introductory Lectures on Psycho-analysis*[4] for the first time and would like to tell you that I not only absorbed their content with much gratitude and full agreement, but also that I admired their wonderful intellectual vigour, clarity and cogency. In old friendship and affection, and with kind regards to you and your family,

Ever yours, [L. Binswanger]

[1] 'Freuds Auffassung des Menschen im Lichte der Anthropologie' [Freud's View of Man in the Light of Anthropology], Binswanger (1936d).
[2] 'Freud und die Verfassung der klinischen Psychologie' [Freud and the State of Clinical Psychology], Binswanger (1936c).
[3] Hotel Regina (built 1896), today Rooseveltplatz 15, Vienna I, not far from the Berggasse.
[4] Freud (1933a).

181F

4 April 1936
Prof. Dr. Freud   Vienna IX, Berggasse 19

Dear Friend,

I had already heard that the Society for Medical Psychology had asked you to deliver an address in Vienna at the celebration of my 80th birthday. I heard it with mixed feelings, but satisfaction at being able to see you again was the strongest component in the mixture. I am plagued enough by old age, but fortunately there is no question of my finding it difficult to receive you in my home.

As for the source of those other, reluctant, feelings, please bear in mind how I dislike on the whole being the object of a 'celebration'. Nothing of the sort will take place in my immediate circle. The opening of the Vienna Society's new home will be the most fitting substitute as an occasion for ceremony.[1] The other arrangements are of no concern to us. And now consider the following: the people from the Academic Society and the speakers they have invited, apart from you and the good Thomas Mann,[2] namely Wagner-Jauregg,[3] Marburg,[4] Pötzl,[5] are neither friends of mine nor are they friends of analysis. They are hostile neutrals, some more hostile, some more neutral, than others. What their motive is for arranging such a celebration is difficult to say. It is certainly not a pure desire to express friendship and recognition. Perhaps, following the American pattern, it is the cult of great age, with the not very respectable intention of gaining publicity. In short, I can take no pleasure in the whole business, nor do I believe in a sudden change of mind and opinion on command. For that reason – I certainly do not wish to tell you what you should or should not say, nor do I want to spoil your pleasure at the task you have undertaken, but I would nevertheless warn you of the situation and ask you to be discreet about intimate details of our friendship in front of these strangers. We have taken our loyalty to each other for granted for a quarter of a century and made little fuss about it.

Please give my kind regards to your wife and daughter. I shall be delighted to see you if I am no worse in May than I am now.

Your old
Freud

[1] The new building of the Viennese Psychoanalytic Society at Berggasse 7 was opened by Ernest Jones on 5 May 1936: 'The Society meetings were to be held there as well as the Vienna Psychoanalytical Institute and Clinic.' Jones (1953–7), Vol. 3, p. 201.

[2] Freud had been in correspondence with Thomas Mann since his lecture 'Die Stellung Freuds in der modernen Geistesgeschichte' [The position of Freud in the modern history of ideas] (1929). Mann visited Freud for the first time on 16 March 1932. Freud's letter of greeting for Mann's 60th birthday ('Thomas Mann, on his Sixtieth Birthday', 1935c) reached him, already in exile, in Switzerland. On 8 May 1936, as part of the celebrations for Freud's 80th birthday, Thomas Mann then gave his lecture 'Freud und die Zukunft' [Freud and the future]; Mann (1936). It was also on his initiative that a collective message of good wishes was sent by a large number of artists on this birthday. Cf. Binswanger's diary report on his visit for Freud's 80th birthday in the Appendix, pp. 239–40 and the editorial remarks in Freud (1988g).

[3] Julius von Wagner-Jauregg (1857–1940), psychiatrist and neurologist, qualified M.D. 1885 in Vienna, where he continued to work until his appointment as Professor at Graz in 1889. He returned to the University of Vienna in 1893 and remained there until his retirement in 1928. He is best known for his discovery of a treatment for general paresis (syphilitic infection of the brain, which was fatal before Wagner-Jauregg's discovery) that involved inducing malaria infection into his patients, for which he was awarded the Nobel Prize in 1927. Cf. R.W. Lundin, in Corsini (1994), Vol. 4, p. 169. On Wagner-Jauregg in relation to Freud, see Gicklhorn J. (1957), Illing (1958) and Eissler (1979) and Wagner-Jauregg's *Reminiscences* (1950).

[4] Otto Marburg (1874–1948) qualified in neurology in 1905, honorary Professor 1912, Professor without Chair, 1916, Principal of Neurological Institute 1919; cf. Kauders (1948); Minkowski (1950).

[5] Otto Pötzl (1877–1962), qualified in psychiatry and neurology in 1911, after 1912 a member of the Vienna Psychoanalytic Society, honorary Professor 1920, ordinary Prof. in Prague 1922, Vienna 1928. As Wagner-Jauregg's successor in 1928, he put an end to Vienna University's disowning of psychoanalysis which had reigned up to that time, and supported Freud's students as far as possible. However, his attitude to psychoanalysis remained ambivalent all his life (Mühlleitner, 1992). Cf. also Harrer and Hoff (1968).

182B

Bödele bei Dornbirn, 8 April 1936

Dear Professor Freud,

Lest this letter, too, strike you as a 'mixed pleasure', I am sending it home first to have it 'translated' onto a typewriter, which will save you the bother of having to decipher the original!

I am here working at my usual retreat for ten days,[1] occupying myself this time entirely with you. I was tremendously pleased to see your handwriting once again and to hear that you are well, for your friendship is one of my life's most precious possessions. Your reservations about my lecture have in no way diminished the pleasure I shall have in delivering it. In the first place I scarcely think that the people you mentioned will be among my audience. The last time it consisted mostly of young people; young people were probably responsible for the invitation, and it is to youth above all that I want to address myself. In the second place, I would remind you of some lines by Goethe with which you are familiar and of which I shall be thinking during my address:

'Was klagst Du über Feinde?
Sollten solche je werden Freunde,
Denen das Wesen, wie Du bist,
Im Stillen eine ewiger Vorwurf ist?'

[Why do you complain of foes? Could those to whom a man like you is an eternal, silent reproach, ever become your friends?][2]

That is how you have always thought and lived! But I do realise that a *celebration* amongst 'enemies' does not appeal to you. Regardless of point 1, I shall perform my task quite without ceremony, you

Bödeli b. Thun.
8. IV. 36.

Lieber Herr Professor!

Damit Ihnen dieser Brief nicht auch eine „gemischte Freude" ist, welche ich ihnen meist nachsende, nur ihnen in die Schreib-maschine übersetzen zu lassen. Also ersparen Sie sich die Mühe der Lektüre des Originals! Ich bin für 10 Tage in meiner gewohnten Weltabkommene, diesmal ganz leidenschaftlich mit Schnee. Ihre Schrift: zeigt die alle einmal vor Augen zu haben und zu hören, dass es Ihnen gut ...

First and last pages of a letter from Binswanger to Freud, 8 April 1936.

can rest assured of that! In the third place, it never occurred to me to reveal intimate details of our friendship. I should have framed my request more precisely: I was thinking of a few, probably just two, of your comments that are relevant, one made during a conversation on the Semmering (for the essay)[3] and one from a letter of 1912,[4] in which I have found valuable amplifications of your scientific work. – If at all possible I should like to be present at the opening of the Viennese premises. I shall probably be arriving on the 5th after all, as I must leave on the evening of the 8th.

The pleasure of seeing you and your family again outweighs my pleasure at delivering the address, although they go together.

In old and cordial friendship,

Yours, [L. Binswanger]

[1] Mountain Hotel Bödele bei Dornbirn; cf. note 2 to 176F. According to his diary Binswanger was there from 4–18 April 1936.
[2] Goethe: *West-Eastern Divan*, (book of aphorisms).
[3] Binswanger (1936c), pp. 177ff.
[4] Binswanger (1936d), p. 292 (65F of this edition).

183B

Kreuzlingen, 4 May 1936

Dear Professor Freud, my dear and esteemed friend,
This ceremonial form of address is not a prelude to congratulations, as I know that you attach no importance to those, and as my congratulations are to be reflected in the content and spirit of my lecture. The address will come straight from the heart, in memory of everything we have been through together and of what you mean to me both as scientist and friend.

To my regret, I see that of course you were right after all, and the celebration seems to be taking on a markedly official air. All the same, I shall play my part plainly and simply. You well know that my object is not to eulogise but to present a purely factual appraisal and discussion.

To my great pleasure, my wife has decided to come along after all. This gives the whole affair decidedly more 'charm'. She is very much looking forward to seeing you again, if only for a moment. We shall not be arriving in Vienna until late on 6 May. It would probably be best if we could be allowed to see you during the 8th, that is, after the lecture. We shall be at the Hotel Regina. I shall no doubt be meeting your daughter after the lecture.

With kind regards,

In grateful friendship,
Yours, [L. Binswanger]

Binswanger's Sixth Visit (including the lecture) to Vienna, 6 to 9 May 1936

Binswanger also reported on this visit in his *Reminiscences* (1956c, pp. 95–6 in the English edition, 1957), based on diary entries, whose original text appears in the Appendix, p. 239–40.

184B

1 October 1936

Dear Professor Freud,

I am sending you my Viennese lecture today to complete your record of your 80th birthday. It is my homage to an older, wiser, far superior friend and intellect, a monument to our friendship of almost 30 years and a frank avowal of our points of agreement and of difference.

I was glad and happy to see you again and to feel that we are still close to each other.

With kind regards and best wishes to you, your dear wife, sister-in-law and daughter.

As always, yours, [L. Binswanger]

My wife sends her kind regards to you and your family

185F

8 October 1936
Prof. Dr. Freud   Vienna IX, Berggasse 19

Dear Friend,

What a pleasant surprise your lecture was![1] Those who heard it and told me about it were evidently unmoved; it must have been too difficult for them. Reading it, I was delighted by your elegant language, your erudition, the breadth of your outlook, your tact in contradiction. As is well known, one can put up with any amount of praise.

Of course, I still do not believe you. I have never ventured beyond the ground floor and basement of the building. – You maintain that if one changes one's point of view one can also see a higher floor, in which there live such distinguished guests as religion, art, etc. You are not alone in this; most cultivated specimens of *homo natura*[2] think likewise. You are the conservative in this respect, and I the revolutionary. If I still had a lifetime of work ahead of me, I should dare to assign a home in my lowly little house to those highborn personages. I have already done so for religion since coming across the category 'neurosis of mankind'.[3] But we are probably speaking at cross purposes and it will take centuries before our differences are settled.

In cordial friendship and with kind regards to your wife,

Yours, Freud

[1] Freud had not been able to attend the official birthday celebrations because he was unwell and so met the lecture for the first time in its written form.
[2] Binswanger had spoken in his lecture (1936d, p. 266) of *homo natura*, of men as nature, as the formative idea of Freud's scientific thinking.
[3] See *The Future of an Illusion* (1927c).

186B

19 October 1936

Dear Professor Freud,

Many thanks for your kind letter in which, I think, you let me off rather lightly. The fact that my lecture left most of the audience unmoved is something I was aware of immediately and that did not surprise me. But then I did not write my lecture with a view to instant effect. Still, there was one face in front of me that followed my arguments with keen interest, that of Pötzl. As he told me afterwards, my references to Goethe in particular accorded with his own views of you. The reason Goethe cropped up so often in my lecture is, incidentally, not just objective, but also because I have never found it hard to place Goethe and yourself side by side and to think of you together. The reason is your incorruptible and undeviating independence of judgement in all spheres of life and in all situations, reflecting your very personality and destiny. This similarity occasionally makes itself felt even in your style.

Häberlin has written to me that he hopes that his life's work might one day receive a similar tribute, one that could only have sprung from personal affection.[1] I merely report this to show that others, too, felt that despite differences of opinion my pen was guided by personal affection and respect.

I have just returned from holiday, spent partly in Bödele and partly in Locarno,[2] during which not much work was done. When I am on holiday, I always think I shall never be able to get over the fate that befell my son, rather a silly expression, since fate happens to be there for the purpose of being borne, and we are moulded and fashioned by it.

My wife was very pleased to receive your regards and returns them most cordially.

In loyalty and friendship,

Yours, [L. Binswanger]

[1] Häberlin wrote to Binswanger on 9 October 1936: 'Your celebration lecture gave me a great deal of pleasure. In spite of all criticism it really said the best that can be said about Freud. To be able to do that really requires "personal affection" – and I wish for myself one day nothing better than such an honour. The Freudian bias is fully expressed as much in its bias as also in its – one can say – magnificence.' Häberlin (1997), p. 260.

[2] Binswanger was in Bödele bei Dornbirn from 15 to 30 September 1936 and from 2 to 13 October in Locarno at the Hotel Esplanade, and from 10 October, together with his wife.

187B

18 March 1938

Dear Professor Freud,

I read your last two articles in the *International Journal of Psycho-Analysis* with great interest and pleasure.[1] I also recently read your daughter's book;[2] it is very clearly and meticulously written and I have learnt a number of things from it.

The purpose of these lines is for me to let you know that you would be welcome to come here as soon as you feel the need for a change of air.[3] Last night I rang Pastor Pfister to find out more about your state of health, but he had no further details. You know, of course, that your Swiss friends are thinking of you and are ready to help at any time.

My wife and I have such very pleasant and abiding memories of our last visit to you, and both send you our kind regards.

In old loyalty and friendship,

Yours, [L. Binswanger]

Sigmund Freud, 1938, waiting for permit to leave Vienna.

[1] 'Analysis Terminable and Interminable' (1937c) and 'Construction in Analysis' (1937d).
[2] Anna Freud, *Das Ich und die Abhehrmechanismen* (1936) [The Ego and the Mechanisms of Defence].
[3] Binswanger meant resettlement in Switzerland in view of the *Anschluss* of Austria with Nazi Germany on 13 March. It is clear from correspondence and diaries that by early 1933 he must already have perceived the shocking extent of the dismissals and persecution of Jewish doctors and had no illusions about the persecution now to be expected in Austria.

188B

5 July 1938

Dear Professor Freud,
I felt greatly relieved when I heard that you had arrived safely in England. My thoughts, which in any case are never far from you, have been with you particularly often of late. I never doubted that you would face the changing times and even harassment with psychoanalytic calm, but I was nevertheless worried, knowing of your precarious situation.

I should be very pleased to hear, from anyone in your company, whether your wife, your daughter and your sister-in-law are with you in England and how you have settled down there. My kind regards to all your family including your sons.

As for us, I can only say that my family and I are very well, and that I have too much rather than too little work.

Though Germany has presently ceased sending us patients almost entirely and though Spain must, of course, be forgotten for the time being, the cases that nowadays come to a clinic like ours make particularly heavy work. However, I continue to steal from my practical duties the time I need for scientific study.

These lines are only to let you know that I think of you in cordial friendship and in gratitude,

Yours, [L. Binswanger]

P.S. Many kind regards to Ernest Jones.

189F

19 July 1938

Prof. Dr. Freud   39 Elsworthy Road, London N.W.3

Dear Dr. Binswanger,

Many thanks for your good wishes! I knew they were bound to come.

I am here in temporary quarters together with my wife, sister-in-law, who is unfortunately ill, my daughter Anna, my married daughter[1] and her husband, and my son Martin. My son Ernst has been living here for over four years and is doing well as an architect. Despite all the difficulties of our new surroundings – every detail of life in England is different – we should be feeling quite well if the news from Vienna, and the fact that we are unable to render help to all those who need it so urgently, allowed of any such feeling of well-being. My son and son-in-law are looking for jobs and a living but have not yet been successful. There are no restraints on the practice of analysis in England and our English group has given us a very cordial reception.[2]

I was glad to hear that all of you are well and send my kind regards to you and your family.

Yours,
Freud

215

[1] Mathilde Hollitscher; cf. Jones (1953–7), Vol. 3, p. 243.
[2] Cf. also the letter Freud wrote to Jones on 7 March 1939 on the occasion of the 25th anniversary of the British Psychoanalytical Society, Jones (1953–7), Vol. 3, p. 260 and, in a different translation, in Freud (1993e), p. 769.

190B
[To Anna Freud]

23 August 1938

Dear Fräulein Anna,

Frau Dr. *Grete Ruben*,[1] an analyst trained in Berlin, a very intelligent and trustworthy lady whom I have known very well for many years, a non-Aryan, has now had to give up her flourishing psychoanalytic practice in Milan and is thinking of going to England. She may perhaps appeal to you in person. I would commend her to you most strongly as a very bravely struggling woman and mother. You can rely on her in every respect, both professionally and personally.

Please tell your dear father that he gave me *very* great pleasure with his letter from England. Since scarcely a day goes by that I do not think of him, his letter was happy new proof of his friendship, and a great relief.

With kindest regards to your parents and to yourself,

Yours most sincerely, [L. Binswanger]

[1] Margarete Ruben (...–1981), Psychoanalyst, her membership of the Italian Psycho-analytic Society was formally transferred to the British on 6 November 1940; she emigrated to Los Angeles in the 1950s. Anna Freud wrote a Preface to her book *Parent Guidance in the Nursery School*, New York, 1960. [I am indebted to Jill Duncan of the British Institute of Psycho-Analysis for most of this information. T.R.]

Letters After Freud's Death

191B
[To Martha and Anna Freud]

2 October 1939

Dear Frau Professor Freud, Dear Fräulein Anna.

I had to take some time to assimilate the news of the death of your dear husband and father[1] before I felt able to write to you, since in losing him it was as if I had lost a close member of my own family. Hence I find it very hard to offer you my condolences like an outsider. I feel very close to you right now, as if I were one of you, like a son or brother. You may gauge the extent of my sympathy, if you will, by the fact that, after the death of your husband and father, I feel even more closely attached to you than before. I have no wish to intrude upon your grief, it is as sacred to me as is the memory of him who has departed.

You know that it was not just his scientific accomplishment and genius that bound me to him, nor his crucial influence on my entire scientific career. Much more decisive was that I was deeply receptive, over the decades, to the greatness and the indomitable spiritual and moral force of his personality. But underlying all that was my love for him, which from the day of our first meeting in Vienna in 1907 has remained unchanged to this day. It was my greatest good fortune that your husband and father was sensible to this love and that he responded to it with unfailing friendship. In our correspondence, nothing made me happier than his statement a few years ago that we had kept faith with each other for twenty-five years.[2] But above all I shall never forget that in 1913 he interrupted his strenuous professional round to visit me here in Kreuzlingen after I had told him that I was seriously ill.

That visit was one of the most remarkable demonstrations of personal friendship I have ever experienced. It always distressed me that I was unable to repay this act of friendship with a similar act of my own. There was one occasion when I hoped I might do so, namely when the change took place in Vienna and I wrote to offer him refuge with us.[3] I was, however, happy to learn then that he had been given so affectionate a reception in England. And his last letter from there confirmed that he had not forgotten me.

I vividly remember all my visits to your house in the Bergstrasse [*sic*], and the last one to your villa, whether I came with my wife and my daughter, with Jung or with Häberlin. Your house in the Berg-strasse was a piece of home to me, and even now I look on it as in no way lost in oblivion but as everlastingly full of life. I would like to thank you for having regarded and received me from the start as one of your family.

I should, of course, be very glad if I could at some time be told something of the last weeks of my dearly beloved friend. I only hope that his end was easy.

In your grief, dear Frau Professor, you can nevertheless take pride in having had such a husband and in having created for him such wonderful domestic peace. – Please also convey my sympathy to your sister-in-law[4] and to your children. For you, dear Fräulein Anna, my wish is that you may find your sorrow at your father's passing eased by carrying forward his work and his endeavours.

My wife joins me in this expression of heartfelt condolences and friendly remembrance. I myself send a warm handclasp to you both.

Ever your friend, [L. Binswanger]

[1] Freud had died on 23 September 1939. Cf. the report of his death in Schur (1972), pp. 527–9 and Gay (1988), pp. 649–51.
[2] Cf. 152F.
[3] Cf. 187B.
[4] In error for 'sister', i.e., Minna Bernays who also came to London with the Freuds.

192MF
[Martha Freud to Ludwig Binswanger]

7 November 1939
20 Maresfield Gardens,
London, N.W.3.

[Printed message in English:]
We wish to express our sincere thanks for your expression of sym-pathy shown to us on the death of Sigmund Freud.

October 1939 [October deleted]

[added by hand]

Dear Dr. Binswanger,

Please accept my profound, heartfelt thanks for the warmth and kindness of your letter following our very sad loss. It is only now that we have come to appreciate fully how much he was loved and revered, for we have received touching expressions of this from all over the world. What a good thing, dear Dr. Binswanger, that you knew him when he was still in the prime of life, for at the end he suffered so terribly that even those who would have loved to have kept him forever longed for his release.

And yet how terribly hard it is to have to manage without him: to carry on without all that kindness and wisdom at one's side. It is small consolation for me to know that in the fifty-three years of our marriage we had not one angry word, and that I did my best at all times to spare him everyday worries. Now my life has lost all substance and meaning.

In conclusion, dear Dr. Binswanger, I would only ask that you keep for me some portion of the precious friendship you felt for *him*, and in this hope I remain,

Yours ever, Martha Freud

193B

[Ludwig Binswanger to Martha Freud]

21 November 1939

My dear Frau Professor,

I was so very glad to get your letter and am deeply grateful to you for this sign of personal affection. I am happy to know that it pleases you that my friendship and respect for your dear husband also extend to you and your family. As far as I am concerned, that goes without saying. But your dear husband, too, lives on for me, as vividly as ever. I was very sad to learn that towards the end he suffered so much that you had to look upon his death as a release.

It occurred to me that, one of these days, we might consider publishing a collection of your husband's letters, so that the world may also come to know his purely personal side. I myself have only come to understand him properly through some of his letters. I know that he was extremely reluctant about the publication of purely personal communications, but I almost believe that we owe it to mankind, today more than ever, not to withhold even the personal side of the picture of this great man. But there is no hurry about that, and I consider these suggestions more in the nature of a friendly dialogue between us.

Please remember me to your daughter, your sons and your sister-in-law[1], and accept, my dear Frau Professor, the very kind regards of my wife and of

Yours ever, [L. Binswanger]

[1] In error for 'sister', i.e. Minna Bernays. See also footnote to 191B, p. 220.

194AF
[Anna Freud to Ludwig Binswanger]

20 Maresfield Gardens
London N.W.3
29 December 1939

Dear Dr. Binswanger,
My mother has shown me what you wrote to her about my father's letters. You are quite right, of course, and I had already discussed something similar with Dr. Bibring[1] and Kris.[2] There is naturally no intention of publishing these letters either immediately or in the near future. But I should like to bring them together all the same, originals or copies, whichever the owners prefer. Then in due course it can be decided what is of scientific interest and what is purely personal. I hope to make an appeal for such letters in the next but one issue of the *Zeitschrift*, in which another of my father's posthumous writings is due to appear.[3] Do you think there will be a good response?[4] And may I ask you to intercede with your close associates to send me copies? Anything that is too personal can of course be omitted.

In his lifetime we were all so wasteful of everything he put out, since there was always so much of it. Now one would very much like to collect it all together again.

With kind regards,

Yours, Anna Freud

[1] Eduard [changed to Edward] Bibring (1895–1959), neurologist and psychoanalyst in Vienna, after 1935 co-editor of *International Zeitschrift für Psychoanalyse*, emigrated to London 1938. At the time of this letter he was Secretary to the International

Education Commission; emigrated to Boston 1941. Cf. Deutsch (1959), obituary by
Arthur F. Valenstein in *Int. Jnl. of Psycho-Analysis*, Vol. 41 (1960) pp. 162–3 and
also Mühlleitner (1992), pp. 41–2.

[2] Ernst Kris (1900–1957), art historian and psychoanalyst. Emigrated to London 1938,
played important role as a founding editor of the *Psychoanalytic Study of the Child*,
and as an editor – in collaboration with Anna Freud – of the *Gesammelte Werke* of
Sigmund Freud and an early edition of Freud's letters to Fliess (1950a). Cf. Hoffer
(1957); Ritvo (1957) and (1966) and Mühlleitner (1992), pp. 187–9.

[3] The *Internationale Zeitschrift für Psychoanalyse und Imago* contained in its Vol.
25 (1940) five posthumous works by Freud: (1940a)–(1940e).

[4] No such appeal appeared either in Vol. 25 (1940) or Vol. 26 (1941) of the *Internationale Zeitschrift für Psychoanalyse und Imago*. Indeed, it is possible that the
publication of two Freud letters (1941g), (1941i) in Vol. 26 came about in connection
with the intention expressed here.

195B
[Binswanger to Anna Freud]

11 January 1940

Dear Fräulein Anna,

I was very glad to learn that you and Messrs. Bibring and Kris had
already had the same idea as myself. I am certain that your appeal
will be successful. Needless to say, I shall do my utmost to help see
that it is, but I hardly believe that will be necessary. If I may give
you some advice, then it is to frame the appeal in such a way that it
covers all types of correspondence from your father, and not merely
those of purely scientific or impersonal interest. One day you will have
to resign yourself to the idea of a biography of your father, and for
that it is impossible to collect too much material. I myself remember
very well how deep an impression it made on me when your father
wrote to me about the death of his grandson,[1] who, like one of my
own sons, died of tuberculous meningitis. There was scarcely any
other occasion on which I gained so deep an insight into his character
as I did then, and even though this particular trait is not of paramount
importance, I should nevertheless be happy if posterity were also to
learn something of your father's innermost core, for the sake of which
I loved and revered him so particularly. I should sort the material into
three categories, namely:

1) scientific contributions
    a) to the theory
    b) to the practice of psychoanalysis

2) contributions to the history of the psychoanalytic movement, of its adherents and its opponents

3) biographical items concerning the inner and outer life of your father.

With the warmest regards to yourself, your mother, your aunt and Herr Kris, I remain as ever, dear Fräulein Anna,

Yours sincerely [L. Binswanger]

[1] Cf. 154F, note 2

Ludwig Binswanger, about 1955.

Appendix

Reciprocal Visits between Binswanger and Freud

The correspondence between Freud and Binswanger began after they had met in person and it was later to be interrupted several times because one of them would be visiting the other. These interruptions are indicated within the body of the letters in the appropriate place. Binswanger made a written record of these visits directly afterwards or retrospectively later. Even though these reports cannot make good the gap left by Binswanger's missing letters, they do afford a glimpse into Binswanger's personal impressions of the meetings. Because these notes, as far as they have been published, are no longer easily accessible or have until now not been published at all, they are reproduced below. The report on Binswanger's *first* visit with Freud, which took place before the correspondence began, precedes the letters in this edition.

Binswanger's Second Visit to Vienna, 15 to 26 January 1910[1]

Shortly after this visit to Vienna Binswanger made notes about it for himself, which have survived in the original:

On the day I arrived, I attended Freud's seminar[2] which took place one evening each week from seven till nine. There were about thirty people there, beginners and advanced, some not doctors, no school psychiatrists; mostly young people, apart from the old guard: Sadger, Stekel, Rank, etc.[3] Freud's procedure was to give several participants a subject, on which they would report orally at the next meeting. On the agenda was Shakespeare's *Hamlet*, from which several scenes were considered psychoanalytically, the most thoroughly Scene 2, Act III, in which Hamlet goes to his mother and says, 'O, heart, lose not

thy nature! let not ever / The soul of Nero enter this firm bosom!'
and so on. The speaker concerned cleverly made it plausible that a
sexual attack by Hamlet on his mother can be seen in that scene. The
core complex of the neurosis or, as Freud also called it, family
romance, seems to be detectable even in *Hamlet*. (We know that the
core complex is about incestuous love towards one half of the parental couple, here the mother, with a tendency towards the destruction
of the other, competing [half of the] parental couple, in this case the
father.) Then one of the other speakers analysed in a slightly critical
and very complicated way Hamlet's relationship to his father in the
sense stated and in particular pointed to the division of one person
into several people, which dream interpretation reveals. We know that
in dreams various characteristics of one and the same person can be
represented by different people. Accordingly, here the 'father complex'
points to two people, namely the stepfather and Polonius. I do not
need to go into more detail here about how the father becomes a
stepfather. We know this process from, *inter alia*, Riklin's [*Wunscherfüllung und Symbolik im Märchen*],[4] I mean the origin of the stepmother fairy stories.

I must admit that a shiver ran down my spine when I started listening to this discussion. It was just too strong a ψ [psychic?] invasion.
But I soon saw the legitimacy of such an undertaking; I should say
another such, because we already know an excellent example of the
psychoanalytic examination of a literary work in the *Gradiva*.[5] But I
remember also Freud's fruitful analysis of Oedipus. Freud later told
me personally a short life story of Shakespeare from which it is easy
to see that Shakespeare – as whom, indeed, we must always see
Hamlet – had a severe mother complex. Why should the unconscious
not also be apparent in the case of intensive activity, that is, inspiration? On the contrary, we must say that inspiration does have
considerable significance in the unconscious coming to light. However, the question remains, which was mentioned only briefly in that
meeting and which the young people actually took as read, whether
we may automatically analyse a work of art, e.g. a play, as if it were
a dream. To me it seems that the difference is of only a secondary
nature. I regard such an activity as the one just described, which
presupposes the necessary level-headedness and criticism, as justified.
Freud even said that here we were only dealing with making something more or less plausible, not with the discovery of firm facts! At
the same time he pointed out the exercise value of such investigations.

I should just like to mention an *aperçu* of one of the younger members: he compared that changing scenes in a play, such as had just
occurred with Shakespeare, with the change of scenery in dreams.

After that I took part in one of the Wednesday evenings[6] which
serve as [meetings of] our Psychoanalytic Association. About fifteen
members, almost all doctors, and only a few beginners. It lasted [from]
nine [till] after twelve o'clock. Stekel gave a lecture on obsessional
images.[7] To start with he gave several examples with generally enlight-
ening interpretations. After that he went into a theoretical discussion
of obsessive behaviour, but it was so lacking in clarity that I no longer
remember it. I only know that I was struck by his strong addiction to
generalisation and that everything referred back to doubt, just as in
his book on anxiety hysteria everything refers back to anxiety. With
regard to doubt, he believed he could go further than Freud. While,
as his latest work demonstrates, Freud always prefers to put doubt
down to a doubt between love and hate and has established this
objectively and thoroughly, Stekel believes that other doubts should
also be considered. I still remember that he brought up the doubt
between religious belief and non-belief, understood in the sense of a
primary doubt, out of which, through displacement, a tendency to
brood arises and a doubt of the obsessional neurosis, which in terms
of content was incomprehensible to us. Someone who had been attending more closely pointed out that all that wiped out what Freud had
carefully worked out. As far as I remember, Stekel did not provide a
single ground for his opinion. The lack of clarity in his thinking
showed at one point and I brought it up when giving my opinion[8] on
the lecture. He spoke of a contrast between belief and non-belief,
intellect and affectivity, conscious and unconscious, all in the same
breath! As if belief, intellect and conscious on the one hand and non-
belief, affectivity and unconscious on the other could be inter-
changeable! It is still worth mentioning Stekel's assertion, which he
supported with a good example, that the compulsive impulse can
always be put down to a parental ban or command, of course taking
displacement into account. Personally, because of a lack of experience,
I still cannot form an opinion on the matter.

At the end of a lecture each participant had to give his opinion on
it. The order in which this was done was determined by throwing
dice.[9] Sadger, who got his chance to speak early on, accepted the part
of the lecture based on case material, but cursed the theoretical part
with sharp words. There then developed a long and quite pointless

discussion about the question whether anxiety or doubt was more important in a case of obsessional neurosis. At this point it seemed to me that the lack of psychiatric education of most of the participants was manifesting itself, if only in the terminology, which must be established at the outset if one wishes to communicate something.

The highlight of the evening was Freud's criticism of Stekel's talk. He took Sadger's view, albeit in a milder form. He raised with Stekel the danger of his deductions and rightly emphasised that he could scarcely accept that his (Freud's) expositions on the obsessional neurosis, which had taken years of study, could be enlarged upon after only a few weeks. Freud regarded Stekel as the most gifted 'sleuth of the unconscious' from whom we could all learn; he repeated this often to me. As I said, he did not think much of his theoretical ability. Even in his interpretations he pointed out an error to Stekel, which had arisen out of arbitrary reinterpretation of the *conscious* content of the symptom (gas tap – gasometer). As elsewhere, Freud emphasised that neurotic symptoms should not always be judged only by their conscious 'façades', but first and foremost by their unconscious background. Indeed in this connection I need only remember the contrast between dream content and dream thought. In the example above, Stekel, as we saw, had simply altered the content of the symptom, the conscious façade making the gas tap into a gasometer. Then, of course, even the interpretation did not add up. At this point I made a note of a very wise and meaningful remark of Freud's: 'None of us has acquired the habit of *thinking* about the processes of the ego and consciousness *simultaneously* with those of the repressed and the sexual drive!'

Freud commented on Stekel's assertion that every doubt is a doubt about the ego and every anxiety is a fear of death. He *rejected* both assertions in their generality. He also sought to restore order to the confusion of Stekel's arguments about doubt. For Freud, the real *pathological, compulsive* doubt is always related to reality. It is always a *reality-doubt*, for example, when someone has to ask himself over and over again, 'Did I *really* turn the gas off?' He contrasted the reality-doubt with the expectation-doubt, for example the doubt: 'How can I raise the money for things I have bought?' (Stekel's example). I can also mention here my own example: 'Will the patient find and drink the hyoscine, or not?' In these cases of expectation-doubts Freud spoke, if I remember rightly, of an anxiety delirium. (Past = reality: future = expectation).

For me, Freud's opinion[10] was very valuable because I saw how adept he is at criticism and how with a few words he can bring clarity to the morass and how he endeavours generally to maintain order and scientific discipline among his adherents. Incidentally I came away from the meeting with a good impression because I saw how hard the differences collided with each other and how nobody minced his words and none of the others took offence. Even Freud, for all the respect he commands, is contradicted often enough. Stekel, whom I liked better than I had expected in my resistance against him, protested against each damning criticism and pointed out how much had been thrown out in the group at first, but had later been acknowledged even by Freud. To a large extent Adler took Stekel under his wing.

Then again I was in the seminar with Freud where, because he had forgotten to allocate topics, he gave a lecture himself. It was about the train of thought in Rank's book *The Myth of the Birth of the Hero*,[11] which I assume everybody knew. In a masterful and clear-cut way, he underlined the essentials of the matter, which concerned the nuclear complex as well as the neurosis. Freud was quite taken with the need for and the usefulness of further psychoanalytic research into mythology.

Indeed, it must be emphasised anyway that for Freud the psycho-analysis of the neurotic is but *one* branch of his life's work; it is the side he practises most often, because the opportunity for it arises most often and at the same time it is the side from which a practical use can be obtained. At the same time, however, Freud always views psychoanalysis as a comprehensive science, as a great new research medium which he wants to know how to apply to religion, history and art. Indeed, that is the greatness and the impressiveness of his flight of thought.

Out of the multifarious conversations I was allowed with Freud, I should like to bring up a few more things: firstly his views on the unconscious. In the conversation concerned, I had taken up something he had said at the Wednesday meeting: 'The unconscious is metaphysical, we simply posit it as real!' This sentence certainly says how content Freud was in the matter. He says we proceed *as if* the unconscious were something real, like the conscious. On the *nature* of the unconscious, like a true natural scientist, Freud says nothing, simply because we know nothing about it for certain, but rather only deduce it from the conscious. In his postulation that behind the conscious, which we can experience, lies the unconscious, which can never be experienced directly, he sees a parallel with Kant's postulation of the thing in itself behind the appearance. On another occasion he called the unconscious a more lowly psychic organisation than the conscious. It is known that, like Lipps, he sees in the unconscious the psychic *par excellence*,[12] out of which the conscious develops. The comparison with Kant seems to me to be not quite right when you consider the details. I should like to say that we can experience more of the unconscious and more certainty from the conscious than we can of the thing in itself from the appearance. I also pointed incidentally to Schopenhauer, who after all construes in a purely philosophical way the will behind the conscious, which is, of course, no use to us at all.

I was interested to see how little need of metaphysics the notoriously speculative Freud had. Indeed, one should assume that the person who knows the unconscious best would also have metaphysical thoughts about the unconscious, e.g., *à la* Hartmann. Not so. There is no bridge between Hartmann and Freud. Freud is and remains a conscientious natural scientist who says no more than he has gained from experience. To have that confirmed, though, was the biggest impression of my [second] visit to Vienna. Of course, in matters of the psyche, one does not proceed from a premise, any more than one would in physics or chemistry, without certain 'prejudices'; I just remember the assumption that in matters of the psyche everything can be as precisely determined as in nature.

I found the following expression misleading: 'The unconscious is *metaphysical*, while at the same time it is supposed to be absolutely psychic.' Freud agreed and it quickly became clear that instead of *metaphysical*, one ought to say *metaconscious*. I consider the expression metaphysical unnecessary.

I was interested in Freud's expositions about *fetishism*, which he now treats just as psychoanalytically as the neuroses. This was all the more important to me as I could never quite believe his statement in the third essay on the theory of sexuality that fetishism occupied a special place in relation to the neuroses. He gave me several instructive examples and particularly emphasised the great influence of osphresiophilia in the genesis of fetishism. He put clothes fetishism down, among other things, to scopophilia as well as to the pleasure of looking at the *naked* body. As a result of repression [he said] great importance is attached to the covering, namely clothes.

(Manuscript, 19 pages, S.B. Munich, Cgm 8626, 209.)

Freud's Visit to Kreuzlingen, 25 to 28 May 1912[13]

Binswanger was operated on for a malignant tumour in March 1912, so he must have been in fear of his life. Freud visited him the following Whitsun. In his *Reminiscences* Binswanger wrote about the visit:

Unfortunately I kept no diary at the time, so in recounting the details of this visit I must, with one exception, depend entirely on my memory, which, although it has retained certain details very clearly, has left me completely in the lurch about a great deal. At any rate I can still see Freud getting off the train from St. Margrethen, looking very bright and youthful. I was happy about his coming and only the feeling that I would be unable to recompense him for the sacrifice of his time and trouble weighed on my mind. Freud quickly felt at home amongst us. To my wife he was kindness and consideration itself. He displayed particular interest in my four-year-old son,[14] and his 'great mother fixation' and expressed high hopes for him. We went for walks along the Bay of Constance and once went by car to the Untersee,[15] which particularly enchanted him. We usually had our meals with just the immediate family and also spent one evening at our family seat, where my stepmother, my father's widow,[16] gathered a wide circle of people round Freud. There too I can still see him in front of me. He was particularly light-hearted and talkative. On one occasion I read to him from my work,[17] and I seem to remember getting the impression that he was listening with polite interest but would have much preferred to hear something about analyses than about theoretical research. Once I asked him what he thought of his patients. He replied, 'I could wring all their necks.' My memory certainly does not deceive me here. But despite everything he himself said about his inadequacies as a physician, as is also so conscientiously recorded by Jones, I only half believed him – much too 'impressionistic' about how completely he sacrificed himself for some of his patients. After his return to Vienna, he sent me Victor Hugo's *Notre Dame de Paris*. Since, remarkably, we never spoke of the book subsequently – he had expressly forbidden me to thank him for it – I learned only from Jones'[18] biography that Freud had previously not thought highly of this book, but later preferred it to 'anything in neuropathology', I suppose because of its moving portrayal of the consequences of sexual abstention and the extent of sexual fantasies.

Binswanger (1956c), pp. 42–3

In a letter of 30 May 1912 to Ferenczi, Freud reports on the visit as follows:

[. . .] I really was in Constance from Saturday noon until Monday noon. I had been promising Binswanger a visit for a long time, was received like the dear Lord, also saw Stockmayer and a couple of younger doctors, was in the festive company of the Queen Widow, who sits enthroned on Estate Brun[n]egg above Kreuzlingen. The next estate ten minutes farther up, is Zeppelin's. I saw Arenenberg, where Napoleon the Third spent his youth, on a nice, long automobile trip with Binswanger and Stockmayer on the afternoon of Whitsun, which slowly brightened up. The area around the lake is a garden, Constance[19] is magically, beautifully situated, really at the point on Lake Constance where the Rhine flows out; Hohentwiel, known from Ekkehard,[20] the tower of Radolfzell, the island of Reichenau; everything comes together there.

Of course you know Binswanger to be highly respectable, serious, and honest; he has little talent, knows it, and is very modest. He read aloud to me part of a paper of his, in which $\psi\alpha$ [psychoanalysis] is compared with clinical psychiatry and which is based on good points of view. We also talked about Jung, and he informed me that, although he is close to him as a pupil, he never expects anything from him in the way of personal affection. He [Jung] is not a leader of men, strongly attracts men and then repels them with his coldness and lack of consideration. But he is also irreplaceable.

The three days were very good for me, despite two nights on the train and constant strain there.

(Freud 1992g, Vol. 1, p. 376.)

Binswanger's Third Visit to Vienna
(accompanied by Paul Häberlin), 17 to 18 May 1913[21]

For his report on this visit Binswanger relied upon a letter Häberlin had written him on 10 June 1954:[22]

It is also my recollection that our visit to Freud took place some time in the spring of 1913. Of the actual content of our conversations, however, I remember only three things:

1. I opposed Freud's deduction of the phenomenon of conscience (censorship) from instinct with the argument that a function [*Instanz*] which conferred no decisive authority upon the instinctual drive *as such* could indeed have no instinctual character itself. – But Freud held onto his view, which he later tried to substantiate in 'Narcissism'.[23]
2. Freud asked me if Kant's 'thing in itself' was not the same thing as he (Freud) understood as the 'unconscious'. I said no to this with a laugh and pointed out that the two things were on entirely different levels.
3. Freud expressed the opinion – not *quite* in earnest, though, it seemed to me – that philosophy was the most decent form of sublimation of repressed sexuality, nothing more. In response I put the question, 'What then is science, particularly psychoanalytic psychology?' Whereupon he, visibly a bit surprised, answered evasively: 'At least psychology has a social purpose.'

Perhaps as a fourth point, my question could be mentioned, in which I asked him how it had come about that his oldest and perhaps most gifted disciples, Jung and Adler for example, had just broken with him. He answered, 'They just wanted to be the Pope'.

Finally point 5. I asked why so many psychoanalysts cut a rather adventurous figure. He answered: 'I always thought that the first to snap up my theories would be pigs and speculators.'

As far as I know Freud sent his nephew to stay with me only after our visit.[24]

As we parted, Freud said to me: 'Go along with me as far as you can and, incidentally, let us remain good friends.'

Binswanger's Fourth Visit to Freud on the Semmering, 16 to 17 September 1927[25]

Binswanger's later reports on this visit are based on original diary entries, the text of which follows here:

10th September departed from Braunwald, 11th–18th Vienna, between 15th/16th [actually 17th] Semmering with *Freud*. [...]

In the evening of the 15th left Hertha behind in a very bad room (which I had not seen) in the Grand Hotel, both very depressed. Went out in the night with heavy heart. Next morning (16 September) sat in front of the Südbahnhotel in the sun for hours, because Freud had not expected me so soon and was out. Still felt bad and tired, but in the sun as if on the Riviera. An hour alone with Freud in the afternoon, in the evening with Ferenczi, Laforgue and the Princess of Greece (Bonaparte), earlier Laforgue under fire from all sides because of his scotomisation.[26]

Next day (17 September) alone with Freud from 10 till 12.30. About 3.30 went out in beautiful weather, contemplated the mountains at leisure and their gradual slope down to the fertile living plains. The Semmering itself was for me, even in summer, too much enclosed by the pine trees and monotonous, only the view down to the plain and the terrace of the Südbahnhotel wonderful.

I found *Freud* very cheerful and retaining his former enchanting charm. With nobody else does one feel so small, but nevertheless I was much more free with him this time than ever before. We talked about a lot of personal and of professional matters. He related in detail his views on telepathy, then about the Gi. case and the reasons the treatment had failed. I questioned him again about his perception of the spiritual in man, which he interpreted more in the direction of the 'intellectual functions'. He admitted that it plays a leading role in treatment: 'Yes, spirituality is everything (here)!' 'Indeed, humans knew they had spirit, I had to show them that they also have drive. People are always dissatisfied, cannot rest, always want something whole and completed immediately, but one nevertheless makes a start somewhere and just makes slow progress.' He denied there could be any such thing as an *a priori* religious category. Religion arises out of the need and anxiety of children and of early mankind, there is no doubt about that. With that, he pulled open the drawer of his desk ('Now is the moment to show you something') and produced a neatly written manuscript with the title 'The Future of an Illusion',[27] smiling questioningly at me as he did so. I guess from the context what the title means. As we part, he says with a smile: 'I am sorry I cannot fulfil your religious needs!' I take my leave from him quickly in the firm hope that I shall see him again in life. I felt refreshed and elated from the visit, not only spiritually, but almost physically and am pleased at last to have seen again the man who plays such a big role in my inner life. As I look round and up the steps of the Villa Schüler to see him, he has already disappeared inside the house.

(Diary III, pp. 80–4.)

Binswanger's Fifth Visit to Freud in Vienna, 22 to 23 April 1932[28]

There is also an entry for this visit in Binswanger's diary:

Friday 22nd, from 5 till 6 Hilde and I with *Freud*, who intellectually very lively and completely unchanged in appearance. Told him about Bobi [Robert] and he asked about everything, found Hilde very serious, the next day presented her with another book. Of Bleuler, who had visited him, he said he had 'not grown any more intelligent'. Asked about his sons: they have their destiny. [He] talked about Marie Bonaparte's new book,[29] still very delighted with her. The next day went to see his wife and [her] sister, spoke to them about my unrequited love for Freud. *Very pleased* to have seen him again

(Diary IV, p. 118.)

Binswanger's Sixth Visit (including the lecture) to Vienna, 6 to 9 May 1936[30]

Binswanger had been invited by the Academic Society for Medical Psychology in Vienna to give a lecture for Freud's 80th birthday. He took this opportunity to visit Freud and noted in his diary:

6–12 May 1936. Trip with Hertha to *Vienna* and *Munich*.

On the 6th [May] captivating journey in the morning by car through the spring landscape to Feldkirch, from there by train to Vienna, in constant sunshine through the Austrian countryside I love so much.

7th [May]. […] from 5.30 till 6.30 with *Freud* in his beautiful villa in Grinzing,[31] which completely full of flowers, rhododendrons, roses, carnations, azaleas. He himself very lively and friendly. Took me by the arm, led me back and forth in the large salon and the garden leading off it, asked about everything, and whether I was not nervous about the lecture afterwards at 8.15. Above all about Jung, our first visit, my dreams at that time, I spoke about Bobi. He did not want to accept that in such a case one had control over whether one became neurotic or not, [he said] that did depend upon the constitution. Showed me with satisfaction the wonderful letter of thanks from 300 artists, collected and put together for his birthday by Thomas Mann. Very happy to have seen this respected man and rare great spirit again.

About 8 o'clock [...] was picked up for the lecture in the hall of the Vienna Doctors Association. Wagner-Jauregg, Marburg and Pötzl spoke first, then I on *Freuds Auffassung des Menschen im Lichte der Anthropologie*[32] for about 1 hour 20 minutes. Pötzl my 'saviour' with his extremely intelligent attention. Too difficult and too long for most of them. Hertha and *Leonhard Frank*[33] very satisfied.

8th May. Visited Frau Gi., same old patient[34] who had just been rescued from an unfortunate suicide attempt, creepy case. Afterwards to the Kunsthistorischen [Museum][35] with Hertha [...]. Lunch with Frank and the young academics. [...] After that into the newly opened Analytic Institute. In the evening *Thomas Mann lecture* on Freud and the future.[36] Very wise and instructive, even in its form and in the courage to say things which people like us scarcely think and even if we do, we do not express them.

---

[1] Cf. above p. 29 between letters 22F and 23F.

[2] In Gicklhorn and Gicklhorn (1960), p. 154, this gathering is described as a lecture entitled 'Talks on Neuroses and Psychoanalysis'. No indication is given there of the number of people attending.

[3] In the *Reminiscences* (1956c), p. 5 in the English edition 1957, Binswanger mentioned 'Hitschmann, Federn, Sadger, Adler, Stekel, Rank, etc.'.

[4] [Wish Fulfilment and Symbols in Fairy Stories]. There is a gap in the manuscript here, presumably because Binswanger did not have the book to hand. It was published by the Heller publishing house, Vienna and Leipzig, in 1908.

[5] Freud (1907a) *Delusion and Dream in Jensen's 'Gradiva'*.

[6] Lecture evening of 19 January 1910. In addition to Freud twelve members of the Association were present and apart from Binswanger, the guests were Ludwig Jekels and Louise von Karpinska; see *Minutes*, Vol. II. (1967), pp. 394–403.

[7] In the *Minutes* the subject is given as: 'A Contribution to the Psychology of Doubt'; see *Minutes*, Vol. II. (1967), p. 394. Cf. also Freud's report to Jung: 'Stekel read us a paper on obsessions, it was absolutely frivolous and faulty in method; he was thoroughly heckled, as Binswanger will confirm.' Freud (1974a), p. 291.

[8] Cf. *Minutes*, Vol. II (1967), pp. 400.

[9] However, it states in the *Minutes* that 'the order of the speakers in the discussion is determined by lot' (written at a very early date: 10 Oct. 1906, *Minutes* Vol. I, 1962, p. 6.

[10] Cf. *Minutes*, Vol. II (1967), pp. 400–02.

[11] Rank (1909).

[12] In Greek in the original.

[13] Cf. above, p. 86.

[14] Robert Binswanger, born 1909.

[15] [Binswanger's note:] Cf. in this regard Jones II, p. 104.

[16] [Binswanger's note:] The 'Queen Widow', as he called her jocularly in a letter to Ferenczi. Cf. Jones II, p. 104.

[17] Binswanger (1922a); cf. note 2 to letter 62B.

[18] [Binswanger's note:] Cf. Jones I, p. 201: 'He entered into the spirit of Victor Hugo's *Notre Dame de Paris*, which previously he had not thought highly of, and even said he preferred it to neuropathology.' [Presumably a joke, but not identified as such by Jones. TR].

[19] Cf. note 1 to 163F.

[20] Joseph Victor von Scheffel (1826–86), *Ekkehard. Eine Geschichte aus dem 10. Jahrhundert*, Frankfurt, 1855 [Ekkehard. A story from the 10th century].

[21] See p. 116 above.

[22] Häberlin (1997), pp. 319–20.

[23] Freud (1914c).

[24] This is in answer to Binswanger's question: 'Did not Freud at that time entrust you with a young relative of his, or was that later?' Cf. Freud (1977j), also appears in Häberlin (1997), p. 350: letter of 4 June 1911 to Häberlin asking him to have his nephew Hermann Graf, then aged 14, to stay for a year because he had been disturbed since the death of his father. Hermann went to stay with Häberlin in Basel on 24 August 1910 and attended the Gymnasium (grammar school) there, returning to Vienna at Christmas 1911 (*ibid*, p. 351, note 1)

[25] See p. 189 above.

[26] René Laforgue, 'Verdrängung und Skotomisation' [repression and scotomisation] (1926a); 'Über Skotomisation in der Schizophrenie' [Scotomisation in schizophrenia] (1926b).

[27] Freud (1927c).

[28] Cf. above, p. 202.

[29] Probably Marie Bonaparte, *Aus der Analyse einer mutterlose Tochter* [From the analysis of a motherless daughter] (1931).

[30] Cf. above, p. 211.

[31] Leafy suburb on the northern outskirts of Vienna, at the end of a tram line from the city.

[32] Cf. note 1 to 180B.

[33] Leonhard Frank (1882–1961), German novelist, by this time had already been friends with Binswanger for many years, emigrated in 1933, returned to Germany in 1950.

[34] Cf. 44B, 48B, 49F, 50F.

[35] Major art gallery in Vienna.

[36] Mann (1936).

Chronology of the Letters

Abbreviations of names

AF	Anna Freud	AM	Alphonse Maeder
LB	Ludwig Binswanger	MF	Martha Freud
PH	Paul Häberlin	SF	Sigmund Freud

Abbreviations of letter types

C	Card	H	Handwritten
L	Letter	LC	Lettercard
MS	Manuscript	PC	Postcard
PPC	Picture Postcard	T	Telegram
TD	Telegram draft	TL	Typed letter
TLC	Typed letter (carbon copy or letterbook copy)	VC	Visiting card

	14 January 1908	SF —> LB		VC
	5 January 1909	SF —> LB		L
before	17 January 1909		LB —> SF	L *missing*
	17 January 1909	SF —> LB		L
	28 January 1909	SF —> LB		L
	5 February 1909		LB —> SF	TLC
before	7 February 1909		LB —> SF	T *missing*
	7 February 1909	SF —> LB		L
	27 February 1909		LB —> SF	TLC
	20 March 1909		LB —> SF	TLC
	13 April 1909		LB —> SF	TLC
	16 April 1909	SF —> LB		L
	18 April 1909		LB —> SF	L
	19 April 1909	SF —> LB		L
	23 April 1909		LB —> SF	L
	27 April 1909		LB —> SF	L
	2 May 1909	SF —> LB		L
before	17 May 1909		LB —> SF	MS L? *missing*
	17 May 1909	SF —> LB		L

242

before	25 May 1909		LB —> SF	L *missing*
	25 May 1909	SF —> LB	L
	7 November 1909		LB —> SF	TLC
	3 December 1909	SF —> LB	L
before	31 December 1909		LB —> SF	L *missing*
	31 December 1909	SF —> LB	L
before	7 January 1910		LB —> SF	L *missing*
	7 January 1910	SF —> LB	L
before	12 January 1910		LB —> SF	L *missing*
	12 January 1910	SF —> LB	L
	17 February 1910	SF —> LB	L
before	3 March 1910		LB —> SF	L? *missing*
	3 March 1910	SF —> LB	L
	8 April 1910		LB —> SF	TLC
	9 April 1910	SF —> LB	L
	12 April 1910	SF —> LB	PC
	18 April 1910		AM —> SF	L
	21 April 1910	SF —> AM	L
	12 May 1910		AM —> SF	L
	2 June 1910		AM —> SF	L
	9 June 1910	SF —> AM	L
	3 July 1910	SF —> LB	L
	8 July 1910		LB —> SF	TLC
	10 July 1910	SF —> LB	L
	12 July 1910		LB —> SF	TLC
	20 July 1910		LB —> SF	TLC
	25 July 1910	SF —> LB	L
	16 August 1910		AM —> SF	L
	14 September 1910	SF —> LB	PPC
before	2 October 1910		LB —> SF	L *missing*
	2 October 1910	SF —> LB	L
before	24 October 1910		LB —> SF	H L *missing*
	24 October 1910	SF —> LB	L
before	6 November 1910		LB —> SF	L *missing*
	6 November 1910	SF —> LB	L
	29 November 1910		LB —> SF	TLC
	3 December 1910	SF —> LB	L
before	9 December 1910		LB —> SF	L *missing*
	9 December 1910	SF —> LB	L
before	1 January 1911		LB —> SF	L *missing*
	1 January 1911	SF —> LB	L
	24 January 1911		LB —> SF	TLC
before	30 January 1911		LB —> SF	L? *missing*
	30 January 1911	SF —> LB	L
before	12 February 1911		LB —> SF	L *missing*
	12 February 1911	SF —> LB	L
before	5 March 1911		LB —> SF	L *missing*
	5 March 1911	SF —> LB	L

before	14 March 1911		LB —> SF	L *missing*
	14 March 1911	SF —> LB		L
before	20 April 1911		LB —> SF	L *missing*
	20 April 1911	SF —> LB		L
before	2 May 1911		LB —> SF	H L *missing*
	2 May 1911	SF —> LB		L
before	8 May 1911		LB —> SF	L *missing*
	8 May 1911	SF —> LB		L
before	28 May 1911		LB —> SF	L *missing*
	28 May 1911	SF —> LB		L
	15 June 1911		LB —> SF	TLC
	23 August 1911	SF —> LB		L
before	10 September 1911		LB —> SF	H L *missing*
	10 September 1911	SF —> LB		L
before	23 November 1911		LB —> SF	H L *missing*
	23 November 1911	SF —> LB		L
before	26 December 1911		LB —> SF	L *missing*
	26 December 1911	SF —> LB		L
	5 March 1912		LB —> SF	TLC
	15 March 1912	SF —> LB		L
	2 April 1912	SF —> LB		L
before	14 April 1912		LB —> SF	L *missing*
	14 April 1912	SF —> LB		L
before	16 May 1912		LB —> SF	L *missing*
	16 May 1912	SF —> LB		L
	18 May 1912		LB —> SF	TLC
after	18 May 1912	SF —> LB		T? *missing*
before	14 June 1912		LB —> SF	H L *missing*
	14 June 1912	SF —> LB		L
	29 June 1912		LB —> SF	TLC
	4 July 1912	SF —> LB		L
	22 July 1912	SF —> LB		L
before	29 July 1912		LB —> SF	L *missing*
	29 July 1912	SF —> LB		L
before	2 September 1912		LB —> SF	L *missing*
	2 September 1912	SF —> LB		L
before	22 September 1912		LB —> SF	L *missing*
	22 September 1912	SF —> LB		L
before	15 October 1912		LB —> SF	H L *missing*
	15 October 1912	SF —> LB		L
	20 October 1912		LB —> SF	L
	20 October 1912	SF —> LB		L
	24 October 1912		LB —> SF	TLC
	28 October 1912	SF —> LB		L
before	3 November 1912		LB —> SF	L *missing*
	3 November 1912	SF —> LB		L
	6 November 1912		LB —> SF	TLC
before	28 November 1912		LB —> SF	L *missing*

	28 November 1912	SF —> LB		L
before	16 December 1912		LB —> SF	L *missing*
	16 December 1912	SF —> LB		L
	19 December 1912		LB —> SF	TLC
	1 January 1913	SF —> LB		L
	26 January 1913		LB —> SF	TD
before	20 February 1913		LB —> SF	L *missing*
	20 February 1913	SF —> LB		L
before	25 February 1913		LB —> SF	L? *missing*
	25 February 1913	SF —> LB		L
before	27 March 1913		LB —> SF	L *missing*
	27 March 1913	SF —> LB		L
before	21 April 1913		LB —> SF	L *missing*
	21 April 1913	SF —> LB		PC
before	16 May 1913		LB —> SF	L *missing*
	16 May 1913	SF —> LB/PH		LC
before	24 July 1913		LB —> SF	L? *missing*
	24 July 1913		LB —> SF	TLC
	27 July 1913	SF —> LB		L
before	7 August 1913		LB —> SF	L *missing*
	7 August 1913	SF —> LB		L
before	7 December 1913		LB —> SF	L *missing*
	7 December 1913	SF —> LB		L
before	8 March 1914		LB —> SF	L *missing*
	8 March 1914	SF —> LB		L
before	12 June 1914		LB —> SF	H L *missing*
	12 June 1914	SF —> LB		L
	19 June 1914	SF —> LB		L
	22 June 1914		LB —> SF	TLC
	27 June 1914		LB —> SF	TLC
	22 July 1914		LB —> SF	TLC
	25 July 1914	SF —> LB		L
	28 July 1914		LB —> SF	TLC
before	29 September 1914		LB —> SF	L? *missing*
	29 September 1914	SF —> LB		L
before	10 January 1915		LB —> SF	L *missing*
	10 January 1915	SF —> LB		L
before	1 April 1915		LB —> SF	L *missing*
	1 April 1915	SF —> LB		L
	19 April 1915		LB —> SF	TLC
	24 April 1915	SF —> LB		L
	18 May 1915		LB —> SF	TLC
before	17 December 1915		LB —> SF	L *missing*
	17 December 1915	SF —> LB		L
before	7 May 1916		LB —> SF	L *missing*
	7 May 1916	SF —> LB		VC
before	25 December 1916		LB —> SF	L *missing*
	25 December 1916	SF —> LB		L

before	8 May 1917		LB —> SF	T *missing*
	8 May 1917	SF —> LB		PC
	10 August 1917		LB —> SF	TLC
	20 August 1917	SF —> LB		PC
	21 August 1917	SF —> LB		PC
before	21 April 1918		LB —> SF	L *missing*
	21 April 1918	SF —> LB		L
before	2 January 1919		LB —> SF	2 Ls *missing*
	2 January 1919	SF —> LB		L
	13 February 1919	SF —> LB		T
before	16 February 1919		LB —> SF	L *missing*
	16 February 1919	SF —> LB		L
before	25 December 1919		LB —> SF	Parcel L? *missing*
	25 December 1919	SF —> LB		L
	7 January 1920		LB —> SF	TLC
before	14 March 1920		LB —> SF	C *missing*
	14 March 1920	SF —> LB		L
	20 June 1921		LB —> SF	TLC
	23 June 1921	SF —> LB		L
	15 September 1921		LB —> SF	TLC
	3 November 1921	SF —> LB		L
	8 November 1921		LB —> SF	TLC
	24 November 1921	SF —> LB		PC
	22 April 1922		LB —> SF	TLC
	27 April 1922	SF —> LB		L
before	8 May 1922		LB —> SF	T *missing*
	8 May 1922	SF —> LB		PC
	31 January 1923		LB —> SF	TLC
	7 February 1923	SF —> LB		L
	23 February 1923		LB —> SF	TLC
	28 March 1923		LB —> SF	TLC
before	10 May 1923		LB —> SF	L *missing*
	10 May 1923	SF —> LB		PC
	27 August 1923		LB —> SF	TLC
	3 September 1923	SF —> LB		PC
	19 November 1923		LB —> AF	TLC
	24 November 1923	SF —> LB		TL
	3 January 1924		LB —> SF	TLC
	11 April 1924		LB —> SF	TLC
	27 August 1924		LB —> SF	TLC
	10 September 1924	SF —> LB		TL
	12 January 1925		LB —> SF	TLC
	27 January 1925	SF —> LB		TL
	15 February 1925		LB —> SF	TLC
	22 February 1925	SF —> LB		TL
	4 May 1925		LB —> SF	TLC
	10 May 1925	SF —> LB		VC
	4 May 1926		LB —> SF	TLC

	21 May 1926	SF —> LB		TL
	7 October 1926		LB —> SF	TLC
	15 October 1926	SF —> LB		L
	29 November 1926		LB —> SF	TLC
	4 December 1926	SF —> LB		L
	11 July 1927		LB —> SF	TLC
	15 July 1927	SF —> LB		L
	25 July 1927		LB —> SF	TLC
	28 July 1927	SF —> LB		PC
	24 September 1927		LB —> SF	TLC
	21 February 1928		LB —> SF	TLC
	26 February 1928	SF —> LB		L
before	2 April 1928		LB —> SF	Book, L? *missing*
	2 April 1928	SF —> LB		L
	23 April 1928		LB —> SF	TLC
	7 January 1929		LB —> SF	TLC
	11 January 1929	SF —> LB		L
after	6 April 1929		LB —> SF	H L *missing*
	11/12 April 1929	SF —> LB		L
	3 May 1929		LB —> SF	TLC
	12 May 1929	SF —> LB		LC
	27 December 1929		LB —> SF	TLC
	1 January 1930	SF —> LB		LC
	4 May 1931		LB —> SF	TLC
	10 May 1931	SF —> LB		LC
	13 April 1932		LB —> SF	TLC
after	13 April 1932	SF —> LB		L? T? *missing*
before	5 June 1933		LB —> SF	C? L? *missing*
	5 June 1933	SF —> LB		PC
	12 July 1934		LB —> AF	TLC
	23 July 1934	AF —> LB		TL
	28 July 1934		LB —> AF	TLC
	30 March 1936		LB —> AF	TLC
	4 April 1936	SF —> LB		L
	8 April 1936		LB —> SF	TLC
	4 May 1936		LB —> SF	TLC
	1 October 1936		LB —> SF	TLC
	8 October 1936	SF —> LB		L
	19 October 1936		LB —> SF	TLC
	18 March 1938		LB —> SF	TLC
	5 July 1938		LB —> SF	TLC
	19 July 1938	SF —> LB		L
	23 August 1938		LB —> AF	TLC
	2 October 1939		LB —> MF/AF	TLC
	7 November 1939	MF —> LB		L
	21 November 1939		LB —> MF	TLC
	29 December 1939	AF —> LB		L
	11 January 1940		LB —> AF	TLC

247

List of Illustrations and Facsimiles with Acknowledgement of Sources

p. xii: The Bellevue Sanatorium, main building (seen from the park side). Photographer: Arthur Brugger, Kreuzlingen. BA in the Archive of Tübingen University.

p. xiii: The park of the Bellevue Sanatorium. Photographer: Arthur Brugger, Kreuzlingen. BA in the Archive of Tübingen University.

p. 4: Ludwig Binswanger's wife, Hertha, née Buchenberger, about 1910. Frau Trudi and Dr. Wolfgang Binswanger, Kreuzlingen.

p. 11: Bellevue Sanatorium: dining hall. BA in the Archive of Tübingen University 442/364.

p. 11: Bellevue Sanatorium: entrance hall with a view into the reading room (left) and the entrance to the dining room (right). BA in the Archive of Tübingen University 442/364.

p. 58: Ludwig Binswanger, about 1911. Frau Trudi and Dr. Wolfgang Binswanger, Kreuzlingen

p. 97: Sigmund Freud, circa 1912, on the balcony of Berggasse 19, Vienna. Taken by his son Martin. By permission of Sigmund Freud Copyrights / Mark Paterson and Associates.

pp. 140–1: Binswanger's four oldest children (about 1917); left to right: Ludwig A., b. 1913; Hilde, b. 1911; Wolfgang, b. 1914; Robert, b. 1909. Frau Trudi and Dr. Wolfgang Binswanger, Kreuzlingen.

p. 200: Sigmund Freud, circa 1931. A.W. Freud *et al.*

pp. 208–9: First and last pages of a letter from Binswanger to Freud, 8 April 1936. Reproduced from the original in the Sigmund Freud Copyrights archive at the University of Essex by permission of Sigmund Freud Copyrights / Mark Paterson and Associates.
[This, one of only two surviving handwritten original letters of Binswanger to Freud, exists also in a typed, unsigned version. Because he was away from home and without a secretary, it is probable that, to avoid inflicting his atrocious handwriting on Freud, Binswanger sent the manuscript version to his secretary in Kreuzlingen, who then typed it and posted both versions to Freud, one legible but unsigned, the other illegible but bearing the signature.]

p. 214: Sigmund Freud, 1938, waiting for permit to leave Vienna. A.W. Freud *et al.*

p. 225: Ludwig Binswanger, about 1955. Frau Trudi and Dr. Wolfgang Binswanger, Kreuzlingen.

List of Abbreviations

B.A.   Binswanger Archive (in the University Archive, Tübingen, Germany).

C.W.   C. G. Jung: Collected Works.

FA   Family archive.

FAB   Binswanger family archive (Kreuzlingen, Switzerland).

Freud-Bibliographie   *Freud–Bibliographie mit Werkkonkordanz*, Meyer-Palmedo, Ingeborg, and Fichtner, Gerhard, S. Fischer Verlag, Frankfurt am Main, 2nd edn., 1999.

G.W.   Freud, Sigmund: *Gesammelte Werke,* S. Fischer Verlag, Frankfurt/Main.

Ges. Schriften   Freud, Sigmund: *Gesammelte Schriften* (an early version of the collected works).

Korrespondenzblatt   *Korrespondenzblatt der Internationalen Psychoanalytischen Vereinigung.* Ed. by C.G. Jung and F. Riklin. Nos. 1–6 Zürich 1910–11. Later continued as part of the *Zentralblatt* or the *Zeitschrift.*

Minutes	*Minutes of the Vienna Psychoanalytic Society*, eds. Nunberg and Federn, Volumes 1–4, 1906–18, New York, 1962–74 (*Protokolle der wiener psychoanalytischen Vereinigung*, Frankfurt am Main, 1976-81).
S.E.	*The Standard Edition of the Complete Psychological Works of Sigmund Freud*, London, 1953–66, index volume 1974, transl. from the German under the general editorship of James Strachey.
UB	University library.
WS	Winter semester.
Zeitschrift	*Internationale Zeitschrift für ärtzliche Psychoanalyse*, Vols. 1–26; 1913–41, Leipzig and Vienna until 1917, then Vienna only. Edited by: 1913–1918 Sándor Ferenczi, Otto Rank and Ernest Jones. 1919 Karl Abraham, Sándor Ferenczi, Eduard Hitschmann, Ernest Jones and Otto Rank. 1920–1923 Otto Rank. 1924 Sándor Ferenczi and Otto Rank. 1925–1932 Max Eitingon, Sándor Ferenczi and Sándor Radó. 1933–1935 Paul Federn, Heinz Hartmann and Sándor Radó. 1936 Edward Bibring, Heinz Hartmann and Sándor Radó.
Zentralblatt	*Zentralblatt für Psychoanalyse*, Vols. I–II; 1911–2/1912, Wiesbaden. Editor-in-chief Sigmund Freud. *Zentralblatt für Psychoanalyse. Medizinische Monatsschrift für Seelenkunde*, Vols. III–IV; 3/1912–15, Wiesbaden. Editor-in-chief Sigmund Freud.

Detailed Notes on the Translation

All the letters in this edition have been translated into English by Arnold J. Pomerans, with the exception of the following, which have been either fully or partially translated by Thomas Roberts.

11B	Binswanger to Sigmund Freud, 18 April 1909
13B	Binswanger to Sigmund Freud, 23 April 1909
14B	Binswanger to Sigmund Freud, 27 April 1909
28M	Alphonse Maeder to Sigmund Freud, 18 April 1910
30M	Alphonse Maeder to Sigmund Freud, 12 May 1910
31M	Alphonse Maeder to Sigmund Freud, 2 June 1910
39M	Alphonse Maeder to Sigmund Freud, 16 August 1910
44B	Binswanger to Sigmund Freud, 29 November 1910
65F	Sigmund Freud to Binswanger,14 April 1912 – Extract in [1960a].
68F	Sigmund Freud to Binswanger, 14 June 1912 – part only in AJP translation – translation of one brief passage only from Binswanger (1956c), p. 57
75aB	Binswanger to Sigmund Freud, 20 October 1912 – not in Fischer edition published in German.
90F	Sigmund Freud to Binswanger and Häberlin, 16 May 1913.
122F	Sigmund Freud to Binswanger, 14 March 1920 – last two paragraphs missing from AJP translation – incomplete translation from Binswanger (1956c), pp. 81f.
139B	Binswanger to Anna Freud, 19 November 1923
140F	Sigmund Freud to Binswanger, 24 November 1923
167F	Sigmund Freud to Binswanger, 11 January 1929 – First page reproduced in facsimile in Fischer edition.

Also translated by Thomas Roberts:
Introduction; Binswanger visits; Editorial apparatus.

There are a few small errors in the German edition which have been corrected in the course of translation. So that these may not be interpreted as errors in this edition, they are listed here. The page numbers in the column on the left refer to the German edition.

p. 37, 25B, note 1	Freud (1974a), p. 49, note 2 should read note 4 (note 3 in English edition).
p. 58, 41F, note 3	ref. to (1974a) should read note 3, not 2.
p. 62, 44B, note 2	date should read 29 November 1910, not 20 November [not checked with holograph, but 20 November does not tally with conference date].
p. 65, 46F, note 1	This should not read 'See note 7 to 3F', but should refer the reader to the introduction. It now reads: 'See p. xii of the Introduction'.
p. 78, 54F, note 5	(a) the date of Freud's letter to Jung is 15 June 1911, not 16 June. (b) the dates of Freud's Küsnacht visit were 16–19 Sept.
p. 98, 66F, note 4	'note 3 to 56B' – should read 56F.
p. 101, 68F, note 9	(1960a) page numbers given are those of 1980 revised edition.
p. 109, 73F, note 2	date of Freud letter to Jung should read 30 May 1910, not 1912.
p. 102, 69B, note 1	Pfister died in 1956, not 1856.
p. 120, 82F, note 5	refers to note 2 to 75F, should read 'cf. note 3 to 75F'
p. 138, 96F, note 6	refers to note 4 to 75F, should read 'see note 3 to 75F'
p. 144, 103F, note 5	'five days in Berlin' should read 'five hours in Berlin' – actually an error from the German translation of Jones's biography: see Jones (1953–57) Vol. II, p. 195 in original English edn.
p. 199, 147B, note 3	'Freud (1912e), p. 175f.' Page number incorrect.
p. 224, 170F, note 2	'Jones (1960–62), Vol. 3, pp. 177–9' – should read p. 177.
p. 266, note 3	[now] Freud (1977j).

Bibliography

Abraham, Hilda [1974]: *Karl Abraham; an Unfinished Biography*. London [*Int. Rev. of Psycho-Analysis*. 1974/1].

Abraham, Karl (1916/17): 'Untersuchungen über die früheste prägenitale Entwicklungsstufe der Libido.' In: *Internat. Zschr. ärztl. Psychoanal.*, Vol. 4 (1916/17), pp. 71–97. Pub. in English, London, 1927 as 'The First Pregenital State of the Libido', transl. Douglas Bryan and Alix Strachey, Intro. Ernest Jones, in *Selected Papers of Karl Abraham*, pp. 248–79. (Repr. 1979, 1988).

Adler, Alfred [1910]: 'Die psychische Behandlung der Trigeminusneuralgie.' In: *Zentralblatt,* Vol. 1 (1910), pp. 10–29.

— [1912]: *The Neurotic Constitution*, transl. B. Glueck and J. E. Lind, New York, 1916. Orig. title: *Über den nervösen Charakter*, Wiesbaden.

Aeschebacher, Jörg (1980): 'Wie aus der Spinnwinde eine therapeutische Gemeinschaft wurde. Anfang und Ende der Klinik "Bellevue".' In: *Tagesanzeiger Magazin*, No. 14, 5.4.1980.

Alexander, Franz and Selesnick, Sheldon T. (1965): 'Freud–Bleuler Correspondence.' In: *Arch. Gen. Psychiat.*, Vol. 12 (1965), pp. 1–9

Amitai, Menachem and Cremerius, Johannes (1984): 'Dr. med. Arthur Muthmann. Ein Beitrag zur Frühgeschichte der Psychoanalyse.' In: *Psyche,* Vol. 38, pp. 738–53

Bally, Gustav (1966): 'Ludwig Binswangers Weg zu Freud.' In: *Schweiz. Zschr. Psychol.*, Vol. 25 (1966), pp. 293–308.

Barth, Karl (1948): *David Friedrich Strauß als Theologe,* 1839–1939. 2nd edn, Zollikon.

Bertin, Célia (1982): *Marie Bonaparte: A Life*. London and New York, 1983. First published in French, Paris, 1982.

Bianchini, Marco Levi (1940): 'Die psychoanalytische Traumtheorie in einem Distichon aus dem dritten nachchristlichen Jahrhundert.' In: *Internat. Zschr.*

ärztl. Psychoanal u. Imago, Vol. 25, pp. 409–17. ('The psychoanalytic theory of dreams as contained in a couplet of the third century AD') Abstract by August Stärcke in *Int. J. Psycho-Anal*, 22 (1941), pp. 79–80.

Binswanger, Ludwig (1907-08a): 'Diagnostische Assoziationsstudien. XI. Beitrag: Über das Verhalten des psychogalvanischen Phänomens beim Assoziationsexperiment.' In: *J. Psychol. Neurol.* 10 (1907), pp. 149–81; 11 (1908), pp. 65–95, 133–53. (Also med. dissertation, Zürich.)

— (1909a): 'Versuch einer Hysterie-Analyse.' In: *Jb. psychoanal. psychopathol. Forsch.* Vol. 1, No. 1, pp. 174–318; No. 2, pp. 319–56.

— (1911a) 'Analyse einer hysterischen Phobie.' In: *Jb. psychoanal. psychopathol. Forsch.* 3 (1911), pp. 229–308.

— (1913a) 'Bemerkungen zu der Arbeit Jaspers': Kausale und "verständliche" Zusammenhänge zwischen Schicksal und Psychose bei der Dementia praecox (Schizophrenie).' In: *Internat. Zschr. ärztl. Psychoanal.* 1 (1913), pp. 383–90.

— B[uchner], L[othar] [pseudonym] (1914a): 'Klinischer Beitrag zur Lehre vom Verhältnisblödsinn' [A clinical contribution to the theory of pseudo-dementia.], *Zschr. Psychiatr.* 71 (1914), pp. 587–639. This English translation of the title is taken from the bibliography, based on data provided by Michael Balint, to the English edition of Ferenczi's *Further Contributions to the Theory and Technique of Psychoanalysis* (London, 1949), p. 468. Sándor Ferenczi wrote a review of the work, which appeared in the *Zeitschrift* Vol. 3 (1915), p. 59. No English publication of either the paper itself or Ferenczi's review of it has been traced.

— (1920): *Psychoanalyse und klinische Psychiatrie* (Paper given at the 6th International Psychoanalytical Congress in Den Haag, 8–11 September 1920.) In: *Internat. Zeitschrift artzl. Psychoanal.* Vol. 7 (1920a), pp. 137–65. Also in English transl.: 'Psycho-analysis and clinical psychiatry.' [Abstract] In: *Internat. J. Psychoanal.* Vol.1, p. 357.

— (1922a): *Einfuhrung in die Probleme der allgemeinen Psychologie.* Berlin.

— (1923): [Review of] Hoop, J. H. van der, *Character and the Unconscious: a Critical Exposition of Freud and Jung.* London and New York.

— (1924a) 'Einführung in die Psychoanalyse.' In: *Siglo med.* 73 (1924), pp. 388, 417–18, 447–8.

— (1926a): 'Erfahren, Verstehen, Deuten in der Psychoanalyse.' In: *Imago* 12, pp. 223–37. ['Experience, understanding and interpretation in psychoanalysis' – no English pub.]

— (1927b) 'Eröffnungsrede des Präsidenten.' [70. Versammlung des Schweiz. Vereins für Psychiatrie in Bern, 27. November 1926.] In: *Schweiz. Arch. Neurol. Psychiat.* 20 (1927), pp. 173–5.

— (1928c) 'Lebensfunktion und innere Lebensgeschichte'. [Based on a lecture given 6 Dec. 1927 'Hirnrinde' [cerebral cortex] Society in the Physiological Institute of Berlin.] In: *Mschr. Psychiat. Neurol.* 68 (1928c), pp. 52–79.

— (1928e) *Wandlungen in der Auffassung und Deutung des Traums von den Griechen bis zur Gegenwart.* Berlin: Springer.

— (1930): 'Traum und Existenz.' In: *Neue Schweiz. Rdsch.*, pp. 673–85, 766–79.

— (1930a): 'Dream and Existence'; in Engl. transl. in Foucault & Binswanger: 'Dream and Existence', transl. from German by Jacob Needleman, in *Being-in-the-World: Selected Papers of Ludwig Binswanger*, New York, 1963, pp. 222–48, reprinted in spec. issue of *Rev. Existential Psychol. & Psychiat.*, 19, no. 1, pp. 81–105, Seattle, 1986. Orig. title: 'Traum und Existenz', in: *Neue Schweiz. Rdsch.*, Zurich, Vol. IX, 1930, pp. 673–85; 766–79.

— (1931–3a): 'On the flight of ideas.' / 'Uber Ideenflucht.' In: *Schweiz. Arch. Neurol. Psychiat.* 27 (1931), pp. 202–17; 28 (1932), pp. 18–72, 183–202; 29 (1932), pp. 1–38, 193–252; 30 (1933), pp. 68–85.

— (1932a) 'Ernest Wenger † 4. Nov. 1888 – 18. Feb. 1932.' In: *Schweiz. Arch. Neurol. Psychiat.* 29 (1932), pp. 356–60.

— (1936c) 'Freud und die Verfassung der klinischen Psychiatrie.' In: *Schweiz. Arch. Neurol. Psychiat.* 37 (1936), pp. 177–99. Also in *Ausgewählte Vorträge und Aufsätze*, Vol. 2.

— (1936d): *Freuds Auffassung des Menschen im Lichte der Anthropologie.* In: *Nederl. Tijdschr. Psychol.* Vol. 4, Nos 5/6, pp. 266–301. Also in *Ausgewählte Vorträge und Aufsätze*, Vol. 1.

— (1941b): 'On the relationship between Husserl's phenomenology and psychological insight.' In: *Philos. and Phenomenol. Research* 2, pp. 199–210.

— (1942b) *Grundformen und Erkenntnis menschlichen Daseins.* Zurich.

— (1944–45a): 'Der Fall Ellen West. Eine anthropologisch-klinische Studie.' In: *Schweiz. Arch. Neurol. Psychiat.* 53 (1944), pp. 255–77; 54 (1944), pp. 69–117, 330–60; 55 (1945). pp. 16–40. English transl. (1958): 'The case of Ellen West: an anthropological–clinical study.' (Transl. W. M. Mendel and J. Lyons.) In: May, Rollo *et al.* (eds), *Existence: a New Dimension in Psychiatry and Psychology.* New York, pp. 237–364.

— (1945a): 'Uber die manische Lebensform.' In: *Schweiz. Med. Wschr.*, Vol. 75, pp. 49–52. English transl. (1964): 'On the manic mode of being-in-the-world' in: Straus, E.W. (ed.), *Phenomenology Pure and Applied.* Pittsburgh, pp. 127–41.

— (1949a) 'Die Bedeutung der Daseinsanalytik Martin Heideggers für das Selbstverständnis der Psychiatrie.' In: *Martin Heideggers Einfluß auf die Wissenschaften.* Berne, pp. 58–72.

— (1951e): 'Symptom und Zeit. Ein kasuistischer Beitrag.' In: *Schweiz. Med. Wschr.*, Vol. 81, pp. 510–12. English transl. by George Kastner: 'Symptom and time: a casuistic contribution.' In: *Existential Inquiries*, Vol. 1. No. 2, pp. 14–18

— (1955): 'Existential analysis and psychotherapy.' In: *Acta pyschother.* 3 (Suppl.) pp. 311–16. Also in: *Progress in Psychotherapy*, F. Fromm-Reichmann and J. L. Moreno (eds) (1956). Vol. 1, pp. 144–8.

— (1956a) 'Dr. Martha Wenger, Zürich (1890–1955).' [Obituary.] In: *Schweiz. Arch. Neurol. Psychiat.* 78 (1956a), pp. 386–7.

— (1956c): *Erinnerungen an Sigmund Freud.* Berne. English transl. by Norbert Guterman (translation amended for the current edition) (1957): *Sigmund Freud: Reminiscences of a Friendship*, London and New York.

— (1957b) 'Mein Weg zu Freud.' In: Alexander, Franz [et al]: *Freud in der Gegenwart.* A lecture cycle at the Universities of Frankfurt and Heidelberg in commemoration of the centenary of Freud's birth. Frankfurt (*Frankfurter Beiträge zur Soziolologie.* Vol. 6), pp. 207–27.

— (1957c): *Schizophrenie.* Pfullingen. [Reprint of five *Studien zum Schizophrenieproblem*, 5th ed., with a new Introduction].

— (1957e) *Zur Geschichte der Heilanstalt Bellevue. 1857–1957.* Kreuzlingen.

— (1958a): 'Daseinsanalyse, Psychiatrie, Schizophrenie.' In: *Schweiz. Arch. Neurol. Psychiat.* Vol. 81, pp. 1–8. Also in: *Beiträge zur Schizophrenielehre der Zürcher Psychiatrischen Universitätsklinik Burghölzli (1902–71)*, Darmstadt (1979, pp. 213–22. English transl.: 'Existential analysis, psychiatry, schizophrenia,' in:. *Existent. Psychiatr.*, Vol. 1 (1960), pp. 157–65

— (1958b):'Daseinsanalyse und Psychotherapie [II]. In: *Aktuelle Psychotherapie*, E. Speer (ed.) (Papers from the 7th Lindauer Pyschotherapy Conference, Munich, pp. 7–10. Also in: *Psycholanal. Rev.* Vol. 45 (1958). pp. 79–83.

— (1958c): 'The existential analysis school of thought.' (Transl. E. Angel) In: May, Rollo *et al.*, *Existence: a New Dimension in Psychiatry and Psychology.* New York, pp. 191–213.

— (1958d): 'Insanity as life-historical phenomenon and as mental disease: the case of Ilse.' (Transl. E. Angel) In: *ibid.*, pp. 214–36.

— (1959a) 'Dank an Edmund Husserl.' In: *Edmund Husserl, 1859–1959. Recueil commémoratif publié à l'occasion du centenaire de la naissance du philosophe.* Den Haag 1959, pp. 64–73.

— (1959b) 'Martin Heidegger und die Psychiatrie.' In: *Neue Zürcher Zeitung* 27. Sept. 1959, Beil. Literatur und Kunst, p. 5.

— (1960a): *Melancholie und Manie. Phänomenologische Studien.* Pfullingen.

— (1963): *Being-in-the-World: Selected Papers of Ludwig Binswanger.* (Transl. and with a critical Intro. by Jacob Needleman.) New York and London.

[Binswanger, Ludwig] (1966): *In memoriam Ludwig Binswanger, Dr. med., Dr med. et phil. h.c. 13 April 1881 bis 5 Februar 1966.* Kreuzlingen.

[Binswanger, Ludwig A.] (1978): *In memoriam Ludwig A. Binswanger,* pub. privately, Kreuzlingen.

Bircher, Ralph (1959): *Bircher-Benner. Bahnbrecher der Ernährungslehre und Heilkunde. Leben und Lebenswerk.* Zürich and Bad Homburg.

Bjerre, Poul (1911): 'Zur Radikalbehandlung der chronischen Paranoia.' In *Jb. psychoanal. psychopathol. Forsch.*, Vol. 3, pp. 795–847.

Blankenburg, Wolfgang (1977): 'Die Daseinsanalyse.' In: *Die Psychologie des 20. Jahrhunderts.* Vol. 3: *Freud und die Folgen (II).* ed. Dieter Eicke. Zürich, pp. 941–64.

Blauner, Jacob (1957): 'Existential Analysis. L. Binswanger's Daseinsanalyse.' In: *Psychoanal. Rev.* Vol. 44, pp. 51–64.

Bleuler, Eugen (1893): [Review of] Charcot, Jean-Martin: *Poliklinische Vorträge*, Vol. 1, Leipzig and Vienna, (Transl. into German and addl footnotes by Sigmund Freud). In: *Münch. med. Wschr.,* Vol. 40, p. 826.

— (1896): [Review of] Breuer, Josef and Freud, Sigmund: *Studien über Hysterie* [Freud 1895d], Leipzig, Vienna, 1892–94. In: *Münch. med. Wschr.* Vol. 43, pp. 524ff. Engl. transl. in Kiell, Norman (1988): *Freud Without Hindsight: Reviews of His Work, 1893–1939*, Madison, CT, pp. 73–4.

— (1907): *Über die Psychologie der Dementia praecox. Ein Versuch,* Halle.

— (1910a): 'Die Psychoanalyse Freuds. Verteidigung und Kritische Bemerkungen.' In: *Jb. f. psychoanal. u. psychopathol. Forsch.*, Vol. 2, pp. 623–730.

— (1910b): 'Freud'sche Theorien in der IV. Jahresversammlung der Gesellschaft deutscher Nervenärzte, Berlin 6–8 October 1910.' [On Oppenheim's attacks on psychoanalysis.] In: *Zentralblatt*, Vol. 1, pp. 424–7.

— (1911): *Dementia praecox, oder Gruppe der Schizophrenien.* Leipzig and Vienna. English transl. by Joseph Zinkin (1950): *Dementia praecox or the Group of Schizophrenias,* New York.

— (1931): Dr. Fritz Ris†, Direktor der Pflegeanstalt Rheinau. (Obituary). In: *Schweiz. Arch. Neurol. Psychiat.* 27 (1931), pp. 184–6.

Blum, E. (1967): 'Anthropology and psychoanalysis.' In: *Jahrbuch für Psychologie, Psychotherapie und medizinische Anthropologie,* Vol. 15, pp. 225–35.

Bodenheimer, A.R. (1957): [Review of] Binswanger, Ludwig: *Erinnerungen an Sigmund Freud.* Bern. In: *Schweiz. Arch. Neurol. Psychiat.,* Vol. 79, p. 201.

Bollnow, Otto Friedrich (1967): *Dilthey. Eine Einführung in seiner Philosophie.* 3rd edn, Stuttgart.

Bonaparte, Marie (1931): *Aus der Analyse einer mutterlosen Tochter. Zwei Beispiele zur psychoanalytischen Kasuistik.* Vienna.

Bori, Pier Cesare (1990): 'Oskar Pfister, "pasteur à Zurich" et analyste laïque.' In: *Rev. internat. hist. psychanal.,* Vol. 3, pp. 129–43.

Boring, Edward G. (1950): *A History of Experimental Psychology,* 2nd edn, New York.

Boudier, H.S. (1990): *Ontmoeting. Correspondentie v. F.J.J. Buytendijk met Ludwig Binswanger* [Encounter. Correspondence of F.J.J. Buytendijk with Ludwig Binswanger], transl. into Dutch and annotated by Henk Struyker Boudier. Kerckebosch, (*Carolingia Impressa*, 13). [This item catalogued in German edition as Binswanger, Ludwig (1990a).]

Bourguignon, André (1977): 'La correspondance entre Freud et Laforgue 1923–37', Paris. In: *Nouvelle Rev. de Psychanal.* 15, pp. 251–314. Not publ. in English, but there are significant extracts from the correspondence in Bertin (1982).

Bovet, Theodor (1971): Alphonse Maeder†. In: *Neue Zürcher Zeitung,* 2. Feb., midday edn, p. 25.

Brauchlin, E. (1957): 'Zum 75. Geburtstag von Alphons Maeder.' In: *Schweiz. Zschr. Psychol.* 16, p. 225.

Braun, H.J. (1971): *Ludwig Feuerbachs Lehre vom Menschen.* Stuttgart.

Broekman, J.M. (1965): 'Phänomenologisches Denken in Philosophie und Psychiatrie.' In: *Confin. Psychiatr.,* Vol. 8, pp. 165–87.

Brome, Vincent (1978): *Jung.* London.

Brunner, Conrad (1911): 'Dr. Robert Binswanger.' In: *Corr.-Bl. Schweiz. Ärzte,* 41, pp. 437–40.

Burlingham, Michael John (1989): *The Last Tiffany; A Biography of Dorothy Tiffany Burlingham.* New York.

Cargnello, Danilo (1948): 'Amore, amicizia, aggressivita ed ipseità nella antropologia esistenzialista di Ludwig Binswanger.' In: *Riv. Psicol.* No. 4.

— (1949): 'Antropoanalisi e psicoanalisi.' In: *Arch. Piscol. Neurol. Psichiatr.,* Vol. 10, No. 4.

— (1956): 'From Psychoanalytic Naturalism to Phenomenological Anthropology (*Daseinsanalyse*): From Freud to Binswanger.' In: *The Human Context,* Vol. 1, No.1, August 1968. [1st pub. in Italian, 1956.] Incl. biographical note on Binswanger by Binswanger, Herbert.

— (1966): 'Ludwig Binswanger (1881–1966).' In: *Arch. Psiol. Neurol. Psichiatr.,* Vol. 27, 2, pp. 106–10.

— (1968): 'From Psychoanalytic Naturalism to Phenomenological Anthropology (Daseinsanalyse): From Freud to Binswanger,' London. In: *The Human Context*, Vol. 1, No.1, August 1968, pp. 71–92, includes a biographical note on Ludwig Binswanger by Binswanger, Herbert; orig. German text pp. 71–2; English text, translated by Arnold Pomerans, pp. pp. 72–3.

— (1981): 'Ludwig Binswanger e il problema della schizofrenia – Prima parte.' In: *Rivista Sperimentale di Freniatria e Medicina Legale della Alienazioni Mentali*, Vol. 105, pp. 7–75.

Carotenuto, Aldo (ed.) (1980): *A Secret Symmetry; Sabina Spielrein between Jung and Freud*, New York, 1982. 1st pub. in Italian as *Diario di una segreta simmetria – Sabina Spielrein tra Jung e Freud*. Rome, 1980.

Chauzard, Jacques; Payonne-Lidbom, A. de la (1988): 'A propos d'une correspondance récemment découverte entre Freud et Bjerre.' In: *Frénésie*, Vol. 2, No. 5, pp. 97–113.

Coles Robert (1992): *Anna Freud. The Dream of Psychoanalysis*, Reading, MA.

Colpe, Carl (1967): 'Der Arzt im Zwiegespräch. Erinnerung an Ludwig Binswanger, gestorben am 5. Februar 1966.' In: *Landarzt*, vol 43, 6, pp. 277–83.

Cooper, John W. (1979): 'The philosophical foundations of Ludwig Binswanger's existential psychiatry.' In: *Dissertation Abstracts International*, Vol. 40, 2-A, pp. 897–8.

Corsini, Raymond J. (ed.) (1994): *Encyc. of Psychology*, 2nd edn, New York and Chichester.

Costa, Alessandro (1987): *Binswanger. Il mondo come progetto*. Rome (*Interpretazioni*, 17).

Craig, Erik (1988): '*Daseinsanalysis*: A Quest for Essentials. Special Issue: Psychotherapy for freedom: The daseinsanalytic way in psychology and psychoanalysis.' In: *Humanistic Psychologist*, Vol. 16, pp. 1–21.

Csorba, Janos (1984): 'Analysis of Existence vs. Psychoanalysis.' In: *Bull. South. California Psychoanal. Inst.*, No 71, pp. 6–8.

Delgado, Honorio (1967): 'Ludwig Binswanger' (obituary). In: *Rev. Neuropsiquiatr.*, Vol 30, 2, pp. 216–7.

Deutsch, Felix (1946–7): 'Hanns Sachs 1881–1947.' In: *Amer. Imago*, Vol. 4, No. 2, pp. 3–11.

— (1957): 'Edward E. Hitschmann 1871–1957.' In: *Psychoanal. Quart.*, Vol. 26, pp. 536–8.

— (1959): 'Edward Bibring 1894–1959.' In: *Psychoanal. Quart.*, Vol. 28, p. 78.

Dilthey, Wilhelm (1894): 'Ideen über eine beschreibende und zergliedernde Psychologie.' In: *Gesammelte Schriften*. 5th imp., Vol. 5. Stuttgart and Göttingen, pp. 139–240.

Dusen, Wilson van, Ansbacher, Heinz L. (1960): 'Adler and Binswanger on Schizophrenia.' In: *J. Individual Psychology*, Vol. 16, pp. 77–80

Edelheit, Henry (1967): 'Binswanger and Freud.' In: *Psychoanal. Quart.*, Vol. 36, pp. 85–90.

Eggert, Gertrude H. (1977): *Wernicke's works on Aphasia. A sourcebook and review.* The Hague, Paris, New York. (*Early Sources in Aphasia and Related Disorders*. Vol. 1) (*Janua linguarum*. Ser. maior. 28).

Eidelberg, Ludwig (1970): 'Tribute to Dr. Theodor Reik.' In: *Psychoanal. Rev.*, Vol. 57 pp. 531–4.

Eissler, K.R. (1958): 'Julius Wagner-Jaureggs Gutachten über Sigmund Freud und seine Studien zur Psychoanalyse.' In: *Wien. klin. Wschr.,* Vol. 70, pp. 401–07. To an extent incorporated in Eissler (1979). Abstract by Hans Kleinschmidt in *Annl. Survey of Psychoanal.,* ed. J. Frosch, 1958.

— (1979): *Freud as an Expert Witness: The Discussion of War Neuroses between Freud and Wagner-Jauregg,* transl. by Christine Trollope, New York. (Orig. title: *Freud und Wagner-Jauregg vor der Kommission zur Erhebung militärischer Pflichtverletzungen.* Vienna.)

— (1982): *Psychologische Aspekte des Briefwechsels zwischen Freud und Jung.* Stuttgart–Bad Cannstatt. (*Jahrbuch der Psychoanalyse,* supplmt 7). This essay on the psychological aspects of the Freud–Jung correspondence is incorporated, in condensed form in 'C.G. Jung, a witness, or, The unreliability of memories', section 2 of *Three Instances of Injustice,* Madison, CT, 1993.

[Eitingon] (1950): *Max Eitingon in memoriam* (ed. Max Wulff), Israeli Psychoanal. Soc., Jerusalem.

Ellenberger, Henri F. (1970): *The Discovery of the Unconscious: The History and Evolution of Dynamic Psychiatry,* New York.

Elrod, Norman (1989): *Freud und die französische Revolution,* Zürich.

Ewald, C.A., Heffter, A. (1911): *Handbuch der allgemeinen und speziellen Arzneiverordnungslehre.* 14th edn, Berlin.

Fabricius, H. (1973): 'Psychologen, die Schule machten. IV. Gemeinschaftspsychologie – Adler – Seif – Künkel (1889–1956).' In: *Schwest. Rev.* Vol. 11, No. 12, pp. 11–14.

Fechner, Gustav Theodor (1846): *Über das höchste Gut.* Leipzig.

— (1860–89): *Elements of Psychophysics.* Vol. 1, transl. from the German by Helmut E. Adler, ed. Davis H. Howes and Edwin G. Boring, New York.

Figueroa, Cave Gustavo (1982): 'El analisis existencial de la esquizofrenia en Ludwig Binswanger.' In: *Revista Chilena de Neuro-Psiquiatria,* Vol. 20, pp. 13–23.

[Fischer, Isidor] (1938): *Geschichte der Gesellschaft(der Ärzte in Wien 1837– 1937.* Vienna.

Fischer, Isidor (ed.) (1962): *Biographisches Lexikon der hervoragenden Ärzte der letzten fünfzig Jahre. Zugleich Fortsetzung des Biographischen Lexikons der hervorragenden Ärzte aller Zeiten und Völker.* 2/3rd edn. Vols. 1–2. Munich, Berlin.

Foucault, Michel (1954): 'Dream and Existence.' In: *Rev. Existential Psychol. & Pyschiat.* (special issue), Vol. 19, No. 1, 1986. Contains Foucault's 'Dream, Imagination and Existence', pp. 31–78 (F.'s 'La rêve et l'existence' appeared originally as the Intro. to the French translation of Binswanger's *Traum und Existenz.* Paris, 1954. Transl. by Forrest Williams). Also contains Binswanger (1930a).

— (1962): *Mental Illness and Psychology.* Transl. from the French by Alan Sheridan, New York, 1976. Orig. title: *Maladie mentale et psychologie,* Paris. Also repr. Berkeley, CA, 1987.

Frank, Claudia (1983): 'Entwurf eines ganzheitlichen Menschenverständnisses einschließlich einer diesem entsprechenden Methode am Beispiel von Ludwig Binswanger – Analyse und Kritik.' Med. dissertation. Würzburg.

Freud, Anna (1936): *The Ego and the Mechanisms of Defence.* London, 1937. First publ. in German, 1936. English transl. by Cecil Baines.

Freud, Ernst *et al* (1976): *Sigmund Freud. His Life in Pictures and Words*, ed. Ernst Freud; Lucie Freud and Ilse Grubrich-Simitis, with biog. sketch by K.R. Eissler, German texts transl. by Christine Trollope; New York and London, 1978, first publ. in German 1976.

Freud, Sigmund, jointly with Rie, Oscar (1891a): 'Clinical study of the hemilateral cerebral paralysis in children', Vienna (*Beiträge zur Kinderheilkunde*, No. 3); abstracts in *S.E.*, Vol. III, pp. 239, 241–2, 245–7.

Freud, Sigmund (1891b): 'On the Interpretation of the Aphasias; A critical study' [transl. James Strachey], *S.E.*, Vol. XIV, pp. 206–15 (part only). (Earlier Engl. title: 'On Aphasia; A critical study'. Transl. E. Stengel, London 1953.)

— (1892–94a): Preface and footnotes to Freud's German transl. of Jean-Martin Charcot: *Leçons du mardi à la Salpêtrière 1887–8*; Leipzig, Vienna. Formerly (1892–94). *S.E.*, Vol. I, pp. 133–7 (the Preface) and 137–43 (extracts from the footnotes).

— (1895a): review of Edinger, Ludwig, *Eine neue Theorie über die Ursachen einiger Nervenkrankheiten insbesondere der Neuritis und der Tabes* (1894). *Wiener klin. Rundschau*, Vol. 9, pp. 27ff. (Not published in English.)

— (1895c [1894]): 'Obsessions and phobias. Their psychical mechanism and their aetiology'. *S.E.*, Vol. III, pp. 74–84.

— (1895d): *Studies on Hysteria*. jointly written with Breuer, Joseph. N.B. Foreword to 2nd edition under 1909e. *S.E.*, Vol. II (entire volume).

— (1900a): *The Interpretation of Dreams*. *S.E.*, Vols. IV, V, pp. 1–625. [The pagination of these two volumes is continuous.]

— (1901a): *On Dreams*. *S.E.*, Vol. V, pp. 633–86. Published as a shortened veresion of (1900a), of which it is now usually considered a part.

— (1901b) *The Psychopathology of Everyday Life*. *S.E.*, Vol. VI (entire volume).

— (1905c): *Jokes and their Relation to the Unconscious*. *S.E.*, Vol. VIII (entire volume).

— (1905d): *Three Essays on the Theory of Sexuality*. *S.E.*, Vol. VII, pp. 135–243.

— (1905e [1901]): 'Fragment of an Analysis of a case of Hysteria'. *S.E.*, Vol. VII, pp. 7–122. Part of Dora case. (1905e), (1910h), (1912d), (1918a).

— (1906f): 'Contribution to a Questionnaire on Reading'. *S.E.*, Vol. IX, pp. 245–7. Formerly (1907d).

— (1907a [1906]): 'Delusion and Dream in Jensen's "Gradiva",' *S.E.* vol. IX, pp. 7–93.

— (1909b): 'Analysis of a Phobia in a Five-year-old Boy'. *S.E.*, Vol. X, pp. 5–147.

— (1909d): 'Notes upon a Case of Obsessional Neurosis' (the 'Rat Man' case). *S.E.*, Vol. X, pp. 155–249.

— (1910a [1909]): *Five Lectures on Psycho-Analysis*. *S.E.*, Vol. XI, pp. 7–55.

— (1910b [1909]): Preface to Sándor Ferenczi: *Psychoanalysis Essays*. *S.E.*, Vol. IX, p. 252.

— (1910c): *Leonardo da Vinci – a Memory of his Childhood*. *S.E.*, Vol. XI, pp. 63–137.

— (1910d): 'The Future Prospects of Psycho-Analytic Therapy'. *S.E.*, Vol. XI, pp. 141–51.

— (1910h): 'A Special Type of Choice of Object made by Men'. *S.E.*, Vol. XI, pp. 165–75; part of 'Contributions to the Psychology of Love' (1910h),

(1912d), (1918a [1917]).

— (1910k): 'Wild Psycho-Analysis'. *S.E.*, Vol. XI, pp. 221–7.

— (1911b): 'Formulations regarding the Two Principles in Mental Function'. *S.E.*, Vol. XII, pp. 218–26.

— (1911c [1910]): 'Psycho-Analytic Notes on an Autobiographical Account of a Case of Paranoia' (the Schreber case). *S.E.*, Vol. XII, pp. 9–79.

— (1911e): 'The Handling of Dream-Interpretation in Psycho-Analysis'. *S.E.*, Vol. XII, pp. 91–6.

— (1911j [1910]): transl. into German of and additional footnote to James J. Putnam: 'On the Etiology and Treatment of the Psychoneuroses'. *S.E.*, Vol. XVII, p. 271 (the footnote only). (Putnam's paper 1st pub. *Boston Med. Surg. J.*, 1910).

— (1912b): 'The Dynamics of Transference'. *S.E.*, Vol. XII, pp. 99–108.

— (1912d): 'On the Universal Tendency to Debasement in the Sphere of Love'. *S.E.*, Vol. XI, pp. 179–90. ('Contributions to the Psychology of Love') – (1910h), (1912d), (1918a [1917]).

— (1912e): 'Recommendations to Physicians Practising Psycho-Analysis'. *S.E.*, Vol. XII, pp. 111–20.

— (1912–13a): *Totem and Taboo: Some points of agreement between the mental lives of savages and neurotics. S.E.*, Vol. XIII, pp. vii, xiiiff, 1–161.

— (1913a): 'An Evidential Dream'. *S.E.*, Vol. XII, pp. 269–77.

— (1913b): Introduction to Oskar Pfister, *The Psychoanalytic Method. S.E.*, Vol. XII, pp. 329–31.

— (1913f): 'The Theme of the Three Caskets'. *S.E.*, Vol. XII, pp. 291–301.

— (1913i): 'The Disposition to Obsessional Neurosis'. *S.E.*, Vol. XII, pp. 317–26.

— (1913j): 'The Claims of Psycho-Analysis to Scientific Interest'. *S.E.*, Vol. XIII, pp. 165–90.

— (1913m [1911]): 'On Psychoanalysis'. *S.E.*, Vol. XII, pp. 207–11.

— (1914b): 'The Moses of Michelangelo'. *S.E.*, Vol. XIII, pp. 211–36.

— (1914c): 'On Narcissism: an Introduction'. *S.E.*, Vol. XIV, pp. 73–102.

— (1914d): 'On the History of the Psycho-Analytic Movement'. *S.E.*, Vol. XIV, pp. 7–66.

— (1914g): 'Remembering, Repeating and Working Through' [part of: 'Further Recommendations…']. *S.E.*, Vol. XII, pp. 147–56.

— (1915a[1914]): 'Observations on Transference Love' [part of: 'Further Recommendations…']. *S.E.*, Vol. XII, pp. 159–71.

— (1915b): 'Thoughts for the Times on War and Death'. *S.E.*, Vol. XIV, pp. 275–300. First publ. in English as *Reflections on War and Death*, transl. Brill and Kuttner, 1918.

— (1915c): 'Instincts and their Vicissitudes'. *S.E.*, Vol. XIV, pp. 117–40.

— (1915d): 'Repression'. *S.E.*, Vol. XIV, pp. 146–58.

— (1915e): ''The Unconscious'. *S.E.*, Vol. XIV, pp. 166–204.

— (1915i): 'Wir und der Tod.' In: *Zweimonats-Bericht für die Mitglieder der österr. israel. Humanitätsverein, B'nai Brith*, Vol. 18 [1915], No. 1, pp. 41–51; reprinted in *Psyche*, Vol. 45 (1991), pp. 97–142. Not publ. in English, but see the discussion of the first draft of 'Death and Ourselves' in Ilse Grubrich-Simitis (1966): *Back to Freud's Texts*, transl. from the German by Philip Slotkin, London and New Haven, pp. 131–4.

— (1916–17a [1915–17]): *Introductory Lectures on Psycho-Analysis. S.E.*, Vols. XV–XVI, Formerly [1916–17]. English transl. Joan Riviere (1922): *General Introduction to Psycho-Analysis*; James Strachey, *S.E.*, XV–XVI (entire volumes), [1963].

— (1916–17g [1915]): 'Mourning and Melancholia'. *S.E.*, Vol. XIV, pp. 243–58. Previously [1917e].

— (1918b (1914)): 'From the History of an Infantile Neurosis' (the 'Wolf Man' case). *S.E.*, Vol. XVII, pp. 7–122.

— (1919a [1918]): 'Lines of Advance in Psycho-Analytic Therapy'. *S.E.*, Vol. XVII, pp. 159–68.

— (1919b): 'James J. Putnam †' (obituary). *S.E.*, Vol. XVII, p. 271.

— (1919c): 'A Note on Psycho-Analytic Publications and Prizes'. *S.E.*, Vol. XVII, pp. 267–9.

— (1919h): 'The Uncanny'. *S.E.*, Vol. XVII, pp. 219–56.

— (1920c): 'Dr. Anton von Freund †' (obituary). *S.E.*, Vol. XVIII, p. 267.

— (1920f): 'Supplements to the Theory of Dreams'. *S.E.*, Vol. XVIII, p. 4.

— (1920g): 'Beyond the Pleasure Principle'. *S.E.*, Vol. XVIII, pp. 69–143.

— (1921c): 'Group Psychology and the Analysis of the Ego'. *S.E.*, Vol. XVIII.

— (1922b [1921]): 'Some Neurotic Mechanisms in Jealousy, Paranoia and Homosexuality'. *S.E.*, Vol. XVIII, pp. 223–32.

— (1923b): *The Ego and the Id. S.E.*, Vol. XIX, pp. 12–59.

— (1924c): 'The Economic Problem of Masochism'. *S.E.*, Vol. XIX, pp. 159–70.

— (1924d): 'The Dissolution of the Oedipus Complex'. *S.E.*, Vol. XIX, pp. 173–9. Earlier English title: 'The Passing of the Oedipus Complex' (transl. Joan Riviere).

— (1925d [1924]): 'An Autobiographical Study'. *S.E.*, Vol. XX, pp. 7–70.

— (1926b): 'Karl Abraham †' (obituary). *S.E.*, Vol. XX, p. 277.

— (1926d [1925]): *Inhibitions, Symptoms and Anxiety. S.E.*, Vol. XX, pp. 87–172.

— (1927c): *The Future of an Illusion. S.E.*, Vol. XXI, pp. 5–56.

— (1933a [1932]): *New Introductory Lectures on Psycho-Analysis. S.E.*, Vol. XXII, pp. 5–182.

— (1935c): 'Thomas Mann, on his sixtieth birthday' (letter of April 1935). In: *S.E.*, Vol. XXII, p. 255.

— (1937c): 'Analysis Terminable and Interminable'. *S.E.*, Vol. XXIII, pp. 216–53.

— (1937d): 'Construction in Analysis'. *S.E.*, Vol. XXIII, pp. 257–69.

— (1940a [1938]): *An Outline of Psycho-Analysis, S.E.*, Vol. XXIII, pp. 144–207.

— (1940b [1938]): 'Some Elementary Lessons in Psycho-analysis' (in German with English title) *S.E.*, Vol. XXIII, pp. 281–6.

— (1940c [1922]): 'Medusa's Head'. *S.E.*, Vol. XVIII, pp. 273–4.

— (1940d [1892]): 'On the Theory of Hysterical Attacks'. *S.E.*, Vol. I, pp. 151–4. Jointly written with Breuer, Josef.

— (1940e [1938]): 'Splitting of the Ego in the Process of Defence'. *S.E.*, Vol. XXIII, pp. 275–8.

— (1941g [1936]): draft of a letter to Thomas Mann (29 Nov. 1936), In: Jones (1953–7), Vol. 3, p. 492.

— (1941h [1939]): letter to Charles Berg, in facsimile in 'War in the Mind. The Case Book of a Medical Psychologist', *An Introduction to the Practical Application of Modern Psychology*, London, 1941, p. 6

— (1941i [1873]): letter to Emil Fluss, 16 Jun. 1873, pub. in *Imago*, 1941. Facsimile, ill. no. 31, pp. 76–7, with English transl. by Christine Trollope, p. 326, in Freud (1976).

— (1950a [1887–1902]): *The Origins of Psycho-Analysis; Letters to Wilhelm Fliess, Drafts and Notes 1887–1902*. S.E., Vol. I, pp. 177–280. Since published in unabridged form (1985) as *The Complete Letters of Sigmund Freud to Wilhelm Fliess, 1887–1904*; ed. Jeffrey Moussaieff Masson, Cambridge, MA.

— (1956l) [1911–38]): Letter to Theodor Reik and two references (c. 1934, 3 Jul. 1938). In: Reik, Theodor (1956): *The Search Within. The Inner Experiences of a Psychoanalyst,* New York, pp. 75f., 172f., 630–57.

— (1960a [1873–1939]): *The Letters of Sigmund Freud 1873–1939*, ed. Ernst L. and Lucie Freud, transl. from the German by Tania and James Stern, London.

— (1963a [1909–39]): *Psychoanalysis and Faith – the Letters of Sigmund Freud and Oskar Pfister*, ed. Heinrich Meng and Ernst L. Freud, transl. from the German by Eric Mosbacher, London, 1960. Also pub. New York, 1960 as: *Psychoanalysis and Faith – Dialogues with the Rev. Oskar Pfister.*

— (1965a [1907–26]): *A Psychoanalytic Dialogue; The Letters of Sigmund Freud and Karl Abraham 1907–1926*, ed. and transl. from the German by Hilda Abraham and Ernst Freud.

— (1966a [1912–36]): *Sigmund Freud and Lou Andreas-Salomé Letters*, ed. Ernst Pfeiffer, transl. from the German by William and Elaine Robson-Scott, London, 1972.

— (1968a [1927–39]): *Correspondence Sigmund Freud–Arnold Zweig*, ed. Ernst L. Freud, transl. from the German by William and Elaine Robson-Scott, London and New York, 1970 (1st pub. in German, 1968).

— (1971a [1909–16]): *James Jackson Putnam and Psychoanalysis; Letters between Putnam and Freud, Ernest Jones, William James, Sándor Ferenczi and Morton Prince 1877–1917*, ed. and intro. by Nathan G. Hale, Jr. Transl. of German texts by Judith Bernays Heller. Cambridge, MA.

— (1974a [1906–13]): *The Freud–Jung Letters*, ed. William McGuire, transl. from the German by Ralph Manheim and R.F.C. Hull; Princeton, NJ. German edition (Frankfurt, 1974) further edited by Wolfgang Sauerländer.

— (1977h), Bourgignon, André (ed.): 'La correspondance entre Freud et Laforgue.' In: *Nouv. Rev. Psychanal.*, Vol. 15, pp. 233–314. The correspondence between Freud and René Laforgue, transl. into French; not pub. in full in English, but extensively quoted in Bertin (1982).

— (1977i [1924–29]): Four letters to Abel de Castro (4 Jul. 1924, 22 Sep.1927, 28 Sep. 1928, 26 Sep. 1929). In: *Internat. Rev. Psycho-Analysis*, Vol. 6 (1979), pp. 437–40. Do Valle et al: 'Four recently discovered letters by Freud to a Portuguese Correspondent. A contribution to the pre-history of psycho-analysis in Portugal.'

— (1977j [1910-15]): 7 letters to Paul Häberlin (only 2 in full) in Kamm, Peter: *Paul Häberlin, Leben und Werk*, vol. I, pp. 254–7, 387ff., Thun, 1977. Also printed in Häberlin (1997).

— (1977k): Letter to Ludwig Binswanger and Paul Häberlin (16. 5. 1913) in Kamm, Peter: *Paul Häberlin, Leben und Werk*, Vol. I, Thun, p. 256. Formerly designated 1987h; also printed in Häberlin (1997).

— (1983a [1921–39]): Letters to Smith Ely Jelliffe. In: Burnham, John C. (ed.);
McGuire, William (ed. of letters): *Jelliffe: American Psychologist and
Physician; Part 1, His Correspondence with Sigmund Freud and C. G. Jung*,
Chicago.

— (1985a [1915]): *Overview of the Transference Neurosis / A Philogenetic
Fantasy* ed. Grubrich-Simitis, Ilse, Cambridge, MA. English transl. by Hoffer,
Axel and Hoffer, Peter T.

— (1985c) *The Complete Letters of Sigmund Freud to Wilhelm Fliess; 1887–
1904*, Cambridge, Mass.

— (1987c [1908–38]): Correspondence Sigmund Freud–Stefan Zweig (not pub. in
English). In: Zweig, Stefan, *Briefwechsel mit Hermann Bahr, Sigmund Freud,
Rainer Maria Rilke und Arthur Schnitzler*, ed. Hans-Ulrich Lindken *et al*,
Frankfurt am Main.

— (1988g [1929–37]): 4 letters to Thomas Mann (not publ. in English). In :
Mann, Thomas: *Briefwechsel mit Autoren*, ed. Hans Wysling, Frankfurt am
Main.

— (1989a [1871–81, 1910]): *Letters of Sigmund Freud to Eduard Silberstein
1871–1881*, ed. Walter Boehlich. (English transl. by Arnold J Pomerans,
Cambridge, MA, 1990.)

— (1992g [1908–33]) *Correspondence of Sigmund Freud and Sándor Ferenczi*,
ed. Eva Brabant, Ernst Falzeder and Patrizia Giampieri-Deutsch with Intro. by
André Haynal. English transl. by Peter J. Hoffer, Cambridge, MA, Vol. I
1993, Vol. II 1996, Vol. III 2000.

— (1993e); Paskauskas, R. Andrew (ed.): *The Complete Correspondence of
Sigmund Freud and Ernest Jones, 1908–1939*, Cambridge, MA.

— (1996g): *Lettres de famille de Sigmund Freud et des Freud de Manchester
1911–1938*, ed. Thomas Roberts, Paris. French transl. by Claude Vincent;
English. ed. in prepn under the title *Vienna and Manchester, The
Correspondence between Sigmund Freud and Sam Freud, 1911–1938*.

Friedländer, A.A. (1910a): 'Hysteria and Modern Psychoanalysis', *J. Abnormal
Psycholog.* Vol. 5 (1911), pp. 297–319. Orig. title: 'Hysterie und moderne
Psychoanalyse.' In: *Psychiatr.-neurol. Wschr.* 11 (1910), pp. 393–6, 406–08,
424–6, 435–6.

— (1910b): (review of) L. Binswanger, 'Versuch einer Hysterieanalyse.' In: *Zschr.
Psychol. Physiol. Sinnesorg.,* 1 pt. 57 (1910), pp. 148f.

Gargiolli, Maria Guiseppina (1966): 'Ludwig Binswanger filosofo e psichiatra.'
In: *Med. nei Sec.,* vol 3, no. 4, pp. 41–6.

Gay, Peter (1988): *Freud: a Life for Our Time*, New York.

Geinitz, Wolfgang (1986/87): 'Hans Prinzhorn. Das unstete Leben eines ewig
Suchenden.' In: *Hestia*, pp. 39–64.

Gicklhorn, Josef (1957): 'Julius Wagner-Jaureggs Gutachten über Sigmund Freud
und seine "Studien zur Psychoanalyse".' Eine wissenschaftsgeschichtliche
Notiz. In: *Wien. klin. Wschr.,* Vol. 69 (1957), pp. 533–7.

Gicklhorn, Josef, Gicklhorn, Renée (1960): *Sigmund Freuds akademische
Laufbahn im Lichte der Dokumente.* Vienna and Innsbruck.

Gidal, Tim N. (photographs); Friedrich, Volker (ed.) (1990): *Die Freudianer auf
dem 13. Internationalen Psychoanalytischen Kongreß 1934 in Luzern.* Munich
and Vienna.

Gius, E., Benna, L., De Sanctis, R. (1975): *L'Antropoanalisi di Ludwig Binswanger come superamento del pensiero freudiano*. Brescia, La Scuola, Rome.

Graber, Gustav Hans (1962): 'Dr Alphons Maeder zum 80. Geburtstag.' In: *Schweiz Zschr. Psychol.* (Bern), Vol. 21 (1962), No. 14, p. 10.

Grinstein, Alexander (1977): *Sigmund Freud's Writings: A Comprehensive Bibliography*. New York.

Häberlin, Paul (1997) ed. Luczak, Jeannine: *Paul Häberlin–Ludwig Binswanger Briefwechsel 1908–1960*. Basle.

Hale, Nathan G. Jr. (ed.) (1971): *Freud in America. Vol. I: Freud and the Americans. The Beginnings of Psychoanalysis in the United States 1876–1917*. New York.

Handlbauer, Bernhard (1990): *Die Adler–Freud Kontroverse*, Frankfurt am Main, 1990. 'Von "schlämpfigen Konflikten" und "großen Neurosen" – Ein neuer Blick auf die Freud-Adler Kontroverse' in *Beiträge zur Individualpsychologie*, Vol. 22 (1996), pp. 33–47. The content of the 1996 paper is incorporated in the English edition of the 1990 book *The Freud–Adler Controversy*, Oxford, 1998.

Harmat, Paul (1988): *Freud, Ferenczi und die ungarische Psychoanalyse*. Tübingen.

Harrer, Gehart, Hoff, Hans (1968): 'Otto Pötzl zum Gedenken' (with portrait). In: *Wien. klin. Wschr.*, Vol. 80, pp. 826–7.

Haupt, Emil (1858): *Zweiter Bericht über das Institut für Electricität, Heilgymnastik, Kiefernadel- und Kaltwasserbäder in Nassau a.d. Lahn*. Wiesbaden.

Havens, Leston L. (1972): 'The development of existential psychiatry.' In: *J. of Nervous and Mental Disease*, Vol. 154, pp. 309–31.

Haymann, Hermann (1925): 'Schmerzen als Frühsymptome der Dementia praecox.' In: *Arch. Psychiatr. Nervenkh.*, Vol. 74, pp. 416–26.

Haynal, André (1987): *The Technique at Issue: Controversies in Psychoanalysis: from Freud and Ferenczi to Michael Balint*, transl. from the French by Elizabeth Holder. London, 1988. (Orig. title: *La technique en question*. Paris.)

Hekking, Christian F. (1986): 'Die Daseinsanalyse Ludwig Binswanger Voraussetzungen eines Denkmodells und seine Tauglichkeit als therapeutisches Instrument', diss. Freiburg im Breisgau.

Herberhold, Ulrich (1978): 'Theodor Ziehen. Ein Psychiater der Jahrhundertwende und sein Beitrag zur Kinderpsychiatrie...'; med. diss. Freiburg.

Herzog, Max (1991): 'Der Begründer der Daseinsanalyse. Ludwig Binswanger' (1881–1966). In: *Neue Zürcher Zeitung* (foreign edn.), 15 Nov., p. 44.

Hirschmüller, Albrecht (1978a): *The Life and Work of Josef Breuer; Physiology and Psychoanalysis*. New York, 1989. Originally pub. in German as: *Physiologie und Psychoanalyse in Leben und Werk Josef Breuers*. Berne.

— (1978b): 'Nina R: Eine bisher unbekannte Krankengeschichte Sigmund Freuds und Josef Breuers aus der Entstehungszeit der *Studien über Hysterie*.' Includes letters: 5.3.1889 Nina R to Richard von Krafft-Ebing; 7.1.1994 Sigmund Freud to Robert Binswanger; 12.3.1994 and 23.3.1994 Josef Breuer to Robert Binswanger. In: *Jb. der Psychoanal.*, Vol. 10, pp. 136–68.

Hitschmann, Eduard (1911): *Freud's Theories of the Neuroses*, transl. by C. R. Payne, with Intro. by Ernest Jones, New York, 1919. Orig title: *Freuds*

Neurosenlehre. Nach ihrem gegenwärtigen Stande zusammenfassend dargestellt. Vienna and Leipzig, 1911.

— (1914): 'Über Träume Gottfried Kellers.' In: *Internat. Zschr. ärztl. Psychoanal.*, Vol. 2, pp. 41–3.

— (1915/16): 'Gottfried Keller, Psychoanalytische Behauptungen und Vermutungen über sein Wesen und sein Werk.' [I] In: *Imago*, Vol. 4, pp. 223–47 and 274–316. Abstract in *Psycho-Anal. Rev.*, Vol. 9 (1922), pp. 257–81 ('Gottfried Keller, psychoanalytical statements and suppositions concerning his nature and his work').

— (1919): *Gottfried Keller. Psychoanalyse des Dichters, seiner Gestalten und Motive.* Leipzig, etc.

Hoche, Alfred (1910): 'Eine psychische Epidemie unter Ärzten.' In: *Med.Klinik,* Vol. 6, pp. 1007–10.

Hoff, Hans (1962): 'In memoriam Otto Pötzl.' In: *Wien. klin. Wschr.*, Vol. 74, pp. 369–70 (includes portrait).

Hoffer, Willi (1957): 'Obituary. Ernst Kris 1900–1957.' In: *Internat. J. Psychoanal.*, Vol. 38, pp. 359–62.

— (1958a): 'Obituary. Edward E. Hitschmann 1871–1957.' In: *Internat. J. Psychoanal.*, Vol. 39, pp. 614–15.

— (1958b): 'Oskar Pfister 1873–1956' (obituary) In: *Internat. J. Psychoanal.*, Vol. 39, pp. 616–17.

[Hoffer] (1969): 'Willi Hoffer. 1897–1967' (obituary). In: *Internat. J. Psycho-Anal.*, Vol. 50, pp. 261–8.

Holt, H. (1966): 'Ludwig Binswanger (1881–1966): a tribute.' In: *J. Existent.* Vol. 6, pp. 93–6.

Illing, Hans A. (1958): 'Freud and Wagner-Jauregg.' In: *Amer. Imago*, Vol. 15, pp. 267–73.

L'Italia nella Psicoanalisi (1989)*: L'Italia nella Psicoanalisi.* [Italy in Psychoanalysis]. Ideazione e direzione scientifica: Arnaldo Novelletto. Rome 1989 (*Treccani Cataloghi, 6*).

Jaffé, Aniela (ed.) (1977): *C. G. Jung; Word and Image.* Princeton, NJ, 1979. Orig. German title: *C. G. Jung; Bild und Wort*, Olten. Transl. by Krishna Winston.

Jarchov, Inge (1980): 'Die Prinzhorn-Sammlung.' In: *Die Prinzhorn-Sammlung. Bilder, Skulpturen, Texte aus Psychiatrischen Anstalten (c. 1890–1920).* Königstein im Taunus, pp. 15–27. (Exhibition catalogue.)

Jaynes, Julian (1971): 'Fechner, Gustav Theodor.' In: *Dictionary of Scientific Biography* (ed. Charles Coulston Gillispie), Vol. 4. New York, pp. 556–9.

Jelgersma, Gerbrandus (1914): 'Ongeweten Geestesleven.' ('Unconscious mental life.') Lecture given in commemoration of 339th anniversary of Leiden University, 9 February 1914; Leipzig, Vienna (Supp. to *Int. Zschr. f. ärztliche Psychoanal.*, 1).

Jones, Ernest (1911): 'Remarks upon Dr. Morton Prince's Article: "The Mechanism and Interpretation of Dreams".' In: *J. of Abnormal Psychology*, Vol. 5 (1911), pp. 328–36.

— (1940): 'Otto Rank †' (obituary). In: *Internat J. Psycho-Anal.*, Vol. 21, pp. 112–13.

— (1943): 'Max Eitingon †' (obituary). In: *Internat J. Psycho-Anal.*, Vol. 24, pp. 190–2.

— (1953–7): *Sigmund Freud – Life and Work*. 3 volumes, London.

— (1959): *Free Associations. Memories of a Psycho-Analyst*. London.

Jung, Carl Gustav (1906a); with Riklin, Franz, catalogued in English as (1918a), C.W. 2.1: 'The Associations of Normal Subjects' (Part 1 of *Studies in Word Association*). Orig. title: *Diagnostische Assoziationsstudien: Beiträge zur experimentellen Psychopathologie*. Vol. 1, Leipzig.

— (1908a): 'Die Inhalt der Psychose' (lecture), Leipzig and Vienna (*Schriften zur angewandten Seelenkunde, H. 3*). (G.W.3). Given as a lecture at Zurich Town Hall 16 Jan. 1908. The English version, *The Content of the Psychoses* (1916a, 14) transl. by M. D. Eder from an expanded German version of 1914.

— (1910q), catalogued in English as (1916a, 5): 'A Contribution to the Psychology of Rumour', C.W. 4.4, pp. 176–90. Orig. title: 'Ein Beitrag zur Psychologie des Gerüchtes', *Zentralblatt*, Vol. 1 (1911), issue 3, pp. 81–90.

— (1911a), [parts 1 & 2 publ. together in book form by Franz Deuticke, Leipzig and Vienna, catalogued as (1912a), the Engl. version as (1916b)]: 'Psychology of the Unconscious. A Study of the Transformations and Symbolisms of the Libido. A Contribution to the History of Thought,' C.W., 5. Orig. title: 'Wandlungen und Symbole der Libido. Beiträge zur Entwicklungsgeschichte des Denkens'. (Part 1). In: *Jb. psychoanal. psychopathol. Forsch.*, Vol. 3 (1911), pp. 120–227.

— (1912c), [together with (1911a), catalogued in English as (1916b): 'Psychology of the Unconscious. A Study of the Transformations and Symbolisms of the Libido. A Contribution to the History of Thought', C.W., 5. Orig. title: 'Wandlungen und Symbole der Libido'. (Part 2). In: *Jb. psychoanal. psychopathol. Forsch.*, Vol. 4 (1912), pp. 162–464.

— (1913a), catalogued in English as (1913b), (9 lectures given at Fordham University, New York, Sept. 1912). 'The Theory of Psychoanalysis', written in German and transl. for Jung's delivery in New York by Edith and M. D. Eder and Mary Moltzer; 1st. pub. in 5 issues of *Psychanal. Rev.*, 1913–15; C.W., 4.9, pp. 88–226. Orig. title: 'Versuch einer Darstellung der psychoanalytischen Theorie.' 1st publ. in: *Jb. psychoanal. psychopathol. Forsch.*, Vol. 5, p. 307–441; G.W. 4.

Kamm, Peter (1977–1981): *Paul Häberlin. Leben und Werke*. Vols. 1–2, Zürich.

Kauders, Otto (1948): 'Professor Dr. Otto Marburg.' In: *Wien. klin. Swchr.*, Vol. 60, pp. 461–2. (Includes portrait.)

Kimmisch, Hans (1978): 'Anthropologie und Menschlichkeit. Der Beitrag Ludwig Binswangers zur Humanisierung der Psychiatrie,' med. diss., Göttingen.

Kisker, K.P. (1961): 'Die phänomenologische Wendung Ludwig Binswangers. Erläuterungen und kritische Bemerkungen zu seinem Buch. "Melancholie und Manie".' In *Jb. Psychol. Psychother.*, Vol. 8, pp. 142–53.

Kittel, Ingo-Wolf (1986): 'Arthur Kronfeld zur Erinnerung. Schicksal und Werk eines jüdischen Psychiaters und Psychotherapeuten in drei deutschen Reichen.' In *Exil*. Vol. 6, pp. 58–65.

Klaesi, Jakob (1946): 'Prof Dr. Hans W. Maier †, 25. Juli 1882 bis 25 März 1945.' In: *Schweiz. Arch. Neurol. Psychiatr.*, Vol. 57, pp. 1–6 (obituary)

Korrespondenzblatt (1910–11): *Korrespondenzblatt der Internationalen Psycho-analytischen Vereinigung*, ed. C. G. Jung and F. Riklin, Nos. 1–6, Zürich. Later continued as part of *Zentralblatt* or *Zeitschrift*.

Kos, Wolfgang (1984): *Über den Semmering. Kulturgeschichte einer künstlichen Landschaft*. Vienna.

Kraepelin, Emil (1983): *Memoirs*, eds. H. Hippius, G. Peters and D. Ploog, transl. from the German by Cheryl Wooding-Deane. New York, 1987. Orig. pub. as *Lebenserinnerungen*, Berlin, 1983.

Kraus, Friedrich, Brugsch, Theodor (eds.) (1919–27): *Spezielle Pathologie und Therapie innerer Krankheiten*. Vols. 1–11, Berlin and Vienna.

Krienen, Heinz-Peter (1982): *Ludwig Binswangers Versuch einer existential-ontologischen Grundlegung des psychopathologischen Daseins: Geschichte und aktuelle Situation*. Frankfurt am Main, Berne. (*Europäische Hochschulschriften: Series 20, Philosophie*, Vol. 92).

Kronfeld, Arthur (1911): 'Über die psychologischen Theorien Freuds und verwandte Anschauungen.' In *Arch. ges. Psychol.*, Vol. 22, pp. 130–248.

Kuhn, Roland (1956): 'Ludwig Binswanger.' In: *Internat. Bodensee-Zeitschrifte*, Vol. 5, pp. 81–4.

— (1961): 'Dr Ludwig Binswanger zum 80. Geburtstag.' In: *Schweiz. Arch. Neurol. Neurochir. Psychiatr.*, Vol. 88, 1, pp. 5–8.

— (1966): 'Ludwig Binswanger. Die Bedeutung seines Werkes für die Psychiatrie.' In: *Neue Zürcher Zeitung*, 8 Feb. 1966, midday ed., p. 4.

— (1967): 'Ludwig Binswanger (1881–1966).' In: *Schweiz. Arch. Neurol. Neurochir. Psychiatr.*, Vol. 99, 1, pp. 113–17.

— (1968): 'Ludwig Binswanger 13 Apr. 1881 – 5 Feb. 1966.' In: *Bull. Schweiz Akad. Med. Wiss. Suppl. 24*, p. 99.

— (1972): 'Die aktuelle Bedeutung des Werkes von Ludwig Binswanger.' In *Zschr. klin. Psychol. Psychother.*, Vol. 20, pp. 311–21.

— (1981): 'Erinnerungen an Ludwig Binswanger.' In: *Der Psychiater Dr. med. Ludwig Binswanger und das Sanatorium Bellevue*, with contributions from Roland Kuhn, Emil Staiger and Jörg Aeschbacher. Kreuzlingen. (*Vereinigung Heimatmuseum Kreuzlingen, Beiträge zur Ortsgeschichte*, no. 21), pp. 7–14.

Laehr, Hans (1907): *Die Anstalten für Psychisch-Kranke in Deutschland, Österreich, der Schweiz und den baltischen Ländern*. 6th edn. Berlin.

Laforgue, René (1926a): 'Verdrängung und Skotomisation.' In: *Internat. Zschr. Psychoanal.*, Vol. 12, pp. 54–65.

— (1926b): 'Scotomisation and Schizophrenia.' In *Internat. J. Psychoanal.*, Vol. 8, pp. 473–8.

Lanczik, Mario Horst (1988): *Der Breslauer Psychiater Carl Wernicke. Werkanalyse und Wirkungsgeschichte als Beitrag zur Medizingeschichte Schlesiens*. Sigmaringen. (*Schlesische Forschungen*, Vol. 2.)

Larese, Dino (1965): *Ludwig Binswanger. Versuch einer kleinen Lebensskizze*. Amriswil. (*Amriswiler Bücherei*.)

Laugwitz, Christian (1986): 'Ludwig Binswanger und Sigmund Freud. Persönliche Beziehung und sachliche Divergenz.' med. dissertation, Würzburg.

Leichtenstern, O. (1880): 'Balneotherapie.' In: *Handbuch der allgemeinen Therapie*, ed. H. v. Ziemssen, Vol. 2, pt. 1, Leipzig.

Lester, David (1971): 'Ellen West's suicide as a case of psychic homicide.' In: *Psychoanalytic Rev.*, Vol. 58, pp. 251–63.

Liebermann, E. James (1985) *Acts of Will. The Life and Work of Otto Rank.* New York.

Liepmann, Hugo (1911): 'Über Wernickes Einfluß auf die klinische Psychiatrie.' In: *Mschr. Psychiatr. Neurol.*, Vol. 30, pp. 1–37.

Lombardo, G.P., Fiorelli, F. (1984): *Binswanger e Freud: malattia mentale e teoria della personalita.* Turin.

Lück, Helmut E. and Mühlleitner, Elke (eds.) (1993): *Psychoanalytiker in der Karikatur*, Munich.

Maldiney, Henri (1963): 'Le dévoilement des concepts fondamentaux de la Psychologie à travers la Daseinsanalyse de L. Binswanger.' In: *Schweiz Arch. Neurol. Neurochir. Psychiatr.*, Vol. 92, pp. 204–17.

— (1989): 'L'existence en question dans la dépression et dans la mélancolie.' ('The existence at stake in depression and melancholia.') 2nd ALEP Conference (1987, Lyon, France). In: *Evolution Psychiatrique*, Vol. 54, pp. 571–94.

Mann, Thomas (1929): 'Die Stellung Freuds in der modernen Geistergeschichte.' In: *Die psychoanalytische Bewegung*, Vol. 1, pp. 3–32.

— (1936): 'Freud und die Zukunft.' Lecture given as part of celebrations of Freud's 80th birthday, at the Viennese Academic Soc. for Medical Psychology, 9 May 1936. English transl: 'Freud and the Future.' In: Mann, Thomas: *Freud, Goethe, Wagner*, New York.

Maraldo, J.C. (1974): *Der hermeneutische Zirkel. Untersuchungen zu Schleiermacher, Dilthey und Heidegger.* Freiburg and Munich.

McGuire, William (1984): 'Jung's complex reactions (1907): Word association experiments performed by Binswanger.' In: *Spring*, pp. 1–34.

Meerwein, Fritz (1979): 'Reflexionen zur Geschichte der Schweizerischen Gesellschaft für Psychoanalyse in der deutschen Schweiz.' In: *Schweiz. Ges. Psycho-anal. Bull.* no. 9, pp. 25–39.

Michaelis, Edgar (1925): *Die Menschheitproblematik der Freudschen Psychoanalyse.* Leipzig.

Minkowski, M. (1950): 'O. Marburg (1874–1948).' In: *Schweiz. Arch. Neurol. Psychiatr.* Vol. 65, pp. 415–20.

Mishara, A.L. (1990): 'The Problem of the Unconscious in the Later Thought of L. Binswanger: A Phenomenological Approach to Delusion in Perception and Communication.' In: *Analecta Husserliana*, Vol. 31, pp. 247–78.

Missriegler, Anton (1928): 'Zum sechzigsten Geburtstag Wilhelm Stekels.' In: *Allg. ärztl. Zschr. Psychother. psych. Hyg.*, Vol. 1, pp. 134–6.

Moellenhoff, Fritz (1966): 'Hanns Sachs 1881–1947. The Creative Unconscious.' In: *Psychoanalytic Pioneers.* Ed. by Franz Alexander, Samuel Eisenstein and Martin Grotjahn. New York and London, pp. 180–99. (Also new edn. with new Intro. by Samuel Eisenstein, New Brunswick, NJ, 1995.)

Mühlleitner, Elke (1992): *Biographisches Lexikon der Psychoanalyse. Die Mitglieder der Psychologischen Mittwoch-Gesellschaft und der Wiener Psychoanalytischen Vereinigung 1902–1938.*, Tübingen.

Murphy, William F. (1964): 'Felix Deutsch, 1884–1964' (obituary). In: *Psychoanal. Quart.*, Vol. 45, pp. 615ff.

Neiser, Emil J. N. (1978): 'Max Eitingon. Leben und Werk.' Doctoral thesis, Johannes Gutenberg-Universität, Mainz.

Neumann, H. (ed.) [1905]: *Jahrbuch der Heil-, Pflege- und Kuranstalten.* Privately published. Berlin.

Nitzschke, Bernd (1988): *Zu Fuß durch den Kopf. Wanderungen im Gedanken-gebirge.* (Selected writings of Herbert Silberens, a miscellany of his life and work.) Tübingen.

Nunberg, Herman, Federn, Ernst (eds), (1962–75): *Minutes of the Vienna Psycho-analytic Society.* Vol. I–IV, New York. *Protokolle der Wiener Psychanalytischen Vereinigung.* Vol. 1–4, Frankfurt am Main 1976–1981. (N.B. The later, German, edition has significantly more annotation and, in some cases, additional text which presumably came to light after the English edition had been published.)

Oppenheim, Hermann (1906): *Psychotherapeutische Briefe.* 2nd edn, Berlin. (3rd edn, Berlin 1910.)

Pellegrino, Raffaele (1986): 'Ideologia e practica nel pensiero di Ludwig Binswanger.' In: *Rivista Sperimentale di Freniatria e Medicina Legale delle Alienaxioni Mentali,* Vol. 110, pp. 915–87.

Peters, Uwe Henrik (1979): *Anna Freud: A Life Dedicated to Children*, New York, 1984, London, 1985. Orig. pub. as *Anna Freud; Ein Leben für das Kind.* Munich, 1979.

Pfister, Oskar (1913): *The Psychoanalytic Method.* Introduction by Sigmund Freud (1913b), transl. from the German by Charles Rockwell Payne, London and New York, 1917. Orig. pub. as *Die psychoanalytische Methode,* Leipzig, 1913.

Pivnicki, Dimitrije (1979): 'Paradoxes of Psychotherapy. In Honor and Memory of Ludwig Binswanger.' In *Confin. Psychiatr.*, Vol. 22, pp. 197–203.

Polak, P. (1953): 'Existenz und Liebe. Ein kritischer Beitrag zur ontologischen Grundlegung der medizinischen Anthropologie durch die "Daseinsanalyse" Binswangers und die "Existenzialanalyse" Frankls.' In: *Jahrb. für Psychologie und psychol. Therapie*, no. 3, pp. 355–64.

Praetorius, Numa (pseud. for Magnus Hirschfeld) (1917/18): (Review of:) Mann, Thomas: *Das Tod in Venedig. Novelle.* (*Death in Venice*), Berlin, 1913. In: *Zschr. Sexualwiss.* Vol. 4, pp. 247–8.

Prince, Morton (1911): 'The Mechanism and Interpretation of Dreams – A Reply to Dr. Jones.' In: *J. of Abnormal Psychology*, Vol. 5, pp. 337–53.

Probst-Frey, Cilly (1979): 'Autismus und Wahn bei Binswanger, Blankenburg und Boss.' Phil. dissertation, Zürich, 1979.

Protti, M. (1974): 'From the phenomenography of Jaspers to the phenomenology of Binswanger.' In: *Neuropsichiatria,* Vol. 30, pp. 294–309.

Putnam, James Jackson (1910a): 'On the Etiology and Treatment of the Psychoneuroses.' In: *Boston Med. and Surg. J.,* No. 163 (21 July 1910). Transl. by Freud as 'Über Ätiologie und Behandlung der Psychoneurosen' (1911).

— (1910b): 'Personal Experience with Freud's Psychoanalytic Method.' In: *J. Nervous and Mental Diseases,* Vol. 37, pp. 657–74.

— Hale, Nathan G. Jr. (ed) (1971): *James Jackson Putnam and Psychoanalysis; Letters between Putnam and Sigmund Freud, Ernest Jones, William James, Sándor Ferenczi, and Morton Prince, 1877–1917.* Cambridge, MA. German texts transl. by Judith Bernays Heller.

Quintana, Manuel (1952): 'Ludwig Binswanger y el análisis existencial.' In: *Rev. Psiquiatr. clin.*, Vol. 1. pp. 93–106.

Raecke, Julius (1916): 'Alois Alzheimer †.' In: *Arch. Psychiatr. Nervenkh.*, Vol. 56, pp. III–VIII.

Rank, Otto (1909): *The Myth of the Birth of the Hero. A Psychological Interpretation of Mythology*, transl. from the German by F. Robbins and Smith Ely Jelliffe, New York, 1914. Orig. pub. as: *Der Mythus von der Geburt des Helden. Versuch einer psychologischen Mythendeutung*, Leipzig and Vienna, 1909 (*Schriften zur angewandten Seelenkunde*, No. 5).

Rattner, Josef (1979): 'Ludwig Binswanger.' In: *Pioniere der Tiefenpsychologie*, ed. Josef Rattner. Vienna, Munich, Zürich, pp. 221–46.

— (ed.) (1981): *Der Weg zum Menschen: Wilhelm Stekel [...]*, Vienna, Munich, Zürich.

Reik, Theodor (1915/16): 'Puberty Rites among Savages. On some similarities in the mental life of savages and neurotics,' in Reik's *Ritual, Psychoanalytic Studies*, transl. by C. A. Douglas Bryan, London and New York, 1931, pp. 91–166. Orig. title: 'Die Pubertätsriten der Wilden. Über einige Übereinstimmungen im Seelenleben der Wilden und der Neurotiker.' In: *Imago*, Vol. 4, pp. 125–44 and 189–222.

— (1956): see Freud (1956l).

Reuter, K.H. (1961): 'Der Mensch in der Psychiatrie. Ludwig Binswanger zum 80. Geburtstag.' In *Ärztl. Praxis*, Vol. 13, pp. 875ff.

Ribi, A. (1971): 'Franz Riklin (1909–1969)' In: *Schweiz. Arch. Neurol. Neurochir. Psychiatr.*, Vol. 109, pp. 127–8.

Riem, Ludger (1987): *Das daseinsanalytische Verständnis in der Medizin. Von seinem Beginn bei Ludwig Binswanger bis zur Gründung des 'Daseinsanalytischen Institutes für Psychotherapie und Psychosomatik (Medard Boss Stiftung)' in Zürich.* Herzogenrath. (*Studien zur Geschichte der Socialmedizin und Psychiatrie*, Vol. 4) – simult. med. dissert., Aachen.

Riklin, Franz (1908): *Wunscherfüllung und Symbolik im Märchen.* Leipzig and Vienna (*Schriften zur angewandten Seelenkunde,* no. 2).

— (1912): 'Ödipus und die Psychoanalyse.' In: *Wissen und Leben,* Vol. 5.

[Riklin] (1938): 'Totentafel.' (Obituary of Franz Riklin.) In: *Neue Zürcher Zeitung*, 7 Dec. 1938, evening edn, p. 8.

Ritvo, Samuel (1957): 'Ernst Kris. 1901–1957.' In: *Psychoanal. Quart.*, Vol. 26, pp. 248–50.

Ritvo, Samuel and Lucille B. (1966) in *Psychoanalytic Pioneers*, ed. Franz Alexander et al. New York. Also new edition with new Introduction by Eisenstein, Samuel, New Brunswick, NJ, 1995.

Roazen, Paul (1973): *Brother Animal. The Story of Freud and Tausk*, Harmondsworth.

Roemling-Wettstein, Doris (1973): 'Extremformen des In-der-Welt-Seins und die ursprüngliche Bedeutung des Mit-Einander-Seins. Die exemplarische Bedeutung von Binswangers Schizophrenieanalysen für die Psychologie.' Phil. dissert., Zürich.

Rohleder, Hermann (1902): *Die Masturbation. Eine Monographie für Ärzte, Pädagogen und gebildete Eltern.* With preface by Herman Schiller, 3rd edn, enlarged and corrected. Berlin.

Romm, Sharon (1983): *The Unwelcome Intruder: Freud's Struggle with Cancer*. New York.

Rosenfeld, Eva M. (1962): 'Hedwig Hoffer. 1888–1961.' (Obituary.) In: *Internat. J. Psycho-Anal.* Vol. 43, p. 477.

Rosenstein, Gaston (1912): 'Eine Kritik (der psychologischen Theorien Freuds).' In: *Jahrbuch,* Vol. 4, pp. 744–99.

Rümke, Henricus Cornelius (1952): 'Die Zukunft der klinischen Psychiatrie. Dr. Alphons Maeder als klinischer Psychiater.' In: *Schweiz. Arch. Neurol. Psychiatr.,* Vol. 70, pp. 351–65.

Sachs, Hanns (1944): *Freud, Master and Friend*, Cambridge, MA.

Sadler, William A., Jr (1926): 'Ludwig Binswanger's Existenial Phenomenology: The Significant Contributions of a Psychiatrist to the Understanding of Man.' Dissert. Cambridge, MA (Harvard, History and Philosophy of Religion).

Sarró, Ramón (1958): Ludwig Binswanger. Fundador del Anàlisis existencial psiquiátrico. In: *IV Congreso Internacional de Psicoterapia* (Barcelona), Nr. 2, 14, pp. 1–2.

Schmidl, Fritz (1959): 'Sigmund Freud and Ludwig Binswanger.' In: *Psychoanal. Quart.,* Vol. 28, pp. 40–58.

Schreber, Daniel Paul (1903): *Memoirs of my Nervous Illness*. Transl. and ed. by Ida MacAlpine and Richard A. Hunter, London, 1955, repr. 1988. Orig. pub in German as: *Denkwürdigkeiten eines Nervenkranken,* Leipzig, 1903; new edn ed. and Intro. by Samuel M. Weber, Frankfurt am Main, Berlin, Vienna, 1973.

Schrenk, Martin (1967): 'Ludwig Binswangers Auseinandersetzung mit Sigmund Freud, ein Stück Wissenschaftsgeschichte.' In: *Confin. Psychiatr.,* Vol. 10, pp. 113–27.

Schultz, Ulrich, Hermanns, Ludger M. (1987): 'Das Sanatorium Schloß Tegel Ernst Simmels – Zur Geschichte und Konzeption der ersten Psychoanalytischen Klinik.' In: *Psychother. med. Psychol.,* Vol. 37, pp. 58–67.

Schur, Max (1972): *Freud: Living and Dying*, New York.

Schwartz, Léonard (1918): 'Alois Alzheimer†.' In: *Schweiz. Arch. Neurol. psychiat.,* Vol. 2, pp. 315–16.

Schwartzman, Riva S. (1986): 'Uma reflexao sobre as psicoterapias humanistas e a analise existencial. A reflection on humanistic psychotherapies and existential analysis.' In: *J. Brasileiro de Psiquiatria,* Vol. 35, pp. 173–180.

Seidler, Eduard (1986): 'Alfred Erich Hocke (1865–1943). Versuch einer Standort-bestimmung.' In: *Freiburger Universitätsbl.,* No. 94, pp. 65–75.

Seidman, Bradley (1983): *Absent at the Creation: The Existential Psychiatry of Ludwig Binswanger*. New York.

Sherman, Murray H. (1970): 'Dr Theodor Reik: A Life Devoted to Freud and Psychoanalysis.' In: *Psychoanal. Rev.,* Vol. 57, pp. 535–43.

Sidis, Boris (1911): 'Fundamental States in Psychoneurosis.' In: *The J. of Abnormal Psychology*, Vol. 5, pp. 320–7.

Simmel, Ernst (1918): *War Neuroses*, New York, 1944. Orig. pub. in German as: *Kriegsneurosen und psychisches Trauma. Ihre geistigen Bezeihungen, dargestellt auf Grund psychoanalytischer, hypnotischer Studien,* Munich and Leipzig, 1918.

Simon, Artur (1972): 'Das Artikulationsproblem aus der Sicht von Alfred Gysi und Hermann Schröder.' Dentistry dissert., Berlin.

Sneessens, Germaine (1966): 'Bibliographie de Ludwig Binswanger.' In: *Rev. philos. Louvain,* Vol. 64, pp. 594–602.

Spiegelberg. H. (1972): *Phenomenology in Psychology and Psychiatry.* Evanston.

Staiger, Emil (1951): 'Dank eines Literarhistorikers' (on Ludwig Binswanger's 70th birthday), in: *Schweiz Arch. Neurol. Psychiat.,* Vol. 67, pp. 82–6.

Stekel, Wilhelm (1911): *The Language of Dreams.* Authorised transl. by James S. van Teslaar, Boston, MA, 1922; orig. pub. in German as: *Die Sprache des Traumes,* Wiesbaden, 1911.

[Stekel] (1940) (anon. obituary). In: *Psychoanal. Rev.,* Vol. 27, p. 506.

Stern, Arthur (1958): 'In memoriam Hermann Oppenheim (1.1.1858–22.5.1919).' In: *Schweiz. Arch. Neurol. Psychiatr.,* Vol. 81, pp. 359–62.

Stern, Paul J. (1976): *C.G. Jung: The Haunted Prophet.* New York, 1976; Munich, Zürich 1977.

Stertz, Georg (1970): 'Karl Bonhoeffer, 1868–1948.' In: *Große Nervenärzte.* Vol. 1, ed. K. Kolle, 2nd enlgd edn, Stuttgart, 1970, pp. 17–26.

Sticker, Georg (1939–40): 'Wunderlich, Roser, Griesinger "die drei Schwäbischen Reformatoren der Medizin".' In: *Sudhoffs Arch.,* Vol. 32 (1939), pp. 217–74, Vol. 33, pp. 1–54.

Storch, Alfred (1961): 'Das Verständnis des menschlichen Daseins und seiner abnormen Gestaltung bei Ludwig Binswanger (Daseinsanalyse und Analyse der konstitutiven Erfahrungsgrundlagen).' In: *Schweiz. Zschr. Psychol.,* Vol. 20, No. 3, pp. 253–65.

Straus, Erwin (1951): 'Ludwig Binswangers zum 70. Geburtstag.' In: *Nervenarzt,* Vol. 22, 12, pp. 169ff.

— (1966): 'Dem Andenken Ludwig Binswangers 1881–1966.' In: *Nervenarzt,* Vol. 37, 12, pp. 529–31.

Szilasi, Wilhelm (1951): 'Die Erfahrungsgrundlage der Daseinsanalyse Binswangers.' In: *Schweiz. Arch. Neurol. Psychiat.* Vol. 67 (1951), pp. 74–82.

Taft, Jessie (1958): *Otto Rank: A biographical study based on notebooks, letters, collected writings, therapeutic achievements and personal associations.* New York.

Taverna, P. (1968): 'The bases of "Daseinsanalyse" from Heidegger to Binswanger, I.' In: *Neuropsichiatria,* Vol. 24, pp. 37–49.

Tellenbach, Hubert (1961): 'Zu Ludwig Binswangers 80. Geburtstag.' In: *Nervenarzt,* Vol. 32, pp. 288–89.

Tögel, Christfried (1989): *Berggasse – Pompeji und Zurück*, Tübingen.

Valenstein, Arthur F.(1960): 'Obituary. Edward Bibring 1895–1959.' In: *Int. Jnl of Psycho-Analysis,* Vol. 41, pp. 162–3.

Vanderpool, John P. (1968): 'The Existential Approach to Psychiatry [Ludwig Binswanger, Victor Frankl].' In: *Texas Rep. Biol. Med.,* Vol. 26, 2, pp.163–71.

Vetter, Heinz (1990): *Die Konzeption des Psychischen im Werk Ludwig Binswangers.* Bern, Frankfurt am Main, New York, Paris. (*Europäische Hochschulschriften, R. 6: Psychologie,* Vol. 313.)

Wagner-Jauregg, Julius (1950): *Lebenserinnerungen, (Reminiscences.)* Edited and enlarged by Leopold Schönbauer and Marlene Jantsch. Vienna.

Walser, Hans H. (1968): *August Forel. Briefe – Correspondance 1864–1927.* Preface by Manfred Bleuler. Bern, Stuttgart.

— (1970): *Hundert Jahre Klinik Rheinau 1867–1967. Wissenschaftliche*

Psychiatrie und praktische Irrenpflege in der Schweiz am Beispiel einer großen Heil- und Pflegeanstalt. Aarau. (*Veröffentlichungen der Schweiz. Gesellschaft für Geschichte der Medizin und der Naturwissenschaften,* 24).

— (1973): 'J. J. Honegger (1885–1911) – Ein Beitrag zur Geschichte der Psychoanalyse.' In: *Schweiz. Arch. Neurol.,* Vol. 112 (1973), pp. 107–113.

— (1976): 'Psychoanalyse in der Schweiz.' In: *Die Psychologie des 20. Jahrhunderts.* Vol. 2: *Freud und die Folgen (I),* ed. Dieter Eicke. Zürich, pp. 1192–1218.

— (1986): 'Wilhelm Griesinger – von der Inneren Medizin zur Psychiatrie.' In: *Gesnerus,* Vol. 43 (1986), pp. 197–204.

Wangerin, Albert, Taschenberg, Otto (eds.) (1895): *Verhandlungen der Gesellschaft Deutscher Naturforscher und Ärzte. 66. Versammlung zu Wien, 24.–28. September 1894,* part 2, 2nd half, Leipzig.

Winnicott, Donald W. (1958): 'Ernest Jones.' (Obituary.) In: *Internat. J. Psycho-Anal.* Vol. 39, pp. 298–304.

Winternitz, Wilhelm (1890): *Die Hydrotherapie auf physiologischer und klinischer Grundlage,* 2nd edn., Vol. 1, Leipzig, Vienna, 1890. Not pub. in English, but a paper by Winternitz, 'Hydrotherapy' is in: *A System of Physiologic Therapeutics,* ed. Solomon S. Cohen, Philadelphia, 1902.

Wolf, Max, Fleischer, Fritz (1910): *Nova therapeutica.* Berlin.

Wollheim, Ernst (1958): 'Friedrich Kraus zum 100. Geburtstag (31.5.58).' In: *Medizinische,* pp. 993–6.

Wyrsch, Jakob (1961): 'Ludwig Binswanger zum 80. Geburtstag.' In: *Psychiatr. Neurol.,* Vol. 141 (1961), pp. 229–33.

— (1966): 'Ludwig Binswanger (1881–1966).' In: *Civitas,* Vol. 21, pp. 645–7.

Wyrsch, Jakob, Walthard, K.M., Bing, R., Minkowski, M., Staehelin, J.E., Steck, H. (1951): 'Verehrter, lieber Freund und Kollege.' (Ludwig Binswanger on his 70th birthday.) In: *Psychiatr. Neurol.,* Vol. 67, pp. 1–4.

Ylla, Luis (1990): 'Philosophic sources underlying diverse aspects which characterise therapeutic communities of psychoanalytic orientation.' In: *Internat. J. of Therapeutic Communities,* Vol. 11, pp. 7–11. (Special Issue: 'Philosophy and the therapeutic community.')

Young-Bruehl, Elisabeth (1988): *Anna Freud: A Biography.* New York.

Ziehen, Theodor (1929): 'Otto Binswanger (Kreuzlingen und Jena)†, 1852–1929.' In: *Schweiz. Arch. Neurol. Psychiatr.,* Vol. 25, pp. 171–4.

Zulliger, Hans (1966): 'Oskar Pfister 1873–1956. Psychoanalysis and Faith.' In: *Psychoanalytic Pioneers,* ed. Franz Alexander *et al.* New York, pp. 169–99. Also new edition with new Intro. by Samuel Eisenstein. New Brunswick, NJ, 1995.

Index